Windows Programmer's Guide to

Resources

Windows Programmer's

Guide to

Resources

Alex Leavens

SAMS
PUBLISHING

A Division of Prentice Hall Computer Publishing
11711 North College, Carmel, Indiana 46032 USA

This book is for my beautiful wife, Shirley Ann. She knows why.
This book is also for my two sons, Miles and Sloan,
twin points of magic and joy.

Publisher
Richard K. Swadley

Managing Editor
Neweleen A. Trebnik

Acquisitions Editor
Joseph Wikert

Development Editor
Ella Davis

Production Editor
Cheri Clark

Copy Editor
Colleen Flanagan

Editorial Coordinator
Bill Whitmer

Editorial Assistants
Rosemarie Graham
Lori Kelley

Formatter
Pat Whitmer

Technical Editor
Mark Solinski

Cover Designer
Kathy Hanley

**Director of Production
and Manufacturing**
Jeff Valler

Production Manager
Corinne Walls

Imprint Manager
Matthew Morrill

Book Designer
Michele Laseau

Production Analyst
Mary Beth Wakefield

Proofreading/Indexing Coordinator
Joelynn Gifford

Graphics Image Specialists
Jerry Ellis, Dennis Sheehan,
Sue VandeWalle

Production
Alys Brosius, Christine Cook,
Terri Edwards, Mark Enochs, John Kane,
Carrie Keesling, Roger Morgan,
Linda Quigley, Caroline Roop,
Sandra Shay, Greg Simsic,
Angie Trzepacz, Julie Walker,
Phil Worthington

Indexer
Sherry Massey

About the Author

Alex Leavens is a software engineer and graphics artist with more than 10 years of experience in designing graphical user interfaces. He has designed products that have sold more than a million copies, and he is one of only a handful of software designers to have his work included in a permanent collection at the National Museum of American History (Smithsonian Institution). He heads the ShadowCat Technologies' product development group, which provides Windows product development support and consulting for a wide range of clients. He can be reached at ShadowCat Technologies, 39120 Argonaut Way, Suite 741, Fremont, CA 94538.

Overview

Contents

Acknowledgments

Lots of people helped make this book happen. My particular thanks go to Ella Davis and Joe Wikert at Prentice Hall, for giving me the opportunity to do it in the first place. Thanks!

Writing an entire book has proved to be an unparalleled learning experience. Of course, in the process of learning, no person stands alone, and I'm certainly no exception. Lots of people helped me along the way. In particular, I'd like to thank Alan Cooper, Peter Eden, Fran Finnegan, Fred Gault, and Mike Geary, as well as many others who contributed insights or ideas that would become the germ of something bigger. Thanks, guys. It's always fun.

Trademarks

All terms mentioned in this book that are known to be trademarks or service marks have been appropriately capitalized. Sams Publishing cannot attest to the accuracy of this information. Use of a term in this book should not be regarded as affecting the validity of any trademark or service mark.

Introduction

This book is about Windows resources—primarily *graphics* resources, bitmaps, icons, and cursors. It goes into a fair bit of depth on how to create these images, manipulate them, and use them in your programs. Although a certain basic understanding of Windows programming is necessary, it isn't necessary to have a good handle on programming graphics to get the most out of this book. Indeed, I discovered much of the material used for this book through painful trial and error in the creation of my own programs.

I liken Windows graphics programming to stumbling around in a room filled with invisible furniture. The first time you enter the room, you keep whacking your shins on the invisible coffee table. After a while, you begin to know where things are, and the number of bruises that you accumulate goes down. Rather than let others share this same fate, I've tried to document, as much as possible, all the little things that go into programming graphics in Windows. Sort of spray-painting the invisible furniture, you might say, or at least putting bumper pads on it.

The Examples in This Book

One of the things I've done is to include lots of sample code about how things work. Sample code is often the best way of learning; you can take something I've done and modify it for your own use, even if you don't fully understand it. In the process of adapting the code, you'll gain the understanding needed to do more complex things. This isn't to say that there isn't a lot of detail in this book; it's just that the more complex objects are built on simpler ones.

The examples in this book are a mixture of C and C++. I've included a fair bit of C++ code, not out of any desire to be programmatically correct, but simply because C++ relieves you of a lot of the effort of building graphics objects in Windows. Much of the work involved in manipulating graphics in Windows is setup and cleanup; you set up the objects at the beginning of a routine, and you clean them up (hopefully!) at the end. This is the kind of thing C++ is almost perfect for; the constructor and destructor routines can implement this behavior transparently. (I'll get on my soapbox for a minute here and

suggest that if you haven't learned C++ yet, now is as good a time as any to start. C++ will give you not only greater programming skills, but a terrific leg up on Windows programming.)

If you are an experienced C++ programmer, you'll discover that I haven't tried to put a C++ wrapper on every graphics display interface (GDI) function. Instead, I've tried to concentrate on building higher-level objects (such as a compatible DC class), which take much of the burden of Windows graphics programming off you. If you do decide to use some of the object classes, you should be aware that the object classes later in the book build on the object classes earlier in the book. The object classes are self-contained, however. Because they don't rely on any third-party object library, they should work with any C++ compiler.

The C examples in this book are compatible with the Microsoft C/C++ compiler, version 7.0; the C++ examples are for use with the Borland C++ compiler, version 3.1. The resource examples in the book can be compiled with either Microsoft's resource compiler (rc.exe) or Borland's Resource Workshop.

Many of the C examples in this book were created using WindowsMaker Professional, from Blue Sky Software. This is a helpful tool for prototyping applications, as well as building the shell of an application very quickly.

The Conventions in This Book

Italic type is used for terms being introduced for the first time.

A special `monospace` font is used for variable names and code listings.

Windows functions are printed in a **`bold monospace`** font.

A special icon is used in the text:

The debug icon indicates things that might cause bugs or problems in the code (that is, things that don't work as advertised in Windows).

Windows Graphics Resources: An Overview

Although there has been a proliferation of Windows programming books in recent months, few of these books have dealt in a significant way with one of the more important areas of Windows programming: managing graphics resources. This book is an attempt to change that situation. By the end of the book, you'll understand what graphics resources are, how to create them, and how to include and manipulate them in your programs. You'll be able to build better looking programs, as well as programs with which a user can more directly interact.

Why are graphics resources so important? Quite simply, they are the *graphics* in a graphical user interface (GUI). Through displayed graphics images that users can manipulate, users get immediate feedback about what a program is doing. This enables them to concentrate on the task they want to accomplish, rather than on how they should go about accomplishing that task. There are many different ways of presenting graphics information to the user; this book concentrates on several of the best known ways.

One common visual metaphor in Windows programming is that of a graphics button. When clicking a button with an image in it, the user knows that the program will respond by performing an action associated with the image. For example, the user knows that clicking a button with an image of an arrow pointing to a diskette causes the program to save the current file.

Although a graphics button is easy for the user to deal with, there is significantly more work involved in programming one. In Chapter 7, "Bitmap Buttons," I show you how programming the application to support the use of a bitmap (graphics) button can be made significantly easier.

This book also contains a utility for creating graphics resources, ICE/Works. This is a scaled-down version of the commercially available product ICE/Works Professional. This utility enables you to manipulate graphics images in ways that you should find useful. I discuss it in more detail in Appendix A.

The Bitmap

At the heart of all graphics resources under Windows is the bitmap. A bitmap is a method of *map*ping a piece of the computer's memory (the *bit*s) onto a graphics image; hence the term *bitmap.* In its simplest form, each bit in a byte is mapped to one pixel of the bitmap. Because a bit can have only two values, 1 and 0, the corresponding pixel can have only two states, on and off. In an idealized bitmap, a 1 is an on-pixel (black), and a 0 is an off-pixel (white). (See Figure 1.1.)

Figure 1.1.
A basic black and white bitmap.

Notice, however, that with only one bit per pixel the number of colors you can display is rather small. Moving to two bits per pixel gives you a bit more flexibility—with two bits, you can have one of four values (0, 1, 2, and 3), which gives you the ability to represent twice as many colors as before. Moving to three bits per pixel again doubles the number of colors you can represent, from 4 to 8. Moving to four bits per pixel lets you represent 16 colors. (See Figure 1.2.)

Each time you add one more bit per pixel, you double the number of colors you can represent. At 8 bits per pixel (1 byte) you can represent 256 colors. By moving to 16 bits (2 bytes) you can represent 65,536 colors, and at 24 bits per pixel (the current maximum under Windows) you can represent a truly mind-boggling 16 *million* colors (16,777,216 to be precise)!

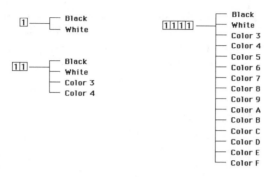

Figure 1.2. The number of colors available when one, two, or four bits are used to represent a single pixel.

Managing Colors (Or, Why More Isn't Always Better)

In the early days of computing, memory was scarce, a precious resource. Thus, devoting large chunks of memory to displaying images was, for the most part, out of the question. Video displays with only 2 or 4 colors were common. Today, however, video cards with half a megabyte (524,288 bytes) or a megabyte (1,048,576 bytes) of video memory are common. This increase in video memory means it is now perfectly reasonable to display 16,256 or even 32,768 colors on-screen at the same time. However, this huge increase in the number of colors that can be displayed confronts you with a different problem: managing all these colors.

Managing colors wasn't a problem when you had only four colors to work with; indeed, there wasn't really anything to manage. The colors corresponded directly to values; when you wanted a color, you used the corresponding value. This direct correspondence between values and colors is called a direct color map. (See Figure 1.3.)

Managing colors when you have 256 colors is rather different, because more than likely, your program isn't going to use all those colors. It might not even use a significant subset of them. Under a direct color mapping scheme, however, you have to be concerned about all the colors, whether or not you're going to use them. The particular colors you want might be scattered throughout the range of values; you might want a couple of colors down around 5, some more around 47, and the rest up near 200.

5

It would be much simpler, of course, if you could specify the colors you were interested in and have them all occur in the same range, ideally starting at 0 and continuing up linearly. With a direct color map, this is impossible. However, by using an *indirect* color map, you can do exactly this.

Figure 1.3.
A direct color map. The value 2 is always mapped to a green pixel.

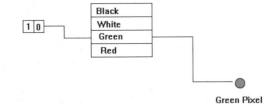

An indirect color map adds a level of indirection to the process of specifying colors. Instead of specifying a color directly (as in a direct color map), your program specifies the place that specifies the color you want. To change the color your program uses, you change only the contents of the place that specifies the color, and this changes the color everywhere.

To make this clearer, imagine a post office with many post office boxes. I hand you the key to box 700 and ask you to get my mail. You go to box 700, and inside it is a pile of mail. This is the equivalent of a direct color map. Under an indirect color map, you wouldn't find a pile of mail inside box 700; instead, you'd find another key, to a different box. You'd take this new key and go to that box to get the mail.

This might not seem like such a big deal; you used the first key to get the second key, which got you the mail. However, it's clear that until you actually open box 700, you have no idea of what box actually holds my mail. (The only thing you do know is that my mail isn't in box 700.) I could put any key I wanted to inside box 700, or even no key at all. More important, I could change which box you would get the mail from simply by changing the key inside box 700. Box 700 is, in effect, a *pointer* to my mail.

Similarly, under an indirect color mapping scheme, you don't specify colors; you specify *pointers* to colors. You can change the colors your program uses at any time simply by changing the pointers. You can even have several different sets of pointers and switch them about according to your needs. A set of these pointers to colors is typically referred to as a *palette*, and under Windows the program that deals with palettes and mapping colors is known as the *Palette Manager.*

The second advantage you gain from using an indirect color map and a palette is that you gain a degree of device independence. Before having some form of Palette Manager, you had to be concerned about the different methods used to represent video information, as well as differing screen resolutions (both in terms of number of pixels and number of colors). With the advent of the Palette Manager under Windows, you can simply specify the number of colors your application uses and let the Palette Manager handle how the colors you specify are actually mapped to whatever hardware is in the machine that your program is being run on.

Windows Bitmaps

As I said earlier, the bitmap is the heart of all Windows graphics resources. The bitmap itself comes in different flavors:

- The device *dependent* bitmap (DDB)

- The device *independent* bitmap (DIB)

- The OS2/PM bitmap

The device dependent bitmap is also known as an old-style bitmap, because it's been around since Windows 1.0. Just as its name implies, it is device dependent, meaning that the organization and format of the bits inside it cannot be determined in advance. This has some important ramifications, as you'll see later.

The device independent bitmap is new with Windows 3.0. In contrast to the device dependent bitmap, it provides a way to exchange images without concern for the device on which they are displayed.

The OS2/Presentation Manager bitmap is really a variation of DIB, although an OS2/PM bitmap contains less information about how it is formatted than a device independent bitmap does.

In general, when you're performing graphics operations in Windows, you're talking to type 1, a device dependent bitmap. This means that, for example, when you're drawing a circle into a device context (discussed in Chapter 2), you're drawing onto the surface of a DDB.

DIBs are used primarily to deal with file-oriented operations. Writing a DIB means that any program which wants to read a bitmap is able to, because all the information needed to properly reconstruct the bitmap is contained in the DIB. Using a DIB is also useful at other times, and I discuss those in Chapter 4, "The Device Independent Bitmap."

OS2/PM bitmaps are used when you're dealing with OS2/Presentation Manager. Because this book is primarily about Windows, I ignore this kind of bitmap for the most part, although I note which calls enable you to read and write this kind of bitmap.

One thing I haven't mentioned up to now that is true of all bitmaps is that they're *rectilinear*. That's a fancy word which means that they're either square or rectangular. Yet there are obviously times when you need a nonrectangular image. This leads to the next type of Windows graphics resource, the icon.

Icons

First, Windows icons are a modified form of bitmap. Whereas a bitmap (DIB or DDB) contains only one image, icons can contain many images. Second, each image in the icon has not one set of bits, but two. The first set of bits defines the actual image (just as the bits in a DIB do). The second set of bits is where the big difference between icons and bitmaps is. This second set of bits is a monochrome bitmap that defines, for the immediately preceding color bitmap, what that bitmap's *transparency* is. (The actual mechanics of how transparency is defined I defer to Chapter 5, "The Icon Resources.") This means that bitmap images no longer need be rectilinear. Using this second image (generally called a *mask image*, or just a *mask*), you can define irregularly shaped bitmaps, with whatever's beneath the bitmap showing through in places. For example, when you're drawing an icon on the desktop, the background mask defines the places where the desktop shows through the icon.

Icons are typically used to represent programs, files, or folders in a system. To run a program from Program Manager or a third-party desktop, a user double-clicks the program's icon. These icons are bound into your program at compile time. I discuss how later. If no icon is bound into your program, Windows uses the default icon (if there is one).

You can do other things with icons besides use them as your program's visual representation. I discuss the details of icons and how they work in Chapter 5.

Cursors

The third type of Windows graphics resource is the cursor. The cursor is the image that corresponds to the mouse on a user's system. When the user moves the mouse, the cursor moves on-screen in response.

Windows provides cursors of its own that you can access with the `LoadCursor()` call. In addition, you can define your own cursors, and load and display these using the same call. Cursors are a very special-purpose object; the only way you use cursors is as a representation of the user's mouse on-screen. Even in this very limited domain, though, cursors still can do several interesting things, which I discuss in Chapter 6, "The Cursor Resource."

Bitmaps, icons, and cursors, then, are the three types of Windows graphics resources. In addition to discussing these in detail in the following chapters, I also give lots of examples along with source code.

On the disk at the back of this book is a copy of ICE/Works, a graphics resource editor for Windows. This tool enables you to create images you can use with many of the examples in this book. Naturally, the version contained herein is limited. Whereas the commercial version reads and writes icons, cursors, and bitmaps, as well as .EXE, .DLL, and .DRV files, this one writes only icon files (although it reads all the other types).

Appendix A contains a brief introduction to ICE/Works. However, the best way to learn to use it is to start playing with it.

The Display Context

Before examining bitmaps (and the objects derived from them), you must first examine the *display context* (DC). A DC defines the properties of how many operations occur onto a bitmap. A display context is to a bitmap what a frame is to a piece of canvas—although you paint on the canvas itself, the frame is what gives the canvas shape and definition. Similarly, although you paint (create) images on a bitmap, the display context associated with that bitmap is what defines many of the properties of the bitmap and what the results of many drawing operations will be.

A display context defines many of the properties that affect how a bitmap is rendered in that display context. This brings up an important point about display contexts (or DCs, which is how I'll refer to them from now on): they come in two distinct flavors. There are *memory* DCs and *screen* DCs.

A screen DC is just what it sounds like—a display context that is attached to a physical screen display (most likely the monitor). This kind of DC defines what the actual output behavior of the bitmap is when it is rendered onto the screen.

A memory DC, by contrast, is not hooked to an output device; however, it mimics the behavior of a particular screen DC, which is. The purpose of a memory DC is to create and manipulate bitmaps in a private off-screen area and then copy that image onto the screen (or to disk, or whatever). Especially with larger and more complex images, it can take a relatively long time to create the image by drawing it using individual GDI calls, whereas a `BitBlt()` call (a method of copying a bitmap from one place to another, discussed in Chapter 3, "The Device Dependent Bitmap") is relatively quick.

In this chapter I discuss the following topics:

■ Display context basics: the screen DC

■ Flavors of display context

■ Using a DC: a simple example

■ The memory or compatible DC

Display Context Basics: The Screen DC

All DC-related operations use and/or return an HDC, or a handle to a display context. An HDC is a fundamental primitive of Windows, and is used by virtually all the GDI functions dealing with graphics.

Getting a DC

The simplest DC to get is a window's DC. This is usually your program's main window, although it also can be the window of a dialog box, or of a child window. You get the DC of a window by using the **GetDC()** call, which returns a handle to a display context (HDC). Using **GetDC()** takes the form

```
HDC   myDC;          // Copy of the DC handle that you can use
...

// Get the handle to the DC of this window

myDC = GetDC ( hWnd );
```

in which hWnd is the window handle of the window whose DC you want to get.

There are two important things to note about **GetDC()**. First, as long as hWnd is a valid window handle, **GetDC()** returns a valid display context. Second, the handle to the DC returned by **GetDC()** is a *handle* to the display context, and not the display context itself. This means that to manipulate the display context, you pass this handle to functions that act on the display context. The HDC acts as a tag, indicating to Windows exactly which DC you are interested in. (Indeed, you can accomplish some very tricky things after you grasp this concept. More on that in a bit.)

Releasing a DC

When you've finished using the HDC, you must give it back to the system. It's not optional. Display context handles are an extremely precious resource in Windows; in fact, there are only five display context handles for the entire system. So if you don't give an HDC back when you're done with it, it's pretty obvious—you've got *BOOM!* bits on the ceiling, and Windows comes to a screeching halt. In fact, failing to give back an HDC when you're done with it is such a catastrophic failure that it's pretty easy to catch—if your program can do exactly five graphics operations before the system locks up, it's pretty certain you're not giving a display context handle back somewhere in your program.

Giving an HDC back when you're done with it is simple; you use the call **ReleaseDC()** and pass it the handle of the window that the DC belongs to, and the handle to the DC itself, like so:

```
HDC        myDC;            // DC handle for us to play with

// Get a handle to the DC of this window

myDC = GetDC ( hWnd );

// Do graphics things here...

// Give the DC back now that you're done.

ReleaseDC ( hWnd, myDC );
```

Getting a DC—Another Method

Using the **GetDC()**/**ReleaseDC()** calls is one way to get and release a handle to a DC for a window (any window). You can also get and release an HDC using the **BeginPaint()** and **EndPaint()** calls. Unlike the **GetDC()**/**ReleaseDC()** calls, which can be used at any time (regardless of whether it makes sense to do so), **BeginPaint()** and **EndPaint()** should only be used in response to a WM_PAINT message.

This is because **BeginPaint()** does more than simply return a handle to a DC; it also sets the clipping region for the window and returns the bounding rectangle of the clipping region. (Note that the bounding rectangle for the clipping region is not the clipping region itself—it's merely the smallest rectangular area that completely contains the clipping region.) This is significantly slower than merely getting the DC of a window. Furthermore, unless **BeginPaint()** is used in response to a WM_PAINT message, both the DC and the clipping region returned are also very likely to be completely invalid.

Just as with **GetDC()**, you must release the handle to the DC that you get from the **BeginPaint()** call. You do this by using the **EndPaint()** call.

13

Flavors of the Display Context

Like most other things in Windows, DCs can come in a variety of flavors, starting out simple and becoming increasingly complex. To understand the different uses of these varieties, take a look at them.

The Common DC: Sharing a DC with Everything

With regard to a window, display contexts come in different flavors. When you create a window, if you don't specify any special information about a DC, the window has a *Common display context*. This is the default.

The client area is everything inside the window frame; the window frame itself, including the various window bits, such as the sizer bars, the system menu button, the title bar, and the minimize and maximize buttons, are all nonclient area objects. It's possible to draw in these parts of a window by getting the DC of the entire area by the `GetWindowDC()` function.

A Common display context is easy to use, but it has some limitations. First, when you want to draw in the client area of your window (see Figure 2.1), you have to retrieve the DC to the window, by using either `GetDC()` or `BeginPaint()`. Second, each time you get the handle to the DC, it's set up with all default attributes. (See Table 2.1 for a list of a DC's attributes and their defaults.) If you make any changes to those defaults, those changes disappear when you release the DC's handle. Thus, unless the default attributes of a DC are OK with you, each time you get the handle to a Common DC you have to write a bunch of code to change the attributes to what you want.

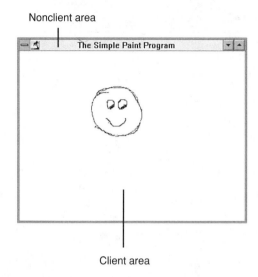

Nonclient area

The Simple Paint Program

Client area

Figure 2.1.
The client area
of a window.

Table 2.1. Default attributes for a display context.

Attribute	Default
Background color	White
Background mode	OPAQUE
Bitmap	No default (Not quite true for **CreateCompatibleDC()**, which has a single-pixel monochrome bitmap created inside it. See **CreateCompatibleDC()** for more details.)
Brush	WHITE_BRUSH
Brush origin	(0,0)
Clipping region	Display surface
Color palette	DEFAULT_PALETTE
Current pen position	(0,0)

continues

Table 2.1. continued

Attribute	*Default*
Drawing mode	R2_COPYPEN
Font	System font
Intercharacter spacing	0
Mapping mode	MM_TEXT
Pen	BLACK_PEN
Polygon filling mode	ALTERNATE
Stretching mode	BLACKONWHITE
Text color	Black
Viewport extent	(1,1)
Viewport origin	(0,0)
Window extent	(1,1)
Window origin	(0,0)

The Class DC: Sharing a DC with Other Windows

If changing a bunch of the default attributes each time you get the DC seems tedious, you can create a window that has a *Class display context*. You do this by specifying the style CS_CLASSDC as one of the window's class attributes before you create it.

A Class display context is a semiprivate resource, which is shared between *all* windows of a particular class. This makes sense, for example, for a bunch of small control windows that all share the same attributes.

A Class display context must be retrieved before you can use it (that is, retrieved with GetDC() or BeginPaint()), but it doesn't have to be released when you're done with it. This is a big change from the Common DC, in which you *must* release the DC when you're done. However, it's often the case that low-level routines you write might not know exactly which window they're dealing with (especially in regard to some of the more atomic graphics operations, such as `BitBlt()`). Therefore, your code should generally assume that it must give a DC back when it's done with it. There's no penalty for doing so with a Class DC or a Private DC (discussed later), and as I mentioned before, it's critical to do so for Common DCs.

> **Tip:** In general, when you're done with a DC, give it back.

Another difference between a Class DC and a Common DC is that a Class DC doesn't get taken out of Windows' DC cache (the five DCs that are available system-wide). This means, however, that using a Class DC type causes your program to use slightly more memory, because Windows allocates a chunk of it (roughly 800 bytes) for your Class DC.

The big advantage of using a Class DC is that any changes you make to the default attributes of the DC are permanent (until you change them again). This means you can make one change to a DC, and all windows which use that DC are affected by the change. The exceptions to this are the clipping region and origin offset; each time you retrieve the DC, Windows updates these values to properly reflect the window whose DC you are retrieving.

The Private DC: A DC of Your Very Own

You can go one step further than a Class DC by giving each window you create its own DC. Doing this means specifying the CS_OWNDC style as one of the window's class attributes before you create the window. This gets you a *Private display context*.

A Private DC is very similar to a Class DC; it's outside of the Windows DC cache, so each time you create a window with this attribute set, you use up an additional 800 bytes (or so) of memory. A Private DC also maintains any changes that you make to its default attributes—when you make a change, it stays changed, unless you change it again.

The big difference between a Private DC and a Class DC is that Class DCs apply to all instances of a particular window class, whereas Private DCs apply to just one instance of a window. This means that a Private DC is not a good choice for a window class that is going to have hundreds of instances (such as a control button), but it is a good choice for a window class that's only going to have one or two instances.

The Window DC: Getting at the Edges

The fourth flavor of DC is somewhat different than the three I've just discussed. It's called a *Window DC,* and it enables you to get at all of a window's display space, not just the client area. Whereas Common DCs, Class DCs, and Private DCs all clip to the client area of a window (or some portion of it), a Window DC gives you access to everything in the window, even stuff like the title bar and borders.

This means two things. If you want to be able to draw into (say) the mover bar or window edges of a window, it's easy to do. On the other hand, unless you know exactly what you're doing, it's going to look *real* ugly. This is one of the reasons `DefWindowProc()` was invented. Do you really want to have to redraw not only your client area, but also your window edges, and title bar, and everything each time you get a `WM_NCPAINT` message? Me neither.

Window DCs are quite useful for doing certain kinds of special effects (such as a pop-up that's always in the title bar of the active window), but are of little use otherwise.

Now that I've thoroughly confused you, it's time for a simple example.

Using a DC: A Simple Example

The following section presents a simple (very simple!) paint program. The program is almost absurdly easy; when you click and hold down the left mouse button inside the SimPaint window, a single black pixel is put at the current mouse position.

Looking at the SimPaint Program

Listings 2.1 through 2.7 show the source code for SimPaint.

Listing 2.1. SIMPAINT.C—C source file for SimPaint.

```c
// SIMPAINT.C
//
// Source code for the simple paint program
//
// Written by Alex Leavens, for ShadowCat Technologies

#include <WINDOWS.H>
#include "SIMPAINT.H"

#include "SIMPAINT.WMC"


BOOL buttonDown = FALSE; // If true, mouse button down

/***************************
 *
 * WinMain()
 *
 * Start-up function for all Windows programs.
 */

    int PASCAL

WinMain(HANDLE  hInstance,       // Current instance of program
        HANDLE  hPrevInstance,   // Previous instance of program (if any)
        LPSTR   lpCmdLine,       // Command line (if applicable)
        int     nCmdShow)        // Window display style (open/iconic)

{
    MSG msg;    // Message passed to your program

    //---------------------------------

    hInst = hInstance;   // Save the current instance

    if (!BLDInitApplication(hInstance,hPrevInstance,&nCmdShow,lpCmdLine))
        return FALSE;

    if (!hPrevInstance)         /* Is there another instance of the task   */
        {
        if (!BLDRegisterClass(hInstance))
            return FALSE;       /* Exits if unable to initialize */
```

continues

Listing 2.1. continued

```
        }

    MainhWnd = BLDCreateWindow(hInstance);
    if (!MainhWnd)                /* Check if the window is created */
        return FALSE;

    ShowWindow(MainhWnd, nCmdShow);   /* Show the window */
    UpdateWindow(MainhWnd);           /* Send WM_PAINT message to window */

    BLDInitMainMenu(MainhWnd);        /* Initialize main menu if necessary */

    while (GetMessage(&msg,      /* Message structure */
        0,                       /* Handle of window receiving the message */
        0,                       /* Lowest message to examine */
        0))                      /* Highest message to examine */
        {
        if (BLDKeyTranslation(&msg))
            continue;
        TranslateMessage(&msg); /* Translates character keys */
        DispatchMessage(&msg);  /* Dispatches message to window */
        }

    BLDExitApplication();       /* Clean up if necessary */

    return(msg.wParam);         /* Returns the value from PostQuitMessage */
}


/******************************************************************/
/*              WINDOW PROCEDURE FOR MAIN WINDOW                 */
/******************************************************************/

    long FAR PASCAL

BLDMainWndProc ( HWND          hWnd,
                 unsigned      message,
                 WORD          wParam,
                 LONG          lParam )
{

    HDC        hDC;       // Handle to your display context

    WORD  mX;       // Mouse x position
    WORD  mY;       // Mouse y position
```

```
//-----------------------

switch (message)
{
case WM_CREATE:                /* Window creation */

    /* Send to BLDDefWindowProc in (.WMC) for controls in main window */
    return BLDDefWindowProc(hWnd, message, wParam, lParam);
    break;

case WM_SETFOCUS:              /* Window is notified of focus change */
    /* Send to BLDDefWindowProc in (.WMC) for controls in main window */
    return BLDDefWindowProc(hWnd, message, wParam, lParam);
    break;

case WM_DESTROY:               /* Window being destroyed */
    PostQuitMessage(0);
    return BLDDefWindowProc(hWnd, message, wParam, lParam);
    break;

case WM_MOUSEMOVE:

 // Only paint if the mouse button is down.

 if ( buttonDown != TRUE )
     break;

 /* Get the current mouse coordinates */

mX = LOWORD(lParam);
mY = HIWORD(lParam);

   hDC = GetDC ( hWnd );        // Get DC of your window

   SetPixel ( hDC,
      mX,
      mY,
      RGB ( 0, 0, 0 ) );  // Draw a black pixel

ReleaseDC ( hWnd,
          hDC );
   break;
```

continues

Listing 2.1. continued

```
case WM_LBUTTONDOWN:

    /* Get the current mouse coordinates */

    mX = LOWORD(lParam);
    mY = HIWORD(lParam);

        buttonDown = TRUE;

        hDC = GetDC ( hWnd );        // Get DC of your window

        SetPixel ( hDC,
            mX,
            mY,
            RGB ( 0, 0, 0 ) );  // Draw a black pixel

     ReleaseDC ( hWnd,
                 hDC );
        break;


    case WM_LBUTTONUP:

        buttonDown = FALSE;
        break;

    case WM_COMMAND:                /* Command from the main window */
        if (BLDMenuCommand(hWnd, message, wParam, lParam))
            break;                  /* Processed by BLDMenuCommand. */
            /* Else default processing by BLDDefWindowProc. */
default:
        /* Pass on message for default processing */
        return BLDDefWindowProc(hWnd, message, wParam, lParam);
    }

    return FALSE;                   /* Returns FALSE if processed */
}
```

Listing 2.2. SIMPAINT.WMC—special include file for SimPaint that handles much of the details of processing Window messages.

```
/*File name: SIMPAINT.WMC                                 */
/*"SIMPAINT" Generated by WindowsMAKER Professional       */
/*Author: Alex Leavens                                    */


/****************************************************************/
/*                  GLOBAL VARIABLES                          */
/****************************************************************/


HANDLE  hInst  = 0;  /* Handle to instance.                  */
HWND    MainhWnd= 0;  /* Handle to main window.               */
HWND    hClient = 0;  /* Handle to window in client area.     */
FARPROC lpClient= 0L; /* Function for window in client area.  */


/****************************************************************/
/*            PROCESSES KEYBOARD ACCELERATORS                 */
/*            AND MODELESS DIALOG BOX KEY INPUT               */
/****************************************************************/


BOOL BLDKeyTranslation(pMsg)
MSG *pMsg;
    {
    return FALSE; /* No special key input                     */
    }


/****************************************************************/
/*        CUSTOM MESSAGE PROCESSING FOR MAIN WINDOW          */
/****************************************************************/


long FAR PASCAL BLDDefWindowProc(hWnd, message, wParam, lParam)
HWND hWnd;                      /* Window handle             */
unsigned message;              /* Type of message           */
WORD wParam;                   /* Additional information     */
LONG lParam;                   /* Additional information     */
    {

    switch (message)
```

continues

23

Listing 2.2. continued

```
        {

    default:
        /* Pass on message for default processing by Windows    */
        return DefWindowProc(hWnd, message, wParam, lParam);
        }
    return FALSE; /* Returns FALSE if not processed by Windows */
    }


/****************************************************************/
/*              PROCESSES ALL MENU ITEM SELECTIONS              */
/****************************************************************/

BOOL BLDMenuCommand(hWnd, message, wParam, lParam)
HWND hWnd;                      /* Window handle                */
unsigned message;               /* Type of message             */
WORD wParam;                    /* Additional information       */
LONG lParam;                    /* Additional information       */
    {

    switch(wParam)
        {

        /* Processing of linked menu items in menu: SIMPAINT   */

        default:
            return FALSE;    /* Not processed by this function. */
        }
    return TRUE;             /* Processed by this function.    */
    }


/****************************************************************/
/*    FUNCTIONS FOR INITIALIZATION AND EXIT OF APPLICATION      */
/****************************************************************/

BOOL BLDInitApplication(hInst,hPrev,pCmdShow,lpCmd)
HANDLE hInst;    /* Handle to application instance.            */
HANDLE hPrev;    /* Handle to previous instance of application. */
int *pCmdShow;   /* Pointer to variable that specifies         */
                 /* how main window is to be shown.            */
LPSTR lpCmd;     /* Long pointer to the command line.          */
    {
    /* No initialization necessary */
    return TRUE;
    }
```

```
BOOL BLDRegisterClass(hInstance) /* Registers the class for the main window */
HANDLE hInstance;
    {
    WNDCLASS WndClass;

    WndClass.style        = 0;
    WndClass.lpfnWndProc  = BLDMainWndProc;
    WndClass.cbClsExtra   = 0;
    WndClass.cbWndExtra   = 0;
    WndClass.hInstance    = hInstance;
    WndClass.hIcon        = LoadIcon(NULL,IDI_APPLICATION);
    WndClass.hCursor      = LoadCursor(NULL,IDC_ARROW);
    WndClass.hbrBackground = CreateSolidBrush(GetSysColor(COLOR_WINDOW));
    WndClass.lpszMenuName  = "SIMPAINT";
    WndClass.lpszClassName = "SIMPAINT";

    return RegisterClass(&WndClass);
    }


HWND BLDCreateWindow(hInstance)  /* Creates the main window */
HANDLE hInstance;
    {
    HWND hWnd;              /* Window handle */
    int coordinate[4];     /* Coordinates of main window */

    coordinate[0]=CW_USEDEFAULT;
    coordinate[1]=0;
    coordinate[2]=CW_USEDEFAULT;
    coordinate[3]=0;

    hWnd = CreateWindow("SIMPAINT",  /* Window class registered earlier  */
          "The Simple Paint Program",          /* Window caption */
        WS_OVERLAPPED¦WS_THICKFRAME¦WS_SYSMENU¦WS_MINIMIZEBOX¦WS_MAXIMIZEBOX,
                              /* Window style */
          coordinate[0],       /* X position */
          coordinate[1],       /* Y position */
          coordinate[2],       /* Width */
          coordinate[3],       /* Height */
          0,                   /* Parent handle */
          0,                   /* Menu or child ID */
          hInstance,           /* Instance */
          (LPSTR)NULL);        /* Additional info */

    return hWnd;
    }
```

continues

Listing 2.2. continued

```c
BOOL BLDInitMainMenu(hWnd)          /* Called just before entering message loop */
HWND hWnd;
    {
    /* No initialization necessary */
    return TRUE;
    }


BOOL BLDExitApplication()           /* Called just before exit of application */
    {
    /* No processing needed at exit for this design */
    return TRUE;
    }


/**********************************************************/
/* ERROR MESSAGE HANDLING (Definitions can be overruled.) */
/**********************************************************/

#ifndef ERRORCAPTION
#define ERRORCAPTION "The Simple Paint Program"
#endif

#ifndef LOADERROR
#define LOADERROR "Cannot load string."
#endif

int BLDDisplayMessage(hWnd,uMsg,pContext,iType)
HWND hWnd;
unsigned uMsg;
char *pContext;
int iType;
    {
    int i, j;
    char Message[200+1];

    if (uMsg)
        {
        if (!LoadString(hInst,uMsg,Message,200))
            {
            MessageBox(hWnd,LOADERROR,ERRORCAPTION,
                    MB_OK¦MB_SYSTEMMODAL¦MB_ICONHAND);
            return FALSE;
            }
        }
```

```
    else
        Message[0]=0;

    if (pContext)
        {
        i = lstrlen(Message);
        j = lstrlen(pContext);
        if (i + j + 1 <= 200)
            {
            lstrcat(Message, " ");
            lstrcat(Message, pContext);
            }
        }

    return MessageBox(hWnd,Message,ERRORCAPTION,iType);
    }

/****************************************************************/
/*          FUNCTIONS FOR DRAWING GRAPHICS BUTTONS          */
/****************************************************************/

BOOL BLDDrawIcon(lpDrawItem,pIconName)
LPDRAWITEMSTRUCT lpDrawItem;
char *pIconName;
    {
    HICON hIcon;

    if (!(hIcon = LoadIcon(hInst,pIconName)))
        {
        BLDDisplayMessage(GetActiveWindow(),BLD_CannotLoadIcon,pIconName,
                        MB_OK | MB_ICONASTERISK);
        return FALSE;
        }
    SetMapMode(lpDrawItem->hDC,MM_TEXT);
    return DrawIcon(lpDrawItem->hDC,0,0,hIcon);
    }


BOOL BLDDrawBitmap(lpDrawItem,pBitmapName,bStretch)
LPDRAWITEMSTRUCT lpDrawItem;
char *pBitmapName;
BOOL bStretch;
    {
    HBITMAP hBitmap;
```

continues

Listing 2.2. continued

```
HDC hMemDC;
BITMAP Bitmap;
int iRaster;

iRaster = GetDeviceCaps(lpDrawItem->hDC,RASTERCAPS);
if ((iRaster&RC_BITBLT)!=RC_BITBLT)
    return FALSE; /* Device cannot display bitmap */

if (!(hBitmap = LoadBitmap(hInst,pBitmapName)))
    {
    BLDDisplayMessage(GetActiveWindow(),BLD_CannotLoadBitmap,pBitmapName,
                    MB_OK | MB_ICONASTERISK);
    return FALSE;
    }

if (!GetObject(hBitmap,sizeof(BITMAP),(LPSTR)&Bitmap))
    {
    DeleteObject(hBitmap);
    return FALSE;
    }
if (!(hMemDC = CreateCompatibleDC(lpDrawItem->hDC)))
    {
    DeleteObject(hBitmap);
    return FALSE;
    }
if (!SelectObject(hMemDC,hBitmap))
    {
    DeleteDC(hMemDC);
    DeleteObject(hBitmap);
    return FALSE;
    }

if (bStretch)
        {
        StretchBlt(lpDrawItem->hDC,
                lpDrawItem->rcItem.left,
                lpDrawItem->rcItem.top,
                lpDrawItem->rcItem.right-lpDrawItem->rcItem.left,
                lpDrawItem->rcItem.bottom-lpDrawItem->rcItem.top,
                hMemDC,
                0,
                0,
```

```
                    Bitmap.bmWidth,
                    Bitmap.bmHeight,
                    SRCCOPY);
        }
    else
        {
            BitBlt(lpDrawItem->hDC,
                    lpDrawItem->rcItem.left,
                    lpDrawItem->rcItem.top,
                    lpDrawItem->rcItem.right-lpDrawItem->rcItem.left,
                    lpDrawItem->rcItem.bottom-lpDrawItem->rcItem.top,
                    hMemDC,
                    0,
                    0,
                    SRCCOPY);
        }
    DeleteDC(hMemDC);
    DeleteObject(hBitmap);
    return TRUE;
    }

/****************************************************************/
/*        FUNCTION FOR CREATING CONTROLS IN MAIN WINDOW        */
/****************************************************************/

HWND BLDCreateClientControls(pTemplateName,lpNew) /* Start-up procedure for
                                                     window in client area */
char    *pTemplateName;
FARPROC lpNew;
    {
    RECT rClient,rMain,rDialog;
    int dxDialog,dyDialog,dyExtra,dtXold,dtYold;
    HANDLE hRes,hMem;
    LPBLD_DLGTEMPLATE lpDlg;
    unsigned long styleold,style;
    HWND hNew;

    if (!IsWindow(MainhWnd))
        return 0;
    if (IsZoomed(MainhWnd))
        ShowWindow(MainhWnd,SW_RESTORE);

    if (IsWindow(hClient))
```

continues

29

Listing 2.2. continued

```
DestroyWindow(hClient); /* Destroy Previous window in client area  */

/* Get access to data structure of dialog box
   containing layout of controls */
if (!(hRes=FindResource(hInst,(LPSTR)pTemplateName,RT_DIALOG)))
    return 0;
if (!(hMem=LoadResource(hInst,hRes)))
    return 0;
if (!(lpDlg=(LPBLD_DLGTEMPLATE)LockResource(hMem)))
    return 0;

/* Change dialog box data structure so it can be used as a window
   in client area */
styleold      = lpDlg->dtStyle;
style         = lpDlg->dtStyle&(CLIENTSTRIP);
lpDlg->dtStyle = lpDlg->dtStyle^style;
lpDlg->dtStyle = lpDlg->dtStyle ¦ WS_CHILD ¦ WS_CLIPSIBLINGS;
dtXold        = lpDlg->dtX;
dtYold        = lpDlg->dtY;
lpDlg->dtX    = 0;
lpDlg->dtY    = 0;

if (!(hNew = CreateDialogIndirect(hInst,(LPSTR)lpDlg, MainhWnd,lpNew)))
    return 0;

/* Restore dialog box data structure. */
lpDlg->dtStyle =styleold;
lpDlg->dtX    = dtXold;
lpDlg->dtY    = dtYold;

UnlockResource(hMem);
FreeResource(hMem);

/* Move and size window in client area and main window */
GetClientRect(MainhWnd,&rClient);
GetWindowRect(MainhWnd,&rMain);
GetWindowRect(hNew,&rDialog);
dxDialog=(rDialog.right-rDialog.left)-(rClient.right-rClient.left);
dyDialog=(rDialog.bottom-rDialog.top)-(rClient.bottom-rClient.top);
BLDMoveWindow(MainhWnd,rMain.left,rMain.top,
         (rMain.right-rMain.left)+dxDialog,
                       (rMain.bottom-rMain.top)+dyDialog,
         TRUE);
MoveWindow(hNew,0,0,
              (rDialog.right-rDialog.left),
```

```
                          (rDialog.bottom-rDialog.top),
                      TRUE);
     GetClientRect(MainhWnd,&rClient);

     /* Compensate size if menu bar is more than one line. */
     if ((rDialog.bottom-rDialog.top)>(rClient.bottom-rClient.top))
         {
         dyExtra=(rDialog.bottom-rDialog.top)-(rClient.bottom-rClient.top);
         BLDMoveWindow(MainhWnd,rMain.left,rMain.top,
                   (rMain.right-rMain.left)+dxDialog,
                   (rMain.bottom-rMain.top)+dyDialog+dyExtra,
                   TRUE);
         }

     ShowWindow(hNew,SW_SHOW);
     hClient=hNew;
     lpClient=lpNew;
     return hClient;
     }

/* Ensure that window is within screen. */
void BLDMoveWindow(hWnd,x,y,nWidth,nHeight,bRepaint)
HWND hWnd;
int  x;
int  y;
int  nWidth;
int  nHeight;
BOOL bRepaint;
     {
     int xMax,yMax,xNew,yNew;

     xMax = GetSystemMetrics(SM_CXSCREEN);
     yMax = GetSystemMetrics(SM_CYSCREEN);
     if ((nWidth<=xMax)&&(x+nWidth>xMax))
         xNew=xMax-nWidth;
     else
         xNew=x;

     if ((nHeight<=yMax)&&(y+nHeight>yMax))
         yNew=yMax-nHeight;
     else
         yNew=y;

     MoveWindow(hWnd,xNew,yNew,nWidth,nHeight,bRepaint);
     return;
     }
```

continues

Listing 2.2. continued

```
/****************************************************************/
/*              FUNCTION FOR SWITCHING MENU SET                 */
/****************************************************************/

BOOL BLDSwitchMenu(hWnd,pTemplateName)
HWND hWnd;
char *pTemplateName;
    {
    HMENU hMenu1,hMenu;
    DWORD style;

    style = GetWindowLong(hWnd,GWL_STYLE);
    if((style & WS_CHILD) == WS_CHILD) /* Called from control
                                          in main window? */
        {
        if (!(hWnd=GetParent(hWnd)))
            return FALSE;
        style = GetWindowLong(hWnd,GWL_STYLE);
        if((style & WS_CHILD) == WS_CHILD) /* No menu in a WS_CHILD window. */
            return FALSE;
        }
    if((style & WS_CAPTION) != WS_CAPTION) /* No menu if no caption.        */
        return FALSE;

    hMenu1 = GetMenu(hWnd);
    if (!(hMenu = LoadMenu(hInst,pTemplateName)))
        {
        BLDDisplayMessage(hWnd,BLD_CannotLoadMenu,pTemplateName,
                        MB_OK | MB_ICONASTERISK);
        return FALSE;
        }

    if (!SetMenu(hWnd,hMenu))
        return FALSE;
    if (hMenu1)
        DestroyMenu(hMenu1);

    DrawMenuBar(hWnd);
    return TRUE;
    }
```

Listing 2.3. SIMPAINT.H—include file for SimPaint.

```
/*File name: SIMPAINT.H                                    */
/*"SIMPAINT" Generated by WindowsMAKER Professional        */
/*Author: Alex Leavens                                     */


/* Give access to handles in all code modules */
extern HANDLE hInst;
extern HWND MainhWnd;

/* Constants for error message strings */
#define BLD_CannotRun          4000
#define BLD_CannotCreate       4001
#define BLD_CannotLoadMenu     4002
#define BLD_CannotLoadIcon     4003
#define BLD_CannotLoadBitmap   4004

#if !defined(THISISBLDRC)

int PASCAL WinMain(HANDLE,HANDLE,LPSTR,int);
long FAR PASCAL BLDMainWndProc(HWND,unsigned,WORD,LONG);
long FAR PASCAL BLDDefWindowProc(HWND,unsigned,WORD,LONG);
BOOL BLDKeyTranslation(MSG *);
BOOL BLDInitApplication(HANDLE,HANDLE,int *,LPSTR);
BOOL BLDExitApplication(void);
HWND BLDCreateClientControls(char *,FARPROC);
BOOL BLDInitMainMenu(HWND);
BOOL BLDMenuCommand(HWND, unsigned , WORD, LONG);
BOOL BLDRegisterClass(HANDLE);
HWND BLDCreateWindow(HANDLE);
int BLDDisplayMessage(HWND,unsigned,char *,int);
BOOL BLDSwitchMenu(HWND,char *);
BOOL BLDDrawBitmap(LPDRAWITEMSTRUCT,char *,BOOL);
BOOL BLDDrawIcon(LPDRAWITEMSTRUCT,char *);
void BLDMoveWindow(HWND,int,int,int,int,BOOL);

/****************************************************************/
/* Variables, types and constants for controls in main window. */
/****************************************************************/

extern HWND hClient;     /* Handle to window in client area.  */
extern FARPROC lpClient; /* Function for window in client area.*/

#dofino CLIENTSTRIP
```

continues

Listing 2.3. continued

```
WS_MINIMIZE¦WS_MAXIMIZE¦WS_CAPTION¦WS_BORDER¦WS_DLGFRAME¦
WS_SYSMENU¦WS_POPUP¦WS_THICKFRAME¦DS_MODALFRAME

typedef struct
  {
  unsigned long dtStyle;
  BYTE dtItemCount;
  int dtX;
  int dtY;
  int dtCX;
  int dtCY;
  } BLD_DLGTEMPLATE;

typedef BLD_DLGTEMPLATE far              *LPBLD_DLGTEMPLATE;

#endif

/* User Defined ID Values             */

/* WindowsMAKER Pro generated ID Values */
```

Listing 2.4. SIMPAINT—makefile for SimPaint.

```
#File name: SIMPAINT - Makefile for Microsoft C 7.0
#"SIMPAINT" Generated by WindowsMAKER Professional
#Author: Alex Leavens

comp= /c /AS /Od /Gw /Zpei /D _WINDOWS /W2

ALL : SIMPAINT.EXE

SIMPAINT.RES : SIMPAINT.RC SIMPAINT.H
    rc -r SIMPAINT.RC

SIMPAINT.OBJ : SIMPAINT.C SIMPAINT.WMC SIMPAINT.H
    cl  $(comp) SIMPAINT.C

SIMPAINT.EXE : SIMPAINT.OBJ  SIMPAINT.DEF SIMPAINT.RES
    LINK @SIMPAINT.LNK
    rc SIMPAINT.RES
```

Listing 2.5. SIMPAINT.DEF—definition file for SimPaint.

```
;File name: SIMPAINT.DEF - Definition file for SimPaint
;"SIMPAINT" Generated by WindowsMAKER Professional
;Author: Alex Leavens


NAME           SIMPAINT
DESCRIPTION    'SIMPAINT the Simple Paint Program by Alex Leavens'
EXETYPE        WINDOWS
STUB           'WINSTUB.EXE'
DATA           MOVEABLE MULTIPLE
CODE           MOVEABLE DISCARDABLE PRELOAD
HEAPSIZE       1024
STACKSIZE      5120
EXPORTS

               BLDMainWndProc
```

Listing 2.6. SIMPAINT.RC—resource file for SimPaint.

```
/*File name: SIMPAINT.RC                                  */
/*"SIMPAINT" Generated by WindowsMAKER Professional       */
/*Author: Alex Leavens                                    */

#define THISISBLDRC

#include <WINDOWS.H>
#include "SIMPAINT.H"


/********************************************************/
/*      Resource code for error message strings         */
/********************************************************/
STRINGTABLE
    BEGIN
        BLD_CannotRun          "Cannot run "
        BLD_CannotCreate       "Cannot create dialog box "
        BLD_CannotLoadMenu     "Cannot load menu "
        BLD_CannotLoadIcon     "Cannot load icon "
        BLD_CannotLoadBitmap   "Cannot load bitmap "
    END
```

Listing 2.7. SIMPAINT.LNK—link for SimPaint.

```
SIMPAINT ,SIMPAINT.EXE ,/align:16 /NOD /map /CO , LIBW SLIBCEW, SIMPAINT.DEF
```

Examining SimPaint

SimPaint illustrates the use of the `GetDC()` and `ReleaseDC()` calls. When the user presses the left mouse button, or moves the mouse (with the left button pressed), SimPaint retrieves the DC of the SimPaint window, uses the `SetPixel()` call to place a black pixel at the mouse position, and then releases the DC. The code responsible for all the painting operations comprises only three Windows calls.

Despite SimPaint's simplicity, there are several points about the program worth noting. One is that when SimPaint retrieves the mouse position (from the `WM_LBUTTONDOWN` and `WM_MOUSEMOVE` messages), the mouse position returned is relative to the client area of the parent window and not the desktop (full-screen) window, as you might expect. Remember that a window's client area has the point (0,0) at the upper-left corner, and the point (x,y) at the lower-right corner.

Getting the mouse position in coordinates relative to the window is very handy because you can simply pass the X and Y mouse coordinates into the `SetPixel()` function; DCs also map their upper-left corner to (0,0) and their lower-right corner to (x,y). Thus, when you retrieve the DC of the SimPaint window, you're automatically retrieving a DC that has the same relative coordinates as the mouse position on-screen. (See Figure 2.2.)

> **Note:** Only if the mapping mode is `MM_TEXT`, which is a valid assumption for all the examples in this book, will the Window DC and the mouse position have the same coordinate system in effect.

Note that there is a direct one-to-one correspondence between the client area of a window and the DC of that window retrieved by `GetDC()`.

The second point to notice about SimPaint is that all the drawing on-screen takes place in response to mouse messages—when the user moves the mouse, the program draws something. In response to the `WM_PAINT` message, however, the program does nothing except call `DefWindowProc()`.

This drawing method makes the paint program very easy to write (as I mentioned, the entire painting operation consists of only three calls to the Windows API), but also very dumb. After the pixel has been placed on the screen by SimPaint, it's fair game. The user can drag another window on top of yours, or Windows itself can cover up part of your screen (through a dialog box or menu). At the point at which the previously covered piece of your window becomes uncovered, Windows sends you a WM_PAINT message.

DC of client area
(GetDC(), BeginPaint())

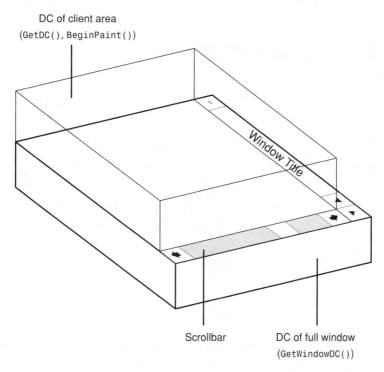

Window Title

Scrollbar

DC of full window
(GetWindowDC())

Figure 2.2. The relationship between the window client area and the hDC of a window.

WM_PAINT is Windows' way of telling your program that part of its display needs redrawing, for whatever reason. In this case, however, you can't redraw the screen, because the program, as it currently stands, remembers nothing about what's been drawn. You obviously need a way of making a copy of the information on the screen, and this is where a memory DC comes into play.

37

The Memory or Compatible DC

A memory DC is a special kind of DC you can use for graphics operations or anything else that requires a DC.

Building a Memory (Compatible) DC

To build a memory DC (also known as a compatible DC), you use the call `CreateCompatibleDC()`. Doing this tells Windows to take a piece of memory and *treat it exactly as if it were a screen*. This is incredibly useful, because you now have an area that looks exactly like a screen and behaves exactly like a screen, but isn't visible. This makes it the perfect place to store images you want to be able to display later.

The way you create a memory, or *compatible*, DC (so named because it's compatible with a screen DC) is

```
HDC  memDC;    // Handle to a compatible (memory) DC
...
memDC = CreateCompatibleDC ( screenDC );
```

in which `screenDC` is a screen DC that you've gotten earlier via one of the methods previously discussed. You now have an off-screen DC that is compatible, in terms of its palette and such, with the screen. One area where it isn't compatible, however, is in its display surface (the bitmap).

Every DC you get—either a screen DC (gotten through `GetDC()`) or a compatible (memory) DC (gotten through `CreateCompatibleDC()`)—has a drawing surface associated with it. For a compatible DC, this is a bitmap. *Every compatible DC you create has a bitmap in it*. In the case of a screen DC, the display surface isn't a bitmap; it's actually a chunk of the physical screen (which is why when you draw on a screen DC's bitmap, it shows up on the screen).

Building a Compatible Bitmap

In the case of a compatible (memory) DC, the bitmap isn't visible. In fact, when you initially create a compatible DC, the bitmap in it is very small—to be exact, it's one pixel big, and monochrome. Naturally enough, you can't do a whole lot with a single-pixel monochrome bitmap (except represent a flea, maybe!), so the first thing to do is create a larger bitmap to go into the compatible DC you've just created. You do this very easily by using the `CreateCompatibleBitmap()` call. (I know, I know, I haven't even gotten to the chapter on bitmaps and I'm already talking about them. Can't be helped, I'm afraid. <grin>)

```
HBITMAP    myBmp;    // Handle to a compatible bitmap

myBmp = CreateCompatibleBitmap ( hDC,     // DC to make bitmap
                                          // compatible with
                                 xSize,   // Width of compatible bitmap
                                 ySize ); // Height of compatible bitmap
```

The first parameter to `CreateCompatibleBitmap()` is the handle to the DC that you want the bitmap to be compatible with. (The second and third parameters, `xSize` and `ySize`, are pretty self-explanatory.) Because the purpose of creating a compatible bitmap is to be able to expand the size of the bitmap in your compatible DC, your first idea is probably to use the handle to the compatible DC that you just created. This is the obvious answer, but it also happens to be the wrong one.

As I mentioned, when you create a compatible DC, it creates a single-pixel monochrome bitmap to go inside the DC. The word *monochrome* is the key—because the `CreateCompatibleBitmap()` call creates a bitmap compatible with the one inside the DC used to create the compatible bitmap. The result of using your compatible DC to create a compatible bitmap is a bigger monochrome bitmap. This is fine if you actually want a monochrome bitmap, but if you're trying to create a bitmap compatible with the screen, you're up a creek, so to speak.

The trick to creating a color bitmap for your compatible DC is to use a *screen* DC to create the compatible bitmap. Because you've already got a screen DC lying around (you used it to create the compatible DC), you can use that one.

Here's how the code looks now:

```
HDC        myDC;     // Compatible DC handle
HBITMAP    myBmp;    // Compatible bitmap handle

myDC = CreateCompatibleDC ( screenDC );
myBmp = CreateCompatibleBitmap ( screenDC,
                                 xSize,
                                 ySize );
```

Both `CreateCompatibleDC()` and `CreateCompatibleBitmap()` use the *screen DC* because you want to create objects that are compatible with the screen. One interesting point to note is that if you create a compatible DC and a compatible bitmap (compatible with the screen), select the compatible bitmap into the compatible DC, and then use the *compatible DC* to create a second compatible bitmap, this second compatible bitmap will be a color bitmap. This is because the format of the bitmap *currently* selected into the DC determines the format of the bitmap created by the `CreateCompatibleBitmap()` call.

Hooking a Bitmap into a DC

Now that you have a compatible DC and a compatible bitmap, the next step is to hook the bitmap into the DC. This is the next place you can run into trouble. When you select an object (such as a bitmap) into a DC, you get back the handle to the object that was in there previously. In this case, you get back the handle of the single-pixel monochrome bitmap that was created when you created the compatible DC.

You might be tempted to ignore this single-pixel monochrome bitmap handle ("Such a leetle bitmap, no?"), but *don't do it*! The reason is very simple—when you're done with a compatible DC, you must destroy it; failing to do so uses up valuable GDI resources. However, if you don't first select the single-pixel monochrome bitmap back into the compatible DC *before* you destroy the DC, that single-pixel monochrome bitmap floats around forever (sort of like the flying Dutchman), cluttering up GDI space, until you reboot your machine.

Doing this once or twice is really no big deal, because this single-pixel monochrome bitmap occupies only 64 bytes of GDI space. (A very good way to tell whether you're leaving these little puppies around is to go into Heap Walker and nose around GDI space. If there are lots of little 64-byte bitmaps that don't appear to belong to anybody, you—or some other app you're running—isn't freeing these resources properly.) However, if you're writing a graphics-intensive application (which you probably are; otherwise you wouldn't be reading this book), you might be creating *hundreds* of compatible DCs. Multiply this small chunk of lost resource by several hundred, and the picture becomes very ugly. Windows comes to a screeching halt.

Tip: The moral is simple: when you're done with a compatible DC, put the original monochrome bitmap back into it before you delete the DC.

Listings 2.8 and 2.9 show a C++ CompatibleDC object that implements all this behavior quite nicely. The constructor and destructor routines make sure that the single-pixel monochrome bitmap is properly saved and restored, with the result that this sort of memory leak goes away without your having to think about it. One of the (many) reasons I like C++ so much is that much of the gruntwork of manipulating Windows can be hidden in object classes like this one.

Note: For those who might not be familiar with C++ yet, here are a few definitions to help you get up to speed.

Object class—A fundamental construct of C++, just as a struct is a fundamental construct of C. An object class is a way of encapsulating data and functions which manipulate that data into a logical object. Ideally, an object class should be treatable as a "black box," with the rest of your program not knowing what's inside the box.

Member function—In C, a structure contains data members; in C++, an object class contains not only data members, but member functions as well. These are the routines that manipulate the data members of the object class.

Instance—In C, when you build a typedef of a struct, you're defining what the structure looks like, but you're not allocating any space for it; you do that only by actually defining a variable of that structure type. Similarly, in C++ when you define an object class, you're only defining the data structure and behavior of the member functions of that class, and not allocating space for it. When you create a particular variable of that object class, you've created an instance of it.

Instantiation—When you create a particular instance of an object class, you're said to have instantiated it.

Constructor—This is a routine that is always called when you instantiate an object class. Every object class has at least one constructor routine (which can be derived from a parent class of the object), and might have more than one. Constructor routines are used to define start-up behavior and initialize data members for an object class.

Destructor—This is a routine that is always called when an object is about to disappear. For example, an instance of an object class that is created inside a routine goes away at the end of that routine. Just before the object goes away, its destructor routine is called. This enables the object class to do any cleanup it needs to do.

Defining a Compatible DC Object Class

Listing 2.8. COMPATDC.H—header file defining the CompatibleDC object class.

```
/* COMPATDC.H
 *
 * Defines a compatible DC class
 *
 * Written by Alex Leavens, for ShadowCat Technologies
 */


#ifndef _ _COMPATDC_H
#define _ _COMPATDC_H

#include <windows.h>
#include "boolean.h"

#ifdef _ _cplusplus

/*---------------- CompatibleDC Code --------------------*/


/*************************************
 *
 * Class: CompatibleDC
 *
 * This class implements a compatibleDC logical object, which you need
 * virtually any time you do anything with bitmaps.
 */

    class

CompatibleDC
{
    private:

        HDC        hDCMem;         // Handle to the compatible DC

        HBITMAP    saveBM;         // Bitmap for saving old mono bitmaps in...

    public:
```

```
    /***********************
    *
    * CompatibleDC() - Constructor
    *
    * Creates a compatible DC
    *
    * Returns: Nothing
    *
    * Args: hDC to be made compatible with
    */

    CompatibleDC( HDC hDC );

    /***************************
    *
    * CompatibleDC() - Constructor
    *
    * Returns: Nothing
    *
    * Args: hDC - device context to make a compatible DC for
    *          newBM - bitmap to select into the compatible DC
    */

    CompatibleDC( HDC      hDC,
            HBITMAP  newBM);

    /********************************
    *
    * ~CompatibleDC() - Destructor
    *
    * Deletes a compatible DC.
    *
    * Returns: Nothing
    *
    * Args: Nothing
    */

~CompatibleDC( void );

/***************************
 *
 * GetCompatDC()
 *
 * Returns a copy of the handle to the compatible DC.
 *
```

continues

Listing 2.8. continued

```
* Returns: handle to the DC
*/

    HDC
GetCompatDC( void );


/*************************
 *
 * SelectBitmapIntoDC()
 *
 * Selects the desired bitmap into the DC
 *
 * Returns: Nothing
 */

    void
SelectBitmapIntoDC ( HBITMAP  newBmp )
{
    saveBM = SelectObject ( hDCMem,
                            newBmp );
}


/*********************
 *
 * RestoreOldBitmap()
 *
 * Before deleting the DC object, this
 * routine will put back in place the old
 * single-pixel mono bitmap that was created
 * when you created the DC, but only if that
 * single-pixel mono bitmap is not currently
 * IN the memory DC.
 *
 * Returns: Nothing
 */

    void
RestoreOldBitmap ( void )
{
    if ( saveBM )
    {
     SelectObject ( hDCMem,
                    saveBM );
```

```
                    saveBM = NULL;
            }
        }
};


//---------------------------------------

#endif // __cplusplus

#endif // __COMPATDC_H
```

Listing 2.9. COMPATDC.CPP—C++ source for implementation of some member functions of the CompatibleDC class.

```
/* COMPATDC.CPP
 *
 * Compatible DC object class
 *
 * Written by Alex Leavens, for ShadowCat Technologies
 */

#include <WINDOWS.H>
#include "boolean.h"
#include "compatdc.h"

#define _EXPORT _export

/*---------------------
 *
 * CompatibleDC::CompatibleDC()
 *
 * Create a compatible (memory) DC with
 * the DC that you've been passed in.
 */

CompatibleDC::CompatibleDC(HDC     hDC)
{
    hDCMem = CreateCompatibleDC( hDC );

    saveBM = NULL;
}
```

continues

45

Listing 2.9. continued

```
/*---------------------------
 *
 * CompatibleDC::CompatibleDC()
 *
 * Create a compatible (memory) DC with the
 * DC that you've been passed in, and select
 * into it the bitmap that was passed in.
 */

CompatibleDC::CompatibleDC(HDC          hDC,
                           HBITMAP      newBM)
{
    hDCMem = CreateCompatibleDC( hDC );

    SelectBitmapIntoDC ( newBM );
}

/*-----------------
 *
 * CompatibleDC::~CompatibleDC()
 *
 * Destructor definition - destroys the compatible
 * DC object. Before it does this, it selects back
 * into the memory DC the single-pixel monochrome
 * bitmap that was created at the instantiation of
 * this memory DC.
 */

CompatibleDC::~CompatibleDC(void)
{
    if (hDCMem)
    {
     RestoreOldBitmap();

     DeleteDC( hDCMem );

     hDCMem = NULL;
    }
}

/****************************
 *
 * CompatibleDC::GetCompatDC()
```

```
 *
 * Returns a copy of the handle to the compatible DC.
 *
 * Returns: handle to the DC
 *
 * Args: Nothing
 */

    HDC
CompatibleDC::GetCompatDC( void )
{
    return hDCMem;
}
```

Examining the CompatibleDC Class

The CompatibleDC class exists to remove much of the burden of creating and manipulating graphics objects in Windows. Because many procedures (such as copying a bitmap) require a compatible DC, it makes sense to create an object that contains all the setup and cleanup code needed.

The CompatibleDC has two data members, hDCMem and saveBM. The data member hDCMem is the handle to the compatible DC that this object class creates. In other words, each instance of a CompatibleDC object saves its compatible DC handle here. The data member saveBM is a space to save the single-pixel monochrome bitmap. (That's the bitmap that is automatically created inside a compatible DC when you create a compatible DC.) This enables you to make sure that this bitmap handle is always saved and restored properly.

Constructor Routines

The CompatibleDC class has two constructor routines. The first one takes a handle to a DC and creates a compatible DC from it. That is, it creates a compatible DC that is compatible with the HDC that's passed in.

The second constructor routine takes both a handle to a DC and a handle to a bitmap. This function creates a compatible DC, saves the handle to the single-pixel monochrome bitmap, and then selects the bitmap that was passed to the compatible DC. This is quite handy; many GDI routines, such as **BitBlt()**, require you to create a compatible DC and select a bitmap into it

47

before you can manipulate the bitmap. This constructor routine provides a single-line method of doing this without your having to worry about the attendant details. (They're already done, and they're always done right.)

The Destructor Routine

The destructor routine takes care of the cleanup details associated with a compatible DC. It checks to make sure that the handle to the compatible DC is valid. If it is, the destructor routine restores the old bitmap back into the compatible DC (see the following section on the RestoreOldBitmap() member function), deletes the compatible DC, and marks the data member hDCMem as being empty. This prevents the object from attempting to delete itself twice.

GetCompatDC()

This function returns a handle to the compatible DC, or NULL if there is no compatible DC in the instance of the class.

SelectBitmapIntoDC()

This function selects the bitmap specified by the newBmp parameter into the compatible DC and saves the old one in the data member saveBM.

RestoreOldBitmap()

This function checks the data member saveBM to see whether it is non-NULL. If it is (that is, if there's a bitmap handle in saveBM), that bitmap is selected back into the compatible DC.

Drawing into a Memory DC

One other point (which is really the main point of this whole exercise of creating compatible DCs and bitmaps) is that after you've created a compatible DC with a bitmap in it, you can draw into it *just as if it were the screen*. You can pass the handle to the compatible DC to every API drawing call that takes an HDC, and Windows happily draws into your off-screen bitmap as though it were a piece of the screen (and this includes clipping it).

You now have all the pieces you need to implement the second version of SimPaint, one that not only enables the user to draw on the screen, but also maintains a copy of the screen image off-screen. Instead of doing nothing in response to a WM_PAINT message, SimPaint now copies its off-screen bitmap back onto the screen, and presto!—you have a fully functional (albeit very limited) paint program.

Updating SimPaint to Use a Memory DC

Listing 2.10 shows the modifications to SIMPAINT.C for the second version of SimPaint, the Simple Paint Program. This listing shows only the changes necessary to SimPaint to make it work with an off-screen bitmap.

Listing 2.10. SIMPAINT.C—updated C source code for SimPaint 2.

```
// SIMPAINT.C
//
// This is SIMPAINT # 2 - Support for an off-screen
// bitmap, and redrawing of the screen in response to
// the WM_PAINT message.
//
// Source code for the simple paint program
//
// Written by Alex Leavens, for ShadowCat Technologies

#include <WINDOWS.H>
#include "SIMPAINT.H"

#include "SIMPAINT.WMC"


BOOL    buttonDown = FALSE;    // If true, mouse button down

HBITMAP offScreenBmp = NULL;  // Handle to your off-screen bitmap

/***************************
 *
 * WinMain()
 *
 * Start-up function for all Windows programs.
 */
```

continues

Listing 2.10. continued

```
    int PASCAL

WinMain(HANDLE  hInstance,          // Current instance of program
        HANDLE  hPrevInstance,      // Previous instance of program (if any)
        LPSTR   lpCmdLine,          // Command line (if applicable)
        int     nCmdShow)           // Window display style (open/iconic)

{
    MSG msg;     // Message passed to your program

    HDC   hDC;   // Handle to screen DC

    DWORD winSize;   // Window size

    //---------------------------------

    hInst = hInstance;    // Save the current instance

    if (!BLDInitApplication(hInstance,hPrevInstance,&nCmdShow,lpCmdLine))
        return FALSE;

    if (!hPrevInstance)           /* Is there another instance of the task   */
        {
        if (!BLDRegisterClass(hInstance))
            return FALSE;         /* Exits if unable to initialize */
        }

    MainhWnd = BLDCreateWindow(hInstance);
    if (!MainhWnd)                /* Check if the window is created */
        return FALSE;

    ShowWindow(MainhWnd, nCmdShow);  /* Show the window */
    UpdateWindow(MainhWnd);          /* Send WM_PAINT message to window */

    BLDInitMainMenu(MainhWnd);       /* Initialize main menu if necessary */

    while (GetMessage(&msg,      /* Message structure */
        0,                       /* Handle of window receiving the message */
        0,                       /* Lowest message to examine */
        0))                      /* Highest message to examine */
        {
        if (BLDKeyTranslation(&msg)) /* WindowsMAKER code for key trans */
            continue;
```

```
        TranslateMessage(&msg); /* Translates character keys */
        DispatchMessage(&msg);  /* Dispatches message to window */
        }

    BLDExitApplication();        /* Clean up if necessary */

    return(msg.wParam);          /* Returns the value from PostQuitMessage */
}

/****************************************************************/
/*            WINDOW PROCEDURE FOR MAIN WINDOW              */
/****************************************************************/

    long FAR PASCAL

BLDMainWndProc ( HWND        hWnd,
                 unsigned    message,
                 WORD        wParam,
                 LONG        lParam )
{

    HDC        hDC;        // Handle to your display context

    HDC        compatDC;   // Handle to a compatible DC

    HBITMAP    oldBmp;     // Handle to bitmap originally in the DC

    WORD   mX;         // Mouse x position
    WORD   mY;         // Mouse y position

    //-----------------------

    switch (message)
    {

    case WM_CREATE:               /* Window creation */

        /* Send to BLDDefWindowProc in (.WMC) for controls in main window */
        return BLDDefWindowProc(hWnd, message, wParam, lParam);
        break;

    case WM_SIZE:        // Window's size has changed

      // Whenever the window changes size, then you need to delete
```

continues

Listing 2.10. continued

```
// the old bitmap (if there is one), and create a new bitmap to
// match the proper size of the window.

hDC = GetDC ( MainhWnd );

// If old bitmap not NULL, delete it.

if ( offScreenBmp )
    DeleteObject ( offScreenBmp );

// The new width is in the low-order word of lParam, and the
// new height is in the high-order word.

offScreenBmp = CreateCompatibleBitmap ( hDC,
                                         LOWORD ( lParam ),
                                         HIWORD ( lParam ) );

compatDC = CreateCompatibleDC ( hDC );   // Create a compatible DC
                                         // for your bitmap

// Select your off-screen bitmap into the compatible DC. Make
// sure that you save the old bitmap that was in the DC!!

oldBmp = SelectObject ( compatDC,
                        offScreenBmp );

// This call zeroes out (erases) whatever's in the bitmap
// (otherwise you just get a chunk of memory, which might look
// interesting on the screen, but is probably NOT what you want!)

PatBlt ( compatDC,
         0,
         0,
         LOWORD ( lParam ),
         HIWORD ( lParam ),
         WHITENESS );

SelectObject ( compatDC, // Put the old bitmap back
               oldBmp ); // into the compatible DC

DeleteDC ( compatDC );          // Get rid of the compatible DC

// Release the DC (must do this for this DC, since you haven't
// defined your drawing window as one with a CLASSDC or OWNDC style)
```

```
    ReleaseDC ( MainhWnd,
                hDC );

    break;


case WM_SETFOCUS:            /* Window is notified of focus change */
    /* Send to BLDDefWindowProc in (.WMC) for controls in main window */
    return BLDDefWindowProc(hWnd, message, wParam, lParam);
    break;

case WM_DESTROY:            /* Window being destroyed */

  // Delete your offScreenBmp

  DeleteObject ( offScreenBmp );

    PostQuitMessage(0);    // You're done...

    return BLDDefWindowProc(hWnd, message, wParam, lParam);
    break;

case WM_PAINT:

  // If you don't have a valid bitmap to paste in, then don't.

    if ( offScreenBmp == NULL )
        return TRUE;        // Message not processed

  // In response to a WM_PAINT message (meaning that some part
  // of your window has been munged), you're going to copy your
  // off-screen bitmap into your window.

{
  PAINTSTRUCT     pntInfo;  // Window repainting information

  int             numBytes; // Dummy return value

  BITMAP          ourBmp;   // Bitmap structure

  //-----------------------------------

  hDC = BeginPaint ( hWnd,
                     (LPPAINTSTRUCT) & pntInfo );
```

continues

Listing 2.10. continued

```
compatDC = CreateCompatibleDC ( hDC );  // Create a compatible DC
                                        // for your bitmap

// Select your off-screen bitmap into the compatible DC. Make
// sure that you save the old bitmap that was in the DC!!

oldBmp = SelectObject ( compatDC,
                        offScreenBmp );

// In order to properly copy the bitmap, you need to retrieve how
// big it is. Do that here.

numBytes = GetObject ( offScreenBmp,
                       sizeof ( BITMAP ),
                       (LPSTR) & ourBmp );

// If you can't get the size of the bitmap, punt.

if ( numBytes == 0 )
{
    MessageBox ( hWnd,
          "Cannot get information about off-screen Bitmap.",
          "SimPaint Error",
          MB_OK );
    return FALSE;
}

// Now copy your off-screen bitmap onto the screen.
// This is done using BitBlt.

BitBlt ( hDC,         // Destination DC (the screen)
         0,           // X value, upper-left corner of dest rectangle
         0,           // Y value, upper-left corner of dest rectangle
         ourBmp.bmWidth,    // Width of bitmap
         ourBmp.bmHeight,   // Height of bitmap
         compatDC,    // Source DC (your off-screen bitmap)
         0,           // Upper-left corner of source, X value
         0,           // Upper-left corner of source, y value
         SRCCOPY );   // Raster operation to perform (source copy)

// Put the old bitmap back into the DC (this is the single-
// pixel monochrome bitmap discussed in the text). Note that
// you don't have to keep track of the handle that the
// SelectObject() call returns this time, because it's the same
```

```
                // handle as is contained in offScreenBmp.

                SelectObject ( compatDC,
                               oldBmp );

                DeleteDC ( compatDC );   // Destroy the compatible DC...

                // Don't forget to release the DC, and let Windows paint again!

                EndPaint ( hWnd,
                           (LPPAINTSTRUCT) &pntInfo );

        }
            break;

        case WM_MOUSEMOVE:

          // Only paint if the mouse button is down.

          if ( buttonDown != TRUE )
               break;

          /* Get the current mouse coordinates */

          mX = LOWORD(lParam);
          mY = HIWORD(lParam);

                hDC = GetDC ( hWnd );       // Get DC of your window

          compatDC = CreateCompatibleDC ( hDC );  // Create a compatible DC
                                                  // for your bitmap

          // Select your off-screen bitmap into the compatible DC. Make
          // sure that you save the old bitmap that was in the DC!!

          oldBmp = SelectObject ( compatDC,
                                  offScreenBmp );

          // Now draw the image on the screen...

                SetPixel ( hDC,
                   mX,
                   mY,
                   RGB ( 0, 0, 0 ) );  // Draw a black pixel
```

continues

Listing 2.10. continued

```
// ...and into your off-screen bitmap.

   SetPixel ( compatDC,
      mX,
      mY,
      RGB ( 0, 0, 0 ) );  // Draw a black pixel

// Put the old bitmap back into the DC (this is the single-
// pixel monochrome bitmap discussed in the text). Note that
// you don't have to keep track of the handle that the
// SelectObject() call returns this time, because it's the same
// handle as is contained in offScreenBmp.

SelectObject ( compatDC,
               oldBmp );

DeleteDC ( compatDC );   // Destroy the compatible DC...

// Release the system DC...

ReleaseDC ( hWnd,
            hDC );
   break;              // Done!

case WM_LBUTTONDOWN:

/* Get the current mouse coordinates */

mX = LOWORD(lParam);
mY = HIWORD(lParam);

   buttonDown = TRUE;

   hDC = GetDC ( hWnd );       // Get DC of your window

compatDC = CreateCompatibleDC ( hDC );  // Create a compatible DC
                                        // for your bitmap

// Select your off-screen bitmap into the compatible DC. Make
// sure that you save the old bitmap that was in the DC!!

oldBmp = SelectObject ( compatDC,
                        offScreenBmp );
```

```
// Now draw the image on the screen...

    SetPixel ( hDC,
        mX,
        mY,
        RGB ( 0, 0, 0 ) );  // Draw a black pixel

// ...and into your off-screen bitmap.

    SetPixel ( compatDC,
        mX,
        mY,
        RGB ( 0, 0, 0 ) );  // Draw a black pixel

// Put the old bitmap back into the DC (this is the single-
// pixel monochrome bitmap discussed in the text). Note that
// you don't have to keep track of the handle that the
// SelectObject() call returns this time, because it's the same
// handle as is contained in offScreenBmp.

SelectObject ( compatDC,
               oldBmp );

DeleteDC ( compatDC );   // Destroy the compatible DC...

// Release the system DC...

ReleaseDC ( hWnd,
            hDC );
    break;


case WM_LBUTTONUP:

    buttonDown = FALSE;
    break;

case WM_COMMAND:                /* Command from the main window */
    if (BLDMenuCommand(hWnd, message, wParam, lParam))
        break;                  /* Processed by BLDMenuCommand. */
        /* Else default processing by BLDDefWindowProc. */
default:
    /* Pass on message for default processing */
    return BLDDefWindowProc(hWnd, message, wParam, lParam);
}
```

continues

Listing 2.10. continued

```
    return FALSE;                  /* Returns FALSE if processed */
}
```

Looking at the Changes to SimPaint

This version of SimPaint is very similar to the first one. The changes I've made are to support the use of the off-screen bitmap. The most interesting things about this version of the program are in the creation of the bitmap itself, which occurs in response to a WM_SIZE message. When the program window is first created, it gets a WM_SIZE message. In this case, the new size represents the size of the window when first opened. It's easy enough to create a compatible bitmap that matches the window's initial screen size.

If the user changes the size of the window, your program receives another WM_SIZE message. At this point, you delete the old bitmap and then create a new bitmap that matches the new window size.

By putting the code for the bitmap creation here, in the WM_SIZE message, I've also neatly addressed the issue of what happens when the user resizes the window. One thing that could be added here is code that creates a new bitmap *before* deleting the old one and then copying the old bitmap into the new one. This would prevent the image from disappearing from the screen when the user resizes the window.

After the bitmap is created, you need to initialize it. The **PatBlt()** call performs this function by copying a pattern of WHITENESS (that is, solid white) into the newly created bitmap. Failing to do this causes the bitmap to be displayed with whatever random stuff is in the bitmap at the time. (You can see this by commenting out the **PatBlt()** call and recompiling the code.)

The WM_PAINT message is now a little more complex, although not too much. The first thing you do is check to make sure you don't have an empty bitmap handle. Trying to use a NULL bitmap handle in calls such as **SelectObject()** and **BitBlt()** is a guaranteed way of giving yourself a UAE!

When you validate that you have a non-NULL bitmap handle, you get the DC of the window (here, using the **BeginPaint()** call). Remember, the WM_PAINT message is the one place where you use **BeginPaint()** and not **GetDC()** to get the hDC of your window and create a compatible DC for it. You select your off-screen bitmap into your compatible DC (making sure to hang on to the handle of the old bitmap that was in the compatible DC so that you can restore it). Now for the actual screen update: Blit from a *source* DC (your compatible DC, which contains your off-screen bitmap) to a *destination* DC (the screen). This copies the off-screen image to the screen.

The other new parts of the program have to do with what happens when the user draws. As before, you draw into your image only in response to a WM_MOUSEMOVE or WM_LBUTTONDOWN message. However, you now draw into two places, rather than just one. The first place is the same as always—the screen.

The second place you draw to is the off-screen bitmap. Fortunately, nothing particularly fancy is required—simply perform a second `SetPixel()` call after you've created an appropriate compatible DC and selected your off-screen bitmap into it.

Finding a Bug Fix for `SetPixel()`: `SetDevicePixel()`

Bug Note: On some 32,768 color drivers, the `SetPixel()` call does not work properly; instead of getting the requested color (the fourth parameter specified by the `SetPixel()` call), you get light gray. A way around this problem is to use the calls `MoveTo()` and `LineTo()` instead. These calls do not take an RGB value directly, but instead use the color of the current pen to determine the color of the pixel or pixels that are set on the screen. Listing 2.11 shows some sample code.

Listing 2.11. A routine that fixes the `SetPixel()` call in 32,768 color mode.

```
// SetDevicePixel()
//
// Sample routine, which replaces the use of SetPixel()
// with a MoveTo()/LineTo() pair.
//
// NOTE: Because of all the calls involved with this operation, this
// routine is fairly slow. Use this routine (or build a similar one)
```

continues

Listing 2.11. continued

```
// only if you know that you're running in 32,768 color mode, and want
// to use the SetPixel() call.
//
// PARAMETERS:
//    hWnd - Window handle to window you want to set a pixel in
//    mX - X position of pixel in window (assumed relative to client area)
//    mY - Y position of pixel in window (assumed relative to client area)
//
// Returns:
//    TRUE - function was successfull
//    FALSE - something went wrong

    BOOL
SetDevicePixel ( HWND      hWnd,
                 int       mX,
                 int       mY,
                 RGB       pixColor )
{
HDC   hDC;       // Screen device context
HPEN myPen;      // Pen for drawing with
HPEN oldPen;     // Holding area for old pen handle

//--------------------------------

myPen = CreatePen ( PS_SOLID,       // Solid pen style
                       1,           // Width of pen (in logical units)
                  RGB ( pixColor ) );  // Defines color to set pixel to
if ( ! myPen )
{
    MessageBox ( hWnd,
             "Cannot create Pen",
             " Graphics error",
             MB_OK );
    return FALSE;
}

hDC = GetDC ( hWnd );     // Get DC of your window
if ( ! hDC )
{
    MessageBox ( hWnd,
             "Cannot get device context",
             " Graphics error",
```

```
                MB_OK );
    return FALSE;
}


oldPen = SelectObject ( hDC,
                        myPen );

// Move the drawing position to the point desired

MoveTo ( hDC,
    mX,
    mY );

// Now draw a line that is one pixel long. Since the LineTo() function
// draws a line from the origin up to but NOT including the end point, the
// result of a LineTo() call that is one bigger than the origin point will
// be a single pixel.

LineTo ( hDC,
    mX + 1,
    mY + 1);

// Reselect old pen

SelectObject ( hDC,
                oldPen );

// Get rid of the pen that you used to draw the point

DeleteObject ( myPen );

// Give the DC back

ReleaseDC ( hWnd,
            hDC );

return TRUE;    // All! done!
}
```

With the addition of an off-screen bitmap, you have the beginnings of a paint program. To give your paint program greater functionality, you need to examine the subject of bitmaps in much greater detail. In Chapter 3, "The Device Dependent Bitmap," I do just that.

Summary

Device contexts are a fundamental part of Windows; they act as the framework that defines a drawing surface. In this way, they enable a program to build a custom set of drawing attributes, or default to the ones that Windows provides. Attributes of a device context include items such as background window color, pen color and style, and current drawing location.

The basic type of device context is the screen DC. This type of device context enables you to talk directly to the screen. When talking to the screen, you use either the `GetDC()`/`ReleaseDC()` function calls or the `BeginPaint()`/`EndPaint()` functions, depending on the type of drawing you are doing.

There are several types of device context that your program can have, and the type is specified by your program's class when you first register it. A Common DC is provided by Windows and has a standard set of default attributes. A Class DC is a DC that is allocated specifically to your application's class and is shared between instances of your application. A Private DC is a DC allocated to each instance of your application. A Window DC enables you to draw on the nonclient portion of your window area.

In SimPaint, the simple paint program, I introduced the idea of drawing onto a device context's surface. The sample source code for SimPaint shows how to get a device context and draw onto it.

The first version of SimPaint brought up the issue of remembering what had been drawn on the screen; simply having a screen copy of the image turned out not to be good enough. Using an off-screen, or memory, DC gives you a way of copying on-screen information to a private data area that you control. This off-screen area can have a bitmap created for it that mimics the screen behavior, and that you can draw into just as though it were a display device.

Function Reference

At the end of each chapter, you'll find a list of functions that I've discussed in the chapter, or that are otherwise useful (or important) for you to know about. This list is not exhaustive; rather, the functions I've documented are ones you'll find useful in building graphics applications. I've also noted areas where you might run into trouble, as well as other useful information on how to use these functions.

CreateCompatibleDC()

HDC CreateCompatibleDC (HDC   hDC   )

WHAT IT DOES:

Creates a memory device context compatible with the device context specified by the hDC parameter. Although the source device context is most often a screen DC, it doesn't have to be; another memory DC can be used as the source.

When a memory DC is created, a single-pixel monochrome bitmap is also created. It is selected into the DC before the handle to the DC is returned by this function.

PARAMETER:

> hDC   Identifies the source DC. If this parameter is NULL, the function creates a memory DC compatible with the system display.

WHAT IT RETURNS:

A handle to the newly created memory device context. If the return value is NULL, the function was unsuccessful.

THINGS TO WATCH FOR:

☐ Memory DCs can be created only for devices that support RC_BITBLT raster capabilities (which can be determined using the **GetDeviceCaps()** function). This means, for example, that you can't create a memory DC for a plotter unless the plotter supports RC_BITBLT operations.

☐ Before you can use a memory DC for drawing operations, you also must create a compatible bitmap and select the bitmap into the memory DC.

☐ When you're done with a memory DC, you must delete it using the DeleteDC() function.

SEE ALSO:

CreateCompatibleBitmap()
SelectObject()
DeleteDC()

CreateDC()

HDC **CreateDC(**   LPSTR   lpDriverName,
                          LPSTR   lpDeviceName,

```
LPSTR        lpOutput,
LPDEVMODE    lpInitData )
```

WHAT IT DOES:

Creates a device context for the specified device. This call is primarily used to create device contexts for printers, but it also can be used to create a device context for the entire screen display, by using the call in this way:

```
HDC  screenDC;

screenDC = CreateDC ( "DISPLAY", NULL, NULL, NULL );
// Returns an HDC to the screen.
```

PARAMETERS:

lpDriverName	Points to the DOS file name of the desired driver. The driver name must be NULL-terminated.
lpDeviceName	Points to a string that names the specific device to be supported.
lpOutput	Points to a NULL-terminated character string that specifies the DOS file or device name for the physical output medium.
lpInitData	Points to a DEVMODE data structure containing device-specific information for the device driver.

WHAT IT RETURNS:

A handle to a DC for the device if the function was successful; otherwise, the return value is NULL.

THINGS TO WATCH FOR:

This call is used principally for output devices other than the display. Using it with the display can sometimes cause unpredictable results, because certain assumed defaults might not be in place.

SEE ALSO:

DeleteDC()

DeleteDC()

```
BOOL DeleteDC( HDC  hDC )
```

WHAT IT DOES:

Deletes the specified device context handle.

PARAMETER:

> hDC   Device context handle to be deleted

WHAT IT RETURNS:

Nonzero if the function was successful, 0 if it was not.

THINGS TO WATCH FOR:

> ▪ This function should be used only for device context handles that you create with the `CreateCompatibleDC()` or `CreateDC()` call. Device context handles that you've gotten from the system by the `GetDC()` call should be released (not deleted) using the `ReleaseDC()` call.

> ▪ Before you delete a compatible DC, it is critical that you first select the original single-pixel monochrome bitmap back into it.

SEE ALSO:

```
CreateCompatibleDC()
GetDC()
ReleaseDC()
CreateDC()
```

GetDC()

```
HDC  GetDC ( HANDLE hWnd )
```

WHAT IT DOES:

Retrieves a handle to the display context of the *client area* of the window associated with the window handle specified by hWnd. You can use this hDC in subsequent GDI operations to paint into the window's client area.

PARAMETERS:

> hWnd   Window handle to the window whose display context you are retrieving.
>
> Depending on what kind of display context is specified for the window when the window is created, `GetDC()` returns one of three kinds of display contexts: Common, Class, or Private.
>
> Common DC   A Common DC comes from the DC cache maintained by Windows (see the following "Things to watch for" section). Each time a Common DC is retrieved, Windows assigns to it a standard set of default drawing attributes. (See Table 2.1.)

Class DC   Both Class and Private DCs are maintained separately from
Private DC   Windows' DC cache, and Windows does not alter any of the
DC's attributes when a handle to the DC is retrieved. Thus,
you can change (for example) the pen of a Private DC, and
release the DC; when you next do a `GetDC()` on the Private DC,
the new pen that you put in is still in place.

WHAT IT RETURNS:

The handle to the DC if Windows is able to get it; otherwise, NULL.

THINGS TO WATCH FOR:

☐ Always check the return value to make sure the hDC you've gotten back
is not NULL; using a NULL DC handle is a great way to generate UAEs
in a hurry.

☐ For Common display contexts (but not Class and Private ones), Windows maintains a cache of DCs; specifically, it maintains five DCs for use
by all programs. This means that you must give a Common DC handle
back when you're done with it, or else you'll chew up a valuable system
resource.

☐ If your program locks up the system after a few graphics operations,
make sure that you're releasing all Common DCs when you're done with
them.

☐ When you retrieve a DC, you're *always* getting back a display surface
relative to the upper-left corner of the client area of the window handle
that you used. This is true even if the window in question is a child
window of another window. For example, you might want to get the DC
of an owner-draw button in a dialog box. Given that the owner-draw
button is a child window of the dialog box, you might believe that the
owner-draw button's DC would start at the same offset that the owner-
draw button's window does from the dialog box window. This is not the
case; a handle to a DC always starts at (0,0) for that particular window.

SEE ALSO:

ReleaseDC()

GetDCOrg()

DWORD   GetDCOrg(HDC hDC)

WHAT IT DOES:

Retrieves the final translation between the screen coordinates and logical coordinates for the *origin* of the device context. That is, this function returns the actual *screen* position that the logical device coordinate of (0,0) maps to (and remember that for most device contexts, this corresponds to the upper-left corner of the *client* area of a window). This is handy to know if you want to be able to figure out exactly where on the screen the device context is located.

PARAMETER:

        hDC   Device context that you want to find out the mapping for

WHAT IT RETURNS:

A DWORD, in which is contained the x and y coordinates of the mapping point, in *device* coordinates. X is in the low word, and Y is in the high word, like so:

```
WORD        xPosition;
WORD        yPosition;
DWORD       posit;

posit = GetDCOrg ( ourDC );    // Where ourDC is the HDC of the desired DC

xPosition = LOWORD ( posit );
yPosition = HIWORD ( posit );
```

THINGS TO WATCH FOR:

This function does not make sense for memory DCs, because they are not mapped to a physical device. Be cautious and make sure that you are actually passing the handle to a device context of a screen DC.

SEE ALSO:

GetWindowDC()

```
HDC  GetWindowDC(   HWND hWnd )
```

WHAT IT DOES:

Retrieves a device context handle for the entire window area, not just the client area. The entire window area includes the menu bar, scroll bars, frames, and other edge pieces of the window.

PARAMETER:

> hWnd   Handle to the window whose Window DC you want

WHAT IT RETURNS:

A handle to the Window DC of the window if the function was successful, and NULL otherwise.

THINGS TO WATCH FOR:

- This function always assigns default attributes to the display context each time it retrieves the DC, regardless of what type of DC the window was created with (that is, Class or Private DC). Previous attributes that were set are lost. (This also means that if you create a pen to draw into a Window DC with, you should also deselect and delete the pen before doing a **ReleaseDC()** on the Window DC.)

- This function always uses one of the DCs from the Windows DC cache; therefore, it is critical that **ReleaseDC()** be called to return this DC after your program is done with it.

- This function is used for special drawing behavior in a program; typically, a program draws to the client area of a window, which is retrieved by using the **GetDC()** function.

- The function **GetSystemMetrics()** can be used to retrieve the dimensions of various parts of the nonclient area such as the caption bar, menu, and scroll bars.

- If your program responds to the WM_NCPAINT message (as opposed to the WM_PAINT message), you can use this function to retrieve the DC of your program's window area.

SEE ALSO:

```
GetDC()
ReleaseDC()
```

ReleaseDC()

```
int ReleaseDC( HWND hWnd,
               HDC  hDC)
```

WHAT IT DOES:

Releases the device context associated with the hDC parameter.

PARAMETERS:

       hWnd   Window handle the DC was retrieved from

       hDC   Handle to the device context to be released

WHAT IT RETURNS:

One if the device context is released; otherwise, zero.

THINGS TO WATCH FOR:

☐ This call only affects window and Common DCs; it has no effect on Class or Private DCs. Because your application must always release a DC of the first two types, it's best to make sure that any call which retrieves a DC eventually calls this function.

☐ Do not use this function to free a DC created with the `CreateCompatibleDC()` or `CreateDC()` function; use instead the `DeleteDC()` call.

SEE ALSO:

```
GetDC()
GetWindowDC()
```

The Device Dependent Bitmap

N ow that you have a handle on device contexts, it's time to get to the real nitty-gritty—the bitmaps. In the next few chapters, I examine the intricacies of bitmaps, the different flavors of them, and how you manipulate them. I also extend the application, SimPaint, to handle reading and writing bitmaps, and I create several new object classes you can use to relieve much of the work of dealing with bitmaps.

As I mentioned previously, there are three basic types of bitmaps:

Device dependent bitmaps (DDB)

Device independent bitmaps (DIB)

OS/2 bitmaps

This chapter covers the first type, the device dependent bitmap, including the following topics:

The device dependent bitmap

Creating and using DDBs

Using bitmaps in a resource

A Bitmap object class in C++

Examining the Device Dependent Bitmap

The device dependent bitmap, commonly referred to as a DDB, is what you typically manipulate in your programs. This is the kind of bitmap that you created for SimPaint, as an off-screen copy of your on-screen image. A DDB is composed of two pieces: the *bitmap header* and the *bits*. The bitmap header looks like this:

```
typedef struct tagBITMAP
    {
        int    bmType;           // Type of image; must be 0
        int    bmWidth;          // Width of bitmap (in pixels)
        int    bmHeight;         // Height of bitmap (in pixels)
        int    bmWidthBytes;     // Width in bytes of the image
        BYTE   bmPlanes;         // # of color planes in the bitmap
        BYTE   bmBitsPixel;      // # of bits per pixel
        LPSTR  bmBits;           // Pointer to the bits of the image
    } BITMAP;
```

This structure defines the way a bitmap looks—its height and width, the number of colors, and where the bits of the bitmap are.

Most of the fields are pretty self-explanatory; bmWidth and bmHeight are the width and height of the bitmap, respectively. Both values are given in *pixel* terms, which means that these values give the actual width and height of the image.

bmBitsPixel defines how many colors the image has. For example, if an image has 4 bits per pixel (bpp), it can have a maximum of 16 colors (4 bits gives 16 possible values, 0–15). Similarly, 8 bits per pixel means a pixel can have 1 of 256 colors; 15 bpp gives you pixels with one of 32,768 colors; and 24 bpp gives you pixels of more than 16 million colors.

The bmWidthBytes field is a bit trickier; it gives the width, *in bytes*, of the image. This value relates to the bmWidth field in the following way: The value you get by multiplying bmWidthBytes × 8 must be the smallest multiple of 16 that is greater than or equal to the value you get by multiplying bmWidth by bmBitsPixel. In other words, the following two equations must be true:

$$(\text{bmWidth} \times \text{bmBitsPixel}) < (\text{bmWidthBytes} \times 8)$$
and $$(\text{bmWidthBytes} \times 8) \text{ modulo } 16 = 0$$

A couple of examples should help make this clear. Suppose you have a bitmap that is 16 pixels wide (it doesn't matter how tall it is), and each pixel requires 4 bits (bmBitsPixel = 4). What value should bmWidthBytes be? It's quite simple, really. Divide 8 (the width of a byte) by 4 bits per pixel. This gives you 2 pixels per byte. Then divide the width of the image in pixels (16) by this number, to give you the width in bytes, which is 8. Thus, an image that is 16 pixels wide and requires 4 bits per pixel requires 8 bytes per horizontal row to hold. bmWidthBytes is then equal to 8.

Take a look at a second example. If the image you just looked at were 17 pixels wide, rather than 16, what would bmWidthBytes be? Again, the image would have 2 pixels per byte. This time, however, when you divide 17 by 2, you still get 8, but with a remainder of 1. Because the width in bytes of the image must be at least big enough to hold the whole image, you need to increase the value of bmWidthBytes, which brings it to 9. When you do this, however, the second equation becomes untrue (that is, (bmWidthBytes × 8) modulo 16 does *not* equal 0), so you need to increase bmWidthBytes by one more, to 10. This satisfies the second equation.

This second example brings to light two important points. One, the value of bmWidthBytes must always be even. Two, the total amount of space in a bitmap can be greater than the actual image contained in it. In this example, you have an extra three pixels worth of blank space on the right side of the bitmap. What's in there? It's undefined; some programs automatically zero out this space, and some don't. In general, it's best not to count on this area being set to any particular value. If you want some value there, you need to set it yourself.

> **Tip:** By the way, you can't clear out the extra pixels by hooking the bitmap into a compatible DC and then drawing into it with a single color (such as black) to zero out the bits. Because GDI knows how big the bitmap is, it automatically clips any graphics operation that you perform to the confines of the bitmap. To get at the area outside the bitmap, you have to lock the handle to the memory and independently set the values.

The last entry in the bitmap header is a long pointer to the bits of the bitmap. Please note: This pointer is not necessarily valid. Some GDI functions that retrieve information about the bitmap *header* (for example, **GetObject()**) do not fill in the bits of the bitmap. Because one sure way to generate a UAE is by attempting to dereference a NULL pointer, it's a good idea to make sure that the pointer is non-NULL before using it.

Creating Bitmaps

There are several ways to create bitmaps. They start out simple and become more complex. Take a look at these methods.

Functions for Creating DDBs

You already saw one way to create a bitmap in the preceding chapter; it's the `CreateCompatibleBitmap()` function, which you used to build a bitmap you could use as a copy of your on-screen image. The one drawback to this function is that it only *creates* a bitmap; it does absolutely nothing else. If you want the bitmap initialized to something, you have to do it yourself. (In fact, if you recall, the first thing you did after you created the compatible bitmap was to copy a pattern of whiteness into it so that it would be blank.)

To create a bitmap that is initialized with an image at creation time, you need to use a different call, `CreateBitmap()`. Unlike `CreateCompatibleBitmap()`, however, this call can create a bitmap of any number of colors. `CreateCompatibleBitmap()` is limited to creating a bitmap that's compatible with the resolution of a particular device context.

`CreateBitmap()` not only lets you create bitmaps of differing numbers of colors, it also lets you initialize the bits of the bitmap. You do this by passing a pointer to an array of bits that represent the image you want created.

A second call, `CreateBitmapIndirect()`, does the same thing `CreateBitmap()` does. Instead of passing in the parameters of the bitmap as arguments to the function, however, you fill in a bitmap header structure with the relevant information and then pass a pointer to this structure to the `CreateBitmapIndirect()` call. (See the Function Reference at the end of the chapter for more details on `CreateBitmapIndirect()`.)

Creating a Monochrome Bitmap by Hand

Creating a monochrome bitmap in this fashion is straightforward. First, you need to create an image, like the one that follows. Using a grid, you can create an image. Next, you need to translate that image into a numerical representation. You do this by converting the pixel image into ones and zeroes. (See Figure 3.1.)

Figure 3.1.
A simple black
and white
bitmap that you
create by hand.

For the image I've created, the bit pattern is like this:

```
0  0  0  0  1  1  1  1    1  1  1  0  0  0  0  0   =  0F  E0
0  0  1  1  1  0  0  0    0  0  1  1  1  0  0  0   =  38  38
0  1  1  0  0  0  0  0    0  0  0  0  1  1  0  0   =  60  0C
0  1  0  0  0  0  0  0    0  0  0  0  0  1  0  0   =  40  04
1  1  0  0  1  0  0  0    0  1  0  0  0  1  1  0   =  C8  46
1  0  0  0  1  0  0  0    0  1  0  0  0  0  1  0   =  88  42
1  0  0  0  1  1  0  0    0  1  1  0  0  0  1  0   =  8C  62
1  0  0  0  0  0  0  0    0  0  0  0  0  0  1  0   =  80  02
1  0  0  0  0  0  0  1    0  0  0  0  0  0  1  0   =  81  02
1  0  0  0  1  0  0  0    0  0  1  0  0  0  1  0   =  88  22
1  1  0  0  1  1  0  0    0  1  1  0  0  1  1  0   =  CC  66
0  1  0  0  0  1  1  1    1  1  0  0  0  1  0  0   =  47  C4
0  1  1  0  0  0  0  0    0  0  0  0  1  1  0  0   =  60  0C
0  0  1  1  1  0  0  0    0  0  1  1  1  0  0  0   =  38  38
0  0  0  0  1  1  1  1    1  1  1  0  0  0  0  0   =  0F  E0
```

Remember that if the image width isn't an even multiple of 16, you need to
pad out the end of it with zeroes. (There's an extra zero at the end of each row
in this image because the image itself is only 15 pixels wide.)

Next, you need to create a data structure to hold the bits:

```
static BYTE    imBits[] =
    {
        0x0F, 0xE0,
        0x38, 0x38,
        0x60, 0x0C,
        0x40, 0x04,
        0xC8, 0x46,
        0x88, 0x42,
        0x8C, 0x62,
        0x80, 0x02,
        0x81, 0x02,
        0x88, 0x22,
        0xCC, 0x66,
```

```
        0x47, 0xC4,
        0x60, 0x0C,
        0x38, 0x38,
        0x0F, 0xE0
    };
```

If you use this structure to create your image, you'll discover that the image you get is a white happy face on a black background, the opposite of what you'd expect. This is because Windows maps 0 bits to black and 1 bits to white, the opposite of the idealized bitmap. To get a black happy face on a white background, use the following version of imBits[]:

```
static BYTE    imBits[] =
    {
        0xF0, 0x1F,
        0xC7, 0xC7,
        0x9F, 0xF3,
        0xBF, 0xFB,
        0x37, 0xB9,
        0x77, 0xBD,
        0x73, 0x9D,
        0x7F, 0xFD,
        0x7E, 0xFD,
        0x77, 0xDD,
        0x33, 0x99,
        0xB8, 0x3B,
        0x9F, 0xF3,
        0xC7, 0xC7,
        0xF0, 0x1F
    };
```

You can also create an initialized data structure containing information about the bitmap, too, like this:

```
static BITMAP imBmp = { 0, 15, 15, 2, 1, 1 };
```

These values correspond to the structure of the bitmap header discussed earlier in the chapter. The very first value is 0, which indicates that this is a bitmap image. (This value is always 0 for device dependent bitmaps). The image is 15 pixels wide and 15 scan lines high, so the next two values are 15. After that comes a 2, which indicates that the image is 2 bytes wide. Finally, because this is a monochrome image, both the number of color planes and the number of bits per pixel are 1.

There are several ways you can create an image using these values. The first is to use **CreateBitmapIndirect()**. If you do, it takes two statements:

```
imBmp.bmBits = (LPSTR) imBits;
hBitmap = CreateBitmapIndirect ( &imBmp );
```

The first statement assigns the address of the image data to the pointer of the bitmap header structure. Then you pass that structure to the **CreateBitmapIndirect()** call, which passes back a handle to a bitmap. This method is a little indirect for what you're doing. It can be useful, though, if you're creating images without knowing in advance what they look like. You also need to be careful using the pointer to the image data. Calling **CreateBitmapIndirect()** immediately after assigning the pointer to your bitmap structure is reasonably safe. Leaving it lying around, though, is more dangerous, because Windows could shift your local data segment, rendering the pointer invalid.

A second method of using **CreateBitmapIndirect()** that avoids this difficulty is to do it this way:

```
hBitmap = CreateBitmapIndirect ( &imBmp );   // Create the bitmap
                                             // first...
SetBitmapBits ( hBitmap,
                (DWORD) sizeof ( imBits ),
                (LPSTR) imBits );
```

This method first creates the bitmap but doesn't set the bits of the image. The second call, **SetBitmapBits()**, does this.

Alternatively, you can do everything in one fell swoop, like so:

```
hBitmap = CreateBitmap ( 15,        // Width (in pixels)
                         15,        // Height (in pixels)
                         1,         // # of color planes
                         1,         // # of bits per pixel
                        (LPSTR) imBits );    // Pointer to the image bits
```

Notice that this method neatly avoids not one but two problems. First, it avoids the problem of having Windows move your data segment. Second, it avoids creating the bitmap structure in the first place. You can specify the desired width and height of the bitmap without worrying about how many bits are going to be needed to pad it out to an even 16-bit boundary. (However, you still have to pad your image bits out to an even boundary.) This method also simplifies things by streamlining the process to one function call.

Creating a bitmap by hand this way is actually less useful than it appears at first blush. Certainly, for monochrome bitmaps there isn't much of a problem; all monochrome bitmaps are the same. If a bit is on, the pixel is black, and if it's off, the pixel is white. (Remember, Windows maps the pixels in the reverse fashion to what you'd expect.) Simple enough. However, as I mentioned

earlier, different displays have different ways of organizing color bitmaps (sometimes radically different methods), which means that in advance you can't build bitmaps for all the different kinds of displays that your program is going to encounter.

The other problem with creating bitmaps this way is that you have to hand-code the image into your program. This gets tedious—I mean, really tedious. The amount of work involved in hand-coding one of these things is astonishing. Isn't there a better way? Absolutely. A much better way of getting a bitmap into your program is to stuff it into a resource and then load it at runtime.

Loading Bitmaps from a Resource

Loading bitmap images from a resource file is a much easier method for getting and using a bitmap than creating one by hand. The first thing you need to do is include the bitmap in the resource file itself.

Including Your Bitmap in a Resource File

Actually, loading bitmaps from a resource is a piece of cake. You need to do a couple of things. First, build your bitmap using a graphics resource editor. Second, include the bitmap in your program's resource file, like this:

```
FOOBAR    BITMAP    FOOBAR.BMP
```

This causes the file FOOBAR.BMP to be included in your resource file, indicate that it's a bitmap resource, and give it the identifier FOOBAR. Although you don't have to give the bitmap the same identifier as the file name to which it corresponds, I find it much easier to keep track of the images (especially when I have a lot of them) by doing so.

Loading a Bitmap from an Executable File

When you compile your program, make sure that your resource file is compiled and included. Finally, to load and use your bitmap, you use the following call:

```
HBITMAP    hBM;        // Handle to a bitmap
...
hBM = LoadBitmap ( hInstance,     // Instance of your application
                "FOOBAR" );    // Name of bitmap to load
if ( !hBM )    // Can't get the bitmap? Punt.
{
    MessageBox ( NULL,
                "Cannot load bitmap",
                "",
                MB_OK );
}

// Do something with the bitmap here (like blit it to the screen)

// Don't forget to clean up the bitmap after you're done with it

if ( hBM )
{
    DeleteObject(hBM);  // Delete object
    hBM = NULL;         // Mark object as deleted
}
```

The `LoadBitmap()` call is used to load a resource from your program. If, for some reason, the bitmap can't be found, you get back a NULL handle. As with almost all Windows calls, it's a wise idea to check this return value before proceeding. If your bitmap is loaded successfully, you're returned a handle to it, which you can use in any call that takes a handle to a bitmap (such as `BitBlt()`).

As with all graphics resources, it's vitally important that you get rid of the bitmap when you're done with it. You do this by using the `DeleteObject()` call, as shown earlier. `DeleteObject()` removes the bitmap from the GDI resource pool. Because the GDI pool is a scarce resource, removing objects when you're done with them ensures that other programs are also able to run.

Naturally, it's time for another example. I've created a small bitmap using ICE/Works, called MRHAPPY.BMP. This bitmap is included in my .rc file and is used in the application. Look at the code, in Listings 3.1 through 3.7.

The Happy App—An Example of Using a Resource Bitmap

Listing 3.1. HAPPY.C—C source code for the Happy App.

```c
/*File name: HAPPY.C                                        */
/*"HAPPY" Generated by WindowsMAKER Professional            */
/*Author: Alex Leavens, for ShadowCat Technologies          */

#include <WINDOWS.H>
#include "HAPPY.H"

#include "HAPPY.WMC"

/***************************
 *
 * WinMain()
 *
 * Start-up function for all Windows programs.
 */

    int PASCAL

WinMain(HANDLE  hInstance,          // Current instance of program
    HANDLE      hPrevInstance,      // Previous instance of program (if any)
    LPSTR       lpCmdLine,          // Command line (if applicable)
    int         nCmdShow)           // Window display style (open/iconic)

{
    MSG msg;    // Message passed to your program

    HDC   hDC;  // Handle to screen DC

    DWORD       winSize; // Window size

    //--------------------------------

    hInst = hInstance;    // Save the current instance

    if (!BLDInitApplication(hInstance,hPrevInstance,&nCmdShow,lpCmdLine))
        return FALSE;

    if (!hPrevInstance)             /* Is there another instance of the task   */
```

```
        {
        if (!BLDRegisterClass(hInstance))
            return FALSE;          /* Exits if unable to initialize        */
        }

    MainhWnd = BLDCreateWindow(hInstance);
    if (!MainhWnd)                 /* Check if the window is created        */
        return FALSE;

    ShowWindow(MainhWnd, nCmdShow);  /* Show the window                     */
    UpdateWindow(MainhWnd);          /* Send WM_PAINT message to window      */

    BLDInitMainMenu(MainhWnd);       /* Initialize main menu if necessary    */

    while (GetMessage(&msg,       /* Message structure                      */
        0,                        /* Handle of window receiving the message */
        0,                        /* Lowest message to examine              */
        0))                       /* Highest message to examine             */
        {
        if (BLDKeyTranslation(&msg)) /* WindowsMAKER code for key trans */
            continue;
        TranslateMessage(&msg); /* Translates character keys              */
        DispatchMessage(&msg);  /* Dispatches message to window           */
        }

    BLDExitApplication();        /* Clean up if necessary                  */

    return(msg.wParam);          /* Returns the value from PostQuitMessage  */
}


/******************************************************************/
/*              WINDOW PROCEDURE FOR MAIN WINDOW                  */
/******************************************************************/

    long FAR PASCAL

BLDMainWndProc ( HWND        hWnd,
                 unsigned    message,
                 WORD        wParam,
                 LONG        lParam )
{

    switch (message)
        {
```

continues

81

Listing 3.1. continued

```
case WM_LBUTTONDOWN:
{

    HBITMAP       oldBmp;         // Bitmap structure
    HBITMAP       happyBmp;       // Handle to happy face bitmap

    WORD          mX;             // Mouse x position
    WORD          mY;             // Mouse y position

    HDC           hDC;            // Handle to the screen DC

    HDC           compatDC;       // Handle to a compatible DC


    //----------------------------------

    /* Get the current mouse coordinates */

    mX = LOWORD(lParam);
    mY = HIWORD(lParam);

       hDC = GetDC ( hWnd );        // Get DC of your window

    compatDC = CreateCompatibleDC ( hDC );  // Create a compatible DC
                                            // for your bitmap

    // Now load the happy face bitmap

    happyBmp = LoadBitmap ( hInst,
                            "MRHAPPY" );

    if ( !happyBmp )
    {
        MessageBox ( hWnd,
                     "Cannot load resource bitmap",
                     "Error",
                     MB_OK );

        // Delete compatible DC if you have one

        if ( compatDC )
            DeleteDC ( compatDC );

        ReleaseDC ( hWnd,
                    hDC );
```

```
        return FALSE;
}


// Select the resource bitmap into the compatible DC so that
// you can copy it...

oldBmp = SelectObject ( compatDC,
                          happyBmp );

// Now copy your off-screen bitmap onto the screen.
// This is done using BitBlt

BitBlt ( hDC,       // Destination DC (the screen)
         mX - 16,   // X value, upper-left corner of dest rectangle
         mY - 16,   // Y value, upper-left corner of dest rectangle
         32,        // Image is 32 pixels wide,
         32,        // 32 pixels high
         compatDC,  // Source DC (your off-screen bitmap)
         0,         // Upper-left corner of source, X value
         0,         // Upper-left corner of source, y value
         SRCCOPY ); // Raster operation to perform (source copy)


// Put the old bitmap back into the DC (this is the single-
// pixel monochrome bitmap discussed in the text). Note that
// you don't have to keep track of the handle that the
// SelectObject() call returns this time, because it's the same
// handle as is contained in offScreenBmp.

SelectObject ( compatDC,
               oldBmp );

DeleteDC ( compatDC );   // Destroy the compatible DC...

// Release the system DC...

ReleaseDC ( hWnd,
            hDC );
}
break;

case WM_CREATE:              /* Window creation                    */
    /* Send to BLDDefWindowProc in (.WMC) for controls in main window */
    return BLDDefWindowProc(hWnd, message, wParam, lParam);
    break;
```

continues

Listing 3.1. continued

```
        case WM_SETFOCUS:              /* Window is notified of focus change     */
            /* Send to BLDDefWindowProc in (.WMC) for controls in main window    */
            return BLDDefWindowProc(hWnd, message, wParam, lParam);
            break;

        case WM_DESTROY:               /* Window being destroyed                 */
            PostQuitMessage(0);
            return BLDDefWindowProc(hWnd, message, wParam, lParam);
            break;

        case WM_COMMAND:               /* Command from the main window           */
            if (BLDMenuCommand(hWnd, message, wParam, lParam))
                break;                 /* Processed by BLDMenuCommand.           */
                /* Else default processing by BLDDefWindowProc.                  */
        default:
            /* Pass on message for default processing                            */
            return BLDDefWindowProc(hWnd, message, wParam, lParam);
            }
        return FALSE;                  /* Returns FALSE if processed             */
        }
```

Listing 3.2. HAPPY.WMC—special include file for the Happy App.

```
/*File name: HAPPY.WMC                                       */
/*"HAPPY" Generated by WindowsMAKER Professional             */
/*Author: Alex Leavens, for ShadowCat Technologies           */


/****************************************************************/
/*                    GLOBAL VARIABLES                        */
/****************************************************************/


HANDLE  hInst   = 0;  /* Handle to instance.                 */
HWND    MainhWnd= 0;  /* Handle to main window.              */
HWND    hClient = 0;  /* Handle to window in client area.    */
FARPROC lpClient= 0L; /* Function for window in client area. */


/****************************************************************/
/*            PROCESSES KEYBOARD ACCELERATORS                 */
/*            AND MODELESS DIALOG BOX KEY INPUT               */
/****************************************************************/


BOOL BLDKeyTranslation(pMsg)
MSG *pMsg;
```

```
    {
    return FALSE; /* No special key input                      */
    }


/*****************************************************************/
/*          CUSTOM MESSAGE PROCESSING FOR MAIN WINDOW          */
/*****************************************************************/

long FAR PASCAL BLDDefWindowProc(hWnd, message, wParam, lParam)
HWND hWnd;                          /* Window handle           */
unsigned message;                   /* Type of message         */
WORD wParam;                        /* Additional information  */
LONG lParam;                        /* Additional information  */
    {

    switch (message)
        {

    default:
        /* Pass on message for default processing by Windows   */
        return DefWindowProc(hWnd, message, wParam, lParam);
        }
    return FALSE; /* Returns FALSE if not processed by Windows */
    }


/*****************************************************************/
/*              PROCESSES ALL MENU ITEM SELECTIONS             */
/*****************************************************************/

BOOL BLDMenuCommand(hWnd, message, wParam, lParam)
HWND hWnd;                          /* Window handle           */
unsigned message;                   /* Type of message         */
WORD wParam;                        /* Additional information  */
LONG lParam;                        /* Additional information  */
    {

    switch(wParam)
        {

        /* Processing of linked menu items in menu: HAPPY  */

        default:
            return FALSE;   /* Not processed by this function. */
        }
    return TRUE;            /* Processed by this function.     */
    }
```

continues

Listing 3.2. continued

```c
/******************************************************************/
/*    FUNCTIONS FOR INITIALIZATION AND EXIT OF APPLICATION     */
/******************************************************************/

BOOL BLDInitApplication(hInst,hPrev,pCmdShow,lpCmd)
HANDLE hInst;     /* Handle to application instance.            */
HANDLE hPrev;     /* Handle to previous instance of application. */
int *pCmdShow;    /* Pointer to variable that specifies
                       how main window is to be shown. */
LPSTR lpCmd;      /* Long pointer to the command line.          */
    {
    /* No initialization necessary */
    return TRUE;
    }


BOOL BLDRegisterClass(hInstance) /* Registers the class for the main window */
HANDLE hInstance;
    {
    WNDCLASS WndClass;

    WndClass.style         = 0;
    WndClass.lpfnWndProc   = BLDMainWndProc;
    WndClass.cbClsExtra    = 0;
    WndClass.cbWndExtra    = 0;
    WndClass.hInstance     = hInstance;
    WndClass.hIcon         = LoadIcon(hInstance,"HAPPY");
    WndClass.hCursor       = LoadCursor(NULL,IDC_ARROW);
    WndClass.hbrBackground = CreateSolidBrush(GetSysColor(COLOR_WINDOW));
    WndClass.lpszMenuName  = "HAPPY";
    WndClass.lpszClassName = "HAPPY";

    return RegisterClass(&WndClass);
    }


HWND BLDCreateWindow(hInstance)  /* Creates the main window              */
HANDLE hInstance;
    {
    HWND hWnd;                    /* Window handle                       */
    int coordinate[4];           /* Coordinates of main window          */

    coordinate[0]=CW_USEDEFAULT;
    coordinate[1]=0;
```

```
        coordinate[2]=CW_USEDEFAULT;
        coordinate[3]=0;

        hWnd = CreateWindow("HAPPY",  /* Window class registered earlier  */
                "The Happy App",            /* Window caption                    */
                WS_OVERLAPPED¦WS_THICKFRAME¦WS_SYSMENU¦WS_MINIMIZEBOX¦WS_MAXIMIZEBOX,
                                    /* Window style                      */
                coordinate[0],      /* X position                        */
                coordinate[1],      /* Y position                        */
                coordinate[2],      /* Width                             */
                coordinate[3],      /* Height                            */
                0,                  /* Parent handle                     */
                0,                  /* Menu or child ID                  */
                hInstance,          /* Instance                          */
                (LPSTR)NULL);       /* Additional info                   */

        return hWnd;
        }


BOOL BLDInitMainMenu(hWnd)       /* Called just before entering message loop */
HWND hWnd;
    {
    /* No initialization necessary */
    return TRUE;
    }


BOOL BLDExitApplication()         /* Called just before exit of application  */
    {
    /* No processing needed at exit for this design */
    return TRUE;
    }

/************************************************************/
/* ERROR MESSAGE HANDLING (Definitions can be overruled.) */
/************************************************************/

#ifndef ERRORCAPTION
#define ERRORCAPTION "The Happy App"
#endif

#ifndef LOADERROR
#define LOADERROR "Cannot load string."
#endif
```

continues

Listing 3.2. continued

```c
int BLDDisplayMessage(hWnd,uMsg,pContext,iType)
HWND hWnd;
unsigned uMsg;
char *pContext;
int iType;
    {
    int i, j;
    char Message[200+1];

    if (uMsg)
        {
        if (!LoadString(hInst,uMsg,Message,200))
            {
            MessageBox(hWnd,LOADERROR,ERRORCAPTION,
                        MB_OK¦MB_SYSTEMMODAL¦MB_ICONHAND);
            return FALSE;
            }
        }
    else
        Message[0]=0;

    if (pContext)
        {
        i = lstrlen(Message);
        j = lstrlen(pContext);
        if (i + j + 1 <= 200)
            {
            lstrcat(Message, " ");
            lstrcat(Message, pContext);
            }
        }

    return MessageBox(hWnd,Message,ERRORCAPTION,iType);
    }

/******************************************************************/
/*           FUNCTIONS FOR DRAWING GRAPHICS BUTTONS          */
/******************************************************************/

BOOL BLDDrawIcon(lpDrawItem,pIconName)
LPDRAWITEMSTRUCT lpDrawItem;
char *pIconName;
    {
    HICON hIcon;
```

```
    if (!(hIcon = LoadIcon(hInst,pIconName)))
        {
        BLDDisplayMessage(GetActiveWindow(),BLD_CannotLoadIcon,pIconName,
                        MB_OK | MB_ICONASTERISK);
        return FALSE;
        }

    SetMapMode(lpDrawItem->hDC,MM_TEXT);
    return DrawIcon(lpDrawItem->hDC,0,0,hIcon);
    }


BOOL BLDDrawBitmap(lpDrawItem,pBitmapName,bStretch)
LPDRAWITEMSTRUCT lpDrawItem;
char *pBitmapName;
BOOL bStretch;
    {
    HBITMAP hBitmap;
    HDC hMemDC;
    BITMAP Bitmap;
    int iRaster;

    iRaster = GetDeviceCaps(lpDrawItem->hDC,RASTERCAPS);
    if ((iRaster&RC_BITBLT)!=RC_BITBLT)
        return FALSE; /* Device cannot display bitmap */

    if (!(hBitmap = LoadBitmap(hInst,pBitmapName)))
        {
        BLDDisplayMessage(GetActiveWindow(),BLD_CannotLoadBitmap,pBitmapName,
                        MB_OK | MB_ICONASTERISK);
        return FALSE;
        }

    if (!GetObject(hBitmap,sizeof(BITMAP),(LPSTR)&Bitmap))
        {
        DeleteObject(hBitmap);
        return FALSE;
        }
    if (!(hMemDC = CreateCompatibleDC(lpDrawItem->hDC)))
        {
        DeleteObject(hBitmap);
        return FALSE;
        }
    if (!SelectObject(hMemDC,hBitmap))
        {
```

continues

Listing 3.2. continued

```
            DeleteDC(hMemDC);
            DeleteObject(hBitmap);
            return FALSE;
            }

    if (bStretch)
            {
            StretchBlt(lpDrawItem->hDC,
                    lpDrawItem->rcItem.left,
                    lpDrawItem->rcItem.top,
                    lpDrawItem->rcItem.right-lpDrawItem->rcItem.left,
                    lpDrawItem->rcItem.bottom-lpDrawItem->rcItem.top,
                    hMemDC,
                    0,
                    0,
                    Bitmap.bmWidth,
                    Bitmap.bmHeight,
                    SRCCOPY);
        }
    else
        {
            BitBlt(lpDrawItem->hDC,
                    lpDrawItem->rcItem.left,
                    lpDrawItem->rcItem.top,
                    lpDrawItem->rcItem.right-lpDrawItem->rcItem.left,
                    lpDrawItem->rcItem.bottom-lpDrawItem->rcItem.top,
                    hMemDC,
                    0,
                    0,
                    SRCCOPY);
        }
    DeleteDC(hMemDC);
    DeleteObject(hBitmap);
    return TRUE;
    }


/****************************************************************/
/*        FUNCTION FOR CREATING CONTROLS IN MAIN WINDOW        */
/****************************************************************/

HWND BLDCreateClientControls(pTemplateName,lpNew) /* Start-up procedure for
                                                     window in client area */
char    *pTemplateName;
FARPROC lpNew;
```

```
{
RECT rClient,rMain,rDialog;
int dxDialog,dyDialog,dyExtra,dtXold,dtYold;
HANDLE hRes,hMem;
LPBLD_DLGTEMPLATE lpDlg;
unsigned long styleold,style;
HWND hNew;

if (!IsWindow(MainhWnd))
    return 0;
if (IsZoomed(MainhWnd))
    ShowWindow(MainhWnd,SW_RESTORE);


if (IsWindow(hClient))
 DestroyWindow(hClient); /* Destroy previous window in client area  */


/* Get access to data structure of dialog box
   containing layout of controls */
if (!(hRes=FindResource(hInst,(LPSTR)pTemplateName,RT_DIALOG)))
    return 0;
if (!(hMem=LoadResource(hInst,hRes)))
    return 0;
if (!(lpDlg=(LPBLD_DLGTEMPLATE)LockResource(hMem)))
    return 0;


/* Change dialog box data structure so it can be used
   as a window in client area */
styleold       = lpDlg->dtStyle;
style          = lpDlg->dtStyle&(CLIENTSTRIP);
lpDlg->dtStyle = lpDlg->dtStyle^style;
lpDlg->dtStyle = lpDlg->dtStyle ¦ WS_CHILD ¦ WS_CLIPSIBLINGS;
dtXold         = lpDlg->dtX;
dtYold         = lpDlg->dtY;
lpDlg->dtX     = 0;
lpDlg->dtY     = 0;


if (!(hNew = CreateDialogIndirect(hInst,(LPSTR)lpDlg, MainhWnd,lpNew)))
    return 0;


/* Restore dialog box data structure. */
lpDlg->dtStyle =styleold;
lpDlg->dtX     = dtXold;
lpDlg->dtY     = dtYold;

UnlockResource(hMem);
```

continues

Listing 3.2. continued

```
        FreeResource(hMem);

        /* Move and size window in client area and main window */
        GetClientRect(MainhWnd,&rClient);
        GetWindowRect(MainhWnd,&rMain);
        GetWindowRect(hNew,&rDialog);
        dxDialog=(rDialog.right-rDialog.left)-(rClient.right-rClient.left);
        dyDialog=(rDialog.bottom-rDialog.top)-(rClient.bottom-rClient.top);
        BLDMoveWindow(MainhWnd,rMain.left,rMain.top,
                (rMain.right-rMain.left)+dxDialog,
                            (rMain.bottom-rMain.top)+dyDialog,
                TRUE);
        MoveWindow(hNew,0,0,
                    (rDialog.right-rDialog.left),
                    (rDialog.bottom-rDialog.top),
                    TRUE);
        GetClientRect(MainhWnd,&rClient);

        /* Compensate size if menu bar is more than one line. */
        if ((rDialog.bottom-rDialog.top)>(rClient.bottom-rClient.top))
            {
            dyExtra=(rDialog.bottom-rDialog.top)-(rClient.bottom-rClient.top);
            BLDMoveWindow(MainhWnd,rMain.left,rMain.top,
                    (rMain.right-rMain.left)+dxDialog,
                    (rMain.bottom-rMain.top)+dyDialog+dyExtra,
                    TRUE);
            }

        ShowWindow(hNew,SW_SHOW);
        hClient=hNew;
        lpClient=lpNew;
        return hClient;
        }


/* Ensure that window is within screen. */
void BLDMoveWindow(hWnd,x,y,nWidth,nHeight,bRepaint)
HWND hWnd;
int  x;
int  y;
int  nWidth;
int  nHeight;
BOOL bRepaint;
    {
```

```
        int xMax,yMax,xNew,yNew;

        xMax = GetSystemMetrics(SM_CXSCREEN);
        yMax = GetSystemMetrics(SM_CYSCREEN);

        if ((nWidth<=xMax)&&(x+nWidth>xMax))
            xNew=xMax-nWidth;
        else
            xNew=x;

        if ((nHeight<=yMax)&&(y+nHeight>yMax))
            yNew=yMax-nHeight;
        else
            yNew=y;

        MoveWindow(hWnd,xNew,yNew,nWidth,nHeight,bRepaint);
        return;
        }

/*****************************************************************/
/*              FUNCTION FOR SWITCHING MENU SET                 */
/*****************************************************************/

BOOL BLDSwitchMenu(hWnd,pTemplateName)
HWND hWnd;
char *pTemplateName;
    {
    HMENU hMenu1,hMenu;
    DWORD style;

    style = GetWindowLong(hWnd,GWL_STYLE);
    if((style & WS_CHILD) == WS_CHILD)     /* Called from control
                                              in main window? */
        {
        if (!(hWnd=GetParent(hWnd)))
            return FALSE;
        style = GetWindowLong(hWnd,GWL_STYLE);
        if((style & WS_CHILD) == WS_CHILD) /* No menu in a WS_CHILD window. */
            return FALSE;
        }
    if((style & WS_CAPTION) != WS_CAPTION) /* No menu if no caption.       */
        return FALSE;

    hMenu1 = GetMenu(hWnd);
    if (!(hMenu = LoadMenu(hInst,pTemplateName)))
```

continues

Listing 3.2. continued

```
    {
    BLDDisplayMessage(hWnd,BLD_CannotLoadMenu,pTemplateName,
                    MB_OK | MB_ICONASTERISK);
    return FALSE;
    }

if (!SetMenu(hWnd,hMenu))
    return FALSE;
if (hMenu1)
    DestroyMenu(hMenu1);

DrawMenuBar(hWnd);
return TRUE;
    }
```

Listing 3.3. HAPPY.H—include file for the Happy App.

```
/*File name: HAPPY.H                                     */
/*"HAPPY" Generated by WindowsMAKER Professional         */
/*Author: Alex Leavens, for ShadowCat Technologies       */


/* Give access to handles in all code modules */
extern HANDLE hInst;
extern HWND MainhWnd;

/* Constants for error message strings */
#define BLD_CannotRun         4000
#define BLD_CannotCreate      4001
#define BLD_CannotLoadMenu    4002
#define BLD_CannotLoadIcon    4003
#define BLD_CannotLoadBitmap  4004


#if !defined(THISISBLDRC)

int PASCAL WinMain(HANDLE,HANDLE,LPSTR,int);
long FAR PASCAL BLDMainWndProc(HWND,unsigned,WORD,LONG);
long FAR PASCAL BLDDefWindowProc(HWND,unsigned,WORD,LONG);
BOOL BLDKeyTranslation(MSG *);
BOOL BLDInitApplication(HANDLE,HANDLE,int *,LPSTR);
```

```
BOOL BLDExitApplication(void);
HWND BLDCreateClientControls(char *,FARPROC);
BOOL BLDInitMainMenu(HWND);
BOOL BLDMenuCommand(HWND, unsigned , WORD, LONG);
BOOL BLDRegisterClass(HANDLE);
HWND BLDCreateWindow(HANDLE);
int BLDDisplayMessage(HWND,unsigned,char *,int);
BOOL BLDSwitchMenu(HWND,char *);
BOOL BLDDrawBitmap(LPDRAWITEMSTRUCT,char *,BOOL);
BOOL BLDDrawIcon(LPDRAWITEMSTRUCT,char *);
void BLDMoveWindow(HWND,int,int,int,int,BOOL);


/****************************************************************/
/* Variables, types, and constants for controls in main window.*/
/****************************************************************/

extern HWND hClient;    /* Handle to window in client area.  */
extern FARPROC lpClient; /* Function for window in client area. */

#define CLIENTSTRIP
WS_MINIMIZE|WS_MAXIMIZE|WS_CAPTION|WS_BORDER|WS_DLGFRAME|WS_SYSMENU|WS_POPUP|
WS_THICKFRAME|DS_MODALFRAME

typedef struct
  {
  unsigned long dtStyle;
  BYTE dtItemCount;
  int dtX;
  int dtY;
  int dtCX;
  int dtCY;
  } BLD_DLGTEMPLATE;

typedef BLD_DLGTEMPLATE far             *LPBLD_DLGTEMPLATE;

#endif


/* User Defined ID Values               */


/* WindowsMAKER Pro generated ID Values */
```

Listing 3.4. HAPPY.RC—resource file for the Happy App.

```
/*File name: HAPPY.RC                                    */
/*"HAPPY" Generated by WindowsMAKER Professional         */
/*Author: Alex Leavens, for ShadowCat Technologies       */

#define THISISBLDRC

#include <WINDOWS.H>
#include "HAPPY.H"

HAPPY  ICON  MRHAPPY.ICO

MRHAPPY BITMAP MRHAPPY.BMP


/*********************************************************/
/*        Resource code for error message strings       */
/*********************************************************/

STRINGTABLE
    BEGIN
        BLD_CannotRun          "Cannot run "
        BLD_CannotCreate       "Cannot create dialog box "
        BLD_CannotLoadMenu     "Cannot load menu "
        BLD_CannotLoadIcon     "Cannot load icon "
        BLD_CannotLoadBitmap   "Cannot load bitmap "
    END
```

Listing 3.5. HAPPY.DEF—definition file for the Happy App.

```
;File name: HAPPY.DEF
;"HAPPY" Generated by WindowsMAKER Professional
;Author: Alex Leavens, for ShadowCat Technologies

NAME        HAPPY
DESCRIPTION 'The Mr Happy App'
EXETYPE     WINDOWS
STUB        'WINSTUB.EXE'
DATA        MOVEABLE MULTIPLE
CODE        MOVEABLE DISCARDABLE PRELOAD
HEAPSIZE    1024
STACKSIZE   5120
EXPORTS

            BLDMainWndProc
```

Listing 3.6. HAPPY.LNK—link file for the Happy App.

```
HAPPY ,HAPPY.EXE ,/align:16 /NOD  , LIBW SLIBCEW, HAPPY.DEF
```

Listing 3.7. HAPPY—makefile for the Happy App.

```
#File name: HAPPY
#"HAPPY" Generated by WindowsMAKER Professional
#Author: Alex Leavens, for ShadowCat Technologies

comp= /c /AS /Os /Gsw /Zpe /D _WINDOWS /W2

ALL : HAPPY.EXE

HAPPY.RES : HAPPY.RC HAPPY.H MRHAPPY.BMP
    rc -r HAPPY.RC

HAPPY.OBJ : HAPPY.C HAPPY.WMC HAPPY.H
    cl  $(comp) HAPPY.C

HAPPY.EXE : HAPPY.OBJ HAPPY.DEF HAPPY.RES
    LINK @HAPPY.LNK
    rc HAPPY.RES
```

Figure 3.2 shows the MRHAPPY.BMP bitmap resource for use with the Happy App.

Figure 3.2.
The MRHAPPY.BMP bitmap resource.

Analyzing the Happy App

This is, by all standards, a pretty loopy little program. The only thing it does, when the left mouse button is clicked, is draw a Mr. Happy Face image underneath the mouse cursor. It accomplishes this by responding to the WM_LBUTTONDOWN message; when it receives this message, it draws the image. (See Figure 3.3 for a screen shot of the Happy App in action.)

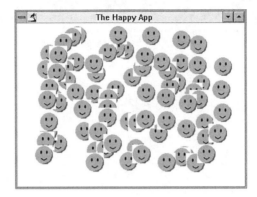

Figure 3.3.
The Happy App
in action.

How does the program draw the image? Really, it's pretty simple. As in SimPaint, the first thing you do is get a screen DC and make a compatible DC of it. Next, you load the bitmap from the resources of the application. As with other resources, it's a good idea to make sure that the resource loaded properly before you try to use it. (The first time I built this app, a message box popped up, telling me that the resource couldn't be loaded. It took a few minutes of head scratching to figure out that I was trying to load the resource named HAPPY when there wasn't one—the resource was MRHAPPY. However, the little check for a successfully loaded resource was much more pleasant—and informative—than the dreaded UAE message.)

After you've successfully loaded the bitmap, you select it into your compatible DC (making sure, of course, to save the old bitmap). Then you blit the image from the compatible DC to your screen DC, using the mouse X and Y position reported by the WM_LBUTTONDOWN message to position the image. This is what makes the bitmap appear at the mouse position.

> **Note:** An interesting aside here—the mouse position reported by the WM_LBUTTONDOWN message (and the other messages that report a mouse position) report the position of the cursor's *hotspot*, that is, the point on the screen over which the cursor's hotspot is located. (See Chapter 6, "The Cursor Resource," for more information regarding a cursor's hotspot.) To successfully center the image around the cursor, you need to subtract half the image's size from the position to which you blit, hence the mX - 16 and mY - 16 as the destination position of the image.

Next, you reselect the old bitmap into the compatible DC, delete the compatible DC, and release the screen DC.

And you're done. Or are you? You probably noticed the error in my code right away, but I didn't, at least not at first. I'm not deleting the resource bitmap when I'm done with it. I'll say it again (not least for my own benefit! <grin>): *Always free a resource when you're done with it.* The proper piece of code for the WM_LBUTTONDOWN message looks like that shown in Listing 3.8.

Listing 3.8. The fixed code for WM_LBUTTONDOWN.

```
case WM_LBUTTONDOWN:
{

    HBITMAP        oldBmp;          // Bitmap structure
    HBITMAP        happyBmp;        // Handle to happy face bitmap

    WORD           mX;              // Mouse x position
    WORD           mY;              // Mouse y position

    HDC            hDC;             // Handle to the screen DC

    HDC            compatDC;        // Handle to a compatible DC


    //---------------------------------------

    /* Get the current mouse coordinates */

    mX = LOWORD(lParam);
    mY = HIWORD(lParam);

       hDC = GetDC ( hWnd );        // Get DC of your window

    compatDC = CreateCompatibleDC ( hDC );  // Create a compatible DC
                                            // for your bitmap
    // Now load the happy face bitmap

    happyBmp = LoadBitmap ( hInst,
                           "MRHAPPY" );

    if ( !happyBmp )
    {
        MessageBox ( hWnd,
```

continues

99

Listing 3.8. continued

```
"Cannot load resource bitmap",
                    "Error",
                    MB_OK );

    // Delete compatible DC if you have one

    if ( compatDC )
        DeleteDC ( compatDC );

    ReleaseDC ( hWnd,
                hDC );

    return FALSE;
}

// Select the resource bitmap into the compatible DC so that
// you can copy it...

oldBmp = SelectObject ( compatDC,
                        happyBmp );

// Now copy your off-screen bitmap onto the screen.
// This is done using BitBlt

BitBlt ( hDC,        // Destination DC (the screen)
         mX - 16,    // X value, upper-left corner of dest rectangle
         mY - 16,    // Y value, upper-left corner of dest rectangle
         32,         // Image is 32 pixels wide,
         32,         // 32 pixels high
         compatDC,   // Source DC (your off-screen bitmap)
         0,          // Upper-left corner of source, X value
         0,          // Upper-left corner of source, y value
         SRCCOPY );  // Raster operation to perform (source copy)

// Put the old bitmap back into the DC (this is the single-
// pixel monochrome bitmap discussed in the text). Note that
// you don't have to keep track of the handle that the
// SelectObject() call returns this time, because it's the same
// handle as is contained in offScreenBmp.

SelectObject ( compatDC,
               oldBmp );

DeleteDC ( compatDC );    // Destroy the compatible DC...
```

```
        // Don't forget to delete the bitmap!!

        DeleteObject ( happyBmp );

        // Release the system DC...

        ReleaseDC ( hWnd,
                    hDC );
    }
        break;
```

SimPaint3—Put On a Happy Face

The Happy App is interesting, but a little frustrating. The happy face appears
only when you click the mouse button, but not when you move the mouse.
Wouldn't it be nice to be able to actually *paint* with the image? (he asked,
rhetorically). Certainly; and Listing 3.9 shows a modified version of SimPaint
that lets you do this. (Only the two files that have changed, SIMPAINT.C and
SIMPAINT.RC are listed. The others are the same as in Chapter 2, "The
Display Context.")

**Listing 3.9. SIMPAINT.C—the new source code for the Happy
Face brush version of SimPaint.**

```
// SIMPAINT.C
//
// This is SIMPAINT # 3 - Painting with a brush loaded as
// a bitmap from a resource file
//
// Source code for the simple paint program
//
// Written by Alex Leavens, for ShadowCat Technologies

#include <WINDOWS.H>
#include "SIMPAINT.H"

#include "SIMPAINT.WMC"


BOOL     buttonDown = FALSE;     // If true, mouse button down
```

continues

Listing 3.9. continued

```c
HBITMAP   offScreenBmp = NULL;      // Handle to your off-screen bitmap

HBITMAP   happyBmp = NULL;          // Handle to your happy face bitmap


/***************************
 *
 * WinMain()
 *
 * Start-up function for all Windows programs.
 */

    int PASCAL

WinMain(HANDLE  hInstance,          // Current instance of program
        HANDLE  hPrevInstance,      // Previous instance of program (if any)
        LPSTR   lpCmdLine,          // Command line (if applicable)
        int     nCmdShow)           // Window display style (open/iconic)

{
    MSG   msg;       // Message passed to your program

    HDC   hDC;       // Handle to screen DC

    DWORD winSize;   // Window size

    //--------------------------------

    hInst = hInstance;    // Save the current instance

    if (!BLDInitApplication(hInstance,hPrevInstance,&nCmdShow,lpCmdLine))
        return FALSE;

    if (!hPrevInstance)         /* Is there another instance of the task   */
        {
        if (!BLDRegisterClass(hInstance))
            return FALSE;       /* Exits if unable to initialize           */
        }

    MainhWnd = BLDCreateWindow(hInstance);
    if (!MainhWnd)              /* Check if the window is created           */
        return FALSE;

    ShowWindow(MainhWnd, nCmdShow);  /* Show the window                     */
```

```
    UpdateWindow(MainhWnd);            /* Send WM_PAINT message to window   */

    BLDInitMainMenu(MainhWnd);        /* Initialize main menu if necessary */

    while (GetMessage(&msg,      /* Message structure                      */
        0,                       /* Handle of window receiving the message */
        0,                       /* Lowest message to examine              */
        0))                      /* Highest message to examine             */
        {
        if (BLDKeyTranslation(&msg)) /* WindowsMAKER code for key trans */
            continue;
        TranslateMessage(&msg); /* Translates character keys              */
        DispatchMessage(&msg);  /* Dispatches message to window           */
        }

    BLDExitApplication();        /* Clean up if necessary                 */

    return(msg.wParam);          /* Returns the value from PostQuitMessage */
}


/****************************************************************/
/*          WINDOW PROCEDURE FOR MAIN WINDOW                  */
/****************************************************************/

    long FAR PASCAL

BLDMainWndProc ( HWND       hWnd,
                 unsigned   message,
                 WORD       wParam,
                 LONG       lParam )
{

    HDC       hDC;        // Handle to your device context

    HDC       compatDC; // Handle to a compatible DC
    HDC       brushDC;  // Handle to a compatible DC for the happy
                        // face bitmap

    HBITMAP   oldBmp;   // Handle to bitmap originally in the DC

    WORD mX;          // Mouse x position
    WORD mY;          // Mouse y position

    //------------------------
```

continues

Listing 3.9. continued

```
switch (message)
{

case WM_CREATE:                /* window creation */

    happyBmp = LoadBitmap ( hInst,
                    "MRHAPPY" );
 if ( !happyBmp )
 {
     MessageBox ( hWnd,
                "Cannot load resource bitmap",
                "Error",
                MB_OK );
 }

    /* Send to BLDDefWindowProc in (.WMC) for controls in main window   */
    return BLDDefWindowProc(hWnd, message, wParam, lParam);
    break;

case WM_SIZE:       // Window's size has changed

// Whenever the window changes size, then you need to delete
// the old bitmap (if there is one) and create a new bitmap to
// match the proper size of the window.

hDC = GetDC ( MainhWnd );

// If old bitmap not NULL, delete it.

if ( offScreenBmp )
    DeleteObject ( offScreenBmp );

// The new width is in the low-order word of lParam, and the
// new height is in the high-order word.

offScreenBmp = CreateCompatibleBitmap ( hDC,
                                        LOWORD ( lParam ),
                                        HIWORD ( lParam ) );

compatDC = CreateCompatibleDC ( hDC );  // Create a compatible DC
                                        // for your bitmap

// Select your off-screen bitmap into the compatible DC. Make
// sure that you save the old bitmap that was in the DC!!
```

```
oldBmp = SelectObject ( compatDC,
                          offScreenBmp );

// This call zeroes out (erases) whatever's in the bitmap
// (otherwise you just get a chunk of memory, which might look
// interesting on the screen, but is probably NOT what you want!)

PatBlt ( compatDC,
         0,
         0,
         LOWORD ( lParam ),
         HIWORD ( lParam ),
         WHITENESS );

SelectObject ( compatDC, // Put the old bitmap back
               oldBmp ); // into the compatible DC

DeleteDC ( compatDC );           // Get rid of the compatible DC

// Release the DC (must do this for this DC, since you haven't
// defined your drawing window as one with a CLASSDC or OWNDC style)

ReleaseDC ( MainhWnd,
            hDC );

break;


case WM_SETFOCUS:             /* Window is notified of focus change     */
    /* Send to BLDDefWindowProc in (.WMC) for controls in main window   */
    return BLDDefWindowProc(hWnd, message, wParam, lParam);
    break;

case WM_DESTROY:              /* Window being destroyed                 */

// Delete your offScreenBmp

if ( offScreenBmp )
    DeleteObject ( offScreenBmp );

if ( happyBmp )
    DeleteObject ( happyBmp );

    PostQuitMessage(0);    // You're done...
```

continues

105

Listing 3.9. continued

```
               return BLDDefWindowProc(hWnd, message, wParam, lParam);
               break;

       case WM_PAINT:

        // If you don't have a valid bitmap to paste in, then don't.

           if ( offScreenBmp == NULL )
               return TRUE;        // Message not processed

        // In response to a WM_PAINT message (meaning that some part
        // of your window has been munged), you're going to copy your
        // off-screen bitmap into your window.

           {
           PAINTSTRUCT    pntInfo;  // Window repainting information

           int            numBytes; // Dummy return value

           BITMAP         ourBmp;   // Bitmap structure

           //-----------------------------------

           hDC = BeginPaint ( hWnd,
                              (LPPAINTSTRUCT) & pntInfo );

           compatDC = CreateCompatibleDC ( hDC );  // Create a compatible DC
                                                   // for your bitmap

        // Select your off-screen bitmap into the compatible DC. Make
        // sure that you save the old bitmap that was in the DC!!

           oldBmp = SelectObject ( compatDC,
                                   offScreenBmp );

        // In order to properly copy the bitmap, you need to retrieve how
        // big it is. Do that here

           numBytes = GetObject ( offScreenBmp,
                                  sizeof ( BITMAP ),
                                  (LPSTR) & ourBmp );

        // If you can't get the size of the bitmap, punt.
```

```
if ( numBytes == 0 )
{
    MessageBox ( hWnd,
                 "Cannot get information about off-screen Bitmap.",
                 "SimPaint Error",
                 MB_OK );
    return FALSE;
}

// Now copy your off-screen bitmap onto the screen.
// This is done using BitBlt

BitBlt ( hDC,                 // Destination DC (the screen)
         0,                   // X value, upper-left corner of dest rectangle
         0,                   // Y value, upper-left corner of dest rectangle
         ourBmp.bmWidth,      // Width of bitmap
         ourBmp.bmHeight,     // Height of bitmap
         compatDC,            // Source DC (your off-screen bitmap)
         0,                   // Upper-left corner of source, X value
         0,                   // Upper-left corner of source, y value
         SRCCOPY );           // Raster operation to perform (source copy)

// Put the old bitmap back into the DC (this is the single-
// pixel monochrome bitmap discussed in the text). Note that
// you don't have to keep track of the handle that the
// SelectObject() call returns this time, because it's the same
// handle as is contained in offScreenBmp.

SelectObject ( compatDC,
               oldBmp );

DeleteDC ( compatDC );   // Destroy the compatible DC...

// Don't forget to release the DC and let Windows paint again!

EndPaint ( hWnd,
           (LPPAINTSTRUCT) &pntInfo );

}
    break;

case WM_MOUSEMOVE:

// Only paint if the mouse button is down.
```

continues

Listing 3.9. continued

```
if ( buttonDown != TRUE )
    break;

/* Get the current mouse coordinates */

mX = LOWORD(lParam);
mY = HIWORD(lParam);

   hDC = GetDC ( hWnd );        // Get DC of your window

compatDC = CreateCompatibleDC ( hDC );  // Create a compatible DC
                                        // for your bitmap

// Now you're going to select the happy face bitmap into
// the compatible DC and use it as a paint brush. You'll
// also keep the old drawing code as a backup, in case you
// can't load the bitmap for some reason.

    // Select your off-screen bitmap into the compatible DC. Make
    // sure that you save the old bitmap that was in the DC!!

    oldBmp = SelectObject ( compatDC,
                            offScreenBmp );

if ( happyBmp )
{
    HBITMAP    saveBmp; // Place to save the bitmap of the
                        // compatible DC

    // Create a compatible DC for the happy face bitmap to go into

    brushDC = CreateCompatibleDC ( hDC );

    if ( brushDC )
    {
        saveBmp = SelectObject ( brushDC,
                                 happyBmp );

    // Now blit the happy face image onto the screen...

    BitBlt ( hDC,        // Destination DC (the screen)
             mX - 16,    // X value, upper-left corner of dest rectangle
             mY - 16,    // Y value, upper-left corner of dest rectangle
             32,         // Image is 32 pixels wide,
```

```
          32,        // 32 pixels high
          brushDC,   // Source DC (your off-screen bitmap)
          0,         // Upper-left corner of source, X value
          0,         // Upper-left corner of source, y value
          SRCCOPY ); // Raster operation to perform (source copy)

    // ...and onto your off-screen bitmap

    BitBlt ( compatDC,  // Destination DC (the screen)
             mX - 16,   // X value, upper-left corner of dest rectangle
             mY - 16,   // Y value, upper-left corner of dest rectangle
             32,        // Image is 32 pixels wide,
             32,        // 32 pixels high
             brushDC,   // Source DC (your off-screen bitmap)
             0,         // Upper-left corner of source, X value
             0,         // Upper-left corner of source, y value
             SRCCOPY ); // Raster operation to perform (source copy)

    // Put the old Bitmap back...

    SelectObject ( brushDC,
                   saveBmp );

    DeleteDC ( brushDC );    // ...and kill the compatible DC
  }
}
else
{

    // Now draw the image on the screen...

      SetPixel ( hDC,
        mX,
        mY,
        RGB ( 0, 0, 0 ) );  // Draw a black pixel

    // ...and into your off-screen bitmap.

      SetPixel ( compatDC,
        mX,
        mY,
        RGB ( 0, 0, 0 ) );  // Draw a black pixel

}
```

continues

Listing 3.9. continued

```
// Put the old bitmap back into the DC (this is the single-
// pixel monochrome bitmap discussed in the text). Note that
// you don't have to keep track of the handle that the
// SelectObject() call returns this time, because it's the same
// handle as is contained in offScreenBmp.

SelectObject ( compatDC,
               oldBmp );

DeleteDC ( compatDC );   // Destroy the compatible DC...

// Release the system DC...

ReleaseDC ( hWnd,
            hDC );
   break;              // Done!

case WM_LBUTTONDOWN:

/* Get the current mouse coordinates */

mX = LOWORD(lParam);
mY = HIWORD(lParam);

   buttonDown = TRUE;

   hDC = GetDC ( hWnd );        // Get DC of your window

compatDC = CreateCompatibleDC ( hDC );  // Create a compatible DC
                                        // for your bitmap

    // Select your off-screen bitmap into the compatible DC. Make
    // sure that you save the old bitmap that was in the DC!!

    oldBmp = SelectObject ( compatDC,
                            offScreenBmp );

// Now you're going to select the happy face bitmap into
// the compatible DC and use it as a paint brush. You'll
// also keep the old drawing code as a backup, in case you
// can't load the bitmap for some reason.

if ( happyBmp )
{
```

```
HBITMAP    saveBmp;  // Place to save the bitmap of the
                     // compatible DC

// Create a compatible DC for the happy face bitmap to go into

brushDC = CreateCompatibleDC ( hDC );

if ( brushDC )
{
   saveBmp = SelectObject ( brushDC,
                            happyBmp );

// Now blit the happy face image onto the screen...

BitBlt ( hDC,        // Destination DC (the screen)
         mX - 16,    // X value, upper-left corner of dest rectangle
         mY - 16,    // Y value, upper-left corner of dest rectangle
         32,         // Image is 32 pixels wide,
         32,         // 32 pixels high
         brushDC,    // Source DC (your off-screen bitmap)
         0,          // Upper-left corner of source, X value
         0,          // Upper-left corner of source, y value
         SRCCOPY );  // Raster operation to perform (source copy)

// ...and onto your off-screen bitmap

BitBlt ( compatDC,   // Destination DC (the screen)
         mX - 16,    // X value, upper-left corner of dest rectangle
         mY - 16,    // Y value, upper-left corner of dest rectangle
         32,         // Image is 32 pixels wide,
         32,         // 32 pixels high
         brushDC,    // Source DC (your off-screen bitmap)
         0,          // Upper-left corner of source, X value
         0,          // Upper-left corner of source, y value
         SRCCOPY );  // Raster operation to perform (source copy)

// Put the old Bitmap back...

SelectObject ( brushDC,
               saveBmp );

DeleteDC ( brushDC );    // ...and kill the compatible DC
}
}
else
{
```

continues

Listing 3.9. continued

```
                // Now draw the image on the screen...

                    SetPixel ( hDC,
                        mX,
                        mY,
                        RGB ( 0, 0, 0 ) );  // Draw a black pixel

                // ...and into your off-screen bitmap.

                    SetPixel ( compatDC,
                        mX,
                        mY,
                        RGB ( 0, 0, 0 ) );  // Draw a black pixel

            }

        // Put the old bitmap back into the DC (this is the single-
        // pixel monochrome bitmap discussed in the text). Note that
        // you don't have to keep track of the handle that the
        // SelectObject() call returns this time, because it's the same
        // handle as is contained in offScreenBmp.

        SelectObject ( compatDC,
                        oldBmp );

        DeleteDC ( compatDC );   // Destroy the compatible DC...

        // Release the system DC...

        ReleaseDC ( hWnd,
                    hDC );
            break;


    case WM_LBUTTONUP:

        buttonDown = FALSE;
        break;

    case WM_COMMAND:              /* Command from the main window        */
        if (BLDMenuCommand(hWnd, message, wParam, lParam))
            break;               /* Processed by BLDMenuCommand.        */
            /* Else default processing by BLDDefWindowProc.             */
    default:
```

```
        /* Pass on message for default processing                    */
        return BLDDefWindowProc(hWnd, message, wParam, lParam);
    }

    return FALSE;                    /* Returns FALSE if processed    */
}
```

Listing 3.10. SIMPAINT.RC—the resource file for SimPaint3, the Happy Face version of SimPaint.

```
/*File name: SIMPAINT.RC                                 */
/*"SIMPAINT" Generated by WindowsMAKER Professional      */
/*Author: Alex Leavens                                   */

#define THISISBLDRC

#include <WINDOWS.H>
#include "SIMPAINT.H"

MRHAPPY BITMAP MRHAPPY.BMP

/********************************************************/
/*      Resource code for error message strings         */
/********************************************************/

STRINGTABLE
    BEGIN
        BLD_CannotRun          "Cannot run "
        BLD_CannotCreate       "Cannot create dialog box "
        BLD_CannotLoadMenu     "Cannot load menu "
        BLD_CannotLoadIcon     "Cannot load icon "
        BLD_CannotLoadBitmap   "Cannot load bitmap "
    END
```

Figure 3.4 shows the Happy Face version of SimPaint. Notice the difference in the two versions: whereas the HappyApp simply has multiple copies of the image on the screen (corresponding to mouse presses), the new version of SimPaint has worm trails of the image behind it (left as the mouse is moved and the button is held down).

Figure 3.4.
Screen shot of
the Happy Face
version of
SimPaint (using
a bitmap as
a brush).

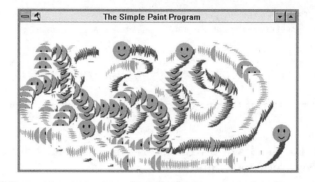

One thing I did in the new version of SimPaint: if the program was unable to load the bitmap resource, I opted to continue, only drawing a single pixel in the old fashion. This bullet-proofing is much friendlier for the user. It also means that if something does go wrong, the user is more likely to be able to save his or her work, if a reasonable default behavior has been provided.

Steps in Creating and Using a Resource Bitmap

Now that you've seen a resource bitmap in action, I'll recap the steps you need to take to use a resource bitmap in your program:

1. Create the bitmap using an editor (such as ICE/Works Pro).

2. Include the bitmap in your resource file.

3. Compile your resource file and your program to include the bitmap.

4. In your program load the bitmap using the `LoadBitmap()` call.

5. Manipulate the bitmap somehow.

6. Delete the bitmap when you're done with it.

There are several interesting things about loading resources. In all the example code I listed previously, I'm making the assumption that you're loading a bitmap resource out of your program's own executable file; however, it doesn't have to be this way. The first parameter to the `LoadBitmap()` call is a handle to an instance of the application containing the bitmap you want to load. It's certainly easy to use your own instance handle here, but you're not precluded from using other instance handles.

Resource-Only DLLs

Why would you want to use other instance handles? One very good reason is the creation of a *resource-only DLL*. This is a dynamic link library that contains nothing except a dummy initialization procedure and a bunch of graphics resources. This is a very handy way of encapsulating all your graphics resources into one file, separated from your main program's .exe file. There are some advantages and disadvantages of doing this.

One advantage is that your .exe file is smaller without a bunch of graphics resources loaded into it. This means that it loads and comes up running more quickly (although there is a small delay when your program tries to access any of these graphics resources). Another advantage is one that you accrue during development: by separating the resources out of your main program, the time that it takes the resource compiler to bind your program's resources is significantly reduced. If your graphics resources rarely change (at least in comparison to source code changes), you can enjoy a big-time savings by doing this.

One disadvantage to putting your graphics resources in a separate file is that it's easier to lose them. If a user tries to copy just your executable file to a different system, without copying your DLL, your application won't be able to display any of the graphics in the DLL when the application is run on the new system. Using an integrated install program, however, can solve this problem.

Another disadvantage is that loading a resource from a different application requires a little more work than loading one from your own. For one thing, you need to get a handle to an instance of the other application. Here's a piece of sample code that loads a bitmap called SPLASH from a resource in a DLL called graphics.dll:

```
HANDLE    dllInst;
HBITMAP   dllBmp;

dllInst = LoadLibrary ( "graphics.dll" );

if ( dllInst < 32 )
{
    MessageBox ( NULL,
                 "Error: Cannot load bitmap from resource dll",
                 "",
                 MB_OK );
    return;
}
```

115

```
dllBmp = LoadBitmap ( dllInst,
                      "SPLASH" );
if ( ! dllBmp )
{
    MessageBox ( NULL,
                 "Error: Cannot load bitmap",
                 "",
                 MB_OK );
    return;
}

// Use the loaded bitmap here

DeleteObject ( dllBmp );
```

You use the **LoadLibrary()** call to get a handle to an instance of the resource DLL you've created. The **LoadLibrary()** call loads the DLL (if it isn't already loaded) and returns a handle to the instance of the DLL. DLLs are always single-instance, which brings up another benefit to using resource-only DLLs. By using one, you can have a single copy of your images, regardless of how many instances of your application are running. You not only save space in your executable, but in memory as well.

If you use this method of loading resources (this technique works not only for bitmaps, but for any other type of resource as well), you need to make sure not only that the resource loads properly, but that your program is able to find the DLL to load the resource from. This is to guard against your DLL file being missing. (By the way, the **LoadLibrary()** call returns a variety of different error codes you can use to determine the kind of error encountered. See **LoadLibrary()** in the Function Reference at the end of the chapter.)

By the way, loading a library also requires you to free it when you're done. This is done with the **FreeLibrary()** function call.

Bitmap: A Bitmap Object Class

Now that you've seen how you can access the bitmaps by putting them into resource files, take a look at a couple of pieces of code. The first is an object class I created for ICE/Works. It's a very basic bitmap class that does only a couple of things. From this basic bitmap class I've derived several useful (well, to me, anyway! <grin>) graphics objects.

Deriving Other Objects from Bitmap

The first of these is a ResourceBitmap class, which is an object that knows how to load itself out of a resource. One useful thing about the ResBitmap class is that its destructor routine takes care of removing the bitmap from the GDI resource pool; you won't have to worry about leaving a bitmap lying around, cluttering up GDI when your application terminates. This is one of the more difficult details in Windows programming: if you're using many bitmaps in your program (as graphics buttons, for example), it's very easy to fail to delete one or two of them when your program terminates. At this point, those bitmaps are like the Flying Dutchman, doomed forever to wander the GDI pool with no hope of being removed—at least until the user resets the machine! The base Bitmap object class also implements some useful behavior that I'll discuss; for example, a bitmap object (as well as all objects derived from it) knows how to render itself into a device context.

Source Code to the Bitmap and ResBitmap Classes

Listing 3.11. BITMAP.H—class definitions and inline functions for Bitmap and ResBitmap object classes.

```
/* BITMAP.H
 *
 * Bitmap object class for C++
 *
 * Contains various object classes which are useful
 * in dealing with bitmaps.
 *
 * Written by Alex Leavens, for ShadowCat Technologies
 */


#ifndef __BITMAP_H

#define __BITMAP_H

#include <windows.h>
```

continues

Listing 3.11. continued

```c
#include "compatdc.h"

#ifdef __cplusplus

/****************************************
 *
 * Class: Bitmap
 *
 * This is the basic bitmap class; it
 * simply contains a handle to a bitmap,
 * and a way to get at it.
 */

    class

Bitmap
{
    //--------------- PROTECTED ------------

    protected:

     HBITMAP hBitmap;            // Handle to the instance of the bitmap

         int
     GetBitmap(BITMAP FAR * lpbm); // Get bitmap object info


    //------------- PUBLIC --------------------

    public:

       /*----------------------------
        *
        * Bitmap() - Default constructor, simply
        * sets the bitmap handle to NULL.
        *
        * Returns: Nothing
        *
        * Args: Nothing
        */

       Bitmap ( void ) { SetHandle ( NULL ); }    // Constructor
```

```
   /*-------------------------------
    *
    * Bitmap() - Non-default constructor.
    * Given a bitmap handle, will copy the
    * handle into the internal variable hBitmap.
    *
    * Returns: Nothing
    *
    * Args: nHBM - handle to the bitmap to set this instance to
    */

Bitmap ( HBITMAP nHBM ) { SetHandle ( nHBM ); }

/*------------------------
 *
 * ~Bitmap() - Destructor routine, cleans up after a bitmap.
 *
 * Returns: Nothing
 *
 * Args: None
 */

   ~Bitmap(void);                    // Destructor

  /*----------------------------
   *
   * SetHandle() - Sets the handle of the bitmap to the
   * handle of the bitmap that's been passed in.
   *
   * Returns: Nothing
   *
   * Args: nHBM - handle to the bitmap to set this bitmap to
   */

   void
SetHandle ( HBITMAP nHBM ) { hBitmap = nHBM; }

  /*-----------------------------
   *
   * DeleteSelf()
   *
   * Deletes the bitmap
   *
   * Returns: Nothing
   *
```

continues

Listing 3.11. continued

```
      * Args: None
      */

         void
      DeleteSelf( void );

      /*------------------------
       *
       * DisplaySelf()
       *
       * Displays the bitmap into the DC you've been
       * passed, at the requested x and y coords.
       *
       * Returns: Nothing
       *
       * Arguments:    hDC - DC to display into
       *               xStart - upper-left corner, x
       *               yStart - upper-left corner, y
       */

         void
      DisplaySelf( HDC        hDC,
                   short      xStart,
                   short      yStart );

  /*----------------------------------
   *
   * GetSize()
   *
   * Gets the size of the bitmap and returns a
   * point structure, indicating the lower-right corner
   *
   * Returns: POINT - lower-right corner of bitmap
   *
   * Arguments: None
   */

         POINT
  GetSize( void );

  /*----------------------------
   *
   * GetBitmapHandle() - returns a handle to the bitmap
   *
```

```
          * Returns: Handle to the bitmap
          *
          * Args: None
          */

          HBITMAP
      GetBitmapHandle ( void ) {   return hBitmap; }
};

/********************************************
 *
 * Class: ResBitmap
 *
 * Definition of a ResBitmap class,
 * which is a derivative of the standard
 * bitmap class. A ResBitmap object
 * deals strictly with a Bitmap loaded
 * as a resource from the .exe file.
 */

    class

ResBitmap : public Bitmap
{

  //--------------- PUBLIC --------------

  public:

    /*-------------------------
     *
     * ResBitmap() - Default constructor (no arguments)
     */

    ResBitmap( void );

    /*-------------------------
     *
     * ResBitmap() - Constructor
     */

    ResBitmap( HANDLE     hInstance,
               LPSTR      lpszBitmapName );
```

continues

Listing 3.11. continued

```
    /*----------------------
     *
     * No destructor needed, since parent class (Bitmap)
     * handles it.
     */

    ~ResBitmap( void );


    /*-----------------
     *
     * LoadSelf() - Will load self if not already loaded
     */

     BOOL
    LoadSelf( HANDLE      hInstance,
              LPSTR       lpszBitmapName );

};

/*--------------------------------------------------*/

#endif    // __cplusplus

#endif    // __BITMAP_H
```

Listing 3.12. BITMAP.CPP—C++ source code for member functions of the Bitmap and ResBitmap object classes.

```
/* BITMAP.CPP
 *
 * C++ Bitmap object class
 *
 * Written by Alex Leavens, for ShadowCat Technologies
 */

#include <WINDOWS.H>

#define _EXPORT _export

/*-----------------------
 *
```

```
 * Bitmap::GetBitmap()
 *
 * Private Function, not to be accessed by nonmembers
 *
 *     Will do a GetObject on
 *     the bitmap and return the result
 *
 * Returns: Positive or 0 if successful
 *          -1 if failure
 *
 * Args: Pointer to a BITMAP structure to be filled in
 */

    int
Bitmap::GetBitmap( BITMAP FAR * lpbm )
{
    if (lpbm == NULL  ¦¦
        !hBitmap)          // If pointer NULL, or no bitmap,
    {                      // then punt
        return -1;
    }

    return GetObject( hBitmap,
                      sizeof( BITMAP ),
                      (LPSTR) lpbm );
}


/*--------------------------------
 *
 * Bitmap::~Bitmap() - Destructor
 *
 * Cleans up the instance of a bitmap object.
 *
 * Returns: Nothing
 *
 * Arguments: Nothing
 */

Bitmap::~Bitmap( void )
{
    DeleteSelf();
}


/*------------------------
 *
 * Bitmap::DeleteSelf()
 *
```

Listing 3.12. continued

```
* Deletes the bitmap
*
* Returns: Nothing
*
* Args: Nothing
*/

    void
Bitmap::DeleteSelf( void )
{

    // If handle isn't NULL, then delete the object.

    if (hBitmap != NULL)
    {
     DeleteObject( hBitmap ); // Delete bitmap

     hBitmap = NULL;                    // Mark handle as NULL so you don't
                                        // try to delete it again.
    }
}


/****************************
 *
 * Bitmap::DisplaySelf()
 *
 * Display routine for the Bitmap class and derived classes.
 * This routine takes the bitmap handle internal to a
 * particular instantiation of the bitmap object, and displays
 * it in the requested DC. It also takes an X,Y offset, which
 * can be used to position the bitmap at some point other than
 * the upper-left corner of the target DC.
 *
 * Returns: Nothing
 *
 * Args: hDC    - target DC to copy (display) the bitmap in
 *       xStart - X offset (from upper left) of the target DC
 *       yStart - Y offset (from upper left) of the target DC
 */

    void
Bitmap::DisplaySelf( HDC hDC,                // Target DC to display in
                     short    xStart = 0,    // X offset in target DC
                     short    yStart = 0 )   // Y offset in target DC
```

```
{
    POINT       ptSize;          // Size of memoryDC

    /*------------------------*/

    // If no bitmap, punt immediately.

    if ( !hBitmap )
        return;

    // First thing, create a compatible DC, and select the bitmap
    // into it.

    CompatibleDC MemoryDC( hDC,
                           hBitmap );

    // If you couldn't create the memory DC, punt. (This is a
    // REAL BAD THING to have happen, and probably means that
    // Windows has been hosed in an irretrievable way.)

    HDC hDCMem = MemoryDC.GetCompatDC();

    if ( !hDCMem )
        return;

    // Get the size of the bitmap

    ptSize = GetSize( );       // Get size of bitmap

    // Now copy the bitmap from the source (your memory DC)
    // to the destination (the target DC handle passed in)
    // Use the size of the bitmap (retrieved above) as the
    // destination size (i.e., draw the whole bitmap), and
    // draw it at the point specified by (xStart, yStart),
    // which by default is (0,0).

    BitBlt( hDC,
            xStart,
            yStart,
            ptSize.x,
            ptSize.y,
            hDCMem,
            0,
            0,
            SRCCOPY );
```

continues

Listing 3.12. continued

```
    // Destructor routine for compatibleDC class will take care
    // of selecting your bitmap out of the DC and putting the single-pixel
    // mono bitmap back in. (That's what's so great about object classes,
    // you can encapsulate the behavior _there_, so you don't have to worry
    // about it _here_. Truly the right answer).
}


/*------------------------------
 *
 * Bitmap::GetSize()
 *
 * Gets the size of the bitmap and returns a
 * point structure, indicating the lower-right corner
 *
 * Returns: POINT - lower-right corner of bitmap
 *
 * Arguments: None
 */

    POINT
Bitmap::GetSize( void )
{
    BITMAP      bm;
    POINT       ptSize;

    /*---------------------------*/

    // Get information about this instance of a bitmap.
    // If the information routine failed, or there is
    // no bitmap, then return a size of zero; otherwise
    // return the current size.

    if ( GetBitmap( &bm ) <= 0 )
    {
        ptSize.x = 0;
        ptSize.y = 0;
    }
    else
    {
        ptSize.x = bm.bmWidth;   // Copy the height info into a POINT
        ptSize.y = bm.bmHeight;  // structure, and pass it back.
    }

    return ptSize;        // Return size of the bitmap...
```

```
}

/*********************************
 *
 * ResBitmap::ResBitmap()
 *
 * DEFAULT constructor function (no arguments)
 * for the derived class Res(ource) bitmap. This
 * function is used when another class includes
 * a ResBitmap object(s) as a member of the other class;
 * in that case, you need a default constructor (which takes
 * no arguments).
 *
 * Returns: None
 *
 * Args: None
 */

ResBitmap::ResBitmap( void )
{
    SetHandle ( NULL );
}

/*********************************
 *
 * ResBitmap::ResBitmap()
 *
 * Constructor function for derived class Res(ource)Bitmap.
 *
 * Returns: Nothing
 *
 * Args: hInstance - instance of the app that has the resource
 *       lpszBitmapName - string containing the name of the bitmap
 *                        to load.
 */


ResBitmap::ResBitmap( HANDLE  hInstance      = NULL,
                      LPSTR   lpszBitmapName = NULL ) : Bitmap()
{
    SetHandle ( NULL );

    LoadSelf ( hInstance,
               lpszBitmapName );
}
```

continues

Listing 3.12. continued

```
/*----------------------------
 *
 * ResBitmap::~ResBitmap()
 *
 * Destructor for ResBitmap()
 *
 * Returns: Nothing
 *
 * Args: None
 */


ResBitmap::~ResBitmap( void )
{
    DeleteSelf();
}


/************************
 *
 * ResBitmap::LoadSelf()
 *
 * Causes a resource bitmap object to load itself if
 * it hasn't already. If the resource bitmap already has
 * something in it, then you simply return.
 *
 * Returns: TRUE - Resource loaded OK
 *          FALSE - resource didn't load OK, or there was a problem
 *                  in the parameter list.
 *
 * Args: hInstance - instance of the application containing the resource
 *       lpszBitmapName - name of the bitmap to load
 *
 */

    BOOL
ResBitmap::LoadSelf( HANDLE    hInstance,
                     LPSTR     lpszBitmapName )
{

    // First, make sure that the bitmap handle doesn't already have
    // something in it...

    if ( hBitmap )
    {
```

```
            MessageBox ( NULL,
                         "Attempting to load bitmap into non-NULL handle",
                         "ResBitmap class",
                         MB_OK );

       return FALSE;
   }

   // Validate the pointer and the instance
   // handle before attempting to load the object

   if (lpszBitmapName == NULL ¦¦
       *lpszBitmapName == NULL ¦¦
       hInstance == NULL)           // No string or instance?
   {                                // Punt.
       return FALSE;
   }

   // OK, everything's valid; let's try to
   // load the thing...

   else
   {

        // Attempt to load the bitmap out of the resource

       hBitmap = LoadBitmap( hInstance,
                             lpszBitmapName );

    // If no bitmap, then nuke

    if (!hBitmap)
    {
        MessageBox ( hWnd,
                     "Cannot load bitmap from resource",
                     "ResBitmap class",
                     MB_OK );

        return FALSE;
    }
    else
        return TRUE;  // Bitmap loaded OK.
    }
}
```

Examining the Bitmap Object Class

Although relatively straightforward in implementation, the Bitmap class supports some useful functionality not present in other C++ object classes for Windows. To understand this functionality, examine the class in more detail.

Purpose of the Bitmap Object Class

The basic purpose of the Bitmap class is really quite simple: to associate the bitmap data with routines that handle that data, and to encapsulate all of that in a black box, away from everything else. This is, by the way, nothing unique to this class—one of the fundamental purposes of C++ is facilitate just this kind of data/function association and encapsulation.

Another design methodology that I used in creating the Bitmap class (and most of the other classes in this book) was that of simplicity; instead of making one very complex, general-purpose object, I created several very simple objects and then derived more complex objects from these simple base classes. Doing this enabled me to focus on the particular behavior of the object I was creating, helping me to build fast, streamlined, robust objects that were reusable (another benefit of C++).

I've also tried to design objects that would help solve real-world Windows problems. The Bitmap class (and the classes derived from it) evolved out of a need to have a set of objects that would alleviate some problems I was encountering trying to build large, graphically oriented applications.

One of the problems I was encountering in building graphics applications was the sheer amount of overhead in dealing with the graphics objects themselves. Every time I wanted to manipulate a bitmap, I'd do the same thing:

1. Get a screen DC.

2. Create a compatible DC.

3. Create a compatible bitmap.

4. Select the bitmap into the compatible DC.

5. Manipulate the bitmap in some fashion.

6. Select the bitmap out of the compatible DC, and put back the old bitmap.

7. Delete the compatible DC.

8. Delete the bitmap (depending on what I was doing).

9. Release the screen DC.

In this process only one of the steps involved (step 5) had anything to do with what I actually wanted to accomplish, which was diddling the bitmap in some way or another.

Now, admittedly, I've lumped a bunch of different things together under the heading of "manipulate the bitmap in some fashion." Quite often this involves several complex manipulations of the drawing space. Equally often, however, I'd be doing only one or two straightforward things to the bitmap, and at that point the amount of code involved in setting up the system to actually do the operation and then cleaning up after I was done was vastly overwhelming what I really wanted to achieve. And given that I was writing a graphics application, this sort of setup/cleanup code was everywhere!

The Benefits of C++ (A Brief Interlude)

When I first moved to C++, it was very obvious that this was the perfect sort of thing to encapsulate in an object. In fact, the first object class I built was the Bitmap object class. In doing so, I was able to shrink my source code significantly. (I chopped out about 8,000 lines in a 100,000-line app.)

There is another benefit that might not be quite as obvious: by building a Bitmap object class, and then using instances of that object everywhere rather than inline code, I was able to get rid of the problem of code cut and copyitis. This is a very familiar problem to everyone—it's when you cut and paste source code from one module to another, which happens a lot with setup and cleanup code. Often when you do this, there are some minor flaws you have to go back and fix in part of the code. Then the trick becomes propagating that change through *every single place* where you copied the original setup code to. This is almost by definition a bug waiting to happen.

I'll give you an example. When I first built ICE/Works, I was completely unaware that I had to delete a bitmap resource I'd loaded from my executable file. As a result, when my program exited, I'd leave behind several dozen small bitmaps in the GDI pool. Eventually, Windows would come to a halt, because the GDI pool would be filled up by all these little bitmaps I'd left lying around.

When I finally discovered this problem, I had to go back through my program and find every place in the source where I was using a resource bitmap and make sure that I was deleting it after I was done with it. This process took a good two weeks. It was most definitely not fun. Even after I was done, it turned out that I wasn't deleting resource bitmaps in all the places I was using them— the beta testers found another couple of bitmaps I'd managed to miss.

C++ changes this. Instead of having to change code in dozens of places, you have to change the code in only one place—the routines of the object class itself. In this case, all I had to do was go into the destructor routine of my resource Bitmap object class and make sure that a bitmap deleted itself before it went away. Instantly (well, with one recompilation), my problem disappeared, and disappeared for good. By definition, every place in my program that used a resource bitmap now automatically deleted itself, and I had to change only one routine. That feature alone was worth it to me to switch to C++.

Anyway, I've ranted and raved long enough about the benefits of C++. Take a look at the Bitmap object class. As you can see, it's a simple object, but it has some very useful behaviors, not the least of which is that it cleans up after itself.

Constructor Routines

The Bitmap object class has two constructor routines. One, the default, simply sets the handle of the object class to NULL. The other constructor routine is used when you already have a bitmap handle created. (One example might be retrieving a bitmap from the clipboard.) This version of the constructor takes the bitmap handle passed into the constructor and copies it to the internal variable hBitmap.

Destructor Routine

The Bitmap class has only one destructor routine, but it's a handy one—it deletes the bitmap (only if the handle is non-NULL), which ensures that all system resources used by the bitmap are freed. This is an example of automatic cleanup. Nowhere in your code do you have to explicitly delete a bitmap; when you're through with a bitmap object, it deletes itself!

SetHandle()

This member function sets the handle of the bitmap to the handle that's passed in. It does no checking to see whether the current handle is NULL. (A good idea for development might be to wrap this in debug code; I chose not to do this for reasons of speed.)

DeleteSelf()

This function deletes the bitmap in the instance of the Bitmap object class. This routine is provided as a way of explicitly deleting a bitmap in an instance of an object class without deleting the instance of the object class.

DisplaySelf()

The Bitmap::DisplaySelf() routine takes three PARAMETERS: a handle to a DC, and an X and Y position within that device context. It then draws the bitmap into that DC at the requested (X,Y) position. (See Figure 3.5.) This routine is far and away the most complex member function of the Bitmap class.

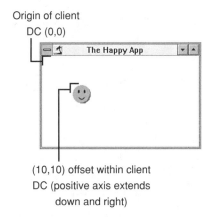

Origin of client
DC (0,0)

The Happy App

(10,10) offset within client
DC (positive axis extends
down and right)

Figure 3.5.
The relationship between a DC and the requested offset position of a drawn bitmap.

Take a look at the function in detail. To begin with, the parameters xStart and yStart are both defined as defaulting to 0. C++ enables you to define default values for parameters in functions, which is certainly convenient. In this case, calling the DisplaySelf() with just an hDC causes the bitmap to be displayed into that DC starting at the upper-left corner, (0,0). Because this is what you want to do 90 percent of the time, it's a very useful default behavior.

The first thing you do inside the member function proper is to make sure that the bitmap handle is non-NULL. This prevents you from trying to select a NULL bitmap handle into a DC.

Next, instantiate a CompatibleDC object (I discussed the CompatibleDC object class in Chapter 2) with the device context handle you've been passed, and the handle to your bitmap. This causes a compatible DC to be built and your bitmap to be selected into it. (As you'll remember, it also causes the single-pixel mono bitmap to be saved by the CompatibleDC object.)

Next, make sure that the compatible DC was properly created, by checking its handle; this also gets a copy of the handle for the **BitBlt()** call.

After ensuring that the compatible DC is good, get the size of your bitmap, using the member function GetSize(). Using this size and the handle to your newly created compatible DC, you make the **BitBlt()** call. The destination is the hDC you've been passed. (Remember that hDC is the device context that you want to copy your bitmap to.) The source is your compatible DC, which has your bitmap selected into it. The starting position in the destination DC is specified by xStart, yStart, and the size by ptSize.x and ptSize.y, which you filled in with the GetSize() call. Because you simply want to copy the bitmap, you use the raster op SRCCOPY, which specifies that the **BitBlt()** should simply copy the source bitmap and overwrite what's in the destination.

That's the end of the routine. Note that you have to do absolutely no cleanup, because the destructor routine of the CompatibleDC class takes care of it for you. It selects your bitmap out of the compatible DC (by selecting the original monochrome pixel bitmap back in), and then deletes the compatible DC, which gets rid of both the monochrome pixel bitmap and the DC itself.

GetSize()

This routine returns the size of the bitmap in the instance of the class in a POINT structure. The width of the image is in point.x, and the height of the image is in point.y. If there isn't a bitmap currently in this instance of the class (that is, the bitmap handle is NULL), the size returned is (0,0).

GetBitmapHandle()

This function returns a copy of the handle to the bitmap currently in the instance of the class. It is NULL if there isn't a valid bitmap in the instance.

Using the Bitmap Class: An Example

OK, you're going to hate me for this, I admit it. But what I'm going to show you illustrates just how powerful class objects can be. If you remember SimPaint from the preceding chapter, remember that in the last version of the program, you added some code to support an off-screen bitmap. One of the messages you added code for was the WM_PAINT message, which had the responsibility of copying your off-screen bitmap to the screen when needed. Listing 3.13 shows the code fragment for the WM_PAINT message.

Listing 3.13. Code fragment of the WM_PAINT message from version 2 of SimPaint.

```
case WM_PAINT:

// If you don't have a valid bitmap to paste in, then don't.

    if ( offScreenBmp == NULL )
        return TRUE;        // Message not processed

// In response to a WM_PAINT message (meaning that some part
// of your window has been munged), you're going to copy your
// off-screen bitmap into your window.

{
PAINTSTRUCT     pntInfo;  // Window repainting information

int             numBytes;    // Dummy return value

BITMAP          ourBmp;      // Bitmap structure

//-----------------------------------

hDC = BeginPaint ( hWnd,
                  (LPPAINTSTRUCT) & pntInfo );

compatDC = CreateCompatibleDC ( hDC );  // Create a compatible DC
                                        // for your bitmap

// Select your off-screen bitmap into the compatible DC. Make
// sure that you save the old bitmap that was in the DC!!
```

continues

Listing 3.13. continued

```
oldBmp = SelectObject ( compatDC,
                            offScreenBmp );

// In order to properly copy the bitmap, you need to retrieve how
// big it is. Do that here

numBytes = GetObject ( offScreenBmp,
                          sizeof ( BITMAP ),
                          (LPSTR) & ourBmp );

// If you can't get the size of the bitmap, punt.

if ( numBytes == 0 )
{
    MessageBox ( hWnd,
                "Cannot get information about off-screen Bitmap.",
                "SimPaint Error",
                MB_OK );
    return FALSE;
}

// Now copy your off-screen bitmap onto the screen.
// This is done using BitBlt

BitBlt ( hDC,              // Destination DC (the screen)
         0,                // X value, upper-left corner of dest rectangle
         0,                // Y value, upper-left corner of dest rectangle
         ourBmp.bmWidth,   // Width of bitmap
         ourBmp.bmHeight,  // Height of bitmap
         compatDC,         // Source DC (your off-screen bitmap)
         0,                // Upper-left corner of source, X value
         0,                // Upper-left corner of source, y value
         SRCCOPY );        // Raster operation to perform (source copy)

// Put the old bitmap back into the DC (this is the single-
// pixel monochrome bitmap discussed in the text). Note that
// you don't have to keep track of the handle that the
// SelectObject() call returns this time, because it's the same
// handle as is contained in offScreenBmp.

SelectObject ( compatDC,
                oldBmp );

DeleteDC ( compatDC );    // Destroy the compatible DC...
```

```
        // Don't forget to release the DC and let Windows paint again!

        EndPaint ( hWnd,
                   (LPPAINTSTRUCT) &pntInfo );


        }
            break;
```

OK, here's where building the class objects really pays off. Watch: Listing 3.14 shows the same code for handling the WM_PAINT message, only it's written in C++ using the object classes.

Listing 3.14. Code fragment showing implementation of the WM_PAINT message using the Bitmap object class.

```
    case WM_PAINT:

        // In response to a WM_PAINT message (meaning that some part
        // of your window has been munged), you're going to copy your
        // off-screen bitmap into your window.

        PAINTSTRUCT     pntInfo;        // Window repainting information
        //-----------------------------------

        hDC = BeginPaint ( hWnd,
                           (LPPAINTSTRUCT) & pntInfo );

        // Create a Bitmap object, and put your off-screen bitmap handle
        // into it.

        Bitmap     paintBM ( offScreenBmp );

        // Have the bitmap object display itself onto the DC that you got back from
        // the BeginPaint() call. Note that you only pass in the hDC, which means
        // that the default values for the X and Y starting display position will
        // be in effect. (The default display position is (0,0).)

        paintBM.DisplaySelf( hDC );

        // Zero out the handle of the bitmap so that the destructor routine
        // doesn't delete it

        paintDM.SetHandle ( NULL );
```

continues

137

Listing 3.14. continued

```
// Don't forget to release the DC, and let Windows paint again!

EndPaint ( hWnd,
          (LPPAINTSTRUCT) &pntInfo );

}
    break;
```

Compare the two listings; they do exactly the same thing. The C version takes more than three times as much code to do the same thing as the C++ version does (nine logical lines of code versus three). In addition, it's a lot more likely that the C version will have a bug in it (especially if the code was copied from somewhere else). In addition, the C++ version is virtually automatic—everything happens as a result of building the object class and requesting that it display itself!

Examining the ResBitmap Object Class

Resource bitmaps are a fairly obvious derivative of the Bitmap class. Device bitmaps loaded from a resource file share many of the same characteristics with memory bitmaps. It makes sense to derive a Resource bitmap class from the base Bitmap class.

Purpose of the ResBitmap Class

As I mentioned earlier, the ResBitmap class is an extension of the Bitmap class that provides specific functionality for loading bitmaps out of resource files. It inherits the Bitmap class's capability of rendering itself onto the screen, as well as all the other behavior of the Bitmap class. (The former is probably the single most important inherited behavior, given the fact that resource bitmaps are almost always used for displaying graphics objects in a program.)

Constructor Routines

There are two constructor routines for the ResBitmap class: a default routine that takes no arguments and sets the internal bitmap handle to NULL, and an explicit constructor that takes two arguments and attempts to load the bitmap resource. The second constructor takes the arguments

```
HANDLE    hInstance;
LPSTR     lpszBitmapName;
```

in which hInstance is the instance handle to the module containing the bitmap resource. As I mentioned, this doesn't have to be the instance handle of your application; it can be the instance handle of any valid module.

lpszBitmapName is a pointer to a string that contains the name of the resource to load. This is the name you assigned to the bitmap when you compiled it with a resource compiler. Here's an example of using the ResBitmap class:

```
ResBitmap fooBmp ( hInst,
                   "FOOBAR" );
```

You could then take this resource bitmap and place it on the screen, like this:

```
HDC   screenDC;

screenDC = GetDC ( hWnd );

if ( screenDC )
{
    fooBmp.DisplaySelf ( screenDC,
                         0,
                         0 );

    ReleaseDC ( hWnd,
                screenDC );
}
```

Note that by putting the **ReleaseDC()** call inside the test for whether the DC was obtained, you avoid the problem of trying to release a NULL DC.

Destructor Routines

The destructor routine for the ResBitmap class simply calls the base class routine DeleteSelf(), which takes care of deleting the bitmap. Because the call that's performed (**DeleteObject()**) works for either kind of bitmap, you could

let the base class destructor take care of the entire operation and not even provide a destructor routine for the ResBitmap class. Personally, however, I like the symmetry of providing both constructor and destructor for each class I build.

LoadSelf()

This routine is the main component of the ResBitmap class. It attempts to load the bitmap specified by the string lpszBitmapName from the module specified by the hInstance parameter. If the instance handle, the pointer to the string, or the contents of the string are NULL, the routine returns a FALSE. If all the parameters are valid, the routine attempts to load the bitmap out of the module.

If the bitmap is loaded successfully, the routine returns a TRUE. If the bitmap fails to load, the routine posts an alert box and returns a FALSE. After a bitmap resource has been successfully loaded, it can be used via the base Bitmap class just as any other bitmap would be.

Summary

There are several kinds of bitmaps. The one you use most often in your programs is the device dependent bitmap, or DDB. This form of bitmap is designed to work directly with the Windows API. When you draw on a bitmap (via a memory device context), you are drawing on this form of bitmap.

Using a bitmap is easy. You can construct one by hand by encoding the bits in an array and then calling one of several routines to create the bitmap. Doing this, however, is time-consuming. It also presents the difficulty of having an image that is specific for only one kind of device (typically, one kind of screen device). To get around this limitation, you can use a resource bitmap, which is a bitmap stored in your application's executable file. You can also create a resource-only DLL, which contains resources your application wants to access.

I discussed several new object classes, the Bitmap class, and the ResBitmap (or resource bitmap) class. These classes implement much of the basic behavior of Windows bitmaps in a very transparent way. In addition, they provide a level of safety that straight C code cannot match. By using the constructor and destructor routines to implement useful behavior, they remove much of the drudgework of building bitmap objects and prevent GDI space corruption via unfreed objects.

Function Reference

This section of the chapter details the various function calls used in dealing with bitmaps. Although it does not pretend to be all-encompassing, it does list all the bitmap functions you are likely to find useful, as well as details on their use, and things to watch for.

BitBlt()

```
BOOL BitBlt(    HDC     hdcDest,
                int     nXDest,
                int     nYDest,
                int     nWidth,
                int     nHeight,
                HDC     hdcSrc,
                int     nXSrc,
                int     nYSrc,
                DWORD   dwRop)
```

WHAT IT DOES:

Copies a bitmap from a source DC (specified by the hdcSrc parameter) to a destination DC (specified by the hdcDest parameter). The bitmap copied is the one that's selected into the source DC at the time of the **BitBlt()** call.

PARAMETERS:

hdcDest	Handle to the destination device context
nXDest	Upper-left corner of destination, X value
nYDest	Upper-left corner of destination, Y value
nWidth	Width of the bitmap (in logical units)
nHeight	Height of the bitmap (in logical units)
hdcSrc	Handle to the source device context
nXSrc	Upper-left corner of source bitmap, X value
nYSrc	Upper-left corner of source bitmap, Y value
dwRop	Raster operation to perform (see "Things to watch for")

WHAT IT RETURNS:

Nonzero if the bitmap is drawn successfully, or zero if the bitmap is not drawn (error).

THINGS TO WATCH FOR:

☐ If the raster operation being performed doesn't include a source, the hdcSrc parameter must be NULL.

☐ The dwRop specifies what raster operation is going to take place. You can perform various operations, as summarized in the following table. Note that this is not a complete list of operations that can be performed.

Code	Description
BLACKNESS	Turns all output black.
DSTINVERT	Inverts the destination bitmap.
MERGECOPY	Combines the pattern and the source bitmap by using the Boolean AND operator.
MERGEPAINT	Combines the inverted source bitmap with the destination bitmap by using the Boolean OR operator.
NOTSRCCOPY	Copies the inverted source bitmap to the destination.
NOTSRCERASE	Inverts the result of combining the destination and source bitmaps by using the Boolean OR operator.
PATCOPY	Copies the pattern to the destination bitmap.
PATINVERT	Combines the destination bitmap with the pattern by using the Boolean XOR operator.
PATPAINT	Combines the inverted source bitmap with the pattern by using the Boolean OR operator. Combines the result of this operation with the destination bitmap by using the Boolean OR operator.
SRCAND	Combines pixels of the destination and source bitmaps by using the Boolean AND operator.
SRCCOPY	Copies the source bitmap to the destination bitmap.
SRCERASE	Inverts the destination bitmap and combines the result with the source bitmap by using the Boolean AND operator.
SRCINVERT	Combines pixels of the destination and source bitmaps by using the Boolean XOR operator.

Code	Description
SRCPAINT	Combines pixels of the destination and source bitmaps by using the Boolean OR operator.
WHITENESS	Turns all output white.

If your application uses **BitBlt()** to copy pixels from one window to another window or from a source rectangle in a window to a target rectangle in the same window, you should set the CS_BYTEALIGNWINDOW or CS_BYTEALIGNCLIENT flag when registering the window classes. By aligning the windows or client areas on byte boundaries, you're ensuring that all **BitBlt()** operations occur on byte-aligned rectangles. This means that your **BitBlt()** calls are significantly faster than if you don't byte-align your window and rectangles.

GDI transforms the nWidth and nHeight parameters, once by using the destination device context and once by using the source device context. If the resulting extents do not match, GDI uses the **StretchBlt()** function to compress or stretch the source bitmap as necessary. If destination, source, and pattern bitmaps do not have the same color format, the **BitBlt()** function converts the source and pattern bitmaps to match the destination. The foreground and background colors of the destination bitmap are used in the conversion.

When the **BitBlt()** function converts a monochrome bitmap to color, it sets white bits (1) to the background color and black bits (0) to the foreground color, using the foreground and background colors of the *destination* DC.

To convert color to monochrome, **BitBlt()** sets pixels that match the background color to white and sets all other pixels to black. This is using the foreground and background colors of the *source* DC to determine black and white. Needless to say, this usually doesn't look very good.

The foreground color is the current text color for the specified device context, and the background color is the current background color for the specified device context.

Not all devices support the **BitBlt()** function. To determine whether a device supports it, call the **GetDeviceCaps()** function, specifying the RASTERCAPS value.

SEE ALSO:

PatBlt()
StretchBlt()
StretchDIBits()

CreateBitmap()

```
HBITMAP CreateBitmap(    int                nWidth,
                         int                nHeight,
                         UINT               cbPlanes,
                         UINT               cbBits,
                         const void FAR *   lpvBits)
```

WHAT IT DOES:

Creates a DDB-style bitmap of the specified width and height, as well as the specified number of color planes and bits per pixel. Optionally, it also sets the bits if the lpvBits parameter is non-NULL.

PARAMETERS:

nWidth   Specifies the width in pixels of the bitmap to create.

nHeight   Specifies the height in pixels of the bitmap to create.

cbPlanes   Specifies the number of color planes for the bitmap (device specific).

cbBits   Specifies the number of bits per pixel for the bitmap (device specific).

lpvBits   Pointer to an array of bits to initialize the bitmap with. If this value is NULL, the bitmap is not initialized.

WHAT IT RETURNS:

A handle to a DDB bitmap if the function is successful, or NULL if it isn't.

THINGS TO WATCH FOR:

☐ Because the format of a color bitmap is highly device specific, this function must be used with caution when creating color bitmaps. It is much better to load the bitmap as a resource, or read it in as a DIB and convert it.

☐ Your application should call **DeleteObject()** to delete the bitmap when you're done with it.

SEE ALSO:

```
BitBlt()
CreateBitmapIndirect()
CreateCompatibleBitmap()
CreateDIBitmap()
CreateDiscardableBitmap()
DeleteObject()
SelectObject()
```

CreateBitmapIndirect()

```
HBITMAP CreateBitmapIndirect( BITMAP FAR *    lpbm)
```

WHAT IT DOES:

Creates a device dependent bitmap, using the BITMAP structure passed into the call. Similar to `CreateBitmap()`, but you have to fill in the structure first, and then execute this call. Useful for creating DDB-format bitmaps when you don't know in advance what the bitmap is going to look like (for example, reading a DDB from disk).

PARAMETER:

lpbm   Pointer to the structure containing the information about the bitmap

WHAT IT RETURNS:

A handle to a DDB bitmap if the function is successful, and NULL if it fails.

THINGS TO WATCH FOR:

☐ Your application should call `DeleteObject()` to delete the bitmap when you're done with it.

☐ Some functions (such as `GetObject()`) do not fill in the pointer to the bits parameter of the BITMAP structure (the last parameter in the structure). In this case, the `CreateBitmapIndirect()` call won't fill in the bits of the bitmap. At this point you can use a GDI call (such as `BitBlt()`) to fill in the bits, or set them using `SetBitmapBits()`, for DDBs, or `SetDIBits()`, for DIBs.

SEE ALSO:

```
BitBlt()
CreateBitmap()
CreateCompatibleBitmap()
```

```
CreateDIBitmap()
DeleteObject()
GetObject()
```

CreateCompatibleBitmap()

```
HBITMAP CreateCompatibleBitmap(    HDC  hdc,
                                   int  nWidth,
                                   int  nHeight)
```

WHAT IT DOES:

Creates a DDB-style bitmap that's compatible with the screen device specified by the hdc parameter. Note that the hdc parameter doesn't have to be a screen DC itself, but can be an indirect reference to a screen DC (that is, the hdc parameter can be a DC that was created by using the **CreateCompatibleDC()** function).

PARAMETERS:

hdc   Handle to the device context to make the bitmap compatible with

nWidth   Width of the bitmap to be created

nHeight   Height of the bitmap to be created

WHAT IT RETURNS:

A value identifying a DDB-style bitmap if the function is successful. Otherwise, it is NULL.

THINGS TO WATCH FOR:

☐ For noncompatible DC devices (that is, the screen, and not a memory DC), the bitmap created by the **CreateCompatibleBitmap()** function has the same format as the device for which it has been created. It can be selected as the current bitmap for any memory device that is compatible with the one identified by hdc.

☐ If hdc specifies a compatible DC, the bitmap created has exactly the same format as the bitmap that's currently selected into the compatible DC. This means that if you create a compatible DC but don't select some form of color bitmap into it, the **CreateCompatibleBitmap()** function creates a monochrome bitmap of the indicated size.

☐ Your application should call **DeleteObject()** to delete the bitmap when you're done with it.

SEE ALSO:

```
CreateBitmap()
CreateBitmapIndirect()
CreateDIBitmap()
DeleteObject()
SelectObject()
```

DeleteObject()

```
BOOL DeleteObject( HANDLE    hObject)
```

WHAT IT DOES:

Deletes the object specified by the hObject parameter. This object must have been created through some GDI call (for example, **CreateBitmap()**). GDI objects that can be deleted by this function are pens, brushes, fonts, bitmaps, regions, and palettes.

PARAMETER:

> hObject   Handle to the object to be deleted

WHAT IT RETURNS:

TRUE if the object was deleted, and FALSE if the handle is not valid or the object is currently selected into a DC.

THINGS TO WATCH FOR:

☐ Make sure that the object you're deleting has been selected out of all device contexts before you attempt to delete it.

☐ After this function call, the handle specified by the hObject parameter is no longer valid, but it is not NULL. Be sure to zero out any copies of this handle that you have in your application; for example:

```
DeleteObject ( foo );
foo = NULL;
```

☐ When you delete a pattern brush, the bitmap associated with the brush is not deleted; you must delete the bitmap separately.

SEE ALSO:

```
SelectObject()
```

GetBitmapBits()

```
LONG GetBitmapBits( HBITMAP        hBM,
                    LONG           cbBuffer,
                    void FAR *     lpvBits)
```

WHAT IT DOES:

Copies the bits of the specified bitmap into the buffer pointed to by lpvBits. Because the parameter hBM is a DDB, the format of the bits that are copied into the buffer cannot be determined in advance and will be device-specific.

PARAMETERS:

hBM   Handle to the bitmap whose bits this function retrieves

cbBuffer   Number of bytes to copy from the bitmap

lpvBits   Pointer to the buffer to put the bits into

WHAT IT RETURNS:

A value specifying how many bytes were actually copied to the buffer. It is zero if there's an error.

THINGS TO WATCH FOR:

☐ Your application should use the **GetObject()** function to determine how many bytes to copy from the bitmap.

☐ Because the source bitmap is a DDB, the bytes returned in the buffer are in *device specific* format. This format cannot be determined in advance, and your application should not make assumptions about what it will be. (Just because you're running on VGA doesn't mean everyone else is.)

SEE ALSO:

```
GetObject()
SetBitmapBits()
```

GetObject()

```
int GetObject( HANDLE        hObject,
               int           cbBuffer,
               void FAR *     lpvObject)
```

WHAT IT DOES:

Retrieves information about the specified object pointed to by the `hObject` parameter and places it in the buffer pointed to by the `lpvObject` buffer.

PARAMETERS:

`hObject`	Handle to the object about which you want information
`cbBuffer`	Number of bytes to copy to the buffer
`lpvObject`	Pointer to the buffer that's going to get the information

WHAT IT RETURNS:

A value indicating how many bytes were actually placed in the buffer. It's zero if there was an error.

THINGS TO WATCH FOR:

☐ The buffer that you allocate to receive the information must be big enough to hold the information (otherwise you get a UAE).

☐ If you're retrieving information about a bitmap, this function call only fills in the size (width and height) and color format (number of planes and bits per pixel) of the bitmap. To get the bits themselves, you need to use the `GetBitmapBits()` function.

☐ If you're retrieving information about a logical palette, this call returns the number of entries in the palette. To get the actual LOGPALETTE structure data that defines the palette, you need to call the `GetPaletteEntries()` function.

SEE ALSO:

GetBitmapBits()
GetPaletteEntries()

GetPixel()

```
COLORREF GetPixel( HDC  hdc,
                   int  nXPos,
                   int  nYPos)
```

WHAT IT DOES:

Returns the COLORREF value of the pixel at the specified point in the specified device context.

PARAMETERS:

hdc   Device context from which to retrieve the pixel

nXPos   X position of the pixel to get

nYPos   Y position of the pixel to get

WHAT IT RETURNS:

The COLORREF value of the pixel at the specified point, or − 1 if the point is not in the clipping region of the specified device context.

THINGS TO WATCH FOR:

Not all devices support the **GetPixel()** function.

SEE ALSO:

SetPixel()

LoadBitmap()

```
HBITMAP LoadBitmap( HINSTANCE hinst,
                    LPSTR     lpszBitmap)
```

WHAT IT DOES:

Loads a bitmap resource from the specified instance of an application, or loads one of the predefined system bitmaps.

PARAMETERS:

hinst   Handle to the instance of the application to load the bitmap from.

lpszBitmap   Pointer to the string specifying the name of the bitmap to load. This parameter can also consist of the resource identifier in the low word, and zero in the high word. You can use the MAKEINTRESOURCE macro to create this value. Doing this enables you to load bitmaps by resource value, rather than name (if you've defined your resources numerically, and not alphabetically).

WHAT IT RETURNS:

A handle to the specified resource bitmap if the function is successful; if the function fails, the return value is NULL.

THINGS TO WATCH FOR:

- If the identified bitmap does not exist, the function fails.

- If there is not enough memory to load the bitmap, the function fails.

- Your application should call `DeleteObject()` to delete the bitmap when you're done with it. Unlike other resources (with which you're not supposed to delete stock objects), this also applies to any of the stock bitmaps listed under the following bulleted item. That is, you must call the `DeleteObject()` function to delete a bitmap, even if it's a stock bitmap loaded using one of the listed values.

- To load a stock bitmap, the `hinst` parameter must be set to NULL, and the `lpszBitmap` parameter must be set to one of the following values:

```
OBM_BTNCORNERS
OBM_BTSIZE
OBM_CHECK
OBM_CHECKBOXES
OBM_CLOSE
OBM_COMBO
OBM_DNARROW
OBM_DNARROWD
OBM_DNARROWI
OBM_LFARROW
OBM_LFARROWD
OBM_LFARROWI
OBM_MNARROW
OBM_OLD_CLOSE
OBM_OLD_DNARROW
OBM_OLD_LFARROW
OBM_OLD_REDUCE
OBM_OLD_RESTORE
OBM_OLD_RGARROW
OBM_OLD_UPARROW
OBM_OLD_ZOOM
OBM_REDUCE
OBM_REDUCED
OBM_RESTORE
OBM_RESTORED
OBM_RGARROW
OBM_RGARROWD
OBM_RGARROWI
OBM_SIZE
OBM_UPARROW
OBM_UPARROWD
```

```
OBM_UPARROWI
OBM_ZOOM
OBM_ZOOMD
```

▢ Bitmap names that begin with `OBM_OLD` represent bitmaps used by Windows versions prior to 3.0.

▢ The bitmaps identified by `OBM_DNARROWI`, `OBM_LFARROWI`, `OBM_RGARROWI`, and `OBM_UPARROWI` are new for Windows 3.1. These bitmaps are not found in device drivers for previous versions of Windows. Note that the constant `OEMRESOURCE` must be defined before including WINDOWS.H in order to use any of the `OBM_` constants.

SEE ALSO:

`DeleteObject()`

LoadLibrary()

```
HINSTANCE LoadLibrary(    LPSTR      lpszLibFileName)
```

WHAT IT DOES:

The `LoadLibrary()` function returns an instance handle for the specified library module. If the module has not yet been loaded, the function loads the library module from the specified file. If the module has already been loaded, this function increments the module's reference count.

Parameter:

`lpszLibFileName`   Pointer to a NULL-terminated string that names the library file to be loaded

WHAT IT RETURNS:

If the function is successful, the return value identifies the instance of the loaded library module. Otherwise, it is a value less than 32 that specifies the error. The following list describes the error values returned by this function:

Value	Meaning
0	Out of memory
2	File not found
3	Path not found
5	Attempt to dynamically link to a task

Value	Meaning
6	Library requires separate data segments for each task
10	Incorrect Windows version
11	Invalid .EXE file (non-Windows .EXE or error in .EXE image)
12	OS/2 application
13	DOS 4.0 application
14	Unknown .EXE type
15	Attempt in protected (standard or 386 enhanced) mode to load an .EXE created for an earlier version of Windows
16	Attempt to load a second instance of an .EXE containing multiple, writable data segments
17	Attempt in large-frame EMS mode to load a second instance of an application that links to certain nonshareable DLLs already in use
18	Attempt in real mode to load an application marked for protected mode only

THINGS TO WATCH FOR:

☐ This function increments the reference count for the particular library module by one.

☐ Multiple applications can access a library module by using this function. The library module in question is loaded only once.

☐ After your application is done using the library module, free it using the `FreeLibrary()` function. This decrements the reference count for the particular library module. The module is actually discarded only when the reference count reaches zero.

SEE ALSO:

PatBlt()

```
BOOL PatBlt(    HDC      hdc,
                int      nLeftRect,
                int      nTopRect,
```

```
int      nwidth,
int      nheight,
DWORD    fdwRop)
```

WHAT IT DOES:

Copies a pattern to the bitmap that's currently selected into the specified device context.

PARAMETERS:

hdc Target DC to be blasted

nLeftRect X position of the upper-left corner of the destination rectangle

nTopRect Y position of the upper-left corner of the destination rectangle

nwidth Width (in logical units) of the destination rectangle

nheight Height (in logical units) of the destination rectangle

fdwRop Raster operation to perform

The possible raster ops are

Value	Meaning
PATCOPY	Copies pattern to destination bitmap.
PATINVERT	Combines destination bitmap with pattern using the Boolean XOR operator.
PATPAINT	Paints the destination bitmap.
DSTINVERT	Inverts the destination bitmap.
BLACKNESS	Turns all output black.
WHITENESS	Turns all output white.

Where a pattern is specified (as in PATCOPY), the current brush is used as the pattern.

WHAT IT RETURNS:

TRUE if the bit pattern is drawn, and FALSE otherwise.

THINGS TO WATCH FOR:

☐ The `PatBlt()` function provides only a subset of the full raster op codes. If raster ops other than the ones listed are desired, a different call (such as `BitBlt()`) must be used.

☐ Not all devices support `PatBlt()`; use the `GetDeviceCaps()` to determine whether the particular device in question does.

SelectObject()

```
HANDLE SelectObject(   HDC      hdc,
                       HANDLE   hObject)
```

WHAT IT DOES:

Selects the object specified by the hObject parameter into the device context specified by the hdc parameter. The new object replaces the object of the same type that was previously selected in the DC.

PARAMETERS:

hdc   Specifies the device context to select the object into

hObject   Specifies the object to be selected into the device context

WHAT IT RETURNS:

The handle to the object that was previously selected into the device context. It is NULL if there was an error.

THINGS TO WATCH FOR:

☐ This function works on several different types of GDI objects; the handle to the object that is returned is always a handle to the same type of object that's being set. Thus, if you select a bitmap object into a DC, you get back the handle of the bitmap that was previously selected into the DC.

☐ The function works on the following list of GDI objects, each of which must have been created using the listed GDI calls.

Object	Functions
Bitmap	`CreateBitmap()`, `CreateBitmapIndirect()`, `CreateCompatibleBitmap()`, `CreateDIBitmap()`
Brush	`CreateBrushIndirect()`, `CreateDIBPatternBrush()`, `CreateHatchBrush()`, `CreatePatternBrush()`, `CreateSolidBrush()`

Object	Functions
Font	`CreateFont()`, `CreateFontIndirect()`
Pen	`CreatePen()`, `CreatePenIndirect()`
Region	`CreateEllipticRgn()`, `CreateEllipticRgnIndirect()`, `CreatePolygonRgn()`, `CreateRoundRectRgn()`, `CreateRectRgn()`, `CreateRectRgnIndirect()`

☐ If the `hObject` parameter specifies a region, this function does the same thing as the `SelectClipRgn()` function, in which case the return value from this function is the same as from that function. (See the following table.)

Value	Meaning
COMPLEXREGION	New clipping region has overlapping borders.
ERROR	Device context or region handle is not valid.
NULLREGION	New clipping region is empty.
SIMPLEREGION	New clipping region has no overlapping borders.

☐ If there is an error, the previously selected object of the specified type stays selected into the DC.

☐ Using this call to select a font, pen, or brush for your application causes the system to allocate space for that object in your application's data segment. Because data segment space is very precious, your application should delete the object (using the `DeleteObject()` call) when you're done with it.

☐ Before deleting a drawing object of the types discussed previously, you must first select the object back out of any DC that it's selected into. You do this by selecting back the original object into the DC, which is why it's vital that the return value from this function be saved for later.

☐ When you are selecting an object into a metafile DC, this function does not return the handle of the previously selected object. In fact, if the DC is a metafile DC, attempting to reselect an old object (gotten from the return value) into the metafile DC causes unpredictable (read: UAE) results. Metafile DCs perform their own cleanup, so you don't need to. (Consistency, that's what I love! <grin>)

▢ You can select a bitmap only into a compatible (memory) DC; further, a bitmap can be selected into only one compatible DC at a time. The format of the bitmap must be either monochrome or compatible with the specified DC; if it isn't, `SelectObject()` returns an error.

SEE ALSO:

`DeleteObject()`

SetBitmapBits()

```
LONG SetBitmapBits( HBITMAP          hbmp,
                    DWORD            cBits,
                    const void FAR * lpvBits)
```

WHAT IT DOES:

Sets the bits of the bitmap specified by the `hbmp` parameter to the bit values pointed to by the `lpvBits` parameter.

PARAMETERS:

hbmp	Handle to the bitmap that's going to have its bits set.
cBits	Number of bytes that the `lpvBits` parameter points to.
lpvBits	Pointer to the bit values to set the bitmap to. Because the bitmap is device specific, these values must match the device-specific format of the bitmap to be of any real use.

WHAT IT RETURNS:

A value specifying the number of bytes used in setting the bitmap's bits. It's zero if the function is unsuccessful.

THINGS TO WATCH FOR:

Because you're setting the bits of a device dependent bitmap, the bits must be in the same format as the bitmap. Because this is impossible to determine in advance, this function call is used primarily for setting the bits of bitmaps you're copying, or for setting the bits of a bitmap you've read from disk.

SEE ALSO:

`GetBitmapBits()`

SetPixel()

```
COLORREF SetPixel( HDC      hdc,
                   int      nXPos,
                   int      nYPos,
                   COLORREF clrref)
```

WHAT IT DOES:

Sets a pixel in the specified DC located at the specified point with the requested color value. The point must be inside the clipping region of the DC.

PARAMETERS:

hdc	Device context whose pixel is to be set
nXPos	X position of pixel to set
nYPos	Y position of pixel to set
clrref	Color value to set pixel to (will be mapped by GDI to nearest color for the color palette currently realized into the DC)

WHAT IT RETURNS:

A value specifying an RGB color value for the color that the point is actually painted. This value can be different from that specified by the clrref parameter if an approximation of that color is used. (This happens when GDI has to map the requested color value to another one that's in the currently realized palette of the DC.) If the function fails (if the point is outside the clipping region) the return value is − 1.

THINGS TO WATCH FOR:

☐ If the point specified is outside of the current clipping region, the function does nothing.

☐ This function fails to work for most 32,768-color drivers used by the Tseng Labs ET4000 Super VGA chip. The results are random and unpredictable. To work around this, use a combination of **MoveTo()**/ **LineTo()**, specifying a pen of the color you want to set. (See Listing 2.11 in Chapter 2 for an example.)

☐ The approximation that GDI uses to map the color requested to a currently available color is more or less accurate, depending on the size of the current palette, and the color that has been requested. (Attempting to map 256 grey scales to 16 VGA colors is obviously not going to be very good.)

Not all devices support this function. You can use the `GetDeviceCaps()` function to determine whether a device supports `SetPixel()`.

SEE ALSO:

GetDeviceCaps()
GetPixel()

SetStretchBltMode()

```
int SetStretchBltMode(   HDC   hdc,
                         int   fnStretchMode)
```

WHAT IT DOES:

Sets the bitmap stretching mode for the specified device context. (For Common and window DCs, this attribute is lost when the DC is released; for Class and Private DCs, this attribute is maintained.) The bitmap stretching mode defines how GDI compresses or expands bitmaps when using the `StretchBlt()` or `StretchDIBits()` functions.

PARAMETERS:

hdc   Device context which is having its bitmap stretching mode set

fnStretchMode   New bitmap stretching mode. The possible settings are as shown:

Value	Meaning
STRETCH_ANDSCANS	Uses the AND operator to combine eliminated lines with the remaining lines. This mode preserves black pixels at the expense of colored or white pixels. This is the default mode.
STRETCH_DELETESCANS	Deletes the eliminated lines. Information in the eliminated lines is not preserved.
STRETCH_ORSCANS	Uses the OR operator to combine eliminated lines with the remaining lines. This mode preserves colored or white pixels at the expense of black pixels.

WHAT IT RETURNS:

A value specifying the previous stretching mode.

THINGS TO WATCH FOR:

☐ The default stretching mode is STRETCH_ANDSCANS.

☐ The STRETCH_ANDSCANS and STRETCH_ORSCANS modes are typically used to preserve foreground pixels in monochrome bitmaps. Typically, the STRETCH_DELETESCANS mode is used to preserve color in color bitmaps.

SEE ALSO:

StretchBlt()
StretchDIBits()

StretchBlt()

```
BOOL StretchBlt(    HDC      hdcDest,
                    int      nXOriginDest,
                    int      nYOriginDest,
                    int      nWidthDest,
                    int      nHeightDest,
                    HDC      hdcSrc,
                    int      nXOriginSrc,
                    int      nYOriginSrc,
                    int      nWidthSrc,
                    int      nHeightSrc,
                    DWORD    fdwRop)
```

WHAT IT DOES:

Takes the bitmap currently selected into the source DC and copies it into the destination DC, shrinking or stretching the bitmap to fit, according to the size parameters given.

PARAMETERS:

hdcDest	Destination device context
nXOriginDest	X coordinate of the upper-left corner of the destination rectangle
nYOriginDest	Y coordinate of the upper-left corner of the destination rectangle
nWidthDest	Width of the destination rectangle
nHeightDest	Height of the destination rectangle
hdcSrc	Source device context

nXOriginSrc	X coordinate of the upper-left corner of the source rectangle
nYOriginSrc	Y coordinate of the upper-left corner of the source rectangle
nWidthSrc	Width of the source rectangle
nHeightSrc	Height of the source rectangle
fdwRop	Raster operation to perform (see "Things to watch for")

WHAT IT RETURNS:

TRUE if the bitmap is successfully drawn, and FALSE otherwise.

THINGS TO WATCH FOR:

☐ The **StretchBlt()** function uses the stretching mode of the destination device context (set by the **SetStretchBltMode()** function) to determine how to stretch or compress the bitmap.

☐ The **StretchBlt()** function stretches or compresses the source bitmap in memory, *then* copies the result to the destination. If a pattern is to be merged with the result, it is not merged until the stretched source bitmap is copied to the destination.

☐ If a brush is used in the raster operation, it is the selected brush in the *destination* device context.

☐ The destination coordinates are transformed according to the destination device context's mapping mode and position. The source coordinates are transformed according to the source device context's mapping mode and position.

☐ If destination, source, and pattern bitmaps do not have the same color format, **StretchBlt()** converts the source and pattern bitmaps to match the destination bitmaps. The foreground and background colors of the destination device context are used in the conversion.

☐ If **StretchBlt()** must convert a monochrome bitmap to color, it sets white bits (1) to the background color and black bits (0) to the foreground color. To convert color to monochrome, it sets pixels that match the background color to white (1) and sets all other pixels to black (0). The foreground and background colors of the device context with color are used.

☐ **StretchBlt()** creates a mirror image of a bitmap if the signs of the nWidthSrc and nWidthDest or nHeightSrc and nHeightDest parameters differ. If nWidthSrc and nWidthDest have different signs, the function creates a

161

mirror image of the bitmap along the x-axis. If nHeightSrc and nHeightDest have different signs, the function creates a mirror image of the bitmap along the y-axis.

 If the specified destination rectangle is an even integer multiple of the source rectangle (that is, if the destination rectangle is twice as big, four times as big, and so on), this function fails.

The fdwRop specifies what raster operation is going to take place. You can perform various operations, as summarized in the following table. Note that this is not the complete list of operations that can be performed.

Code	Description
BLACKNESS	Turns all output black.
DSTINVERT	Inverts the destination bitmap.
MERGECOPY	Combines the pattern and the source bitmap by using the Boolean AND operator.
MERGEPAINT	Combines the inverted source bitmap with the destination bitmap by using the Boolean OR operator.
NOTSRCCOPY	Copies the inverted source bitmap to the destination.
NOTSRCERASE	Inverts the result of combining the destination and source bitmaps by using the Boolean OR operator.
PATCOPY	Copies the pattern to the destination bitmap.
PATINVERT	Combines the destination bitmap with the pattern by using the Boolean XOR operator.
PATPAINT	Combines the inverted source bitmap with the pattern by using the Boolean OR operator. Combines the result of this operation with the destination bitmap by using the Boolean OR operator.
SRCAND	Combines pixels of the destination and source bitmaps by using the Boolean AND operator.
SRCCOPY	Copies the source bitmap to the destination bitmap.
SRCERASE	Inverts the destination bitmap and combines the result with the source bitmap by using the Boolean AND operator.

Code	Description
SRCINVERT	Combines pixels of the destination and source bitmaps by using the Boolean XOR operator.
SRCPAINT	Combines pixels of the destination and source bitmaps by using the Boolean OR operator.
WHITENESS	Turns all output white.

SEE ALSO:

```
BitBlt()
SetStretchBltMode()
StretchDIBits()
```

The Device Independent Bitmap

The device dependent bitmap (DIB) is the type of bitmap manipulated by GDI in your application. However, it suffers from the limitation that you can't save it to disk and use it later easily. Although you certainly can save the image to disk, what you are saving is a device-specific image; if you want to take that image to a different device, you might not be able to read it back in. Enter the device independent bitmap.

Topics I cover in this chapter are

Differences between the DIB and the DDB

The format of a DIB

Reading and writing a DIB

The MalleableBitmap class, a C++ class that implements useful DIB functions

The DIB Data Structures

The device independent bitmap is very similar to a DDB in many ways. It specifies an image using an array of bits to map that image. As with a DDB, the format of that array is unknown in advance. However, unlike the DDB, the DIB specifies not only an image, but all the information necessary to interpret that image. It does this using the following series of header structures.

The BITMAPFILEHEADER Structure

This structure defines what the beginning of a DIB looks like on disk. In memory, you won't have one of these puppies, but if you want your application (and others) to be able to identify it as a DIB when you write it to disk, you must create one of these for the beginning. The structure of a BITMAPFILEHEADER is as follows:

```
typedef struct tagBITMAPFILEHEADER    {

        WORD   bfType;              // Type of object; set to "BM".
        DWORD  bfSize;              // Size of the file, in bytes.
        WORD   bfReserved1;         // Reserved, set to zero.
        WORD   bfReserved2;         // Reserved, set to zero.
        DWORD  bfOffBits;           // Offset, in bytes, from this structure
                                    // to the actual bitmap in the file.


        } BITMAPFILEHEADER;
```

This structure is pretty straightforward; all it really does is define what the file is and how big it is. The first field, bfType, is used to specify this as a DIB-format file. This value must be set to the string "BM", which is encoded in a word as 0x4f42 (for Intel-style processors). The next field, bfSize, defines how big the file is (in bytes).

The third and fourth fields are reserved and should be set to zero. Presumably, Microsoft has future plans for them. The final field, bfOffBits, is a little trickier. It is the number of bytes, starting from the beginning of the file, to where the *actual bits for the image* are located. Because other things come before that information (palette information and such, which you'll get to in a minute), this appears to be a fairly useful pointer to have lying around, because it means you can get at the bits of the image immediately, without having to read in the palette information and such. In practice, I don't know of any app that does this; it's simple enough to read all the other information in as well and process it.

Immediately following this structure is either a BITMAPINFO structure or a BITMAPCOREHEADER structure. The BITMAPINFO structure defines the header information for a DIB, whereas the BITMAPCOREHEADER structure defines header information for an OS2/PM-format DIB. Virtually all the functions discussed in this chapter work on either function.

Because all of these structures can prove more than a little confusing, I've provided a road map of how they all fit together. (See Figure 4.1.)

The layout of a memory DIB is exactly the same as a file DIB, except the first field (the BITMAPFILEHEADER) is not present.

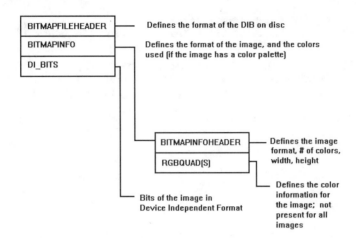

Figure 4.1.
The compo-
nents of a DIB
and how they
fit together.

The BITMAPINFO Structure

This structure defines the format of a DIB. Really, it's a way of referring to the two structures it contains: the BITMAPINFOHEADER structure, which defines the details of the DIB (such as width, height, and so on), and the RGBQUAD structure, which defines the palette. The structure of BITMAPINFO is as follows:

```
typedef struct tagBITMAPINFO {

    BITMAPINFOHEADER    bmiHeader;          // Information about the DIB
    RGBQUAD             bmiColors[1];       // Beginning of the color
                                            // palette

} BITMAPINFO;
```

The first time I saw this structure, I was somewhat confused, because I knew that DIBs contained more than a single RGB entry that defined the palette. In addition, depending on the way the DIB was formatted by the application that wrote it, the bmiColors might not even refer to RGB values, but instead to palette indexes into the currently selected palette. Further, if the DIB image is a 16-million-color image, it won't contain any palette!

For right now, ignore the issue and come back to it after you've explored the other header structures in more detail.

The BITMAPINFOHEADER Structure

This structure is really the guts of the DIB. It defines the size of the image, as well as how many colors it uses, indicates whether it's compressed, and provides other information. The structure looks like this:

```
typedef struct tagBITMAPINFOHEADER
    {
        DWORD   biSize;              // # of bytes required by this
                                     // structure.
        DWORD   biWidth;             // Width of the image, in pixels.
        DWORD   biHeight;            // Height of the image, in pixels.
        WORD    biPlanes;            // # of planes for the target
                                     // device. Must be set to 1 (one).
        WORD    biBitCount;          // # of bits per pixel. Must be
                                     // 1, 4, 8, or 24.
        DWORD   biCompression;       // Specifies the compression used
                                     // (if any).
        DWORD   biSizeImage;         // Size of the image, in bytes.
        DWORD   biXPelsPerMeter;     // Horizontal resolution of the
                                     // image in pixels per meter.
        DWORD   biYPelsPerMeter;     // Vertical resolution of the
                                     // image, in pixels per meter.
        DWORD   biClrUsed;           // # of colors in the color table
                                     // used by the image.
        DWORD   biClrImportant;      // # of colors that are important
                                     // in displaying the image.
    } BITMAPINFOHEADER;
```

Elements of the BITMAPINFOHEADER

Most of the fields in the structure are fairly straightforward. The first three, biSize, biWidth, and biHeight, define the size of this header (that is, the BITMAPINFOHEADER structure), the width of the image (in pixels), and the height of the image (in pixels).

It might seem a little odd at first to have the first element of the structure be a number defining how big the rest of the structure is. However, this size value is the only thing that enables your application to distinguish between a Windows DIB and an OS2/PM DIB; the sizes of the two structures are different. (Honestly, you'd think they just would've used a tag byte or something. Maybe IBM wouldn't let them.)

The next field, biPlanes, is somewhat of a puzzle. Although it seems to indicate the number of planes the image uses in a given device, a la a DDB, it must always be set to one.

The next field, biBitCount, is very important, because it defines the total number of colors this bitmap can have. It can have only one of the four following values: 1, 4, 8, or 24. Each of these values specifies how many bits per pixel are used in representing the image.

If the value is 1, the bitmap is monochrome; this also means bmiColors must contain two entries. For monochrome bitmaps, each bit in the bitmap represents a pixel. If the bit is clear (that is, 0), the pixel is displayed with the color of the first entry in the bmiColors table. If the bit is set (that is, 1), the pixel has the color of the second entry in the table. Although typically these two colors are black and white, there's no reason they have to be.

If the value is 4, the bitmap has a maximum of 16 colors, and bmiColors contains up to 16 entries (although it contains only as many colors as are specified by the biClrImportant field). In a 16-color bitmap, each pixel is represented by a nibble (a nibble is half of a byte), which holds an index into the color table. For example, suppose the first byte of a 16-color DIB contains the value 0x3C. The first pixel of the image would be color number 4 (as defined by the color table), and the second pixel would be color number 13. (The color table is zero referenced.)

If the value is 8, the bitmap has a maximum of 256 colors, and the bmiColors member contains up to 256 entries. In a 256-color bitmap, each byte of the DIB represents a single pixel.

Finally, if the value is 24, the bitmap is a 16-million-color bitmap (2^{24}). This is also known as a true color bitmap. In this case, the DIB doesn't have any palette entries (that is, bmiColors is NULL). Pixels are represented by three bytes, each of which corresponds to one of 256 colors of blue, green, and red, respectively.

The next field is biCompression; it defines how (or whether) the image is compressed. There are three different possibilities. The first, BI_RGB, indicates that the image isn't compressed; each byte of the image is there. The second and third possibilities are BI_RLE8 (for bitmaps that use eight bits per pixel) and BI_RLE4 (for bitmaps that use four bits per pixel), each of which indicates a form of run-length encoding (RLE) of the image. I discuss the compression in more detail later.

The next field, biSizeImage, defines how big the image of the DIB is, in bytes. Although you might think the width multiplied by the height multiplied by the number of bytes per pixel the image takes would give you the total size of

the image in bytes, you'd be mistaken. Just as with a DDB, a DIB's image bytes must be padded out to a boundary. In the case of the bits of a DIB, the bytes are packed but must be zero-padded out to the nearest LONG boundary. This doesn't mean, however, that DIBs cannot span segments—they can (good thing, too, or otherwise it wouldn't be possible to load really big ones into memory).

The next two fields, biXPelsPerMeter and biYPelsPerMeter, can be used in scaling the device to an absolute screen size (for example, to ensure that the image looks the same size on any display, regardless of the size of the screen). In practice, however, I've found most applications and most DIBs just leave these fields empty.

The biClrUsed field is next. It enables an image to specify how many colors it uses. Just because an image can potentially contain, for instance, 32,768 colors doesn't mean it uses all of them. This field indicates how many colors of the total number of possible colors the DIB uses. If it's zero, the image uses all the possible colors.

Finally, the biClrImportant field specifies the number of colors important in displaying the image. I'm not sure what this field is actually good for—I've looked at a lot of DIBs, and none of them I've seen has used it yet. If the value is 0 (which it has been for all the DIBs I've seen), all the colors are important.

Compressing the Image

The notion of compressing bitmap images probably seemed like a better idea when this spec was thought up than it does now. With 100-meg hard drives becoming cheaper by the day, there seems little reason (to me, at least) for compressing 16-color images, at least in everyday use.

Having said that, I will cheerfully admit there are a couple of circumstances under which you might want to compress your images. One instance is if you have a graphics application that uses a lot of images (last time I checked, ICE/Works used something like 100K for images, with about half of that being taken up by bitmap buttons). In that case, you might save space by compressing the images. As a result, you'd have a smaller .exe file (or resource DLL, if that's what you were using). Another use might be for a bulletin board system (BBS) with lots of images; compressing the images lets you put more images on the system.

Note: Using compressed images to the DIB-related calls of windows is actually faster than using uncompressed images. Apparently this is because GDI simply lets the device driver take the run-length encoding and use it to decompress on the fly. This certainly seems like an excellent reason to use compressed DIBs—hey, it speeds things up!

Like most things in life, there's a catch—the RLE decompression of DIBs is, on some video drivers, broken. (Or maybe it's the compression side that's broken—I haven't quite been able to figure it out.) Again, the main culprits are many of the 32,768 Tseng labs drivers.

As usual, there's no way to tell in advance whether, when you hand a compressed DIB to the driver, you're going to get the right answer back, or whether it's *BOOM!* bits on the ceiling. If you're writing a commercial app, this basically means you're going to have to either forget about compressing the images or do it yourself, by hand.

OK, you might ask, "So how do I compress the image?" Really, it's pretty simple—you take the image and reduce the number of bytes it uses. How do you do this without losing data? You (or more accurately, your app) looks for a series of repeating bytes. In this case, you look for a series of pixels on a scan line that are the same color, called a *run* (the RLE schema used by Windows works only on horizontal scan lines). You then replace the series of bytes with two values, one that describes the color of the run of pixels, and one that describes the *length* of the run—hence the term *run-length encoding*.

For example, suppose you have a scan line that contains 20 yellow bytes, all in a row. If yellow is the fourth entry in your color palette, you could reduce this set of 20 pixels to

```
0x14 0x04
```

in which the first value (20) indicates how many pixels there are, and the second value (4) indicates what their color is. Windows uses a similar schema for its RLE methods.

BI_RLE8, the first method, is used for compressing 256-color images. It can compress images in either of two modes: *encoded* or *absolute*. Both of these modes can occur anywhere in a bitmap, and their use is not mutually exclusive. That is, a part of a bitmap can be in encoded mode, and part of it can be in absolute mode.

Encoded RLE is similar to the method just discussed. It consists of two bytes: the first byte holds the run count, and the second byte holds the color of the run. In addition, the first byte can be set to zero, which acts as a flag byte. When the first byte is set to zero, the second byte takes on a different meaning, according to this table:

Second Byte	Meaning
0	End of line.
1	End of bitmap.
2	Delta; the two bytes immediately following are unsigned values that indicate the horizontal and vertical offset of the next pixel from the current pixel position.
03-FF	Switch to absolute mode—this value indicates the number of unencoded pixels that immediately follow this one.

Here are some examples of RLE-encoded streams:

Compressed Stream	Uncompressed Values
05 07 05 03 02 02	07 07 07 07 07 03 03 03 03 03 02 02
04 03	03 03 03 03
04 09 00 01	09 09 09 09 <end of bitmap>
02 08 00 00	08 08 <end of line>
03 06 00 05 8E 4F 43 44 48	06 06 06 8E 4F 43 44 48
03 41 00 02 04 02	41 41 41 <move right 5 pixels, and down 2 pixels>

As you can see, absolute mode is basically a way of indicating a series of absolute values (that is, uncompressed pixels). This makes sense if you stop and think about it. If you don't have any runs of same-color pixels, but have instead pixels that are different colors in a row, encoding these would actually *increase* the amount of space! Absolute mode is a way of indicating that you have a series of unencoded pixels coming up. In absolute mode, runs must be aligned on a word boundary.

Most of the previous examples are obvious and straightforward (if you're into this kind of thing). The only one that seems really off the wall is mode 00 02, which is the "move over and down" mode. What the heck is this good for? Interestingly enough, it's good for doing *diffs* of an image! If you've got a sequence of images that are mostly the same, but in which a few little pieces change, you can store the whole sequence by completely specifying the first image and then specifying only the changes to that image for the subsequent images. Well, why on earth would you want to do that? One good reason is *animation*—in cell (or frame) animation, most things stay the same, and only a few bits change. This compression technique enables you to store lots of animations in a very compact space.

BI_RLE4 works in much the same way as does BI_RLE8. It also uses both encoded and absolute modes, and it has the same tag values as shown previously in the table of values for encoding (that is, when the run count is zero). It, too, uses two bytes to compress runs of pixels; however, the method it uses to compress information in encoded mode is somewhat different.

The first byte is the same; that is, it holds the number of pixels in the run. The second byte, however, breaks down like this:

> High nibble (low four bits)—color index of the even pixels of the run
>
> Low nibble (high four bits)—color index of the odd pixels of the run

(The high and low nibbles are seemingly swapped because of the Intel architecture.) Thus, pixels 0, 2, 4, 6, 8, and so on are drawn using the color specified by the high nibble. Pixels 1, 3, 5, 7, 9, and so on are drawn using the color specified by the low nibble.

This schema seems a little odd, but it actually enables this method to compress more patterns. Rather than only single-color runs (which is the only kind the BI_RLE8 compression can handle), it can handle runs of both a single color and two alternating colors.

As with BI_RLE8, absolute mode runs must be aligned on word boundaries.

Translating Between DIB and DDB

Because the whole point of a DIB is to enable you to read and write bitmap images in a device independent way, there must be some way of converting DIBs to DDBs and vice versa. Indeed there is, but the conversion process is subject to constraints, caveats, and just plain gotchas that can make the process less than straightforward.

Translating from DIB to DDB

First, take a look at the routines that translate from a DIB to a DDB; that is, from a disk bitmap to a memory bitmap. Actually, there's only one routine: `CreateDIBitmap()`. This routine works much the same way that `CreateBitmap()` works, except instead of creating a DDB from a set of already existing bits, it uses a handle to a DIB. Here's an example:

```
HBITMAP      ddbBitmap;              // DDB bitmap handle
HDC          screenDC;

screenDC = GetDC ( NULL );          // Get the DC of the
                                    // system window

ddbBitmap = CreateDIBitmap (  screenDC,
                              lpBmpInfoHeader,
                              CBM_INIT,
                              lpDIBBits,
                              lpBmpInfo,
                              DIB_RGB_COLORS );
```

Take a look at this example. First, to convert an image to a DDB, you need a device context that defines what a DDB looks like in the current display system. The DC is very important in this regard, because it defines exactly how GDI is going to map the DIB color scheme to the current color scheme. This hints at something else `CreateDIBitmap()` does, which is *convert* the DIB format to a DDB format. How does it do this? It takes the color palette of the DIB, and the currently selected color palette of the device context, and maps each pixel of the DIB from the former palette to the latter.

For example, if you have a DIB with 256 shades of grey, and a standard VGA palette in your DC, `CreateDIBitmap()` does its best to map all 256 grey scales to corresponding shades in the VGA palette (which are 4 shades of grey: black, dark grey, light grey, and white). As you might expect, such a mapping doesn't work very well.

Most of the time this mapping conflict won't be a big deal. Usually, you're more interested in being able to load a DIB of some standard color scheme into a display that has the same (or very similar) palette map. In these cases, the matching from one to the other works very smoothly.

Other things you need to pass to the `CreateDIBitmap()` routine include a pointer to the BITMAPINFOHEADER of the DIB (this is the `lpBmpInfoHeader` parameter). Because the beginning of a DIB in memory is exactly this, it's pretty easy to get this pointer—just lock the memory block containing the DIB, and pass the resulting pointer into the function.

The flag indicated by CBM_INIT indicates whether the `CreateDIBitmap()` call should actually fill in the bits of the bitmap from the DIB. You might be asking why you *wouldn't* want this to happen, given what this call is used for. The big reason for doing this is so that you can have the video driver on the system fill in the `biSizeImage` field. This saves you from having to figure out how big this image is going to be. (Given that sometimes the driver doesn't fill in the right answer, and you have to do it anyway, it might be simpler just to always calculate it!)

Next, pass in a pointer to the actual bits of the DIB. This is calculated as

```
lpbi + lpbi->biSize + PaletteSize ( lpbi );
```

in which `lpbi` is a pointer to the DIB chunk (that is, a LPBITMAPINFOHEADER pointer). This calculation says that the bits of the image start at the base pointer, plus the size of the DIB header, plus the size of the palette of this DIB, which is, in fact, where the bits of the DIB are defined as starting.

After that comes another pointer, this time to the BITMAPINFO structure. Because this is the same thing as the pointer to the BITMAPINFOHEADER of the DIB, you can pass in the same pointer you pass in parameter 2 (the `lpBmpInfoHeader` parameter). However, you have to cast it differently, specifically to a LPBITMAPINFO pointer. A BITMAPINFO struct is a structure containing two more structs: the BITMAPINFOHEADER struct and the RGBQUAD[] struct. Because the BITMAPINFOHEADER struct is the first element in the BITMAPINFO struct, a pointer to the latter is, by definition, a pointer to the former.

The final parameter indicates whether the palette of the DIB holds real RGB values or merely indexes to the currently selected palette. Most of the time (for DIBs you read from disk, anyway), this is going to be DIB_RGB_COLORS. That's because unless a DIB is under your exclusive control (in which case you know in advance exactly what palette you use), setting the flag to DIB_PAL_COLORS is risky. By doing so, you're indicating that the DIB you're creating doesn't refer to the RGB colors in the color table, but to the colors in the *current palette*. Unless you know in advance what other apps have in their color palette (and whether it's the same as what's in yours), it's unlikely you can match them. That's because most apps aren't going to have your color palette installed.

In any case, if you want to make DIBs that are usable by every application, set this flag to `DIB_RGB_COLORS`.

Well, that's it—now you can create a memory bitmap (DDB) from a disk bitmap (DIB). In the example application that follows, I've created a whole set of routines that let you read and write DIBs. I discuss some of the other pieces of legerdemain when you get to that app. Before I do that, however, you can look at the flip side of the coin, which is translating a DDB into a DIB. This is actually a bit trickier than transforming a DIB into a DDB.

Translating from DDB to DIB

Well, you've gone one way, from the DIB to a DDB. Now you can get a DIB into memory, but you can't get it back out. The next step is to convert a memory bitmap (a DDB) into a DIB. This process is a little more complex than simply reading in a DIB and creating a memory bitmap from it. Rather than detail the entire procedure (which is documented in the example source code in the module `DIBS.C`, routine `DibFromBitmap()`), I'm simply going to hit the highlights, of which there's really only one: **GetDIBits()**. This is the call that transforms the DDB into the DIB. Here's what it looks like in action:

```
BITMAPINFOHEADER     bi;
BITMAPINFOHEADER FAR *lpbi;
  ...
bi.biSize              = sizeof(BITMAPINFOHEADER);
bi.biWidth             = bm.bmWidth;
bi.biHeight            = bm.bmHeight;
bi.biPlanes            = 1;
bi.biBitCount          = biBits;
bi.biCompression       = biStyle;
bi.biSizeImage         = 0;
bi.biXPelsPerMeter     = 0;
bi.biYPelsPerMeter     = 0;
bi.biClrUsed           = 0;
bi.biClrImportant      = 0;
  ...
dibReturn = GetDIBits(   hdc,
                         hbm,
                         0,
```

```
            (WORD)bi.biHeight,
            (LPSTR)lpbi + (WORD)lpbi->biSize +
                PaletteSize(lpbi),
            (LPBITMAPINFO)lpbi,
            DIB_RGB_COLORS);
```

I've left out quite a few details here (they're discussed later), but the main point is this: you create a BITMAPINFOHEADER structure that defines what the DIB is going to look like; then you call **GetDIBits()**, and it converts the DDB bitmap you pass into a DIB that corresponds to the information you provided in the DIB header block (the BITMAPINFOHEADER structure). This seems innocuous enough until you stop and think about it. There's nothing that says you have to create a DIB that's the same color format as the one of the DDB that you're converting. You might be running in 32,768-color mode, but if you set the biBitCount field to 4, you get a 16-color DIB!

> **Caution:** I don't advise doing a direct translation from 32,768 to 16 colors, because the translation down from 32,768 colors to 16 colors is broken in many super VGA drivers.

The only fields you need to set are the ones specifying the width, height, and bit count. All the others you can leave blank (although you need to fill some of them in before you write the DIB out to disk), and the **GetDIBits()** fills them in with the appropriate information. That's it—that's the magic. You can create a DIB of any number of colors you want, regardless of how many colors the current device supports, simply by specifying the proper number of colors in the header of the DIB before you create it. Seems pretty simple, eh? But it isn't documented *anywhere,* near as I can figure. It's like the old joke about hiding something in plain sight, I guess.

Anyway, you now know the secret of creating DIBs to write to disk—build a header with the number of colors you want your DIB to be, and let **GetDIBits()** take care of the rest.

A Few Cautionary Words

Before you go on and explore the demo app I've created, I want to touch on a few points about using DIBs and DDBs.

Caution: Conversions are forever. This means that after you translate a DIB image to a DDB (memory) bitmap, you have lost *forever* the original DIB information (unless you keep the DIB lying around in memory also). This is OK, if the DIB's resolution happens to match the resolution of the current memory device. But for cases in which you're doing things like converting from a 256-color bitmap to a 16-color bitmap, it's history. *To preserve all the information of the DIB, you must keep the DIB itself around.* (This isn't hard to do, given the routines that I'm going to show you.)

Tip: Don't believe everything you see. As I've already mentioned, some video drivers (which are the ones finally responsible for performing the translations of DIB to DDB and back) *don't work* when handed something oddball. Sure, they've been designed to work properly with DIBs that are the same resolution as the current memory device—but they might or might not have been tested to work with other memory devices. So if you hit a land-mine, don't instantly assume it's your code.

The DibShow App: Source Code

Whew! I didn't think I was going to make it through all of that. Having given you all the basics for how a DIB works, it's now time to give you another example that shows how you can actually manipulate one. It's time for (drumroll, please) the DibShow App! This app builds on all the things I've talked about so far, and actually implements a very simple DIB reader/writer. It enables you to load DIBs into memory and display them in the window of the app. It also lets you write out a DIB to a file. Listings 4.1 through 4.11 show the full source code to the DibShow App.

Listing 4.1. DIBSHOW.C—source code for the DibShow App, a DIB reader and displayer.

```
/*File name: DIBSHOW.C                                   */
/*"DIBSHOW" Generated by WindowsMAKER Professional       */
/*Author: Alex Leavens, for ShadowCat Technologies       */

#include <WINDOWS.H>
#include "DIBSHOW.H"

#include "dibs.h"
#include "filedlg.h"

#include "externs.h"

#include "DIBSHOW.WMC"


HANDLE                  bmpInfoHand;
LPBITMAPINFOHEADER      lpBInfo;


/****************************************************************/
/*                   WinMain FUNCTION                          */
/****************************************************************/

int PASCAL WinMain(hInstance, hPrevInstance, lpCmdLine, nCmdShow)
HANDLE hInstance;                /* Current instance               */
HANDLE hPrevInstance;            /* Previous instance              */
LPSTR lpCmdLine;                 /* Command line                   */
int nCmdShow;                    /* Show-window type (open/icon)   */
    {
    MSG msg;                     /* Message                        */

    hInst = hInstance;           /* Saves the current instance     */

    if (!BLDInitApplication(hInstance,hPrevInstance,&nCmdShow,lpCmdLine))
        return FALSE;

    if (!hPrevInstance)          /* Is there another instance of the task   */
        {
        if (!BLDRegisterClass(hInstance))
            return FALSE;        /* Exits if unable to initialize  */
        }

    MainhWnd = BLDCreateWindow(hInstance);
```

continues

Listing 4.1. continued

```
    if (!MainhWnd)                /* Check if the window is created      */
        return FALSE;

    ShowWindow(MainhWnd, nCmdShow);  /* Show the window                  */
    UpdateWindow(MainhWnd);          /* Send WM_PAINT message to window  */

    BLDInitMainMenu(MainhWnd);       /* Initialize main menu if necessary */

    while (GetMessage(&msg,       /* Message structure                   */
        0,                        /* Handle of window receiving the message */
        0,                        /* Lowest message to examine           */
        0))                       /* Highest message to examine          */
        {
        if (BLDKeyTranslation(&msg)) /* WindowsMAKER code for key trans */
            continue;
        TranslateMessage(&msg);   /* Translates character keys           */
        DispatchMessage(&msg);    /* Dispatches message to window        */
        }
    BLDExitApplication();         /* Clean up if necessary               */
    return(msg.wParam);           /* Returns the value from PostQuitMessage */
    }


/****************************************************************/
/*              WINDOW PROCEDURE FOR MAIN WINDOW                */
/****************************************************************/

long FAR PASCAL BLDMainWndProc(hWnd, message, wParam, lParam)
HWND hWnd;                        /* Window handle                       */
unsigned message;                 /* Type of message                     */
WORD wParam;                      /* Additional information              */
LONG lParam;                      /* Additional information              */
    {

    switch (message)
        {

    case WM_CREATE:               /* Window creation                     */

        lpBInfo = (HPBITMAPINFOHEADER)AllocAndLockMem(&bmpInfoHand,
                                        sizeof(BITMAPINFOHEADER));

        /* Make a proc instance for the callback hook for the open
         * file dialog box.
         */
```

```
        lpfnFileOpenHook = MakeProcInstance((FARPROC)FileOpenHook, hInst);

        if (lpfnFileOpenHook == NULL)
            return FALSE;

        // Allocate space for the file buffer

        dibChunk = (LPFOCHUNK)AllocAndLockMem(&dibFChunkHand,
                                              sizeof(FOCHUNK));

        /* Send to BLDDefWindowProc in (.WMC) for controls in main window  */
        return BLDDefWindowProc(hWnd, message, wParam, lParam);
        break;

case WM_SETFOCUS:              /* Window is notified of focus change      */
        /* Send to BLDDefWindowProc in (.WMC) for controls in main window  */
        return BLDDefWindowProc(hWnd, message, wParam, lParam);
        break;

case WM_DESTROY:               /* Window being destroyed                  */

        // Unlock and free the file access chunk

        GlobalUnlock(dibFChunkHand);
        GlobalFree(dibFChunkHand);

        // Free bitmap if it's there...

        if (globalDIBHnd)
            GlobalFree(globalDIBHnd);

        PostQuitMessage(0);
        return BLDDefWindowProc(hWnd, message, wParam, lParam);
        break;

case WM_PAINT:
{
    HDC             screenDC;
    PAINTSTRUCT     pNt;

    //----------------

    screenDC = BeginPaint (hWnd,
                           &pNt);
```

continues

Listing 4.1. continued

```
if (screenDC && globalDIBHnd)
{
    DibBlt ( screenDC,
             0,
             0,
             lpBInfo->biWidth,
             lpBInfo->biHeight,
             globalDIBHnd,
             0,
             0,
             (LONG)SRCCOPY);
}

if (screenDC)
    EndPaint(hWnd,
             &pNt);
}

break;

case WM_COMMAND:                /* Command from the main window          */
    switch ( wParam )
    {
        case IDM_Save:          // Save the current DIB into a new file
        {
            SaveNativeFile ( hWnd,
                             message,
                             wParam,
                             lParam );
        }
        break;

        case IDM_Open:
        {
            HDC                         screenDC;
            BITMAPINFOHEADER            bi;

            //-------------------

            OpenNativeFile(hWnd,
                           message,
                           wParam,
                           lParam);

            if (globalDIBHnd)
```

```
                        {
                  if ( DibInfo ( globalDIBHnd,
                                &bi ) )
                        {

                        // Size ourselves to the size of the DIB

                        InvalidateRect ( MainhWnd,
                                            NULL,
                                            TRUE );
                        MoveWindow ( hWnd,
                                    30, 30,
                                    bi.biWidth + 50,
                                    bi.biHeight + 50,
                                    TRUE );

                        UpdateWindow(hWnd);

                        screenDC = GetDC ( hWnd );

                        if (screenDC)
                        {
                            DibBlt ( screenDC,
                                        0,
                                        0,
                                        bi.biWidth,
                                        bi.biHeight,
                                        globalDIBHnd,
                                        0,
                                        0,
                                        (LONG)SRCCOPY);

                                ReleaseDC ( hWnd,
                                            screenDC );
                        }
                    }
                }
            }
        }

    if (BLDMenuCommand(hWnd, message, wParam, lParam))
        break;                  /* Processed by BLDMenuCommand.           */
        /* Else default processing by BLDDefWindowProc.                   */
default:
    /* Pass on message for default processing                            */
```

continues

Listing 4.1. continued

```
        return BLDDefWindowProc(hWnd, message, wParam, lParam);
        }
    return FALSE;                    /* Returns FALSE if processed         */
    }
```

Listing 4.2. DIBSHOW.WMC—special include file for the DibShow App.

```
/*File name: DIBSHOW.WMC                                    */
/*"DIBSHOW" Generated by WindowsMAKER Professional          */
/*Author: Alex Leavens, for ShadowCat Technologies          */


/**************************************************************/
/*                  GLOBAL VARIABLES                        */
/**************************************************************/

HANDLE  hInst   = 0;  /* Handle to instance.                */
HWND    MainhWnd= 0;  /* Handle to main window.             */
HWND    hClient = 0;  /* Handle to window in client area.   */
FARPROC lpClient= 0L; /* Function for window in client area. */

LPFOCHUNK       dibChunk;          /* Pointer to DIB file chunk */
HANDLE          dibFChunkHand;     /* Handle to DIB file chunk  */

FARPROC         lpfnFileOpenHook; /* Hook for open file dialog */
HANDLE          globalDIBHnd-0;   /* Handle to global DIB      */

/**************************************************************/
/*          PROCESSES KEYBOARD ACCELERATORS                 */
/*              AND MODELESS DIALOG BOX KEY INPUT            */
/**************************************************************/

BOOL BLDKeyTranslation(pMsg)
MSG *pMsg;
    {
    return FALSE; /* No special key input                    */
    }


/**************************************************************/
/*        CUSTOM MESSAGE PROCESSING FOR MAIN WINDOW         */
/**************************************************************/
```

```
long FAR PASCAL BLDDefWindowProc(hWnd, message, wParam, lParam)
HWND hWnd;                       /* Window handle              */
unsigned message;                /* Type of message           */
WORD wParam;                     /* Additional information     */
LONG lParam;                     /* Additional information     */
    {

    switch (message)
        {

    default:
        /* Pass on message for default processing by Windows  */
        return DefWindowProc(hWnd, message, wParam, lParam);
        }
    return FALSE; /* Returns FALSE if not processed by Windows */
    }


/******************************************************************/
/*            PROCESSES ALL MENU ITEM SELECTIONS              */
/******************************************************************/

BOOL BLDMenuCommand(hWnd, message, wParam, lParam)
HWND hWnd;                       /* Window handle              */
unsigned message;                /* Type of message           */
WORD wParam;                     /* Additional information     */
LONG lParam;                     /* Additional information     */
    {

    switch(wParam)
        {

        /* Processing of linked menu items in menu: DIBSHOW    */

        default:
            return FALSE;    /* Not processed by this function. */
        }
    return TRUE;             /* Processed by this function.    */
    }


/******************************************************************/
/*    FUNCTIONS FOR INITIALIZATION AND EXIT OF APPLICATION    */
/******************************************************************/

BOOL BLDInitApplication(hInst,hPrev,pCmdShow,lpCmd)
HANDLE hInst;   /* Handle to application instance              */
```

continues

Listing 4.2. continued

```
bi.HANDLE hPrev;   /* Handle to previous instance of application. */
int *pCmdShow;  /* Pointer to variable that specifies how main */
                /* window is to be shown.                    */
LPSTR lpCmd;    /* Long pointer to the command line.         */
    {
    /* No initialization necessary */
    return TRUE;
    }


BOOL BLDRegisterClass(hInstance) /* Registers the class for the main window */
HANDLE hInstance;
    {
    WNDCLASS WndClass;

    WndClass.style        = 0;
    WndClass.lpfnWndProc  = BLDMainWndProc;
    WndClass.cbClsExtra   = 0;
    WndClass.cbWndExtra   = 0;
    WndClass.hInstance    = hInstance;
    WndClass.hIcon        = LoadIcon(NULL,IDI_APPLICATION);
    WndClass.hCursor      = LoadCursor(NULL,IDC_ARROW);
    WndClass.hbrBackground = CreateSolidBrush(GetSysColor(COLOR_WINDOW));
    WndClass.lpszMenuName  = "DIBSHOW";
    WndClass.lpszClassName = "DIBSHOW";

    return RegisterClass(&WndClass);
    }


HWND BLDCreateWindow(hInstance)  /* Creates the main window           */
HANDLE hInstance;
    {
    HWND hWnd;                 /* Window handle                     */
    int coordinate[4];         /* Coordinates of main window        */

    coordinate[0]=CW_USEDEFAULT;
    coordinate[1]=0;
    coordinate[2]=CW_USEDEFAULT;
    coordinate[3]=0;

    hWnd = CreateWindow("DIBSHOW",  /* Window class registered earlier  */
            "DIB Shower, by Alex Leavens",     /* Window caption            */
```

```
                  WS_OVERLAPPED¦WS_THICKFRAME¦WS_SYSMENU¦WS_MINIMIZEBOX¦
                  WS_MAXIMIZEBOX,
                                      /* Window style                        */
                  coordinate[0],      /* X position                          */
                  coordinate[1],      /* Y position                          */
                  coordinate[2],      /* Width                               */
                  coordinate[3],      /* Height                              */
                  0,                  /* Parent handle                       */
                  0,                  /* Menu or child ID                    */
                  hInstance,          /* Instance                            */
                  (LPSTR)NULL);       /* Additional info                     */

      return hWnd;
      }


BOOL BLDInitMainMenu(hWnd)      /* Called just before entering message loop */
HWND hWnd;
      {
      /* No initialization necessary */
      return TRUE;
      }


BOOL BLDExitApplication()       /* Called just before exit of application  */
      {
      /* No processing needed at exit for this design */
      return TRUE;
      }

/************************************************************/
/* ERROR MESSAGE HANDLING (Definitions can be overruled.) */
/************************************************************/

#ifndef ERRORCAPTION
#define ERRORCAPTION "Untitled"
#endif

#ifndef LOADERROR
#define LOADERROR "Cannot load string."
#endif


int BLDDisplayMessage(hWnd,uMsg,pContext,iType)
HWND hWnd;
```

continues

CHAPTER 4

Listing 4.2. continued

```c
unsigned uMsg;
char *pContext;
int iType;
    {
    int i, j;
    char Message[200+1];

    if (uMsg)
        {
        if (!LoadString(hInst,uMsg,Message,200))
            {
            MessageBox(hWnd,LOADERROR,ERRORCAPTION,
                        MB_OK|MB_SYSTEMMODAL|MB_ICONHAND);
            return FALSE;
            }
        }
    else
        Message[0]=0;

    if (pContext)
        {
        i = lstrlen(Message);
        j = lstrlen(pContext);
        if (i + j + 1 <= 200)
            {
            lstrcat(Message, " ");
            lstrcat(Message, pContext);
            }
        }

    return MessageBox(hWnd,Message,ERRORCAPTION,iType);
    }


/******************************************************************/
/*              FUNCTIONS FOR DRAWING GRAPHICS BUTTONS           */
/******************************************************************/

BOOL BLDDrawIcon(lpDrawItem,pIconName)
LPDRAWITEMSTRUCT lpDrawItem;
char *pIconName;
    {
    HICON hIcon;

    if (!(hIcon = LoadIcon(hInst,pIconName)))
```

```
        {
        BLDDisplayMessage(GetActiveWindow(),BLD_CannotLoadIcon,pIconName,
                        MB_OK | MB_ICONASTERISK);
        return FALSE;
        }

    SetMapMode(lpDrawItem->hDC,MM_TEXT);
    return DrawIcon(lpDrawItem->hDC,0,0,hIcon);
    }


BOOL BLDDrawBitmap(lpDrawItem,pBitmapName,bStretch)
LPDRAWITEMSTRUCT lpDrawItem;
char *pBitmapName;
BOOL bStretch;
    {
    HBITMAP hBitmap;
    HDC hMemDC;
    BITMAP Bitmap;
    int iRaster;

    iRaster = GetDeviceCaps(lpDrawItem->hDC,RASTERCAPS);
    if ((iRaster&RC_BITBLT)!=RC_BITBLT)
        return FALSE; /* Device cannot display bitmap */

    if (!(hBitmap = LoadBitmap(hInst,pBitmapName)))
        {
        BLDDisplayMessage(GetActiveWindow(),BLD_CannotLoadBitmap,pBitmapName,
                        MB_OK | MB_ICONASTERISK);
        return FALSE;
        }

    if (!GetObject(hBitmap,sizeof(BITMAP),(LPSTR)&Bitmap))
        {
        DeleteObject(hBitmap);
        return FALSE;
        }
    if (!(hMemDC = CreateCompatibleDC(lpDrawItem->hDC)))
        {
        DeleteObject(hBitmap);
        return FALSE;
        }
    if (!SelectObject(hMemDC,hBitmap))
        {
        DeleteDC(hMemDC);
```

continues

Listing 4.2. continued

```
        DeleteObject(hBitmap);
        return FALSE;
        }

    if (bStretch)
            {
            StretchBlt(lpDrawItem->hDC,
                    lpDrawItem->rcItem.left,
                    lpDrawItem->rcItem.top,
                    lpDrawItem->rcItem.right-lpDrawItem->rcItem.left,
                    lpDrawItem->rcItem.bottom-lpDrawItem->rcItem.top,
                    hMemDC,
                    0,
                    0,
                    Bitmap.bmWidth,
                    Bitmap.bmHeight,
                    SRCCOPY);
        }
    else
        {
            BitBlt(lpDrawItem->hDC,
                    lpDrawItem->rcItem.left,
                    lpDrawItem->rcItem.top,
                    lpDrawItem->rcItem.right-lpDrawItem->rcItem.left,
                    lpDrawItem->rcItem.bottom-lpDrawItem->rcItem.top,
                    hMemDC,
                    0,
                    0,
                    SRCCOPY);
        }
    DeleteDC(hMemDC);
    DeleteObject(hBitmap);
    return TRUE;
    }


/*****************************************************************/
/*          FUNCTION FOR CREATING CONTROLS IN MAIN WINDOW        */
/*****************************************************************/

HWND BLDCreateClientControls(pTemplateName,lpNew) /* Startup procedure for */
                                                  /* window in client area */
char    *pTemplateName;
FARPROC lpNew;
```

```
{
RECT rClient,rMain,rDialog;
int dxDialog,dyDialog,dyExtra,dtXold,dtYold;
HANDLE hRes,hMem;
LPBLD_DLGTEMPLATE lpDlg;
unsigned long styleold,style;
HWND hNew;

if (!IsWindow(MainhWnd))
    return 0;
if (IsZoomed(MainhWnd))
    ShowWindow(MainhWnd,SW_RESTORE);


if (IsWindow(hClient))
 DestroyWindow(hClient); /* Destroy Previous window in client area  */

/* Get access to data structure of dialog box containing
   layout of controls */
if (!(hRes=FindResource(hInst,(LPSTR)pTemplateName,RT_DIALOG)))
    return 0;
if (!(hMem=LoadResource(hInst,hRes)))
    return 0;
if (!(lpDlg=(LPBLD_DLGTEMPLATE)LockResource(hMem)))
    return 0;

/* Change dialog box data structure so it can be used as a
   window in client area */
styleold       = lpDlg->dtStyle;
style          = lpDlg->dtStyle&(CLIENTSTRIP);
lpDlg->dtStyle = lpDlg->dtStyle^style;
lpDlg->dtStyle = lpDlg->dtStyle | WS_CHILD | WS_CLIPSIBLINGS;
dtXold         = lpDlg->dtX;
dtYold         = lpDlg->dtY;
lpDlg->dtX     = 0;
lpDlg->dtY     = 0;

if (!(hNew = CreateDialogIndirect(hInst,(LPSTR)lpDlg, MainhWnd,lpNew)))
    return 0;

/* Restore dialog box data structure. */
lpDlg->dtStyle =styleold;
lpDlg->dtX     = dtXold;
lpDlg->dtY     = dtYold;
```

continues

191

Listing 4.2. continued

```
UnlockResource(hMem);
FreeResource(hMem);

/* Move and size window in client area and main window */
GetClientRect(MainhWnd,&rClient);
GetWindowRect(MainhWnd,&rMain);
GetWindowRect(hNew,&rDialog);
dxDialog=(rDialog.right-rDialog.left)-(rClient.right-rClient.left);
dyDialog=(rDialog.bottom-rDialog.top)-(rClient.bottom-rClient.top);
BLDMoveWindow(MainhWnd,rMain.left,rMain.top,
          (rMain.right-rMain.left)+dxDialog,
                      (rMain.bottom-rMain.top)+dyDialog,
        TRUE);
MoveWindow(hNew,0,0,
                (rDialog.right-rDialog.left),
                (rDialog.bottom-rDialog.top),
                TRUE);
GetClientRect(MainhWnd,&rClient);

/* Compensate size if menu bar is more than one line. */
if ((rDialog.bottom-rDialog.top)>(rClient.bottom-rClient.top))
    {
    dyExtra=(rDialog.bottom-rDialog.top)-(rClient.bottom-rClient.top);
    BLDMoveWindow(MainhWnd,rMain.left,rMain.top,
              (rMain.right-rMain.left)+dxDialog,
              (rMain.bottom-rMain.top)+dyDialog+dyExtra,
              TRUE);
    }

ShowWindow(hNew,SW_SHOW);
hClient=hNew;
lpClient=lpNew;
return hClient;
}


/* Ensure that window is within screen. */
void BLDMoveWindow(hWnd,x,y,nWidth,nHeight,bRepaint)
HWND hWnd;
int  x;
int  y;
int  nWidth;
int  nHeight;
BOOL bRepaint;
```

```
    {
    int xMax,yMax,xNew,yNew;

    xMax = GetSystemMetrics(SM_CXSCREEN);
    yMax = GetSystemMetrics(SM_CYSCREEN);

    if ((nWidth<=xMax)&&(x+nWidth>xMax))
        xNew=xMax-nWidth;
    else
        xNew=x;

    if ((nHeight<=yMax)&&(y+nHeight>yMax))
        yNew=yMax-nHeight;
    else
        yNew=y;

    MoveWindow(hWnd,xNew,yNew,nWidth,nHeight,bRepaint);
    return;
    }

/*****************************************************************/
/*              FUNCTION FOR SWITCHING MENU SET                 */
/*****************************************************************/

BOOL BLDSwitchMenu(hWnd,pTemplateName)
HWND hWnd;
char *pTemplateName;
    {
    HMENU hMenu1,hMenu;
    DWORD style;

    style = GetWindowLong(hWnd,GWL_STYLE);
    if((style & WS_CHILD) == WS_CHILD)       /* Called from control
                                                in main window? */
        {
        if (!(hWnd=GetParent(hWnd)))
            return FALSE;
        style = GetWindowLong(hWnd,GWL_STYLE);
        if((style & WS_CHILD) == WS_CHILD) /* No menu in a WS_CHILD
                                              window. */
            return FALSE;
        }
    if((style & WS_CAPTION) != WS_CAPTION) /* No menu if no
                                              caption. */
        return FALSE;
```

continues

Listing 4.2. continued

```
hMenu1 = GetMenu(hWnd);
if (!(hMenu = LoadMenu(hInst,pTemplateName)))
    {
    BLDDisplayMessage(hWnd,BLD_CannotLoadMenu,pTemplateName,
                    MB_OK | MB_ICONASTERISK);
    return FALSE;
    }

if (!SetMenu(hWnd,hMenu))
    return FALSE;
if (hMenu1)
    DestroyMenu(hMenu1);

DrawMenuBar(hWnd);
return TRUE;
}
```

**Listing 4.3. DIBS.C—routines to manipulate DIBs, for the
DibShow App.**

```
/* DIBS.C
 *
 * Routines for handling DIBs (device independent bitmaps)
 *
 * Written by Alex Leavens, for ShadowCat Technologies
 */

#include <windows.h>

#include "dibshow.h"
#include "dibs.h"
#include "filedlg.h"
#include "externs.h"


/************************
 * OpenDIB()
 *    Open a DIB file and create a MEMORY DIB, a memory handle
 *    containing BITMAPINFO, palette data, and the bits.
 *
 * Parameters:
 *    szFile - file name to open
```

```
 *
 * Returns:
 *    A handle to the DIB if everything went OK, NULL if it didn't.
 *
 * Assumptions:
 *    This routine can support cursor, icon, and bitmap formats of a DIB.
 */

    HANDLE
OpenDIB (LPSTR szFile)
{
    unsigned            fh;

    HANDLE              hdib;

    OFSTRUCT            of;

    BOOL        gotIt;

    BITMAPINFOHEADER        bi;

    /*----------------------------------------*/

    /* Open the file and read the DIB information */

    fh = OpenFile(szFile,
                &of,
                OF_READ);

    if (fh == -1)
    {
        MessageBox ( NULL,
                    "Can't open image file",
                    "DIB routines",
                    MB_OK );

        return NULL;
    }

    // Now read in the information about the file

    hdib = ReadDibBitmapInfo ( fh );

    /* If you don't have a handle to the bitmap, punt. */
```

continues

Listing 4.3. continued

```
    if (!hdib)
        return NULL;

    /* Now read the image bits here... */

    hdib = ReadDIBBits(fh,
                            hdib);

    _lclose(fh);    /* Close the file handle */

    return hdib;
}
/**********************************
 * ReadDIBBits()
 *     Given a handle to a bitmap that's already been filled with the
 *     header stuff of a DIB, and a file handle, this routine will read the
 *     actual bits of the DIB into a memory chunk.
 *
 * Parameters:
 *     fh - file handle to open
 *     hdib - handle to the DIB
 *
 * Returns:
 *     TRUE - you read it
 *     FALSE - you didn't
 *
 * Assumptions:
 *     The routine is atomic.
 */

    HANDLE WINAPI
ReadDIBBits(unsigned        fh,
            HANDLE          hdib)
{
    BITMAPINFOHEADER        bi;
    HPBITMAPINFOHEADER  lpbi;

    DWORD                   dwLen = 0;
    DWORD                   dwBits;

    HANDLE              h;

    /*---------------------------*/
```

```
/* Get the size, # colors, etc., of the DIB */

DibInfo(hdib,
        &bi);

/* Calculate the memory needed to hold the DIB */

dwBits = bi.biSizeImage;

dwLen  = bi.biSize + (DWORD)PaletteSize (&bi) + dwBits;

/* Try to increase the size of the bitmap info. buffer to hold the DIB */

h = GlobalReAlloc(hdib,
                  dwLen,
                  GHND);

/* If you didn't get enough memory for the image, then punt... */

if (!h)
{
    GlobalFree(hdib);
    return NULL;
}

/* Lock the memory down... */

lpbi = (HPBITMAPINFOHEADER)GlobalLock(h);

/* Read the bits... */

lread(fh,
    (LPSTR)lpbi +
        (WORD)lpbi->biSize +
        PaletteSize(lpbi),
     dwBits);

/* Unlock the memory... */

GlobalUnlock ( h );

return h;
}
```

continues

Listing 4.3. continued

```
/**********************************
 * WriteDIB()
 *   Writes a DIB to a file
 *
 * Parameters:
 *    szFile - file name to write the DIB to
 *    hdib - handle to the DIB to write
 *
 * Returns:
 *    TRUE - Success
 *    FALSE - "Houston, we have a problem"
 */

    BOOL
WriteDIB (LPSTR           szFile,
          HANDLE hdib)
{
    BITMAPFILEHEADER      hdr;
    HPBITMAPINFOHEADER  lpbi;

    int                  fh;
    OFSTRUCT             of;

    DWORD                 dwLen;

    /*----------------------------------------*/

    if (!hdib)
        return FALSE;

    fh = OpenFile (szFile, &of, OF_CREATE¦OF_READWRITE);
    if (fh == -1)
    {
        MessageBox ( NULL,
                     "Can't open file for writing",
                     "DIB routines",
                     MB_OK );

        return FALSE;
    }

    lpbi = (HPBITMAPINFOHEADER)GlobalLock (hdib);

    /* Fill in the fields of the file header */
```

```
        hdr.bfType              = BFT_BITMAP;
        hdr.bfSize              = GlobalSize (hdib) + sizeof (BITMAPFILEHEADER);
        hdr.bfReserved1     = 0;
        hdr.bfReserved2     = 0;
        hdr.bfOffBits           = (DWORD)sizeof(BITMAPFILEHEADER) + lpbi->biSize +
                            PaletteSize(lpbi);


    /* Write the file header */
    _lwrite (fh,
            (LPSTR)&hdr,
            sizeof (BITMAPFILEHEADER));


    /* Calculate the exact length of the image */

    if (lpbi->biSizeImage != 0 &&
        lpbi->biSize != 0 &&
        PaletteSize(lpbi) != 0)
    {
        dwLen = lpbi->biSizeImage +
                lpbi->biSize +
                PaletteSize(lpbi);
    }
    else
    {
        dwLen = GlobalSize( hdib );
    }


    /* Write the DIB header and the bits */
    lwrite (fh,
            (LPSTR)lpbi,
            dwLen);


    GlobalUnlock (hdib);
    _lclose (fh);

    return TRUE;
}


/*****************************
 * DibInfo()
 *      Retrieves the information about the DIB and puts it
 *      into the memory block pointed to.
 *
 * Parameters:
 *      hbi - Handle to the memory containing the DIB header
```

continues

Listing 4.3. continued

```
*       lpbi - pointer to the memory block to put the information in
*
* Returns:
*       TRUE - success
*       FALSE - "Houston, we have a problem"
*/

    BOOL
DibInfo (HANDLE                 hbi,
        HPBITMAPINFOHEADER      lpbi)
{
    if (hbi)        // If no handle, punt
    {
        // Lock the memory handle

        *lpbi = *(HPBITMAPINFOHEADER)GlobalLock (hbi);

        // Fill in the default fields. Notice that
        // this routine will NOT work for OS2/PM-style headers

        if (lpbi->biSize != sizeof (BITMAPCOREHEADER))
        {
            // If you don't have a size, figure out what it would be

            if (lpbi->biSizeImage == 0L)
            {
                lpbi->biSizeImage =
                WIDTHBYTES(lpbi->biWidth*lpbi->biBitCount) * lpbi->biHeight;
            }

            // If you don't have a number of colors, figure
            // out how many you're using

            if (lpbi->biClrUsed == 0L)
            {
                lpbi->biClrUsed = DibNumColors (lpbi);
            }
        }

        // Unlock the memory handle

        GlobalUnlock (hbi);

        // Return success
```

```
            return TRUE;
        }

        // Return failure

        return FALSE;
    }


/********************************
 * ReadDibBitmapInfo()
 *     Will read a file in DIB format and return a global HANDLE
 *     to its BITMAPINFO. This function will work with both
 *     OS2/PM DIBs (BITMAPCOREHEADER) and DIB DIBs (BITMAPINFOHEADER)
 *     bitmap formats, but will always return a DIB-style BITMAPINFO.
 *
 * Args:
 *     fh - handle to the file
 *
 * Returns:
 *     A handle to the BITMAPINFO of the DIB in the file (or NULL)
 *
 * Assumptions:
 *     That everything you do in here is going to work.
 */

    HANDLE
ReadDibBitmapInfo (int      fh)
{
    DWORD        off;
    HANDLE       hbi = NULL;
    int          size;
    int          i;
    WORD         nNumColors;

    RGBQUAD FAR         *pRgb;
    BITMAPINFOHEADER    bi;
    BITMAPCOREHEADER    bc;
    HPBITMAPINFOHEADER lpbi;
    BITMAPFILEHEADER    bf;
    DWORD               dwWidth = 0;
    DWORD               dwHeight = 0;
    WORD         wPlanes, wBitCount;

    //----------------------------
```

continues

Listing 4.3. continued

```
    if (fh == -1) // Punt on no file handle
        return NULL;

    /* Reset file pointer and read file header */
    off = _llseek(fh, 0L, SEEK_CUR);
    if (sizeof (bf) != _lread (fh, (LPSTR)&bf, sizeof (bf)))
        return FALSE;

    /* Do you have an RC HEADER? */
    if (!ISDIB (bf.bfType)) {
        bf.bfOffBits = 0L;
        _llseek (fh, off, SEEK_SET);
    }
    if (sizeof (bi) != _lread (fh, (LPSTR)&bi, sizeof(bi)))
        return FALSE;

    nNumColors = DibNumColors (&bi);

    /* Check the nature (BITMAPINFO or BITMAPCORE) of the info. block
     * and extract the field information accordingly. If a BITMAPCOREHEADER,
     * transfer its field information to a BITMAPINFOHEADER-style block.
     */
    switch (size = (int)bi.biSize){
        case sizeof (BITMAPINFOHEADER):
            break;

        case sizeof (BITMAPCOREHEADER):

            bc = *(BITMAPCOREHEADER*)&bi;

            dwWidth   = (DWORD)bc.bcWidth;
            dwHeight  = (DWORD)bc.bcHeight;
            wPlanes   = bc.bcPlanes;
            wBitCount = bc.bcBitCount;

            bi.biSize            = sizeof(BITMAPINFOHEADER);
            bi.biWidth               = dwWidth;
            bi.biHeight      = dwHeight;
            bi.biPlanes      = wPlanes;
            bi.biBitCount    = wBitCount;

            bi.biCompression     = BI_RGB;
            bi.biSizeImage       = 0;
            bi.biXPelsPerMeter   = 0;
```

```
        bi.biYPelsPerMeter    = 0;
        bi.biClrUsed          = nNumColors;
        bi.biClrImportant     = nNumColors;

         _llseek (fh, (LONG)sizeof (BITMAPCOREHEADER) -
                        sizeof (BITMAPINFOHEADER), SEEK_CUR);
        break;

    default:
        /* Not a DIB! */
        return NULL;
}


/* Fill in some default values if they are zero */
if (bi.biSizeImage == 0){
    bi.biSizeImage = WIDTHBYTES ((DWORD)bi.biWidth * bi.biBitCount)
                    * bi.biHeight;
}
if (bi.biClrUsed == 0)
    bi.biClrUsed = DibNumColors(&bi);

/* Allocate for the BITMAPINFO structure and the color table. */
hbi = GlobalAlloc (GHND, (LONG)bi.biSize + nNumColors * sizeof(RGBQUAD));
if (!hbi)
    return NULL;
lpbi = (HPBITMAPINFOHEADER)GlobalLock (hbi);
*lpbi = bi;

/* Get a pointer to the color table */
pRgb = (RGBQUAD FAR *)((LPSTR)lpbi + bi.biSize);
if (nNumColors){
    if (size == sizeof(BITMAPCOREHEADER)){
        /* Convert an old color table (3 byte RGBTRIPLEs) to a new
         * color table (4 byte RGBQUADs)
         */
        _lread (fh, (LPSTR)pRgb, nNumColors * sizeof(RGBTRIPLE));

        for (i = nNumColors - 1; i >= 0; i--){
            RGBQUAD rgb;

            rgb.rgbRed      = ((RGBTRIPLE FAR *)pRgb)[i].rgbtRed;
            rgb.rgbBlue     = ((RGBTRIPLE FAR *)pRgb)[i].rgbtBlue;
            rgb.rgbGreen    = ((RGBTRIPLE FAR *)pRgb)[i].rgbtGreen;
            rgb.rgbReserved = (BYTE)0;
```

continues

203

Listing 4.3. continued

```
                    pRgb[i] = rgb;
                }
            }
             else
                _lread(fh,(LPSTR)pRgb,nNumColors * sizeof(RGBQUAD));
        }

        /* Reseek the file pointer to the beginning of the DIB... */

        if (bf.bfOffBits != 0L)
        {
            SeekDouble(NULL,
                fh,
                (DWORD)off + bf.bfOffBits,
                SEEK_SET);
        }

        GlobalUnlock(hbi);
        return hbi;
}
/************************
 * PaletteSize()
 *    Calculates the palette size in bytes, for either OS2/PM-style
 *    headers or standard DIB headers. (OS2/PM headers use 3 bytes RGBTRIPLEs,
 *    and DIBs use 4 byte RGBQUADS.)
 *
 * Returns:
 *    Size in bytes of the palette
 *
 * Args:
 *    pv - pointer to a BITMAPINFOHEADER
 */

    WORD
PaletteSize (VOID FAR * pv)
{
    HPBITMAPINFOHEADER lpbi;
    WORD        NumColors;

    lpbi     = (HPBITMAPINFOHEADER)pv;
    NumColors = DibNumColors(lpbi);

    if (lpbi->biSize == sizeof(BITMAPCOREHEADER))
        return NumColors * sizeof(RGBTRIPLE);
```

```
        else
            return NumColors * sizeof(RGBQUAD);
}
/*************************
 * DibNumColors()
 *     Determines how many colors are in the DIB by looking
 *     at the biBitCount field in the info block.
 *
 * Returns:
 *     Number of colors in the DIB.
 *
 * Params:
 *     pv - pointer to a BITMAPINFOHEADER
 */

    WORD
DibNumColors (VOID FAR * pv)
{
    int             bits;
    HPBITMAPINFOHEADER      lpbi;
    LPBITMAPCOREHEADER      lpbc;

    lpbi = ((HPBITMAPINFOHEADER)pv);
    lpbc = ((LPBITMAPCOREHEADER)pv);

    /* With the BITMAPINFO format headers, the size of the palette
     * is in biClrUsed, whereas in the BITMAPCORE-style headers, it
     * is dependent on the bits per pixel ( = 2 raised to the power of
     * bits/pixel).
     */
    if (lpbi->biSize != sizeof(BITMAPCOREHEADER)){
        if (lpbi->biClrUsed != 0)
            return (WORD)lpbi->biClrUsed;
        bits = lpbi->biBitCount;
    }
    else
        bits = lpbc->bcBitCount;

    switch (bits){
        case 1:
                return 2;
        case 4:
                return 16;
        case 8:
                return 256;
```

continues

Listing 4.3. continued

```
             default:
                      /* A 24 BitCount DIB has no color table */
                      return 0;
      }
}
/**************************
 * DibFromBitmap()
 *    Creates a global memory block in the DIB format that's converted
 *    from the DDB that's passed in.
 *
 * Returns:
 *    A handle to the memory block containing the DIB
 *
 * Args: (See function list)
 */


    HANDLE
DibFromBitmap (HBITMAP       hbm,      /* Handle to the (DDB) bitmap */
                DWORD        biStyle,  /* Palette style to create */
                WORD         biBits,   /* Total bits used (if 0, calculated) */
                HPALETTE     hpal)     /* Handle to palette (if 0, use default) */
{
    BITMAP                bm;
    BITMAPINFOHEADER      bi;
    BITMAPINFOHEADER FAR *lpbi;
    DWORD                 dwLen;
    HANDLE                hdib;
    HANDLE                h;
    HDC                   hdc;

    HPALETTE              savePal;

    int                   dibReturn;

    /*-------------------------------------------------*/

    if (!hbm)            // No bitmap, punt.
    {
         return NULL;
    }

    if (hpal == NULL)    // No palette, use a default one
    {
```

206

```
        hpal = GetStockObject(DEFAULT_PALETTE);
}

// Get information about the bitmap

GetObject(hbm, sizeof(bm), (LPSTR)&bm);

// If no size passed in, figure it out

if (biBits == 0)
    biBits = bm.bmPlanes * bm.bmBitsPixel;

bi.biSize            = sizeof(BITMAPINFOHEADER);
bi.biWidth           = bm.bmWidth;
bi.biHeight          = bm.bmHeight;
bi.biPlanes          = 1;
bi.biBitCount        = biBits;
bi.biCompression     = biStyle;
bi.biSizeImage       = 0;
bi.biXPelsPerMeter   = 0;
bi.biYPelsPerMeter   = 0;
bi.biClrUsed         = 0;
bi.biClrImportant    = 0;

dwLen = bi.biSize + PaletteSize(&bi);

hdc = GetDC(NULL);
savePal = SelectPalette(hdc,hpal,FALSE);

RealizePalette(hdc);    // Force GDI to remap palette

hdib = GlobalAlloc(GHND,dwLen);

if (!hdib)
{
    SelectPalette(hdc,savePal,FALSE);
    ReleaseDC(NULL,hdc);
    return NULL;
}

lpbi = (HPBITMAPINFOHEADER)GlobalLock(hdib);

*lpbi = bi;

/* Call GetDIBits with a NULL lpBits param, so it will calculate the
```

continues

Listing 4.3. continued

```
    * biSizeImage field for you
    */

GetDIBits(hdc,
        hbm,
        0,
        (WORD)bi.biHeight,
        NULL,
        (HPBITMAPINFO)lpbi,
        DIB_RGB_COLORS);

bi = *lpbi;
GlobalUnlock(hdib);

/* If the driver did not fill in the biSizeImage field,
 * make one up
 */

if (bi.biSizeImage == 0)
{
    bi.biSizeImage = WIDTHBYTES((DWORD)bm.bmWidth * biBits) * bm.bmHeight;

    if (biStyle != BI_RGB)
        bi.biSizeImage = (bi.biSizeImage * 3) / 2;
}

/* realloc the buffer big enough to hold all the bits */

dwLen = bi.biSize + PaletteSize(&bi) + bi.biSizeImage;

if (h = GlobalReAlloc(hdib,dwLen,0))
{
    hdib = h;
}
else
{
    GlobalFree(hdib);
    hdib = NULL;

    SelectPalette(hdc,savePal,FALSE);
    ReleaseDC(NULL,hdc);
    return hdib;
}
```

```
        /* Call GetDIBits with a NON-NULL lpBits param, and actually get the
         * bits this time
         */

        lpbi = (HPBITMAPINFOHEADER)GlobalLock(hdib);

        dibReturn = GetDIBits(hdc,
                                hbm,
                                0,
                                (WORD)bi.biHeight,
                                (LPSTR)lpbi + (WORD)lpbi->biSize +
                                PaletteSize(lpbi),
                                (HPBITMAPINFO)lpbi,
                                DIB_RGB_COLORS);

        if (dibReturn == 0)
        {
                GlobalUnlock(hdib);
                hdib = NULL;
                SelectPalette(hdc,savePal,FALSE);
                ReleaseDC(NULL,hdc);
                return NULL;
        }

        bi = *lpbi;
        GlobalUnlock(hdib);

        SelectPalette(hdc,savePal,FALSE);
        ReleaseDC(NULL,hdc);

        return hdib;
}
/*********************
 * BitmapFromDib()
 *    Given a memory DIB, this will create a DDB based on it.
 *    This is actually a tricky little routine, because it uses
 *    the CreateDIBitmap call, which will convert on the fly the DIB
 *    colors to the DDB colors.
 *
 * Returns:
 *    A handle to the DDB created (or NULL)
 *
 * Args: (See function list)
 */
```

continues

209

Listing 4.3. continued

```c
    HBITMAP
BitmapFromDib (HANDLE      hdib,    // Handle of mem block containing DIB
               HPALETTE    hpal)    // Palette to use in creating DDB
{
    HPBITMAPINFOHEADER    lpbi;
    HPALETTE              hpalT;
    HDC           hdc;
    HBITMAP               hbm;

    //--------------------

    if (!hdib)                  // No handle to memory, punt
        return NULL;

    // Lock memory block containing DIB

    lpbi = (HPBITMAPINFOHEADER)GlobalLock(hdib);

    if (!lpbi)
        return NULL;

    // Get a screen DC...

    hdc = GetDC(NULL);

    if (hpal)
    {
        // If they've passed in a palette, you need
        // to select it in here, and make GDI use
        // it. We also need to save the old palette
        // so you can stick it back.

        hpalT = SelectPalette ( hdc,
                                hpal,
                                FALSE);

        RealizePalette(hdc);
    }

    hbm = CreateDIBitmap(hdc,
                (HPBITMAPINFOHEADER)lpbi,
                    (LONG)CBM_INIT,
                (LPSTR)lpbi + lpbi->biSize + PaletteSize(lpbi),
                (HPBITMAPINFO)lpbi,
                    DIB_RGB_COLORS );
```

```
        // If they had a palette, make sure to
        // put the old one back.

        if (hpal)
        {
            SelectPalette(hdc,
                          hpalT,
                          FALSE);
        }

        // Give back the DC, unlock, and go home

        ReleaseDC(NULL,
                  hdc);

        GlobalUnlock(hdib);

        return hbm;    // Return handle to the bitmap
}


/************************
 * DrawBitmap()
 *     Draws the requested bitmap at the desired
 *     location in the DC, using the raster op indicated.
 */

        BOOL
DrawBitmap (HDC            hDC,            /* Destination DC */
            int            x,              /* X offset */
            int            y,              /* Y offset */
            HBITMAP        hbm,            /* Handle to source bitmap */
            DWORD          rop)            /* Raster OP to perform */
{
    HDC            hMemoryDC;
    BITMAP         bm;
    BOOL           f;
    HBITMAP        bmHand;

    /*--------------------------*/

    if (!hDC || !hbm)        /* If either handle is bad, punt */
        return FALSE;

    /* Before you can blit the bitmap, it has to be selected into a device
     * context compatible with the destination. So first, you need
```

continues

Listing 4.3. continued

```
      * to create the compatible DC.
      */

    hMemoryDC = CreateCompatibleDC(hDC);

    /* Select desired bitmap into the memory DC you just created.
     * Also remember the old bitmap handle that used to be in the
     * DC, so that you can restore it after you're done.
     */

    bmHand = SelectObject(hMemoryDC,
                              hbm);

    /* Get information about the bitmap, so that you can blit it properly. */

    GetObject(hbm,
              sizeof(BITMAP),
              (LPSTR)&bm);

    /* Everything's set up--you can now blit the image into the destination
     * DC.
     */

    f = BitBlt(hDC,                 /* Destination DC */
               x,                   /* Destination x offset (if any) */
               y,                   /* Destination y offset (if any) */
               bm.bmWidth,          /* Width of source bitmap */
               bm.bmHeight,         /* Height of source bitmap */
               hMemoryDC,           /* Source DC */
               0,                   /* Source x offset (none) */
               0,                   /* Source y offset (none) */
               SRCCOPY);            /* Copy the bitmap... */

    /* Now select the old bitmap handle back into the memory DC.
     * (Failure to do this will cause a small piece of Windows resource
     * to be lost until reboot time.)
     */

    SelectObject(hMemoryDC,
                    bmHand);

    /* Delete the memory DC so that you're not using up system resources. */

    DeleteDC(hMemoryDC);
```

```
        /* Return status of the BitBlt() call. */

    return f;
}
/*************************
 * DibBlt()
 *    Basically the same thing as BitBlt, but for DIBs.
 */

    BOOL
DibBlt (HDC       hdc,              // Destination DC
        int       x0,               // Upper-left corner, x
        int       y0,               // Upper-left corner, y
        int       dx,               // X extent of rectangle
        int       dy,               // Y extent of rectangle
        HANDLE    hdib,             // Handle to the DIB to draw
        int       x1,               // X offset within DIB
        int       y1,               // Y offset within DIB
        LONG      rop)              // Raster op to use
{
    HPBITMAPINFOHEADER      lpbi;

    LPSTR                   pBuf;

    /*-------------------------------*/

    if (!hdib)
        return PatBlt(hdc,x0,y0,dx,dy,rop);

    lpbi = (HPBITMAPINFOHEADER)GlobalLock(hdib);

    if (!lpbi)
        return FALSE;

    pBuf = (LPSTR)lpbi + (WORD)lpbi->biSize + PaletteSize(lpbi);

    SetDIBitsToDevice (hdc, x0, y0, dx, dy,
                       x1,y1,
                       x1,
                       dy,
                       pBuf,
                       (HPBITMAPINFO)lpbi,
                       DIB_RGB_COLORS );
```

continues

213

Listing 4.3. continued

```
    GlobalUnlock(hdib);
    return TRUE;
}
/*****************************
 * StretchDibBlt()
 *    Basically the same thing as StretchBlt(), but for DIBs.
 *    This code is a wrapper on the StretchDIBits() function; it takes
 *    care of locking the memory block that the DIB is in, and figuring
 *    out where the bits of the DIB are.
 */

    BOOL
StretchDibBlt (HDC       hdc,          // Destination DC
              int       x,            // Upper-left corner, x
              int       y,            // Upper-left corner, y
              int       dx,           // X extent of dest rectangle
              int       dy,           // Y extent of dest rectangle
              HANDLE    hdib,         // Handle to the DIB
              int       x0,           // LOWER-left corner of DIB, x
              int       y0,           // LOWER-left corner of DIB, y
              int       dx0,          // X extent of source rect in DIB
              int       dy0,          // Y extent of source rect in DIB
              LONG      rop)          // Raster op to perform.
{
    HPBITMAPINFOHEADER lpbi;
    LPSTR       pBuf;
    BOOL        f;

    //----------------------------

    if (!hdib) // If no DIB, punt.
        return FALSE;

    // Lock down DIB

    lpbi = (HPBITMAPINFOHEADER)GlobalLock(hdib);

    if (!lpbi)              // Punt on lock failure
        return FALSE;

    // Get address of the bits...

    pBuf = (LPSTR)lpbi + (WORD)lpbi->biSize + PaletteSize(lpbi);
```

```
    // Blit the DIB...

    f = StretchDIBits ( hdc,
                            x, y,
                            dx, dy,
                            x0, y0,
                            dx0, dy0,
                            pBuf, (HPBITMAPINFO)lpbi,
                            DIB_RGB_COLORS,
                            rop);

    // Unlock, and go home.

    GlobalUnlock(hdib);
    return f;
}


/********************
 *  FUNCTION    : lread(int fh, VOID FAR *pv, DWORD ul)
 *
 *  PURPOSE     : Reads data in steps of 32K until all the data has been read.
 *
 *  RETURNS     : 0 - If read did not proceed correctly.
 *                number of bytes read otherwise.
 */

    DWORD PASCAL
lread (int fh, VOID FAR *pv, DWORD ul)
{
    DWORD    ulT = ul;
    BYTE huge *hp = (BYTE huge *)pv;

    while (ul > (DWORD)MAXREAD) {
        if (_lread(fh, (LPSTR)hp, (WORD)MAXREAD) != MAXREAD)
                return 0;
        ul -= MAXREAD;
        hp += MAXREAD;
    }
    if (_lread(fh, (LPSTR)hp, (WORD)ul) != (WORD)ul)
        return 0;
    return ulT;
}


/*************
 *  FUNCTION    : lwrite(int fh, VOID FAR *pv, DWORD ul)
```

continues

Listing 4.3. continued

```
 *
 *  PURPOSE    : Writes data in steps of 32K until all the data is written.
 *
 *  RETURNS    : 0 - If write did not proceed correctly.
 *               number of bytes written otherwise.
 */

    DWORD PASCAL
lwrite (int fh, VOID FAR *pv, DWORD ul)
{
    DWORD     ulT = ul;
    BYTE huge *hp = (BYTE huge *)pv;

    while (ul > MAXREAD) {
        if (_lwrite(fh, (LPSTR)hp, (WORD)MAXREAD) != MAXREAD)
                return 0;
        ul -= MAXREAD;
        hp += MAXREAD;
    }
    if (_lwrite(fh, (LPSTR)hp, (WORD)ul) != (WORD)ul)
        return 0;
    return ulT;
}
/***********************************
 * SeekDouble()
 *    This routine is a wrapper on top of _llseek,
 *    since _llseek can't handle large seek values.
 *
 * Returns:
 *    Number of bytes seeked, or 0 if error.
 *
 * Assumptions:
 *    None, really.
 */

    DWORD FAR PASCAL
SeekDouble(HWND          hWnd,              /* Window handle */
           unsigned      fh,                /* File handle */
           DWORD offset,             /* Amount to seek */
           int           seekStyle)         /* Position to seek from */
{
    DWORD         localOffset;

    LONG  seekResult;
```

```
    LONG   seekVal;

    LONG   runningTotal;

    /*---------------------*/

    /* If no seek, then simply return */

    if (offset == 0)
    {
        return 1;
    }

    /* Size chunk to seek by... */

    seekVal = 0x3FFF;

    /* Now seek in 64K chunks, until you're done. */

    /* If offset is less than 64K, only seek the offset
     * amount and return
     */

    if (offset < (DWORD)seekVal)
    {
        seekResult = _llseek(fh,
                                offset,
                                seekStyle);

        if (seekResult == -1)
        {
            MessageBox ( NULL,
                            "Cannot seek to requested point in file",
                            "Internal error",
                            MB_OK );
            return 0;
        }
        else
            return seekResult;
    }

    /* Offset chunk is bigger than 64K, so break it up into pieces. */

    else
    {
```

continues

Listing 4.3. continued

```
        /* Init count of how many bytes you're offset by. */

        runningTotal = 0;

        /* Seek the first chunk using the requested seek style.
         * All subsequent seeks are going to be SEEK_CURRENT.
         */

        seekResult = _llseek(fh,
                                seekVal,
                                seekStyle);

        if (seekResult == -1)
        {
            MessageBox ( NULL,
                            "Cannot seek to requested point in file",
                            "Internal error",
                            MB_OK );
            return 0;
        }
        else if (seekResult != seekVal)
        {
            MessageBox ( NULL,
                            "Cannot seek to requested point in file",
                            "Internal error",
                            MB_OK );
            return 0;
        }

        /* Now seek the remaining distance... */

        localOffset = offset - seekVal;

        runningTotal += seekVal;

        while (localOffset > 0)
        {
            if (localOffset >= (DWORD)seekVal)
            {
                /* Update running total of # of bytes offset. */

                runningTotal += seekVal;

                /* Attempt to seek another chunk's worth... */
```

```
        seekResult = _llseek(fh,
                              seekVal,
                              SEEK_CUR);
    /* Seek failure? */

    if (seekResult == -1)
    {
        MessageBox ( NULL,
                     "Cannot seek to requested point in file",
                     "Internal error",
                     MB_OK );

        return 0;
    }

    /* Are you where you should be? */

    else if (seekResult != runningTotal)
    {
        MessageBox ( NULL,
                     "Cannot seek to requested point in file",
                     "Internal error",
                     MB_OK );
        return 0;
    }
    else
    {
        localOffset -= seekVal;

        if (localOffset == 0)
            return offset;
    }
}
else
{
    seekResult = _llseek(fh,
                          localOffset,
                          SEEK_CUR);
    if (seekResult == -1)
    {
        MessageBox ( NULL,
                     "Cannot seek to requested point in file",
                     "Internal error",
                     MB_OK );
        return 0;
```

continues

Listing 4.3. continued

```
                    }
                    else if (seekResult != (LONG)offset)
                    {
                        MessageBox ( NULL,
                                     "Cannot seek to requested point in file",
                                     "Internal error",
                                     MB_OK );
                        return 0;
                    }
                    else
                        return offset;
            }
        }
    }

    return 0;
}
/*****************************
 * RewindFile()
 *    Rewinds a file handle to the beginning of the file.
 *    SHOULDN'T be necessary, but...
 *
 * Returns:
 *    TRUE - OK
 *    FALSE - not OK
 *
 * Assumptions:
 *    File is open.
 */

    BOOL FAR PASCAL
RewindFile(HWND           hWnd,
           unsigned       fh)
{
    LONG  seekVal;

    /*-------------------------*/

    seekVal = _llseek(fh,
                      (LONG)0,
                      SEEK_SET);

    if (seekVal != 0)
    {
```

```
        MessageBox ( NULL,
                     "Cannot rewind file",
                     "Internal error",
                     MB_OK );

        return FALSE;
    }

    return TRUE;
}

POINT
GetDIBSize(void)
{
    BITMAPINFOHEADER        bi;

    POINT          pt;

    //------------

    DibInfo(globalDIBHnd,
            &bi);


}
```

Listing 4.4. DIBS.H—header file for DibShow.

```
// DIBS.H
//
// Header file for DIBS.C
//
// Written by Alex Leavens, for ShadowCat Technologies

/* Internal definition for program */
#ifndef HPBITMAPINFOHEADER
#define HPBITMAPINFOHEADER LPBITMAPINFOHEADER
#endif
#ifndef HPBITMAPINFO
#define HPBITMAPINFO LPBITMAPINFO
#endif
```

continues

Listing 4.4. continued

```
/* Flags for _lseek */
#define   SEEK_CUR 1
#define   SEEK_END 2
#define   SEEK_SET 0


/* Header signatures for various resources */
#define BFT_ICON    0x4349    /* "IC" */
#define BFT_BITMAP 0x4d42     /* "BM" */
#define BFT_CURSOR 0x5450     /* "PT" */


/* Macro to determine if resource is a DIB */
#define ISDIB(bft) ((bft) == BFT_BITMAP)


/* Macro to align given value to the closest DWORD (unsigned long) */
#define ALIGNULONG(i)      ((i+3)/4*4)


/* Macro to determine to round off the given value to the closest byte */
#define WIDTHBYTES(i)      ((i+31)/32*4)


#define PALVERSION        0x300
#define MAXPALETTE        256        /* Max. # supported palette entries */


#define MAXREAD   32768                   /* Number of bytes to be read  */
                                          /* during each read operation. */
```

Listing 4.5. FILEDLG.C—file handling routines for the DibShow App.

```
/* FILEDLG.C
 *
 * This module contains routines which handle the common
 * file dialogs for the new Windows 3.1 file dialogs.
 *
 * Written by Alex Leavens, for ShadowCat Technologies
 */

#include <WINDOWS.H>

#include "dibshow.h"
#include "dibs.h"
#include "filedlg.h"

#include "externs.h"
```

```
/*********************************************************************
 *
 *                   FILEOPEN/FILESAVE VARIABLES
 *
 *-------------------------------------------------------------*/

   LPFOCHUNK lpFOChunk;     //Pointer to File Open block
   LPFSCHUNK lpFSChunk;     //Pointer to File Save block

   HANDLE    hfoChunk;      //Handle to File Open block of memory
   HANDLE    hfsChunk;      //Handle to File Save block of memory

char              dibBuffer[256];
char              dibFilter[256] = "DIB Bitmaps¦*.bmp¦¦";

/**********************************************************************
 *  Function:  FormatFilterString(void)                              *
 *                                                                   *
 *   Purpose:  To initialize the gszFilter variable with strings from *
 *             the string table. This method of initializing gszBuffer *
 *             is necessary to ensure that the strings are contiguous  *
 *             in memory--which is what COMMDLG.DLL requires.         *
 *                                                                   *
 *   Returns:  BOOL  TRUE if successful, FALSE if failure loading string *
 *                                                                   *
 *  Comments:  The string loaded from the string table has some wild  *
 *             character in it. This wild character is then replaced   *
 *             with NULL. Note that the wild char can be any unique    *
 *             character the developer chooses, and must be included   *
 *             as the last character of the string. A typical string   *
 *             might look like "Write Files(*.WRI)¦*.WRI¦" where ¦ is   *
 *             the wild character in this case. Implementing it this    *
 *             way also ensures the string is doubly NULL terminated,   *
 *             which is also a requirement of this lovely string.      *
 *                                                                   *
 *   History:  Date      Reason                                       *
 *             --------  --------------------------------            *
 *             11/19/91  Created                                      *
 **********************************************************************/

   BOOL NEAR
FormatFilterString()
{
   WORD  wCtr;
```

continues

Listing 4.5. continued

```c
    WORD  wStringLen;
    char  chWildChar;

    /*------------------------------------*/

    wCtr = 0;

    chWildChar = '¦';

    while (dibFilter[wCtr])
    {
        if (dibFilter[wCtr]==chWildChar)
            dibFilter[wCtr]=0;
        wCtr++;
    }

    return(TRUE);
}

/****************************************************************************
 *  Function:  InitializeStruct(WORD, WORD, LPSTR)                         *
 *                                                                        *
 *   Purpose:  To initialize a structure for the current common dialog.   *
 *             This routine is called just before the common-dialogs      *
 *             API is called.                                             *
 *                                                                        *
 *   Returns:  void                                                       *
 *                                                                        *
 *   Comments:                                                            *
 *                                                                        *
 *   History:  Date      Reason                                           *
 *             --------  ----------------------------------               *
 *             10/01/91  Created                                          *
 ****************************************************************************/


    void NEAR
InitializeStruct(WORD      wCommDlgType,   /* Type of dialog (LOAD or SAVE) */
                 LPSTR     lpStruct)
{

    LPFOCHUNK           lpFOChunk;
    LPFSCHUNK           lpFSChunk;
```

```
WORD                wCtr;
HDC                 hDC;

/*-----------------------*/

switch (wCommDlgType)
{
   case IDC_OPENFILE:

      lpFOChunk = (LPFOCHUNK)lpStruct;

      /* Now format the proper file filter and path... */

      FormatFilterString();      /* Format the filter string */

      /* Specify filter for the files (*.ICO, etc.) */

       lpFOChunk->of.lpstrFilter          = dibFilter;

      /* Specify current file name (if any), and
       * current directory.
       */

      lpFOChunk->of.lpstrFile       = dibChunk->szFile;
      lpFOChunk->of.nMaxFile        = (DWORD)sizeof(dibChunk->szFile);
      lpFOChunk->of.lpstrFileTitle  = dibChunk->szFileTitle;

      *(lpFOChunk->szFile)          = 0;
      *(lpFOChunk->szFileTitle)     = 0;
      lpFOChunk->of.lStructSize     = sizeof(OPENFILENAME);
      lpFOChunk->of.hwndOwner       = (HWND)MainhWnd;
      lpFOChunk->of.hInstance       = (HANDLE)NULL;

      lpFOChunk->of.lpstrCustomFilter = (LPSTR)NULL;
      lpFOChunk->of.nMaxCustFilter    = 0L;

      lpFOChunk->of.nMaxFileTitle     = MAXFILETITLELEN;

      lpFOChunk->of.lpstrTitle        = (LPSTR)NULL;
      lpFOChunk->of.Flags             = OFN_HIDEREADONLY |
                                        OFN_PATHMUSTEXIST |
                                        OFN_FILEMUSTEXIST |
                                        OFN_ENABLEHOOK;
      lpFOChunk->of.nFileOffset       = 0;
      lpFOChunk->of.nFileExtension    = 0;
```

continues

Listing 4.5. continued

```
                  lpFOChunk->of.lpstrDefExt        = (LPSTR)NULL;
                  lpFOChunk->of.lCustData          = 0L;
                  lpFOChunk->of.lpfnHook           = (FARPROC)lpfnFileOpenHook;
                  lpFOChunk->of.lpTemplateName     = (LPSTR)NULL;

                  break;

          case IDC_SAVEFILE:

              lpFSChunk = (LPFSCHUNK)lpStruct;

              /* Now format the proper file filter and path... */

              FormatFilterString();        /* Format the filter string */


               lpFSChunk->of.lpstrFilter          = dibFilter;

              /* Specify current file name (if any), and current directory. */

              lpFSChunk->of.lpstrFile           = dibChunk->szFile;
              lpFSChunk->of.nMaxFile            = (DWORD)sizeof(dibChunk->szFile);
              lpFSChunk->of.lpstrFileTitle      = dibChunk->szFileTitle;

              *(lpFSChunk->szFile)              = 0;
              lpFSChunk->of.lStructSize         = sizeof(OPENFILENAME);
              lpFSChunk->of.hwndOwner           = (HWND)MainhWnd;
              lpFSChunk->of.hInstance           = (HANDLE)NULL;

              lpFSChunk->of.lpstrCustomFilter   = (LPSTR)NULL;
              lpFSChunk->of.nMaxCustFilter      = 0L;
   /*         lpFSChunk->of.nFilterIndex        = 1L; */

              lpFSChunk->of.nMaxFileTitle       = MAXFILETITLELEN;

              lpFSChunk->of.lpstrTitle          = (LPSTR)NULL;
              lpFSChunk->of.Flags               = OFN_OVERWRITEPROMPT;
              lpFSChunk->of.nFileOffset         = 0;
              lpFSChunk->of.nFileExtension      = 0;
              lpFSChunk->of.lpstrDefExt         = (LPSTR)NULL;
              lpFSChunk->of.lCustData           = 0L;
              lpFSChunk->of.lpfnHook            = (FARPROC)NULL;
              lpFSChunk->of.lpTemplateName      = (LPSTR)NULL;

              break;
```

```
    default:

        break;

    }

    return;
}

/****************************************************************************
 *  Function:  AllocAndLockMem(HANDLE *, WORD)                              *
 *                                                                         *
 *   Purpose:  To allocate and lock a chunk of memory for the CD           *
 *             structure.                                                  *
 *                                                                         *
 *   Returns:  LPSTR                                                       *
 *                                                                         *
 *  Comments:                                                              *
 *                                                                         *
 *   History:  Date      Reason                                            *
 *             --------   ----------------------------------               *
 *             10/01/91   Created                                          *
 ****************************************************************************/

    LPSTR FAR
AllocAndLockMem(HANDLE    *hChunk,
                WORD      wSize)
{
    LPSTR lpChunk;

    *hChunk = GlobalAlloc(GHND,
                          wSize);

    if (*hChunk)
    {
        lpChunk = GlobalLock(*hChunk);

        if (!lpChunk)
        {
            GlobalFree(*hChunk);

            MessageBox ( NULL,
                         "Can't lock global memory",
                         "",
                         MB_OK );
```

continues

Listing 4.5. continued

```
                lpChunk = NULL;
        }
  }
  else
  {

        MessageBox ( NULL,
                     "Can't get global memory",
                     "",
                     MB_OK );

        lpChunk = NULL;
  }

  return(lpChunk);
}
/***********************************************************************
*  Function:  FileOpenHook(HWND, unsigned, WORD, LONG)                 *
*                                                                      *
*    Purpose:  This function "hooks" the CD GetOpenFileName() procedure *
*              and enables you to process any messages you want. In this *
*              example, the WM_CTLCOLOR message is being processed to   *
*              give the background of the CD a cool color.              *
*                                                                      *
*    Returns:  BOOL                                                     *
*                                                                      *
*  Comments:  This function must be exported and must have an instance *
*              thunk created for it (i.e., call MakeProcInstance; see   *
*              WM_CREATE processing in the main window procedure above) *
*                                                                      *
*    History:  Date       Reason                                       *
*              --------   ----------------------------------           *
*              10/01/91   Created                                       *
***********************************************************************/

   BOOL FAR PASCAL
FileOpenHook(HWND     hDlg,
             unsigned     message,
             WORD         wParam,
             LONG         lParam)
{
  switch (message)
  {
      case WM_INITDIALOG:
```

```
        return  (TRUE);

    case WM_CTLCOLOR:

        break;

    case WM_COMMAND:
        switch(wParam)
            {
                default:
                    break;
            }
        break;

    default:
        break;
    }

  return  (FALSE);
}


/***********************************
 * OpenNativeFile()
 *    Opens a DIB file, and puts the file name in the allocated buffer
 *
 * Returns:
 *    TRUE - file opened and read successfully
 *    FALSE - Punt.
 *
 * Assumptions:
 *    All file info is held in dibChunk...
 */

    BOOL FAR PASCAL
OpenNativeFile(HWND       hWnd,
               unsigned   message,
               WORD       wParam,
               LONG       lParam)
{
    WORD  wSize;

    char titleBuff[256] = "DIB Viewer - ";

    /*-------------------------------*/
```

continues

Listing 4.5. continued

```
wSize=sizeof(FOCHUNK);

InitializeStruct(IDC_OPENFILE,
                  (LPSTR)dibChunk);

/* Do the file selection dialog box, and get the return values
 * from it. Then process stuff...
 */

if ( GetOpenFileName( &(dibChunk->of) ) )
{
    HANDLE   hFile;
    OFSTRUCT ofstruct;

    /*---------------------*/

    // Check to make sure the file exists

    hFile = OpenFile(dibChunk->of.lpstrFile,
                     &ofstruct,
                     OF_EXIST);

    if (hFile != -1)
    {
        if ( globalDIBHnd )
        {
            GlobalFree ( globalDIBHnd );
        }

        globalDIBHnd = OpenDIB ( dibChunk->of.lpstrFile );

        // If file opened OK, set the window title to
        // the file name.

        if ( globalDIBHnd )
        {
            lstrcat ( titleBuff,
                      dibChunk->of.lpstrFile );

            SetWindowText ( MainhWnd,
                            titleBuff );
        }
    }
    else
```

```
            {
                MessageBox ( NULL,
                                "Cannot open file",
                                "",
                                MB_OK );
            }
        }


        /* User hit cancel, so don't do anything here... */

        else
        {
            /* User cancel or whatever. Punt, basically. */
        }

        return TRUE;
}


/**********************************
 * SaveNativeFile()
 *     Handles saving DIB files
 *
 * Returns:
 *     TRUE - file opened and read successfully
 *     FALSE - Punt.
 *
 * Assumptions:
 *     All file info is held in dibChunk...
 */

    BOOL FAR PASCAL
SaveNativeFile(HWND         hWnd,
                unsigned     message,
                WORD         wParam,
                LONG         lParam)
{
    WORD   wSize;

    /*-------------------------------*/

    wSize=sizeof(FOCHUNK);

    InitializeStruct(IDC_SAVEFILE,
                        (LPSTR)dibChunk);
```

continues

Listing 4.5. continued

```
/* Get file name to save under (and type, as well),
 * and do it.
 */

if ( GetSaveFileName( &(dibChunk->of) ) )
{
    HBITMAP         ddbBmp;           // Handle to DDB bitmap
    HANDLE          dibFromBitmap;    // Handle to new DIB bitmap

    //-------------------------------

    // Create a DDB bitmap from the DIB

    ddbBmp = BitmapFromDib ( globalDIBHnd,
                                NULL );

    // If the bitmap created OK, then create a new
    // DIB from this DDB

    if ( ddbBmp )
    {
        dibFromBitmap = DibFromBitmap ( ddbBmp,
                                            BI_RGB,
                                            0,
                                            0 );

        // If the new DIB was created
        // OK, then write it out...

        if ( dibFromBitmap )
        {
            WriteDIB ( dibChunk->of.lpstrFile,
                        dibFromBitmap );

            GlobalFree ( dibFromBitmap );
        }

        DeleteObject ( ddbBmp );
    }
}

/* User hit cancel, so don't do anything here... */

else
{
```

```
        /* User cancel or whatever. Punt, basically. */
    }

    return TRUE;
}
```

Listing 4.6. FILEDLG.H—header file for DibShow.

```
/* FILEDLG.H
 *
 * Data structs and stuff for supporting the file open dialog stuff...
 */

#ifndef FILE_DIALOGS

#define FILE_DIALOGS

#include <commdlg.h>

/*---------------------------------------------*/


#define IDC_OPENFILE          1
#define IDC_SAVEFILE          2
#define IDC_FIND              3
#define IDC_FINDREPLACE       4
#define IDC_COLORS            5
#define IDC_FONT              6
#define IDC_PRINTDLG          7

#define IDC_ALLOCFAIL         1
#define IDC_LOCKFAIL          2
#define IDC_LOADSTRINGFAIL    3

#define IDC_HELPMSG           2000
#define IDC_FINDREPLACEMSG    2001

#define MAXFILTERBUF          256

#define MAXFILETITLELEN       256
#define MAXFILENAMELEN        256
#define MAXFINDWHATLEN        64
#define MAXREPLACEWITHLEN     64
```

continues

Listing 4.6. continued

```
#define MAXFINDDIRECTIONLEN    24
#define MAXFINDCASELEN         24
#define MAXFINDWORDLEN         26


/*****************************************************************************
*                         FILE OPEN STRUCTURE                               *
*****************************************************************************/

typedef struct tagFOCHUNK
{
     OPENFILENAME of;
     char szFile[MAXFILENAMELEN];
     char szFileTitle[MAXFILETITLELEN];
}
FOCHUNK;

typedef FOCHUNK FAR *LPFOCHUNK;            /* Chunk pointer for reading files */

typedef FOCHUNK FAR *LPFSCHUNK;        /* Chunk pointer for writing files */


#endif
```

Listing 4.7. DIBSHOW—makefile for the DibShow App.

```
#File name: DIBSHOW
#"DIBSHOW" Generated by WindowsMAKER Professional
#Author: Alex Leavens, for ShadowCat Technologies

#comp= /c /AS /Os /Gsw /Zpe /D _WINDOWS /W2
comp= /c /AS /Od /Gw /Zpei /D _WINDOWS /W2


ALL : DIBSHOW.EXE

DIBSHOW.RES : DIBSHOW.RC DIBSHOW.H
    rc -r DIBSHOW.RC

DIBSHOW.OBJ : DIBSHOW.C DIBSHOW.WMC DIBSHOW.H  DIBS.H
    cl  $(comp) DIBSHOW.C

DIBS.OBJ: DIBS.C DIBS.H
    cl $(comp) DIBS.C
```

```
FILEDLG.OBJ: FILEDLG.C FILEDLG.H
    cl $(comp) FILEDLG.C


DIBSHOW.EXE : DIBSHOW.OBJ DIBS.OBJ FILEDLG.OBJ DIBSHOW.DEF DIBSHOW.RES
    LINK @DIBSHOW.LNK
    rc DIBSHOW.RES
```

Listing 4.8. DIBSHOW.DEF—module definition file for the DibShow App.

```
;File name: DIBSHOW.DEF
;"DIBSHOW" Generated by WindowsMAKER Professional
;Author: Alex Leavens, for ShadowCat Technologies


NAME        DIBSHOW
DESCRIPTION 'DIBSHOW generated by WindowsMAKER Professional'
EXETYPE     WINDOWS
STUB        'WINSTUB.EXE'
DATA        MOVEABLE MULTIPLE
CODE        MOVEABLE DISCARDABLE PRELOAD
HEAPSIZE    1024
STACKSIZE   5120
EXPORTS

            BLDMainWndProc
```

Listing 4.9. DIBSHOW.LNK—link file for the DibShow App.

```
DIBSHOW DIBS FILEDLG ,DIBSHOW.EXE ,/align:16 /NOD /map
/CO   , LIBW SLIBCEW COMMDLG, DIBSHOW.DEF
```

Listing 4.10. DIBSHOW.RC—resource file for the DibShow App.

```
/*File name: DIBSHOW.RC                                    */
/*"DIBSHOW" Generated by WindowsMAKER Professional         */
/*Author: Alex Leavens, for ShadowCat Technologies         */


#define THISISBLDRC
```

continuos

Listing 4.10. continued

```
#include <WINDOWS.H>
#include "DIBSHOW.H"


/*********************************************************/
/*              Resource code for menus                 */
/*********************************************************/


DIBSHOW MENU
    BEGIN
    POPUP "&File"
        BEGIN
            MENUITEM  "&Open", IDM_Open
            MENUITEM  "&Save", IDM_Save
        END
    END


/*********************************************************/
/*      Resource code for error message strings         */
/*********************************************************/


STRINGTABLE
    BEGIN
        BLD_CannotRun          "Cannot run "
        BLD_CannotCreate       "Cannot create dialog box "
        BLD_CannotLoadMenu     "Cannot load menu "
        BLD_CannotLoadIcon     "Cannot load icon "
        BLD_CannotLoadBitmap   "Cannot load bitmap "
    END
```

Listing 4.11. EXTERNS.H—external definitions for the DibShow App.

```
// Externs.h - external define file
//
// Written by Alex Leavens, for ShadowCat Technologies

// Variable definitions

#define EXTERN extern;

EXTERN   LPFOCHUNK      dibChunk;          /* Pointer to DIB file chunk */
EXTERN   FARPROC        lpfnFileOpenHook;  /* Hook for open file dialog */
```

```
EXTERN    HANDLE              globalDIBHnd;      /* Handle to global DIB */
EXTERN    HANDLE              dibFChunkHand;     /* Handle to DIB file chunk */

// Function definitions

EXTERN    HANDLE              OpenDIB(LPSTR);
EXTERN    HANDLE WINAPI       ReadDIBBits (unsigned, HANDLE);
EXTERN    BOOL                WriteDIB(LPSTR, HANDLE);
EXTERN    BOOL                DibInfo(HANDLE, HPBITMAPINFOHEADER);
EXTERN    HANDLE              ReadDibBitmapInfo ( int);
EXTERN    WORD                PaletteSize(VOID FAR *);
EXTERN    WORD                DibNumColors(VOID FAR *);
EXTERN    HANDLE              DibFromBitmap(HBITMAP, DWORD, WORD, HPALETTE);
EXTERN    HBITMAP             BitmapFromDib(HANDLE, HPALETTE);
EXTERN    BOOL                DrawBitmap(HDC, int, int, HBITMAP, DWORD);
EXTERN    BOOL                DibBlt(HDC, int, int, int, int, HANDLE, int,
                                     int, LONG);
EXTERN    BOOL                StretchDibBlt(HDC, int, int, int, int, HANDLE,
                                            int, int, int, int, LONG);
EXTERN    DWORD PASCAL        lread(int, VOID FAR *, DWORD);
EXTERN    DWORD PASCAL        lwrite(int, VOID FAR *, DWORD);
EXTERN    DWORD FAR PASCAL    SeekDouble(HWND, unsigned, DWORD, int);
EXTERN    BOOL FAR PASCAL     RewindFile(HWND, unsigned);
EXTERN    BOOL NEAR           FormatFilterString(void);
EXTERN    void NEAR           InitializeStruct(WORD, LPSTR);
EXTERN    LPSTR FAR           AllocAndLockMem(HANDLE *,WORD);
EXTERN    BOOL FAR PASCAL     OpenNativeFile(HWND, unsigned, WORD, LONG);
EXTERN    BOOL FAR PASCAL     SaveNativeFile(HWND, unsigned, WORD, LONG);
```

Figure 4.2 shows the DibShow App in action.

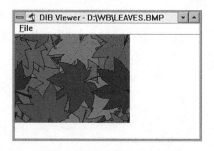

Figure 4.2.
The DibShow
App in action.

Looking at the DibShow App

There's quite a bit going on in the DibShow App, not least of which is the appearance of the new Windows 3.1 common dialog boxes. This is a big change from Windows 3.0 (which didn't have them). These common dialog boxes provide a convenient method of getting file names without your having to write your own file dialog box. If you're running Windows 3.0, you need to copy the commdlg.dll file to your /Windows/system directory.

There are also two menu entries in the DibShow App—one for **File O**pen, and one for **File S**ave. These two menu entries are what trigger all the action. When you hit **File O**pen, it fires off the Open File common dialog box. After that returns, the program tries to open the DIB file you entered. If it's successful, it replaces the old global DIB handle `globalDIBHnd` with a handle to the new DIB that has just been loaded. At this point, you don't have a DDB (memory bitmap) of the image, you just have a handle to the DIB.

To repaint the screen from this DIB, use the routine `DibBlt()`, which is explained in detail later. It performs essentially the same function as **BitBlt()**, but works on DIBs and not on DDBs, the way **BitBlt()** does.

Finally, to save the image, take the DIB, make a memory bitmap (DDB) out of it, and then turn right around and make a new DIB from that memory bitmap, which you then write to disk. Boy, talk about taking the long way around! If you're curious why I didn't just write out the first DIB that I had, it's simple — I wanted to demonstrate how to transform a DIB into a DDB, and then back again.

Now that you've had a brief overview of the structure of the program, look at the routines that are really at the heart of your app.

OpenDIB()

This function basically serves as a wrapper for the functions `ReadDibBitmapInfo()` and `ReadDIBBits()`. Given a file handle, which in this case you got with the Windows 3.1 common File Open dialog box, this routine opens that file, after first checking to see whether the file exists. If the file doesn't exist, it posts an error. Then this routine reads the DIB information about that file into a memory block. Next, it reads the actual bits of the DIB, based on the information it retrieved from the header. After it's done with all this, it returns the handle to the DIB it loaded into memory.

ReadDIBBits()

This routine actually reads the bits of a DIB from a disk file. The first thing it does is find out how big the DIB is, based on its header information. This implies that this information has already been provided (read in somewhere else), which is what the function ReadDibBitmapInfo() does. Next, this routine tries to reallocate the memory block (that's currently holding only the header information) big enough so that it can hold the header, the palette, *and* the bits. If this is successful, the routine locks the memory block and reads the bits of the DIB into that memory block.

WriteDIB()

This routine is very straightforward. Basically, all it does is take an *already-created* DIB in memory and put it to a disk file. Note that I emphasized already-created DIBs, because this routine doesn't create a memory DIB for writing to a disk. That functionality is implemented by the routine DibFromBitmap(). The only vaguely tricky thing here is that this routine creates a file header block for the DIB (a BITMAPFILEHEADER block) based on the DIB, and writes that to disk first, before actually writing the DIB itself.

The other interesting thing is that this routine checks to see whether all the size pieces of the DIB (the biSizeImage field, the biSize field, and the size of the palette) have valid values in them. If they do, it uses those values to determine how many bytes to write to disk. Otherwise, it just uses the size of the memory block.

DibInfo()

This routine returns the header information of a DIB into the BITMAPINFOHEADER struct pointed to by the second parameter. Most of the routines are error checks, simply to make sure you have a valid handle, and so on. After all the validation has been taken care of, the routine calculates the width (in bytes) of the image and multiplies that by the height—this gives the total size (in bytes) of the image.

The routine also fills in the number of colors that the DIB uses, by calling the DibNumColors() routine. For a discussion of the internals of that routine, see the section titled "DibNumColors()."

ReadDibBitmapInfo()

This routine actually reads in the header information of a DIB from disk. First, it tries to read a BITMAPFILEHEADER from disk. If it can't read at least this much, the file can't possibly be a DIB file, and the routine returns. If it reads enough information, the routine checks to see whether the file is a DIB file, using the ISDIB macro—this is where the file type byte, discussed at the beginning of the chapter, is used.

Next, the routine reads in the header information of the DIB. It assumes that the size of the header is that of a DIB (that is, a BITMAPINFOHEADER struct). It also immediately tests to see whether, in fact, the header is a DIB—if it turns out that the DIB is an OS2/PM-format header, the routine must fill in the appropriate information and move the file pointer backward in the file, because OS2/PM headers are smaller than DIB headers.

This accomplished, the routine then determines the number of colors the DIB is using and reads in the appropriate RGB palette table. Finally, it reseeks the file pointer to the beginning of the image in the file, and it returns.

PaletteSize()

This routine is very straightforward. It figures out the size (in bytes) of the palette of a DIB and returns that value. It does this for both Windows-format (standard) DIBs and OS2/PM-format DIBs. It determines whether the DIB is in Windows or an OS2/PM format by checking the size of the DIB header — if the size is equal to that of a BITMAPCOREHEADER (the OS2/PM equivalent of a BITMAPINFOHEADER). It determines the size of the palette based on RGBTRIPLES (three bytes), the method of storing colors in OS2/PM DIBs. If the size of the header isn't equal to a BITMAPCOREHEADER, it's assumed to be a Windows-format DIB, and it returns the size of the palette based on RGBQUADS (four bytes).

This brings up an important reason for filling in the size of the structure at the beginning of a DIB—it is impossible to know what kind of a DIB the image is without it.

The total size of the palette is finally determined by taking the local variable NumColors and multiplying it by the proper size. NumColors is determined by the routine DibNumColors(), which is discussed next.

DibNumColors()

This routine calculates the number of colors a DIB uses; it does this based on the biClrUsed field of the BITMAPINFOHEADER. In the case of a DIB, if biClrUsed is zero, the number of colors used is the same as the total number of colors for the bitmap. This is determined by the value in biBitCount—2, 16, 256, or 16 million colors, corresponding to a value in biBitCount of 1, 4, 8, or 24, repectively. (As discussed in the section on the BITMAPINFOHEADER, these are the only four legal values for the biBitCount field.)

If the size of the DIB header isn't that of a BITMAPINFOHEADER, the DIB is assumed to be an OS2/PM-format DIB, and the bcBitCount field of an OS2/PM BITMAPCOREHEADER is used to determine the total number of colors of the bitmap.

DibFromBitmap()

This routine is one of the most important of the routines in this module, because it's the one that does the actual conversion work. It isn't clear, however, from examining the header of the routine, that it not only converts a memory bitmap (DDB) into a DIB of the same number of colors, but also converts a memory bitmap into a DIB of any valid number of colors you specify. In other words, you can use this routine to create not only, for example, a 16-color DIB from a 16-color DDB, but also a 16-color DIB from a 256-color DDB, or even a 32,768-color DDB—even a 16 million-color DDB! You can also create any other source and target combination, for that matter, because in creating a DIB you are not limited to the resolution of the current display device.

This is a very powerful capability when you've got the hang of it. Look first at the case in which you want to create a DIB of the same number of colors as the current screen resolution.

Although the routine takes four parameters, you really need specify only the first of them, hbm, which is the handle to the memory bitmap. The first thing the routine does is check to make sure you actually have a bitmap, because it wouldn't do much good to try to create a DIB from nothing!

Next, because you're not passing in a palette for the routine to use, it gets a stock palette from the system, using `GetStockObject()`. This routine provides you with a handle to a palette that has the default colors of this display mode in it. (For example, the stock palette of a standard VGA system is the 16 standard VGA colors, black, dark red, dark green, dark blue, and so on up to bright yellow, bright blue, and white.)

After you've gotten a stock palette, you get information about the memory bitmap you're converting, using the `GetObject()` call. (I documented `GetObject()` in Chapter 3, "The Device Dependent Bitmap.") The things you're interested in about the bitmap are its height and width, as well as how many colors it can display at one time.

Next, create a `BITMAPINFOHEADER` that defines the way you want your DIB to look in terms of its height, width, and number of colors. To determine the number of colors the DIB uses, multiply the field `bmPlanes` by `bmBitsPixel`. These are both fields in the `BITMAP` header; you might be surprised to see them simply multiplied together. DIBs always have a plane count of 1, however, which means that the `biBitCount` field actually represents the true number of bits it takes to represent all the colors of the image (1 bit for 2 colors, 4 bits for 16 colors, 8 bits for 256 colors, and 24 bits for 16 million colors). You multiply the two values of the `BITMAP` structure together because a bitmap can be represented in different ways: through a set of bits, all on the same plane, or through a series of bits, spread through multiple planes. It's a device dependent bitmap, which means that you can't rely on its format.

After you calculate the number of colors the DIB holds, fill in the rest of the DIB header. The only fields you're really concerned about are the width and height fields, and the style field, which defines the method of compression (if any) you want the DIB to be created in. If you're compressing the image, it's important to make sure the compression method you choose matches the number of colors in your image. (More on that in a minute.)

Next, calculate how big the DIB is actually going to be. Also get a DC for the display, and select your stock palette into it. Then call the function `RealizePalette()`, which forces Windows to remap the palette into the DC. If you don't do this, the conversion process from the memory bitmap to the DIB won't necessarily be correct. This isn't a problem when you're converting a bitmap to a DIB with the same number of colors; however, when you want to convert a bitmap to a DIB with a different number of colors, this step is very important.

Following this step, allocate enough memory to hold your DIB, and then lock it down. Then make the first of two calls to `GetDIBits()`. The first call is made with the fifth parameter set to NULL, in which case the `GetDIBits()` call only calculates the size of the DIB that results from the parameters you put into the BITMAPINFOHEADER. It puts this value into the header and then returns. Under some circumstances, the `GetDIBits()` routine might not calculate this value, in which case the value in the header is still zero; in this case, you need to calculate it yourself.

After you've gotten the size of the finished set of bits, attempt to reallocate memory to a size that will hold all the pieces (the BITMAPINFOHEADER you've created, the palette, and the bits). This is the format of a file DIB that you write to disk. (See Figure 4.1.)

Now make the second call to `GetDIBits()`, this time with the fifth parameter set to the memory address where you want the routine to put the bits of the image. After the function returns, check the return code to make sure it was successful. If it was, you can unlock the memory handle and return it.

Now that you've created a default DIB, take a look at how you create a DIB that is of a different color format than the current display device. For example, create a 16-color DIB from a 256-color memory bitmap.

First, you need to pass in non-NULL values in the other three parameters of the `DibFromBitmap()` routine. The first of the three (which is the second parameter in the routine, `biStyle`), defines the compression method you want to use. Because you're creating a 16-color DIB, you could choose to set it to be `BI_RLE4`, but to not complicate matters, just leave it as zero. The third parameter to the routine is `biBits`; this is the field that is going to define how many colors your image has. You want a 16-color image, so you pass in a 4 to the routine. This field must be set to one of the allowable values of `biBitCount` in a BITMAPINFOHEADER, so it must be 1, 4, 8, or 24.

You could pass in a NULL for your palette, which means the routine uses a stock palette. However, given that you want to convert from 256 colors to 16, you might want to build a custom palette that more accurately represents the *destination* colors you want to achieve. An important point to note is that the palette selected into the DC that you pass into the `GetDIBits()` function governs what colors appear in your destination DIB. You are, in effect, telling `GetDIBits()`, "Here's the set of colors that you want to map the image to."

The second important point about this is that you don't have to choose a set of 16 colors that corresponds exactly to a set of 16 colors that a display device could render. In other words, you know that the DIB is being mapped to a 16-color palette, and you know that 16-color display devices are usually VGA screens; hence you might assume that the 16 colors you have to map to are the 16 VGA colors. That isn't the case, however. You could create a 16-grey-scale palette, select that into your DC, and have the DIB mapped from 256 colors

to 16 shades of grey. Admittedly, when it comes time to display that image on a VGA display, you could only display 4 shades of grey (black, dark grey, light grey and white), which means that the image would be transformed down again. However, the DIB itself would still have all 16 grey scales internally, and more important, it would be able to display all of those scales on a device that could support it (a 256-color driver, for example). This could prove useful, especially if you wanted to preserve a maximum amount of information in a limited number of colors.

After you've specified the number of colors (and possibly a palette), the routine works identically as before, with two minor changes. If you've specified a bit count (that is, a number of colors), you don't calculate that value based on the DDB you're converting from. And if you specify a nondefault palette, the routine doesn't use a stock palette object.

BitmapFromDib()

This routine performs the conversion in the other direction—from memory DIB (which you've loaded using the OpenDIB() routine) to memory bitmap (DDB). It's significantly simpler than DibFromBitmap(), because it involves less work on your part. Whereas in DibFromBitmap() you could specify the format of the DIB, in this case you can't specify the format of a DDB—it is what it is, and that's that.

One thing you can specify, however, is a nondefault palette. This is useful only if the DIB is stored in DIB_PAL_COLORS mode (that is, the color table of the DIB doesn't specify RGB colors, but indexes into the currently realized palette). Because most real-world bitmaps aren't going to be specified this way, the routine is going to ignore the currently selected palette and do a "best fit" on converting the colors from the DIB into colors in a bitmap the display device can render.

The routine is trivial. You take the handle to the DIB and lock it (failing if either of those actions fail). Then you call the **CreateDIBitmap()** routine, specifying as the third parameter CBM_INIT, which causes the **CreateDIBitmap()** routine to actually fill in the bits of the bitmap. You could also call the routine with this parameter as NULL, in which case you wouldn't get the bits of the bitmap, only the header information for the DDB that would be created: height, width, number of color planes, and so forth. Then you unlock the DIB memory handle and return the handle to the newly created DDB. Simple as that.

DrawBitmap()

This routine provides a handy way of blitting a bitmap (a DDB) onto the screen. It wraps all the actions that you have to do in order to be able to blit a bitmap on-screen. It's also very similar to one of the member functions of the Bitmap class, which I introduced in Chapter 3. In fact, `Bitmap::DisplaySelf()` is virtually identical in behavior to this routine—it creates a compatible DC, selects the bitmap into it, gets the bitmap size, blits the bitmap, selects the bitmap back out, and deletes the compatible DC.

This routine involves a bit more code than the `Bitmap::DisplaySelf()` code, simply because it has to do all the things by hand that the Bitmap and CompatibleDC object classes provide free—automatic initialization at instantiation, and automatic cleanup on deletion. Further, this routine really behaves more like how you would want a Bitmap object (if it were an object) to behave—it simply displays itself and cleans up when it's done instead of having an explicit routine to which you must pass the correct bitmap handle. (There I go again, on my soapbox! <grin>)

DibBlt()

This function provides a quick way of displaying a memory DIB on-screen. It uses the `SetDIBitsToDevice()` routine to accomplish this. `SetDIBitsToDevice()` is the equivalent of `BitBlt()`, but for DIBs. This routine acts as a wrapper on top of that function, providing such services as locking the memory handle of the DIB and calculating the offset to the bits of the image.

StretchDibBlt()

This routine is very similar to the previous one and is the DIB equivalent of `StretchBlt()`. It also provides a way for DIBs to be displayed on the screen, but with the additional functionality of being able to specify a sizing factor that can grow or shrink the DIB. `StretchDibBlt()` uses the `StretchDIBits()` function to accomplish this, and it provides a wrapper on top of the inevitable Lock/Unlock that accompanies global memory handles in Windows 3.0.

The MalleableBitmap Class: Source Code in C++

Given all the behavior of DIBs that I've discussed, it makes sense to encapsulate much of that behavior into an object class, much the same as I did for the base Bitmap class. The new class is the MalleableBitmap class. Derived from the Bitmap class, it performs many of the transformations from DIBs to DDBs as part of its behavior, as well as having the capability of displaying itself on-screen in stretched form.

Because the MalleableBitmap class is derived from the base class Bitmap, it shares more properties with bitmaps (DDBs) than it does with DIBs. That is, you'll note that although there are routines that enable an instance of a MalleableBitmap to render a DIB into itself, there aren't any corresponding routines that let a MalleableBitmap render itself as a DIB. Given the code from the routines in DIBS.C, and this class, can you derive a class which does?

Listings 4.12 through 4.14 show the source code for the MalleableBitmap class.

Listing 4.12. BOOLEAN.H—header file for the MalleableBitmap class.

```
/* BOOLEAN.H
 *
 * Enumerated true/false type
 *
 * Written by Alex Leavens, for ShadowCat Technologies
 *------------------------------------------------------------------------
 */

#ifndef  __BOOLEAN_H

#define  __BOOLEAN_H

/* Logical true/false catagory that's really limited to true/false */

enum    Boolean  {false, true};              // false == 0, true == 1


#endif  // __BOOLEAN_H
```

Listing 4.13. MALLEABL.H—header file for the MalleableBitmap class.

```
// Malleabl.h
//
// Defines for a malleable bitmap class in C++
//
// Written by Alex Leavens, for ShadowCat Technologies

#ifndef __MALLEABLE_BITMAP_H

#define __MALLEABLE_BITMAP_H

#include <windows.h>

#include "boolean.h"

#include "compatdc.h"

#include "bitmap.h"

#ifdef __cplusplus

/*********************************************
 * Class: MalleableBitmap
 *
 * Definition of a MalleableBitmap class,
 * which is a bitmap that knows how to do lots of
 * sophisticated things to itself. (Kinky, eh?)
 */

    class

MalleableBitmap : public Bitmap
{
    public:

        //------------ CONSTRUCTORS ------------

        /*-----------------
         *
         * MalleableBitmap() - Default constructor
         *
         * Returns: Nothing
         *
```

continues

Listing 4.13. continued

```
       * Args: None
       */

      MalleableBitmap ( void ) { SetHandle ( NULL ); }

      /*--------------------
       *
       * MalleableBitmap() - Nondefault constructor
       *
       * Builds a malleable bitmap of the given size,
       * using the specified device context to match to.
       *
       * Returns: Nothing
       *
       * Args: screenDC - screen DC to be made compatible with
       *       xSize - width of the bitmap to create
       *       ySize - height of the bitmap to create
       */

      MalleableBitmap ( HDC      screenDC,
                        WORD    xSize = 1,
                        WORD    ySize = 1 )
      {
          CreateSelfEmpty ( screenDC,
                            xSize,
                            ySize);
      }

      //---------------------------


      /*---------------------
       *
       * ValidateEmptyBitmap()
       *
       * Makes sure that this bitmap doesn't have something
       * already in it.
       *
       * Returns: true - bitmap is empty
       *          false - bitmap is not empty
       *
       * Args: None
       */
```

```
    Boolean
ValidateEmptyBitmap(void);


/*---------------------------------
 *
 * CreateSelfEmpty()
 *
 * Given a screen DC, and a requested
 * x and y size, this routine will create
 * a compatible bitmap of the desired size.
 *
 * Returns: true - bitmap was properly created
 *          false - "Houston, we have a problem"
 *
 * Args: screenDC - screen DC to be made compatible with
 *       xSize - width of the bitmap to create
 *       ySize - height of the bitmap to create
 */

    Boolean
CreateSelfEmpty ( HDC      screenDC,
                  WORD     xSize,
                  WORD     ySize );


/*---------------------------------
 *
 * EraseSelf()
 *
 * This function will cause a malleable bitmap to erase
 * (blank) itself out with whiteness.
 *
 * Returns: Nothing
 *
 * Params: none
 *
 * Assumptions: Sure. Of course.
 */

    void
EraseSelf ( HDC          sourceDC );


/*---------------------------------
 *
 * CopyFromDC()
 *
```

continues

Listing 4.13. continued

```
              * Copies an image from a DC.
              * Uses the requested x and y sizes, and
              * the requested x and y offsets.
              */

              Boolean
          CopyFromDC ( HDC  screenDC,
                         WORD        xSize,
                         WORD        ySize,
                         WORD        xOffset,
                         WORD        yOffset );


      /*--------------------------------
       *
       * WriteBitmapIntoSelf()
       *
       * Given a handle to a bitmap, this
       * function will draw that bitmap into
       * this bitmap.
       */

          Boolean
      WriteBitmapIntoSelf(HDC                   screenDC,
                   HBITMAP        sourceBM);


      /*--------------------------------
       *
       * WriteDIBIntoSelf()
       *
       * Given a handle to a DIB, this function will
       * draw the DIB into the bitmap's internal self.
       */

          Boolean
      WriteDIBIntoSelf(HDC                   screenDC,
                         LPBITMAPINFO   lpBI,
                         LPSTR          lpBits);


      //-----------------------
      //
      // RenderSelfToScreen()
      //
      // Renders the bitmap in the malleable bitmap
      // onto the screen. Uses a DRAWITEMSTRUCT to determine
      // the target location.
```

```
        //
        // xOffset and yOffset determine the offset (if any) from
        // (0,0) that the malleable bitmap will use in drawing itself.
        // I.e., if given (5,5), the MalleableBitmap will draw itself using
        // (5,5) as the source for the upper-left corner, rather than (0,0).

            void
    RenderSelfToScreen ( LPDRAWITEMSTRUCT      lpDrawItem,
                         WORD                  xOffset,
                         WORD                  yOffset );

    //--------------------------
    //
    // CompressSelfToScreen()
    //
    // Displays the bitmap on the screen in compressed form.
    // Uses the current engine size in determining what size to
    // compress the image.

            void
    CompressSelfToScreen ( LPDRAWITEMSTRUCT      lpDrawItem,
                           WORD                  xOffset,
                           WORD                  yOffset );


};

#endif   // __cplusplus

#endif   // __MALLEABLE_BITMAP_H
```

Listing 4.14. MALLEABL.CPP—implementation of member functions of the MalleableBitmap class.

```
// Malleabl.cpp
//
// Member function routines for the malleable
// bitmap object class
//
// Written by Alex Leavens, for ShadowCat Technologies

#include <WINDOWS.H>
#include "SLICE.H"
```

continues

Listing 4.14. continued

```
#define _EXPORT _export

/*---------------------
 *
 * MalleableBitmap::ValidateEmptyBitmap()
 *
 * Makes sure that this bitmap doesn't have something
 * already in it.
 *
 * Returns: true - bitmap was empty
 *          false - bitmap wasn't empty
 *
 * Args: none
 */

    Boolean
MalleableBitmap::ValidateEmptyBitmap(void)
{
    if (GetBitmapHandle() != NULL)
    {
        MessageBox ( NULL,
                     "Bitmap handle is not null",
                     "Malleable bitmap class",
                     MB_OK );

        return false;
    }

    return true;
}
/*------------------------------
 *
 * MalleableBitmap::CreateSelfEmpty()
 *
 * Given a screen DC, and a requested
 * x and y size, this routine will create
 * a compatible bitmap of the desired size.
 *
 * Returns: true/false-success/failure
 */

    Boolean
MalleableBitmap::CreateSelfEmpty ( HDC      screenDC,
                                   WORD  xSize,
                                   WORD  ySize )
```

```
{
    //-------------------

    CompatibleDC  sourceDC ( screenDC );

    // Create a bitmap that the Bits will be put into...

    hBitmap = CreateCompatibleBitmap ( screenDC,
                                            xSize,
                                            ySize );

    // Zero out those bits...

    EraseSelf ( screenDC );
}

/*-------------------------------
 *
 * MalleableBitmap::EraseSelf()
 *
 * This function will cause a malleable bitmap to erase
 * (blank) itself out with whiteness.
 *
 * Returns: Nothing
 *
 * Params: DC to make compatible DC of...
 *
 * Assumptions: Sure. Of course.
 */

    void
MalleableBitmap::EraseSelf ( HDC    sourceDC )
{

    // Make sure that the bitmap is valid before trying
    // to erase it...

    if ( !GetBitmapHandle() )
        return;

    // Create a compatible DC to stick ourselves into

    CompatibleDC  memoryDC( sourceDC,
                                hBitmap );
    // Get the size
```

continues

Listing 4.14. continued

```
    POINT           iSize = GetSize();            // Get size of bitmap

    // Erase the internals by zeroing it out...

    PatBlt ( memoryDC.GetCompatDC(),
             0,
             0,
             iSize.x,
             iSize.y,
             WHITENESS );
}


/*-------------------------------
 *
 * MalleableBitmap::CopyFromDC()
 *
 * Copies an image from a DC.
 * Uses the requested x and y sizes, and
 * the requested x and y offsets.
 */

    Boolean
MalleableBitmap::CopyFromDC ( HDC  screenDC,
                                   WORD      xSize,
                                   WORD      ySize,
                                   WORD      xOffset,
                                   WORD      yOffset )
{
    //----------------------
    //Erase the bitmap ...
    EraseSelf (screenDC);
    //Create a DC for the bitmap to be copied into

    CompatibleDC    destDC ( screenDC,
                                    hBitmap );

    BitBlt ( destDC.GetCompatDC(),
             0,
             0,
             xSize,
             ySize,
             screenDC,
             xOffset,
             yOffset,
             SRCCOPY );
```

```
    return true;
}


/*--------------------------------
 *
 * MalleableBitmap::WriteDIBIntoSelf()
 *
 * Given a handle to a DIB, this function will
 * draw the DIB into the bitmap's internal self.
 *
 * In order for SetDIBits to work right, you
 * have to create the compatible bitmap that you're
 * drawing into using a SCREEN DC (this ensures that
 * you'll get a color bitmap), but use a MEMORY dC
 * for the actual SetDIBits call. (Thanks and a tip
 * of the hatlo hat to Mike Geary for this one! :-))
 *
 * Returns: true/false-success/failure
 */


    Boolean
MalleableBitmap::WriteDIBIntoSelf(HDC                 screenDC,
                                  LPBITMAPINFO   lpBI,
                                  LPSTR          lpBits)
{
    LPBITMAPINFOHEADER    lpBM = (LPBITMAPINFOHEADER)lpBI;

    WORD  imWidth;
    WORD  imHeight;

    /*--------------------*/

    // Make sure that the bitmap handle is empty...

    if (ValidateEmptyBitmap() != true)
        return false;

    // Determine which type of DIB you've got here, a
    // DIB or a COREBMP

    if ( lpBM->biSize == sizeof (BITMAPCOREHEADER) )
    {
        LPBITMAPCOREHEADER lpBC = (LPBITMAPCOREHEADER)lpBI;

        imWidth = lpBC->bcWidth;
```

continues

255

Listing 4.14. continued

```
        imHeight = lpBC->bcHeight;
    }
    else
    {
        imWidth = (WORD)lpBM->biWidth;
        imHeight = (WORD)lpBM->biHeight;
    }

    // Create a compatible MEMORY DC, which you use in the
    // setDIBits call.

    CompatibleDC  memoryDC ( screenDC );

    // Create a bitmap that the Bits will be put into...

    hBitmap = CreateCompatibleBitmap ( screenDC,
                                       imWidth,
                                       imHeight );
    if (!hBitmap)
    {
        MessageBox ( NULL,
                     "Cannot build compatible bitmap",
                     "Malleable bitmap class",
                     MB_OK );
        return false;
    }

    //------------------------
    //
    // Actually set the DI Bits of the image here.
    //
    // NOTE that the compatible bitmap is NOT selected into
    // the device context before doing a setDIBits...

    SetDIBits(memoryDC.GetCompatDC(),           // HDC of source DC
              hBitmap,                           // Handle to bitmap to set
              0,                                 // Starting scan
              imHeight,                          // Height of bitmap
              lpBits,                            // Pointer to image bits
              lpBI,                              // Pointer to DIB Info
              DIB_RGB_COLORS);                   // Use true RGBs from palette

    return true;
}
```

```
/*--------------------------------
 *
 * MalleableBitmap::WriteBitmapIntoSelf()
 *
 * Given a handle to a bitmap, this
 * function will draw that bitmap into
 * this bitmap.
 */

    Boolean
MalleableBitmap::WriteBitmapIntoSelf(HDC        screenDC,
                                     HBITMAP    sourceBM)
{
    /*-----------------------*/

    Bitmap         localBM ( sourceBM );      // Make a copy of the bitmap
                                              // so that you can have your bitmap
                                              // class do its thing

    POINT          sizeBM = localBM.GetSize(); // Get the size of the bitmap...

    // Make sure bitmap doesn't already have something in it...

    if (ValidateEmptyBitmap() != true)
        return false;

    CompatibleDC    sourceMemDC(screenDC,
                                     sourceBM); // Compatible DC for source

    // Now create a bitmap that you can blit into...

    hBitmap = CreateCompatibleBitmap ( screenDC,
                                       sizeBM.x,
                                       sizeBM.y );


    CompatibleDC  destMemDC ( screenDC,
                                     hBitmap );   // Compatible DC for dest

    BitBlt(destMemDC.GetCompatDC(),
           0,
           0,
           sizeBM.x,
```

continues

257

Listing 4.14. continued

```
                sizeBM.y,
                sourceMemDC.GetCompatDC(),
                0,
                0,
                SRCCOPY);

    localBM.SetHandle ( NULL );              // Remove handle from local copy
                                             // of the bitmap; if you leave it
                                             // in there, it'll get clobbered
                                             // when the default destructor gets
                                             // called.
    return true;
}


//-----------------------
//
// MalleableBitmap::RenderSelfToScreen()
//
// Renders the bitmap in the malleable bitmap
// onto the screen. Uses a DRAWITEMSTRUCT to determine
// the target location.
//
// xOffset and yOffset determine the offset (if any) from
// (0,0) that the malleable bitmap will use in drawing itself.
// I.e., if given (5,5), the malleableBitmap will draw itself using
// (5,5) as the source for the upper-left corner, rather than (0,0).

    void
MalleableBitmap::RenderSelfToScreen ( LPDRAWITEMSTRUCT        lpDrawItem,
                                      WORD                    xOffset = 0,
                                      WORD                    yOffset = 0 )
{
    //-------------------

    CompatibleDC    destDC ( lpDrawItem->hDC,
                             hBitmap );

    BitBlt ( lpDrawItem->hDC,
             lpDrawItem->rcItem.left,
             lpDrawItem->rcItem.top,
             lpDrawItem->rcItem.right - lpDrawItem->rcItem.left,
             lpDrawItem->rcItem.bottom - lpDrawItem->rcItem.top,
             destDC.GetCompatDC(),
             xOffset,
```

```
                yOffset,
                SRCCOPY );

}


//---------------------------
//
// MalleableBitmap::CompressSelfToScreen()
//
// Displays the bitmap on the screen in compressed form.

    void
MalleableBitmap::CompressSelfToScreen ( LPDRAWITEMSTRUCT      lpDrawItem,
                                        WORD                  xOffset,
                                        WORD                  yOffset )
{
    CompatibleDC    destDC ( lpDrawItem->hDC,
                                hBitmap );

    POINT               mBmpSize = GetSize();       // Get size of image

    StretchBlt(lpDrawItem->hDC,
             lpDrawItem->rcItem.left,
             lpDrawItem->rcItem.top,
             lpDrawItem->rcItem.right-lpDrawItem->rcItem.left,
             lpDrawItem->rcItem.bottom-lpDrawItem->rcItem.top,
              destDC.GetCompatDC(),
             0,
             0,
             mBmpSize.x,
             mBmpSize.y,
             SRCCOPY);
}
```

Looking at the Malleable Bitmap Class

The Malleable Bitmap class, as you can see, has quite a few member functions. You can look at them here in a little more detail.

ValidateEmptyBitmap()

This routine simply ensures that the instance of the MalleableBitmap is currently empty. It's used in other member functions, as protection, so you can't inadvertently overwrite an existing bitmap handle.

CreateSelfEmpty()

This routine creates a bitmap of the requested size and zeroes it out. This ensures that the bitmap is blank when you want to use it. After the bitmap is created (using CreateCompatibleBitmap()), simply use the member function EraseSelf() to erase the bitmap.

EraseSelf()

This routine blanks out a bitmap by creating a compatible DC, selecting the bitmap into it, and then performing a PatBlt() of WHITENESS on the entire surface of the bitmap.

CopyFromDC()

This routine enables you to copy a portion of the image from a DC to your bitmap. Typically, this is used to grab a portion of the display screen. This can be used to build a basic screen snap-shot program.

WriteDIBIntoSelf()

This routine performs the same functionality as DibFromBitmap() in the DibShow App. It, too, can handle a DIB that's in either Windows or OS2/PM format. It creates a memory DC and creates itself empty (using the CreateSelfEmpty() member function), after which it performs a **SetDIBits()** call, which sets the bits of the bitmap from the DIB.

WriteBitmapIntoSelf()

This is a routine that copies the memory bitmap (DDB) that's passed into the internal bitmap of the instance of the MalleableBitmap object. It does this the way you might expect. First it creates an empty bitmap, into which the bits are going to be copied. Then it creates two compatible DCs, one for the source bitmap to be selected into and one for the destination bitmap to be selected into. (The process of instantiating a CompatibleDC object takes care of both the creation and selection. See the CompatibleDC class in Chapter 2, "The Display Context," for more information.)

After the source and destination DCs have been created, the only thing left to do is a **BitBlt()** from the source to the destination. The destructor routines for CompatibleDC take care of selecting the bitmaps out of the compatible DCs and deleting the DCs.

RenderSelfToScreen()

The RenderSelfToScreen() routine bears a suspicious resemblance to the base class Bitmap::DisplaySelf(). A fair question might be why it exists. If you look closer at the routine, you can see that the basis for having the bitmap render itself is not a DC (which is what the Bitmap::DisplaySelf() uses), but a DRAWITEMSTRUCT. This routine not only enables you to display the bitmap into a DC that you don't know in advance, and put it at any position that you want (just as Bitmap::DisplaySelf() does), but further lets you define the clipping region for the blit, which the base class routine doesn't do. If you note that a DRAWITEMSTRUCT is the structure passed when an owner-draw control needs to be redrawn, you might have a guess as to why I built this function—it's a support routine for the bitmap button and toolbar object classes that are defined later.

CompressSelfToScreen()

This function performs virtually the same function as RenderSelfToScreen(), with the added functionality of being able to fit the source bitmap into the destination rectangle.

Summary

This chapter took a look at DIBs, device independent bitmaps, which provide a way of storing bitmap images in such a fashion that any program running under any resolution can retrieve and display them, even if the results may not be aesthetically pleasing.

One of the most important points about a DIB is that it is just that, a device *independent* method of storing bitmaps. As such, it requires much more information about its makeup to be stored along with it so that other programs can retrieve it properly. This information includes a file header, which identifies what image type the file is; an information header, which defines the size, and the number of colors, of the image; a palette, which defines the colors used by the image; and finally the bits of the image.

Reading and writing DIBs involves a fair bit of preparation. The DibShow App is a simple program that demonstrates the techniques used for reading and writing DIBs.

Because many of the actions that are needed to deal with DIBs are highly specific and repetitive, it makes sense to create an object class that hides these behaviors, just as the Bitmap() object class hides much of the work involved with bitmaps. The MalleableBitmap class hides much of the work involved in dealing with DIBs and provides a further layer that you can use in creating complex graphics applications.

Function Reference

What follows is a list of the functions that deal directly with device independent bitmaps.

CreateDIBitmap()

```
HBITMAP CreateDIBitmap(    HDC                      hdc,
                           BITMAPINFOHEADER FAR *    lpbmih,
                           DWORD                     dwInit,
                           const void FAR *          lpvBits,
                           BITMAPINFO FAR *          lpbmi,
                           UINT                      fnColorUse)
```

WHAT IT DOES:

Creates a DDB-style bitmap from a DIB bitmap and header information. This function is somewhat of a misnomer; it doesn't create a DIB, but rather a DDB-style bitmap. (That is, it creates a device dependent bitmap, and not a device independent one.) This function is useful because you can specify the format of the bits of the bitmap in a device *independent* way, and then have this function convert them to the specific device that your application is running on. Probably most useful for creating memory bitmaps from bitmaps loaded off disk.

PARAMETERS:

hdc	Handle to the device context that defines the format of the bitmap to be created.
lpbmih	Pointer to a BITMAPINFOHEADER structure, which defines the bits in a device *independent* fashion.
dwInit	Indicates whether the bitmap should be initialized. If this value is CBM_INIT, the bitmap is initialized using the information in the next two parameters.
lpvBits	Pointer to an array containing the initial value of the bits of the bitmap.
lpbmi	Pointer to a BITMAPINFO struct, defining the size and color format of the bitmap.
fnColorUse	Specifies how the colors are specified in the BITMAPINFO struct: it can be either DIB_PAL_COLORS or DIB_RGB_COLORS. In the case of DIB_PAL_COLORS, it indicates that the color table of the bitmap is a series of indices into the currently selected color palette; if it's DIB_RGB_COLORS, it indicates that the color table of the bitmap contains literal RGB colors.

WHAT IT RETURNS:

A handle to the DDB created if the function is successful; the return value is NULL if the function fails.

THINGS TO WATCH FOR:

◻ Your application should call **DeleteObject()** to delete the bitmap when you're done with it.

263

- Because this function always creates a bitmap compatible with the DC passed in, you can perform some interesting color transformations on bitmaps by creating a custom palette and selecting the palette into the DC before you call this function.

- You must call this function with a valid screen or compatible DC; unlike some GDI functions that work with a DC of NULL, this function fails if you do not use a valid DC handle.

- This function is very similar to `CreateBitmap()`; however, instead of using a DDB to create the bitmap from, it uses a DIB structure.

SEE ALSO:

```
CreateBitmap()
CreateBitmapIndirect()
CreateCompatibleBitmap()
DeleteObject()
```

GetDIBits()

```
int GetDIBits(    HDC                    hdc,
                  HANDLE                 hbmp,
                  UINT                   nStartScan,
                  UINT                   cScanLines,
                  void FAR *             lpBits,
                  BITMAPINFO FAR *       lpBitsInfo,
                  UINT                   fuColorUse)
```

WHAT IT DOES:

Gets the bits of the DDB-style bitmap specified by the hbmp parameter, and copies them, in DIB fashion, into the buffer pointed to by the parameter lpBits. This call is used for transforming a DDB into a DIB. It is extremely useful!

PARAMETERS:

hdc Handle to the device context used for creating this DIB.

hbmp Handle to the DDB-style bitmap to create the DIB from.

nStartScan Starting scan line of the destination bitmap.

cScanLines Total number of scan lines to get.

lpBits Pointer to the destination buffer that gets the bits of the DIB.

lpBitsInfo   Points to a BITMAPINFO structure defining the DIB.

fuColorUse   Defines how to create the DIB; it can be either DIB_PAL_COLORS or DIB_RGB_COLORS. In the case of DIB_PAL_COLORS, it indicates that the color table of the DIB bitmap is to be created as a series of indices into bits of the DIB image; if it's DIB_RGB_COLORS, it indicates that the color table of the DIB bitmap will contain literal RGB color values.

WHAT IT RETURNS:

The number of scan lines copied from the bitmap, or zero if there's an error.

THINGS TO WATCH FOR:

☐ The values specified in the lpBitsInfo structure *define* how the DIB gets created; thus it's possible to create a 16-color DIB (even if the device your application is running on is in 32,768-color mode) by specifying that the biBitCount field of the structure is 4 (that is, 4 bits per pixel, or 16 colors).

> **Caution:** Not all drivers correctly implement this behavior. In fact, in the example just shown, the driver *fails* to produce the proper bits for an image if going from 32,768 colors to 16 colors (even if the 16 colors specified correspond directly to the standard VGA colors).

☐ By setting the lpBits parameter to NULL, this function fills in the BITMAPINFO structure to which the lpBitsInfo pointer points, but it does not retrieve the bits. (This is slightly silly, because you can also simply do a **GetObject()** on the bitmap and achieve the same thing.)

☐ The bitmap identified by the hBitmap parameter must not be selected into a DC when this function is called (unlike virtually every other function dealing with bitmaps, for which the bitmap must be selected into the DC. I love consistency, don't you? <grin>)

☐ The origin of DIBs is their lower-left corner (not the upper-left corner, like a DDB). This means the cScanLines parameter specifies how many scan lines from the bottom of the DIB upward you want to be copied out of the DDB. (This is OK, though, because most of the time you want to get the bits of the whole image. Just remember, if you're doing something like banding the image, that the two coordinate systems do not match up directly.)

SEE ALSO:

SetDIBits()

SetDIBits()

```
int SetDIBits(    HDC               hdc,
                  HBITMAP           hBitmap,
                  UINT              uStartScan,
                  UINT              cScanLines,
                  const void FAR *  lpvBits,
                  BITMAPINFO FAR *  lpbmi,
                  UINT              fuColorUse)
```

WHAT IT DOES:

This function takes an image specified in a DIB format and sets the bits of a DDB based on it. The function converts the image data in the DIB to one compatible with the DDB.

PARAMETERS:

hdc	Handle to the device context
hBitmap	Handle to the bitmap that's going to get the bits
uStartScan	Starting scan line of the source image
cScanLines	Number of scan lines to convert
lpvBits	Pointer to the bits of the DIB
lpbmi	Pointer to a BITMAPINFO structure containing data about the DIB
fuColorUse	Method of converting the DIB image; this must be either DIB_PAL_COLOR, in which case the color table is taken to be a series of indices into the currently realized logical palette, or DIB_RGB_COLORS, in which case the color table is taken to be explicit RGB values

WHAT IT RETURNS:

The number of scan lines successfully copied, or zero if there's an error.

THINGS TO WATCH FOR:

☐ For **SetDIBits()** to work right, you have to create the compatible bitmap you're drawing into using a SCREEN DC (this ensures you get a color bitmap), but use a MEMORY DC for the actual **SetDIBits()** call. (Thanks and a tip of the hatlo hat to Mike Geary for this one! :-))

☐ Unlike virtually every other call, for which the bitmap must be selected into the DC for the function to work, (for example, **BitBlt()**), the bitmap in this case must not be selected into the DC.

☐ This function also works with DIBs formatted in OS2/PM style (BITMAPCOREINFO style).

☐ The origin for device independent bitmaps is the bottom-left corner of the DIB, not the top-left corner, which is the origin when the mapping mode is MM_TEXT. GDI performs the necessary transformation to display the image correctly. Bloody slow about doing so too, I might add. (Especially in 15-bit or 24-bit mode. Shees, like watching paint peel. Note, though, that it's a lot better for Windows 3.1.)

SEE ALSO:

SetDIBitsToDevice()

SetDIBitsToDevice()

```
int SetDIBitsToDevice(    HDC                hdc,
                          UINT               uXDest,
                          UINT               uYDest,
                          UINT               uWidth,
                          UINT               uHeight,
                          UINT               uXSrc,
                          UINT               uYSrc,
                          UINT               uStartScan,
                          UINT               cScanLines,
                          void FAR *         lpvBits,
                          BITMAPINFO FAR *   lpbmi,
                          UINT               fuColorUse)
```

WHAT IT DOES:

This function does the same thing **SetDIBits()** does, except it sets the bits of a DIB directly to the screen without using an intermediate bitmap and compatible DC. This is essentially the same thing as doing a **SetDIBits()**, using a compatible DC and bitmap, and then performing a **BitBlt()** of the resulting bitmap to the screen.

PARAMETERS:

hdc	Destination DC for the bits; must be a screen DC
uXDest	Upper-left corner of the destination, x-value
uYDest	Upper-left corner of the destination, y-value
uWidth	Width of the rectangle in the DIB to be copied
uHeight	Height of the rectangle in the DIB to be copied
uXSrc	Lower-left corner of the source rectangle in the DIB, x-value
uYSrc	Lower-left corner of the source rectangle in the DIB, y-value
uStartScan	Starting scan line number of the bits pointed to by lpvBits
cScanLines	Number of scan lines to copy to the screen
lpvBits	Pointer to the bits of the DIB
lpbmi	Pointer to a BITMAPINFO structure defining the format of the DIB
fuColorUse	Method of converting the DIB image; this must be either DIB_PAL_COLOR, in which case the color table is taken to be a series of indices into the currently realized logical palette, or DIB_RGB_COLORS, in which case the color table is taken to be explicit RGB values

WHAT IT RETURNS:

The number of scan lines set to the device context.

THINGS TO WATCH FOR:

☐ The uXSrc, uYSrc, uWidth, and uHeight parameters define a rectangle within the full DIB; this rectangle can be either the full DIB or only a partial segment. You can reduce the total amount of memory needed to hold the DIB by putting only a portion of the image into the buffer pointed to by lpvBits, and then repeatedly calling the **SetDIBitsToDevice()** function. This technique is called banding. It's much slower than simply calling the function with the full DIB image, but it does require less memory.

☐ The uXDest and the uYDest parameters enable you to specify an offset within the destination DC where the image is to be drawn; this enables you to paint the image at some point other than the origin of the DC.

■ When mapping DIB images, remember DIBs have as their origin point the lower-left corner of the image, not the upper-left corner, which is the origin point of DDBs and DCs when the mapping mode is MM_TEXT. GDI performs the necessary transformation to display the image correctly, even when banding the image.

■ All coordinates are device coordinates (that is, the coordinates of the DIB) except uXDest and uYDest, which are logical coordinates of the specified DC.

■ This function also works with DIBs formatted in OS2/PM style (BITMAPCOREINFO style).

SEE ALSO:

SetDIBits()

StretchDIBits()

```
int StretchDIBits(    HDC                hdc,
                      UINT               uXOriginDest,
                      UINT               uYOriginDest,
                      UINT               uWidthDest,
                      UINT               uHeightDest,
                      UINT               uXOriginSrc,
                      UINT               uYOriginSrc,
                      UINT               uWidthSrc,
                      UINT               uHeightSrc,
                      const void FAR *   lpvBits,
                      BITMAPINFO FAR *   lpbmi,
                      UINT               fuColorUse,
                      DWORD              fdwRop)
```

WHAT IT DOES:

The StretchDIBits() function moves a device independent bitmap (DIB) from a source rectangle into a destination rectangle, stretching or compressing the bitmap if necessary to fit the dimensions of the destination rectangle.

PARAMETERS:

hdc   Destination device context

uXOriginDest   X-coordinate of the upper-left corner of the destination rectangle

uYOriginDest	Y-coordinate of the upper-left corner of the destination rectangle
uWidthDest	Width of the destination rectangle
uHeightDest	Height of the destination rectangle
uXOriginSrc	X-coordinate of the lower-left corner of the source rectangle
uYOriginSrc	Y-coordinate of the lower-left corner of the source rectangle
uWidthSrc	Width of the source rectangle
uHeightSrc	Height of the source rectangle
lpvBits	Pointer to the array holding the bits of the image of the DIB
lpbmi	Pointer to a BITMAPINFO structure defining the format of the DIB
fuColorUse	Determines how the color information of the DIB should be interpreted
fdwRop	Raster operation to perform

WHAT IT RETURNS:

The number of scan lines copied.

THINGS TO WATCH FOR:

☐ The **StretchDIBits()** function uses the stretching mode of the destination device context (set by the **SetStretchBltMode()** function) to determine how to stretch or compress the bitmap.

☐ The origin of the coordinate system for a device independent bitmap is the lower-left corner. The origin of the coordinates of the destination depends on the current mapping mode of the device context. For MM_TEXT the origin of the destination is the upper-left corner of the DC.

☐ **StretchDIBits()** creates a mirror image of a bitmap if the signs of the uWidthSrc and uWidthDest or uHeightSrc and uHeightDest parameters differ. If uWidthSrc and uWidthDest have different signs, the function creates a mirror image of the bitmap along the x-axis. If uHeightSrc and uHeightDest have different signs, the function creates a mirror image of the bitmap along the y-axis.

SEE ALSO:

SetStretchBltMode()

270

The Icon
Resources

Icons are probably the single most visible type of graphics resource in Windows—every program, whether Windows-based or DOS-based, has an icon associated with it. Although most people think of icons as being a fundamental graphics primitive, they're really not; they're actually just a modified form of DIB. You want to use icons, instead of simply using a bitmap, because an icon gives you something that a bitmap doesn't: *transparency*.

Transparency is the capability to have a piece of a background image show through a foreground image. I'll talk about transparency in more detail in a minute. Topics I cover in this chapter are

☐ Icon resource format

☐ Loading icons from resources

☐ Displaying icons

The Icon Resource File Format

Icon files are laid out in this way:

☐ ICONHEADER (one only)

☐ ICONRCDESCRIPT (one to N copies, one for each icon image)

☐ DIB (N copies; one copy for each icon image)

in which a DIB consists of the following:

☐ BITMAPINFO

☐ Array of bytes that actually define the image

The ICONHEADER Structure

```
typedef struct
{
        WORD icoReserved;         /* Reserved, must be 0 */
        WORD icoResourceType;     /* Resource type, for icons, must be 1 */
        WORD icoResourceCount;    /* Number of images contained in file
                                   * (equal to the number of ICONRCDESCRIPT
                                   * structures which follow it.
                                   */

} ICONHEADER;

typedef ICONHEADER *LPICONHEADER;
```

This structure must be at the beginning of every icon file. It defines, in fact, that the file in question *is* an icon file. The first field, icoReserved, must be 0. The next field, icoResourceType, must be set to 1, to indicate that this is an icon file. The final field, icoResourceCount, defines how many icon images are in this icon file. This brings up an interesting point.

If the icon you're creating is for use as a program icon, the documentation for icon resources mentions that Windows chooses the resolution which most closely matches that of the system the application is being run on (or words to that effect). This might lead you to think you can have only one icon of any particular resolution in an .ico file; for example, only 1 VGA (16-color) icon that's 32x32. Well, that's not the case. There's nothing to prevent you from creating an .ico file with 10, 20, or even 50 icons of the same resolution in it. (One file I downloaded from a BBS had 300 icons in it!) There are drawbacks to doing this, however.

The chief drawback is that you can't attach identifiers to all the icons in the file. When you compile an icon file with the resource compiler (or equivalent tool), you can assign it a string identifier, like this:

```
FOOICON    ICON    FOO.ICO
```

This would give the icon(s) contained in the file FOO.ICO the identifier FOOICON. Or you can give it a numeric identifier, in this fashion:

```
10003    ICON    FOO.ICO
```

This also gives the icon a numerical identifier of 10003. However, when you give an icon file an identifier like this, you can't specify an icon *within* the file, but only the file. When it comes time to load the resource, with the **LoadIcon()**

call, you won't be able to specify which icon to load—Windows tries to find the best fit to the current display attributes. If you've got multiple icons that match, the first one Windows finds gets used.

The only case in which you'd want to put multiple icons of the same resolution into one .ico file would be if you're creating a resource-only DLL. In that case, it doesn't matter that you can't access the icons in the file with the **LoadIcon()** call, because that isn't how Windows does it anyway. For loading icons out of an .EXE or .DLL file (for use with Program Manager), Windows reads the resource headers directly out of the file and loads all the images.

Still, given the extra hassle of doing it this way (I know of no icon editing programs that actually enable you to create multiple icons of the same resolution; ICE/Works certainly won't), there's not much point. It's just about as easy to compile several .ico files into your resources as it is to compile one, and whatever icon editor you're using is a lot less likely to choke on a more standard file format.

In any case, when beyond the ICONHEADER structure, you encounter a number of ICONRCDESCRIPT structures.

The ICONRCDESCRIPT Structure

```
typedef struct
{
      BYTE Width;        /* Width of image in pixels: 16, 32, 64 */
      BYTE Height;       /* Height of image in pixels: 16, 32, 64 */
      BYTE ColorCount;   /* Number of colors in icon: 2, 8, 16 */
      BYTE rByte;        /* Reserved */
      WORD rWord1;       /* Reserved (Used in cursors, X hotspot) */
      WORD rWord2;       /* Reserved (Used in cursors, Y hotspot) */
      DWORD icoDIBSize;  /* Specifies in bytes size of pixel array
                          * for this form of the icon image
                          */
      DWORD icoDIBOffset;    /* Specifies the offset in bytes from the
                             * beginning of the file to the device
                             * independent bitmap for this form
                             * of the icon image
                             */
} ICONRCDESCRIPT;

typedef ICONRCDESCRIPT *LPICONRCDESCRIPT;
```

The ICONRCDESCRIPT structure defines what a particular icon in the icon resource file looks like. This structure has got some immediately familiar fields; Width and Height are certainly no strangers. The interesting thing here is that the width and height of icons can be only 16, 32, or 64 pixels. You might expect that the width and height must have the same value, but that isn't the case. It's perfectly acceptable to have an icon that is 32 pixels wide and 16 pixels high (many CGA icons have these dimensions). The only caveat here is that most display drivers won't handle weird sizes of icons (especially something like 16 wide by 64 high). At one point, there was a rumor that 3.1 would fix the limitations on icon sizes, but it didn't work out that way. *Sigh.*

ColorCount specifies (not surprisingly) the number of colors used by an icon; it must be 2 (for monochrome icons), 8, or 16. If you start playing with icons a great deal, you discover that some icons which are marked as only using 8 colors use, in fact, 16. This leads to the question What's this field good for? The answer is that when Windows attempts to match an icon for the current display driver, it uses this field to determine how many colors an icon uses. It doesn't actually check the icon itself, but only this field.

The next three entries (rByte, rWord1, and rWord2) are reserved and should be set to 0.

After these fields comes icoDIBSize, which contains the size (in bytes) of the DIB for this icon image. That is followed by icoDIBOffset, which specifies in bytes how far into the file the DIB is; that is, this value is the offset, from the beginning of the file, to the DIB for this icon.

After the ICONRCDESCRIPT structure(s) come the DIBs for the icons themselves. Take a look at a simple icon file, which only contains one image. What does the DIB for the icon look like?

To be fair, it's actually two DIBs, not one. The first DIB is the color image for the icon (also known as the XOR image), whereas the second DIB is the monochrome mask (also known as the AND mask). To explain this more fully, I'm going to need to take a moment and explain what a mask is, and why you need one.

Achieving Transparency: Images and Masks

I mentioned in Chapter 1, "Windows Graphics Resources: An Overview," that bitmaps are rectangular images: so many pixels wide and so many pixels down. This is fine as long as all the images you want to draw happen to be rectangular.

It's not so good if the images you want to draw aren't rectangular—and, considering the nature of graphics, that's probably going to be most of the time.

So, what to do? Well, you can attempt to do it by hand. For a nonrectangular image, you can prepare yourself a second image—one that describes how you want the bits of the first image to be displayed. Turn a bit on in the second image, and the corresponding pixel in the first image is displayed when you copy it. Leave a bit off in the second image, and the corresponding bit in the first image won't be displayed when you copy it.

If you create such a second image, you've created what's called a *mask*. A bitmap mask is similar in many ways to a real, physical mask. Just as with a real mask, a bitmap mask can let parts of what's behind it show through while concealing other parts.

A picture should help make this clearer. Take a look at Figure 5.1.

Figure 5.1.
Example of an image combined with a mask.

In this example, I have a filled oval within a rectangle as the image. The mask consists of two rectangles, side by side. The left rectangle is filled with black, whereas the right rectangle is empty and has only a black frame around it. The result of using the mask on the image is shown in the result, at right: the half of the oval underneath the black rectangle appears, but the half under the white rectangle (with the exception of the frame) does not.

Achieving Transparency Under Windows

The previous discussion is a theoretical description of how you'd go about creating a mask for a bitmap image. Now it's time to take a look at the way Windows does it. Here's the process that Windows goes through when it displays an icon.

1. Windows takes the mask image (remember, it's monochrome), and ANDs that with the current background image. The net result of this action is as shown:

Mask Value	Background	Result
On (white)	Background pixel	Background pixel (unchanged)
Off (black)	Background pixel	Black (background pixel erased)

As you can see, by using the mask, you can selectively clear out portions of the background image.

2. After Windows has ANDed the mask to the background, it takes the foreground image (which can be either monochrome or color) and XORs it to the same place in the background that it ANDed the mask, in step 1. This has the following results:

Image Value	Background	Final Result
White	Black (erased)	White
Black	Black (erased)	Black
Color	Black (erased)	Color (unchanged)
White	Background	Inverse of background color
Black	Background	Background color
Color	Background	Result of XORing the background and image colors together

You can see from this the strategy that you need to use. For the parts of the image you want to be displayed, you need to use a background mask pixel of black (that is, the bit is off). This causes the background to be erased in step 1. In step 2, when the pixel at the position is XORed with the background, the final result is the same color (because XORing something with zero yields the original value).

For the parts of the image where you want the background to show through (that is, you want the image to be clear in those spots), you need to use a background mask pixel of white (that is, the bit is on). Additionally, you need to set the *image* pixel at that point to be black. Setting the image pixel to be white gives you the inverse color of the background pixel at that point. Setting the image pixel to some other color gives you the result of XORing the two colors together, which is most likely some sort of weird hybrid.

Take a look at a real icon image to see how this stuff works. Figure 5.2 shows the icon for ICE/Works as it's displayed on-screen. It isn't printed here in color, but you can see what it looks like on your system if you install it into Program Manager. The icon's mask is shown in Figure 5.3.

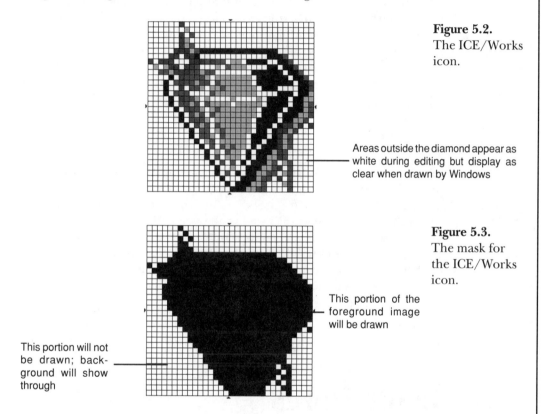

Figure 5.2.
The ICE/Works icon.

Areas outside the diamond appear as white during editing but display as clear when drawn by Windows

Figure 5.3.
The mask for the ICE/Works icon.

This portion of the foreground image will be drawn

This portion will not be drawn; background will show through

Notice that in Figure 5.2 the areas outside of the diamond are displayed as clear (meaning the background shows through); in the figure, they appear as white squares. This is not how they actually appear in the file—in the file, they're black. Remember that for a pixel in the image to be "clear" (that is, let the background show through), you need to have a background pixel of white (which you do) and a foreground pixel of black. As shown previously, you actually get the *inverse* of the background color. Using an icon editor can significantly reduce the headaches involved in creating the image and mask. You can define what the "clear" and "inverse" areas are and let the icon editor worry about how to transform the image properly.

The Icon DIBs

Now that you know how to create a mask for an icon, it's time to look at how the DIBs for the image and the mask are stored in the file. The first DIB stored is the image DIB; this defines the color portion of the image and corresponds to Figure 5.2. Immediately following the color image DIB are the *bits* for the monochrome mask, in DIB format. Note that the monochrome mask is not a full DIB, because it doesn't have a BITMAPINFOHEADER or a color palette. It's only the bits of the mask itself. Thus, the structure of the two DIBs is

```
BITMAPINFOHEADER        colorHead;
RGBQUAD                 colorPal[];
unsigned char           colorImageBits[];
unsigned char           monoMaskBits[];
```

in which colorHead is the BITMAPINFOHEADER that defines the width, height, and so on of the bitmap image. It's a standard DIB header, discussed in great detail in Chapter 4, "The Device Independent Bitmap." One point to note, though, is that the value of the height listed in the header is actually twice the real height of the icon. That is, if an icon is 32 pixels high, the biHeight field of colorHead is 64. This doubling of the height is to allow for the monochrome mask that follows at the end of the color image. To make matters worse, not all icons have this value doubled—most do, but some don't.

The values in colorPal[] define the palette colors for the icon. Immediately following that is colorImageBits[], which defines the color (image) mask of the icon, and monoMaskBits[], which defines the monochrome mask of the icon.

Using Icons

Now that you've seen how to create icons (or at least, what the format of an icon file is), you're probably wondering how to use them in your program. First, you can, if you really want, create an icon by hand. The call is, not surprisingly, **CreateIcon()**. (This is documented in detail in the Function Reference at the end of this chapter.) Unless you're seriously into pain, however, avoid this call—it's just not worth the trouble, because there are much simpler ways of getting an icon into your program.

Loading Icons

By far the easiest way of using icons in your application is to insert them into the resource file, like this:

```
ICONNAME    ICON    ICONFILE.ICO
```

ICONNAME is the string name you use to reference the icon, and *ICONFILE*.ICO is the name of the icon file. As with bitmap and cursor resources, the *ICONNAME* parameter is a *string* you reference in your program, and not a defined constant.

Caution: Failure to get this straight can lead to terribly pernicious and difficult-to-spot bugs.

Let me give you an example. Here's a fragment of an .RC file:

```
#define    FOO_ICON    25

FOO_ICON    ICON    ICONFILE.ICO
```

And here's the code in which I try to use the FOO_ICON:

```
HICON iconHandle;

iconHandle = LoadIcon ( hInst,
                "FOO_ICON" );

if (!iconHandle)
{
    MessageBox ( hWnd,
                "Can't load icon resource",
                "Error",
                MB_OK );
}
```

You've probably noticed that this method won't work—it fails to find the icon because of the #define at the beginning of the resource file. It replaces the FOO_ICON string in the resource file, leading to the string

```
25    ICON    ICONFILE.ICO
```

which is what actually gets compiled. This means that there isn't an icon with the string identifier FOO_ICON, but there is one with the numeric ID of 25. Although this bug is obvious enough when presented like this, it is incredibly harder to catch if you've got a large .RC file that has many items in it. It's even more difficult if you've got external .h files that are included in your .RC file. (I had this happen to me once, and it took me two days to figure out what was happening. I was at the point of debugging the assembly code to see what was wrong when the light bulb finally clicked on.)

As you can see from the code fragment presented, the way you load icons from a resource file is **LoadIcon()**, which is an obvious equivalent to **LoadBitmap()**.

> **Caution:** By the way, one way to screw yourself up really wonderfully is to load a resource with the wrong kind of call—that is, attempt to do something like load a bitmap with the **LoadIcon()** call (or vice versa). It won't work—it won't even come close—but what you get back as a handle won't be NULL, at which point you're a UAE looking for a place to happen. Pass this bogus handle into a routine which needs a real one, and it's *BOOM!* bits on the ceiling....

The first parameter to the **LoadIcon()** call is the instance handle of the application that contains the icon you want. As with other resource calls of the **Load...()** variety, there's no reason you can't use any valid instance handle here, not just your own. This means, of course, that you can put icons into a resource-only DLL or extract them from other running applications, assuming you know the name or ID of the icon.

Just like the **LoadBitmap()** call, the **LoadIcon()** call supports two kinds of resources: private icons, which you load, and system icons, which you can get from Windows. Private icon resources must be destroyed after you're done with them, but system icons must not. Here's a list of the system icons you can get:

IDI_APPLICATION	Default application icon
IDI_ASTERISK	Asterisk (used in informative messages)
IDI_EXCLAMATION	Exclamation point (used in warning messages)
IDI_HAND	Hand-shaped icon (used in serious warning messages).
IDI_QUESTION	Question mark (used in prompting messages)

To load a system icon resource, rather than one of your own, you use **LoadIcon()** this way:

```
HICON sysIcon;

sysIcon = LoadIcon ( NULL,
                     IDI_HAND );
```

Note that the first parameter, which is the handle to the instance of the application you're loading from, is NULL. This is how you let Windows know you want a system icon. The second parameter is one of the constants (defined in windows.h) listed previously.

Displaying Icons

Now that you've got an icon loaded, you'd probably like to display it. For icons, that's quite easy to do, which is a significant change from bitmaps. (Remember some of the machinations you had to go through to display DIBs on the screen in Chapter 4.) The call to display an icon is to **DrawIcon()**. This function takes four parameters: an hDC (the handle of the DC to draw the icon into), an (x,y) position for the upper-left corner of the icon, and a handle to the icon. What could be simpler? Here's an example:

```
DrawIcon ( hDC,
           5,
           5,
           myIcon );
```

IconShow: An Example Program

Of course, it's time for another example program. The IconShow example loads its own icon from within itself and displays it in its main window. It also loads the five system icons and displays them as well. Listings 5.1 through 5.7 show the source.

Listing 5.1. ICONSHOW.C—source code for the IconShow App.

```c
//File name: ICONSHOW.C
//"ICONSHOW" Generated by WindowsMAKER Professional
//Author: Alex Leavens, for ShadowCat Technologies

#include <WINDOWS.H>
#include "ICONSHOW.H"

#include "ICONSHOW.WMC"


//---------------------

// Global variable used to hold a handle to your icon;
// this will be used to draw the icon in the main window

HICON    showIcon;

//**************************************************************
//                      WinMain FUNCTION
//**************************************************************

    int PASCAL
WinMain(HINSTANCE hInstance,
        HINSTANCE hPrevInstance,
        LPSTR      lpCmdLine,
        int        nCmdShow)
{
    MSG msg;                    // Message

    hInst = hInstance;          // Saves the current instance

    if (!BLDInitApplication(hInstance,hPrevInstance,&nCmdShow,lpCmdLine))
        return FALSE;

    if (!hPrevInstance)         // Is there another instance of the task
        {
        if (!BLDRegisterClass(hInstance))
            return FALSE;       // Exits if unable to initialize
        }

    MainhWnd = BLDCreateWindow(hInstance);
    if (!MainhWnd)              // Check if the window is created
        return FALSE;
```

```
        ShowWindow(MainhWnd, nCmdShow);   // Show the window
        UpdateWindow(MainhWnd);           // Send WM_PAINT message to window

        BLDInitMainMenu(MainhWnd);  // Initialize main menu if necessary

        while (GetMessage(&msg,       // Message structure
                      0,              // Handle of window receiving the message
                      0,              // Lowest message to examine
                      0))             // Highest message to examine
            {
            if (BLDKeyTranslation(&msg)) // WindowsMAKER code for key translation
                continue;
            TranslateMessage(&msg); // Translates character keys
            DispatchMessage(&msg);  // Dispatches message to window
            }
        BLDExitApplication();        // Clean up if necessary
        return(msg.wParam);          // Returns the value from PostQuitMessage
}

//***************************************************************
//              WINDOW PROCEDURE FOR MAIN WINDOW
//***************************************************************

    LONG FAR PASCAL
BLDMainWndProc(HWND hWnd,
               UINT message,
               UINT wParam,
               LONG lParam )
{

    switch (message)
    {

    case WM_CREATE:                 // Window creation

        // Load the icon of your application from the resources
        // of the program here.

        showIcon = LoadIcon ( hInst,
                              "ICONSHOW" );

        if ( !showIcon )
        {
            MessageBox ( hWnd,
                        "Cannot load icon from resource",
```

continues

285

Listing 5.1. continued

```
                                "Say what?",
                                MB_OK );
        }

        // Send to BLDDefWindowProc in (.WMC) for controls in main window
        return BLDDefWindowProc(hWnd, message, wParam, lParam);
        break;

    case WM_PAINT:
        {
            PAINTSTRUCT    pS;
            HDC            hDC;

            //------------------------
            // In response to the paint message,
            // you're going to draw your icon into the window; you're
            // also going to draw all the system icons...

            hDC = BeginPaint ( hWnd,
                                    &pS );

            // If you were able to load the icon successfully, then
            // draw it here into your client window.

            if ( showIcon )
            {
                DrawIcon ( hDC,
                            20,
                            20,
                            showIcon );
            }

            // Now load and display the five flavors of system icon
            // that you can get. Note that you embed the LoadIcon() call
            // inside the DrawIcon(), since you don't have to destroy
            // the icons when you're done (they're system icons, which
            // you mustn't destroy).

            DrawIcon ( hDC,
                        60,
                        20,
                        LoadIcon ( NULL, IDI_APPLICATION ) );

            DrawIcon ( hDC,
```

```
                             60,
                             60,
                             LoadIcon ( NULL, IDI_HAND ) );

                 DrawIcon ( hDC,
                             100,
                             60,
                             LoadIcon ( NULL, IDI_QUESTION ) );

                 DrawIcon ( hDC,
                             100,
                             100,
                             LoadIcon ( NULL, IDI_EXCLAMATION ) );

                 DrawIcon ( hDC,
                             100,
                             140,
                             LoadIcon ( NULL, IDI_ASTERISK ) );

                 // Done painting, unlock and return.

                 EndPaint ( hWnd,
                             &pS );
            }
         break;

    case WM_SETFOCUS:             // Window is notified of focus change
         // Send to BLDDefWindowProc in (.WMC) for controls in main window
         return BLDDefWindowProc(hWnd, message, wParam, lParam);
         break;

    case WM_DESTROY:              // Window being destroyed

         // Don't forget to destroy the icon at shutdown time...

         if ( showIcon )
         {
             DestroyIcon ( showIcon );

             // Mark the handle as NULL, so that if, for some odd
             // reason, you try to do this again, you won't be deleting
             // an invalid icon...

             showIcon = NULL;
         }
```

continues

Listing 5.1. continued

```
    PostQuitMessage(0);
    return BLDDefWindowProc(hWnd, message, wParam, lParam);
    break;

    case WM_COMMAND:              // Command from the main window
        if (BLDMenuCommand(hWnd, message, wParam, lParam))
            break;                // Processed by BLDMenuCommand.
        // Else default processing by BLDDefWindowProc.
    default:
        // Pass on message for default processing
        return BLDDefWindowProc(hWnd, message, wParam, lParam);
    }
    return FALSE;                 // Returns FALSE if processed
}
```

Listing 5.2. ICONSHOW.WMC—special include file for IconShow App.

```
//File name: ICONSHOW.WMC
//"ICONSHOW" Generated by WindowsMAKER Professional
//Author: Alex Leavens, for ShadowCat Technologies


//****************************************************************
//                    GLOBAL VARIABLES
//****************************************************************


HBRUSH      hMBrush = 0;       // Handle to brush for main window.
HINSTANCE   hInst   = 0;       // Handle to instance.
HWND        MainhWnd= 0;       // Handle to main window.
HWND        hClient = 0;       // Handle to window in client area.
FARPROC     lpClient= 0L;      // Function for window in client area.


//****************************************************************
//            PROCESSES KEYBOARD ACCELERATORS
//            AND MODELESS DIALOG BOX KEY INPUT
//****************************************************************


BOOL BLDKeyTranslation(MSG *pMsg)
  {
  return FALSE;                 // No special key input
  }
```

```
//****************************************************************
//          CUSTOM MESSAGE PROCESSING FOR MAIN WINDOW
//****************************************************************

LONG FAR PASCAL BLDDefWindowProc(HWND hWnd, UINT message, UINT wParam,
                            LONG lParam )
  {

  switch (message)
    {

        default:
    // Pass on message for default processing by Windows
    return DefWindowProc(hWnd, message, wParam, lParam);
    }
 return FALSE;                 // Returns FALSE if not processed by Windows
  }


//****************************************************************
//             PROCESSES ALL MENU ITEM SELECTIONS
//****************************************************************

BOOL BLDMenuCommand(HWND hWnd, UINT message, UINT wParam, LONG lParam )
{

  switch( LOWORD(wParam) )
    {

    // Processing of linked menu items in menu: ICONSHOW

  default:
    return FALSE;             // Not processed by this function.
    }
 return TRUE;                 // Processed by this function.
    }


//****************************************************************
//    FUNCTIONS FOR INITIALIZATION AND EXIT OF APPLICATION
//****************************************************************

BOOL BLDInitApplication(HANDLE hInst, HANDLE hPrev, int *pCmdShow, LPSTR lpCmd)
 {
 // No initialization necessary
 return TRUE;
 }
```

continues

Listing 5.2. continued

```
// Registers the class for the main window
BOOL BLDRegisterClass( HANDLE hInstance )
 {
 WNDCLASS WndClass;

 hMBrush=CreateSolidBrush(GetSysColor(COLOR_WINDOW));

 WndClass.style         = 0;
 WndClass.lpfnWndProc   = BLDMainWndProc;
 WndClass.cbClsExtra    = 0;
 WndClass.cbWndExtra    = 0;
 WndClass.hInstance     = hInstance;
 WndClass.hIcon         = LoadIcon(hInstance,"ICONSHOW");
 WndClass.hCursor       = LoadCursor(NULL,IDC_ARROW);
 WndClass.hbrBackground = hMBrush;
 WndClass.lpszMenuName  = NULL;
 WndClass.lpszClassName = "ICONSHOW";

 return RegisterClass(&WndClass);
 }


HWND BLDCreateWindow( HANDLE hInstance )  // Creates the main window
{
 HWND hWnd;                  // Window handle
 int coordinate[4];          // Coordinates of main window

 coordinate[0]=CW_USEDEFAULT;
 coordinate[1]=0;
 coordinate[2]=CW_USEDEFAULT;
 coordinate[3]=0;

 hWnd = CreateWindow("ICONSHOW",  // Window class registered earlier
   "IconShow",             // Window caption
   WS_OVERLAPPED|WS_THICKFRAME|WS_SYSMENU|WS_MINIMIZEBOX|WS_MAXIMIZEBOX,
                           // Window style
   coordinate[0],          // X position
   coordinate[1],          // Y position
   coordinate[2],          // Width
   coordinate[3],          // Height
   0,                      // Parent handle
   0,                      // Menu or child ID
   hInstance,              // Instance
   (LPSTR)NULL);           // Additional info
```

```
 return hWnd;
 }


// Called just before entering message loop
BOOL BLDInitMainMenu(HWND hWnd)
 {
 // No initialization necessary
 return TRUE;
 }


BOOL BLDExitApplication()        // Called just before exit of application
 {
 if (hMBrush)
     DeleteObject(hMBrush);
 return TRUE;
 }

//********************************************************
// ERROR MESSAGE HANDLING (Definitions can be overruled.)
//********************************************************

#ifndef ERRORCAPTION
#define ERRORCAPTION "IconShow"
#endif

#ifndef LOADERROR
#define LOADERROR "Cannot load string."
#endif


int BLDDisplayMessage(HWND hWnd, unsigned uMsg, char *pContext, int iType)
   {
   int i, j;
   char Message[200+1];

   if (uMsg)
       {
       if (!LoadString(hInst,uMsg,Message,200))
           {
           MessageBox(hWnd,LOADERROR,ERRORCAPTION,
                   MB_OK|MB_SYSTEMMODAL|MB_ICONHAND);
           return FALSE;
           }
       }
```

continues

291

Listing 5.2. continued

```
    else
        Message[0]=0;

    if (pContext)
        {
        i = lstrlen(Message);
        j = lstrlen(pContext);
        if (i + j + 1 <= 200)
            {
            lstrcat(Message, " ");
            lstrcat(Message, pContext);
            }
        }

    return MessageBox(hWnd,Message,ERRORCAPTION,iType);
    }


//****************************************************************
//            FUNCTIONS FOR DRAWING GRAPHICS BUTTONS
//****************************************************************

BOOL BLDDrawIcon(LPDRAWITEMSTRUCT lpDrawItem, char *pIconName)
 {
 HICON hIcon;

 hIcon = LoadIcon(hInst,pIconName);
 if (!hIcon)
     {
     BLDDisplayMessage(GetActiveWindow(),BLD_CannotLoadIcon,pIconName,
                     MB_OK | MB_ICONASTERISK);
     return FALSE;
     }

 SetMapMode(lpDrawItem->hDC,MM_TEXT);
 return DrawIcon(lpDrawItem->hDC,0,0,hIcon);
 }



BOOL BLDDrawBitmap(LPDRAWITEMSTRUCT lpDrawItem,
                   char *pBitmapName,
                   BOOL bStretch)
 {
 HBITMAP hBitmap;
 HDC hMemDC;
```

```
    BITMAP Bitmap;
    int iRaster;

    iRaster = GetDeviceCaps(lpDrawItem->hDC,RASTERCAPS);
    if ((iRaster&RC_BITBLT)!=RC_BITBLT)
        return FALSE;              // Device cannot display bitmap

    hBitmap = LoadBitmap(hInst,pBitmapName);
    if (!hBitmap)
        {
        BLDDisplayMessage(GetActiveWindow(),BLD_CannotLoadBitmap,pBitmapName,
                MB_OK ¦ MB_ICONASTERISK);
        return FALSE;
        }

    if (!GetObject(hBitmap,sizeof(BITMAP),(LPSTR)&Bitmap))
        {
        DeleteObject(hBitmap);
        return FALSE;
        }
    hMemDC = CreateCompatibleDC(lpDrawItem->hDC);
    if (!hMemDC)
        {
        DeleteObject(hBitmap);
        return FALSE;
        }
    if (!SelectObject(hMemDC,hBitmap))
        {
        DeleteDC(hMemDC);
        DeleteObject(hBitmap);
        return FALSE;
        }

    if (bStretch)
            {
            StretchBlt(lpDrawItem->hDC,
                       lpDrawItem->rcItem.left,
                       lpDrawItem->rcItem.top,
                       lpDrawItem->rcItem.right-lpDrawItem->rcItem.left,
                       lpDrawItem->rcItem.bottom-lpDrawItem->rcItem.top,
                       hMemDC,
                       0,
                       0,
                       Bitmap.bmWidth,
                       Bitmap.bmHeight,
                       SRCCOPY);
```

continues

Listing 5.2. continued

```
    }
else
    {
        BitBlt(lpDrawItem->hDC,
                  lpDrawItem->rcItem.left,
                  lpDrawItem->rcItem.top,
                  lpDrawItem->rcItem.right-lpDrawItem->rcItem.left,
                  lpDrawItem->rcItem.bottom-lpDrawItem->rcItem.top,
                  hMemDC,
                  0,
                  0,
                  SRCCOPY);
    }
DeleteDC(hMemDC);
DeleteObject(hBitmap);
return TRUE;
}


//***************************************************************
//         FUNCTION FOR CREATING CONTROLS IN MAIN WINDOW
//***************************************************************

// Startup procedure for window in client area
HWND BLDCreateClientControls(char *pTemplateName, FARPROC lpNew)
{
 RECT rClient,rMain,rDialog;
 int dxDialog,dyDialog,dyExtra,dtXold,dtYold;
 HANDLE hRes,hMem;
 LPBLD_DLGTEMPLATE lpDlg;
 unsigned long styleold,style;
 HWND hNew;

 if (!IsWindow(MainhWnd))
     return 0;
 if (IsZoomed(MainhWnd))
     ShowWindow(MainhWnd,SW_RESTORE);

 if (IsWindow(hClient))
         DestroyWindow(hClient); // Destroy Previous window in client area

 // Get access to data structure of dialog box containing layout of controls
 hRes=FindResource(hInst,(LPSTR)pTemplateName,RT_DIALOG);
 if (!hRes)
     return 0;
```

```
hMem=LoadResource(hInst,hRes);
if (!hMem)
    return 0;
lpDlg=(LPBLD_DLGTEMPLATE)LockResource(hMem);
if (!lpDlg)
    return 0;

// Change dialog box data structure so it can be
// used as a window in client area
styleold        = lpDlg->dtStyle;
style           = lpDlg->dtStyle&(CLIENTSTRIP);
lpDlg->dtStyle  = lpDlg->dtStyle^style;
lpDlg->dtStyle  = lpDlg->dtStyle | WS_CHILD | WS_CLIPSIBLINGS;
dtXold          = lpDlg->dtX;
dtYold          = lpDlg->dtY;
lpDlg->dtX      = 0;
lpDlg->dtY      = 0;

hNew = CreateDialogIndirect(hInst,(LPSTR)lpDlg, MainhWnd,lpNew);
if (!hNew)
    return 0;

// Restore dialog box data structure.
lpDlg->dtStyle = styleold;
lpDlg->dtX     = dtXold;
lpDlg->dtY     = dtYold;

UnlockResource(hMem);
FreeResource(hMem);

// Move and size window in client area and main window
GetClientRect(MainhWnd,&rClient);
GetWindowRect(MainhWnd,&rMain);
GetWindowRect(hNew,&rDialog);
dxDialog=(rDialog.right-rDialog.left)-(rClient.right-rClient.left);
dyDialog=(rDialog.bottom-rDialog.top)-(rClient.bottom-rClient.top);
BLDMoveWindow(MainhWnd,rMain.left,rMain.top,
    (rMain.right-rMain.left)+dxDialog,
                              (rMain.bottom-rMain.top)+dyDialog,
          TRUE);
MoveWindow(hNew,0,0,
                              (rDialog.right-rDialog.left),
                              (rDialog.bottom-rDialog.top),
                              TRUE);
GetClientRect(MainhWnd,&rClient);
```

continues

Listing 5.2. continued

```c
// Compensate size if menu bar is more than one line.
if ((rDialog.bottom-rDialog.top)>(rClient.bottom-rClient.top))
    {
    dyExtra=(rDialog.bottom-rDialog.top)-(rClient.bottom-rClient.top);
    BLDMoveWindow(MainhWnd,rMain.left,rMain.top,
        (rMain.right-rMain.left)+dxDialog,
        (rMain.bottom-rMain.top)+dyDialog+dyExtra,
        TRUE);
  }


ShowWindow(hNew,SW_SHOW);
hClient=hNew;
lpClient=lpNew;
return hClient;
 }



// Ensure that window is within screen.
void BLDMoveWindow(HWND hWnd, int x, int y,
        int nWidth, int nHeight, BOOL bRepaint)
  {
  int xMax,yMax,xNew,yNew;

  xMax = GetSystemMetrics(SM_CXSCREEN);
  yMax = GetSystemMetrics(SM_CYSCREEN);

  if ((nWidth<=xMax)&&(x+nWidth>xMax))
      xNew=xMax-nWidth;
  else
    xNew=x;

  if ((nHeight<=yMax)&&(y+nHeight>yMax))
      yNew=yMax-nHeight;
  else
      yNew=y;

  MoveWindow(hWnd,xNew,yNew,nWidth,nHeight,bRepaint);
  return;
  }

//************************************************************
//              FUNCTION FOR SWITCHING MENU SET
//************************************************************
```

```
BOOL BLDSwitchMenu(HWND hWnd, char *pTemplateName)
 {
 HMENU hMenu1,hMenu;
 DWORD style;

 style = GetWindowLong(hWnd,GWL_STYLE);
 if((style & WS_CHILD) == WS_CHILD)      // Called from control in main window?
    {
    hWnd=GetParent(hWnd);
    if (!hWnd)
        return FALSE;
    style = GetWindowLong(hWnd,GWL_STYLE);
    if((style & WS_CHILD) == WS_CHILD) // No menu in a WS_CHILD window.
       return FALSE;
    }
 if((style & WS_CAPTION) != WS_CAPTION) // No menu if no caption.
    return FALSE;

 hMenu1 = GetMenu(hWnd);
 hMenu = LoadMenu(hInst,pTemplateName);
 if (!hMenu)
    {
    BLDDisplayMessage(hWnd,BLD_CannotLoadMenu,pTemplateName,
             MB_OK | MB_ICONASTERISK);
    return FALSE;
    }

 if (!SetMenu(hWnd,hMenu))
    return FALSE;
 if (hMenu1)
    DestroyMenu(hMenu1);

DrawMenuBar(hWnd);
return TRUE;
 }
```

Listing 5.3. ICONSHOW.H—include file for the IconShow App.

```
//File name: ICONSHOW.H
//"ICONSHOW" Generated by WindowsMAKER Professional
//Author: Alex Leavens, for ShadowCat Technologies
```

continues

297

Listing 5.3. continued

```c
// Give access to handles in all code modules
extern HINSTANCE hInst;
extern HWND      MainhWnd;

// Constants for error message strings
#define BLD_CannotRun         4000
#define BLD_CannotCreate      4001
#define BLD_CannotLoadMenu    4002
#define BLD_CannotLoadIcon    4003
#define BLD_CannotLoadBitmap  4004


#if !defined(THISISBLDRC)

int  PASCAL WinMain( HINSTANCE hInstance, HINSTANCE hPrevInstance,
                     LPSTR lpCmdLine, int nCmdShow );
LONG FAR PASCAL BLDMainWndProc( HWND hWnd,
                                UINT message,
                                UINT wParam,
                                LONG lParam );
LONG FAR PASCAL BLDDefWindowProc( HWND hWnd,
                                  UINT message,
                                  UINT wParam,
                                  LONG lParam );
BOOL BLDKeyTranslation( MSG *pMsg );
BOOL BLDInitApplication( HANDLE hInst,
                         HANDLE hPrev,
                         int *pCmdShow,
                         LPSTR lpCmd );
BOOL BLDExitApplication( void );
HWND BLDCreateClientControls( char *pTemplateName, FARPROC lpNew );
BOOL BLDInitMainMenu( HWND hWnd );
BOOL BLDMenuCommand( HWND hWnd, UINT message, UINT wParam, LONG lParam );
BOOL BLDRegisterClass( HANDLE hInstance );
HWND BLDCreateWindow( HANDLE hInstance );
int  BLDDisplayMessage(HWND hWnd, unsigned uMsg, char *pContext, int iType );
BOOL BLDSwitchMenu( HWND hWnd, char *pTemplateName );
BOOL BLDDrawBitmap( LPDRAWITEMSTRUCT lpDrawItem,
                    char *pBitmapName, BOOL bStretch );
BOOL BLDDrawIcon( LPDRAWITEMSTRUCT lpDrawItem, char *pIconName );
void BLDMoveWindow( HWND hWnd, int x, int y, int nWidth,
                    int nHeight, BOOL bRepaint );


//***************************************************************
// Variables, types and constants for controls in main window.
//***************************************************************
```

```
extern HWND     hClient;        // Handle to window in client area.
extern FARPROC  lpClient;       // Function for window in client area.

#defineCLIENTSTRIP
WS_MINIMIZE¦WS_MAXIMIZE¦WS_CAPTION¦WS_BORDER¦
WS_DLGFRAME¦WS_SYSMENU¦WS_POPUP¦WS_THICKFRAME¦DS_MODALFRAME

typedef struct
  {
  unsigned long dtStyle;
  BYTE dtItemCount;
  int dtX;
  int dtY;
  int dtCX;
  int dtCY;
  } BLD_DLGTEMPLATE;

typedef BLD_DLGTEMPLATE far  *LPBLD_DLGTEMPLATE;

#endif

#define WMPDEBUG


// User Defined ID Values


// WindowsMAKER Pro generated ID Values
```

Listing 5.4. ICONSHOW.RC—resource file for the IconShow App.

```
//File name: ICONSHOW.RC
//"ICONSHOW" Generated by WindowsMAKER Professional
//Author: Alex Leavens, for ShadowCat Technologies

#define THISISBLDRC

#include <WINDOWS.H>
#include "ICONSHOW.H"

ICONSHOW  ICON  SUNSET.ICO
```

continues

Listing 5.4. continued

```
//*********************************************************
//        Resource code for error message strings
//*********************************************************

STRINGTABLE
  BEGIN
    BLD_CannotRun         "Cannot run "
    BLD_CannotCreate      "Cannot create dialog box "
    BLD_CannotLoadMenu    "Cannot load menu "
    BLD_CannotLoadIcon    "Cannot load icon "
    BLD_CannotLoadBitmap  "Cannot load bitmap "
  END
```

Listing 5.5. ICONSHOW.DEF—module definition file for the IconShow App.

```
;File name: ICONSHOW.DEF
;"ICONSHOW" Generated by WindowsMAKER Professional
;Author: Alex Leavens, for ShadowCat Technologies

NAME          ICONSHOW
DESCRIPTION   'ICONSHOW generated by WindowsMAKER Professional'
EXETYPE       WINDOWS
STUB          'WINSTUB.EXE'
DATA          MOVEABLE MULTIPLE
CODE          MOVEABLE DISCARDABLE PRELOAD
HEAPSIZE      1024
STACKSIZE     5120
EXPORTS
    BLDMainWndProc
```

Listing 5.6. ICONSHOW—makefile for the IconShow App.

```
#File name: ICONSHOW
#"ICONSHOW" Generated by WindowsMAKER Professional
#Author: Alex Leavens, for ShadowCat Technologies

comp= /c /AS /Os /Gsw /Zpe /D _WINDOWS /W2
cc=bcc.exe
```

```
ALL : ICONSHOW.EXE

ICONSHOW.EXE : ICONSHOW.OBJ ICONSHOW.DEF ICONSHOW.RES
  LINK @ICONSHOW.LNK
  rc ICONSHOW.RES

ICONSHOW.RES : ICONSHOW.RC ICONSHOW.H SUNSET.ICO
  rc.exe -r ICONSHOW.RC

ICONSHOW.OBJ : ICONSHOW.C ICONSHOW.WMC ICONSHOW.H
  cl $(comp) ICONSHOW.C
```

Listing 5.7. ICONSHOW.LNK—link file for the IconShow App.

```
ICONSHOW ,ICONSHOW.EXE ,/align:16 /NOD /map /CO  , LIBW SLIBCEW ,ICONSHOW.DEF
```

Figure 5.4 shows the IconShow application in action. Really, this application is pretty simple. You load your own cursor from your resources, with the `LoadIcon()` call. If the call fails, you post a message box alerting the user that the load was unsuccessful. You also check throughout the program to make sure that the global variable showIcon is not NULL. This prevents you from bombing your app by passing in a NULL icon handle to a routine that expects something legitimate.

The other thing to note is that when you display the system icons, you embed the `LoadIcon()` call in the `DrawIcon()` call. In this case, you don't need to destroy the icon when you're done with it (you must not destroy system icons that you've loaded). You therefore can embed the call to load the icon safely within `DrawIcon()`.

Figure 5.4. The IconShow application in action.

Summary

Although icons are a main point of contact with the Windows interface, you can really do only a few things with them compared with the things you can do with a bitmap. You can load an icon from a resource file and display it on-screen. You can also copy an icon, as well as delete one. You can even create one by hand (if you really want to), although the process is extremely laborious.

The big difference between icons and bitmaps is their transparency. If you need to display nonrectilinear images easily, this is a very powerful capability to have. On the other hand, if you don't need to do this, using icons can seriously limit your display options, because there are far fewer ways to display an icon than a bitmap.

Using icons can give you a way of avoiding display device dependency, because you can create multiple resolution icons. In earlier versions of Windows, this was more of a concern than it is now, with the advent of cheap, readily available VGA graphics adapters.

Function Reference

What follows is a list of the functions that deal directly with loading and creating icons within running programs.

CopyIcon()

```
HICON CopyIcon(    HANDLE    hInst,
                   HICON     hIcon)
```

WHAT IT DOES:

Copies the icon whose handle you've passed in with the hIcon parameter.

PARAMETERS:

hInst   Instance handle of the module that's going to copy the icon

hIcon   Handle to the icon to be copied

WHAT IT RETURNS:

A handle to a copy of the icon, or NULL if the function fails.

THINGS TO WATCH FOR:

> Any icon created in this fashion is a private icon resource and must be deleted using the **DestroyIcon()** call. This is true even if the original icon was one of the standard system icons.

SEE ALSO:

CopyCursor()
DestroyIcon()
DrawIcon()

CreateIcon()

```
HICON CreateIcon(      HANDLE      hinst,
                       int         nWidth,
                       int         nHeight,
                       BYTE        bPlanes,
                       BYTE        bBitsPixel,
                       LPSTR       lpANDbits,
                       LPSTR       lpXORbits)
```

WHAT IT DOES:

Creates an icon of the requested width, height, and number of colors, and with the image pointed to by the XOR and AND bitmaps.

PARAMETERS:

hInst	Instance handle of the application doing the creating.
nWidth	Width of the desired icon.
nHeight	Height of the desired icon.
bPlanes	Number of bit planes for the image. This is based on a DDB-style bitmap, and not a DIB one. (See Chapter 3, "Device Dependent Bitmaps," for more information on the format of this field.)
bBitsPixel	Number of bits per pixel for the image. This too is a DDB-based value. (Read Chapter 3 for more information.)
lpANDbits	Pointer to the mask bits of the icon. The mask is always a monochrome bitmap.

lpXORbits   Pointer to the image bits of the icon. The image bits can be any number of colors that's legitimate for a DDB (that is, 2, 8, 16, 256, and so on).

WHAT IT RETURNS:

A handle to the created icon, or NULL if the function isn't successful.

THINGS TO WATCH FOR:

▢ Unlike the DIB drivers, which can handle images of resolutions other than the current one, the `CreateIcon()` call cannot. This means you can't create a monochrome icon with this call if you're running in VGA mode. This wouldn't be so bad if the call returned a NULL if you tried to do this. Unfortunately, it doesn't—it returns a value that *looks* like a valid icon handle but isn't. The first time you try to do something with an icon created under such circumstances, it's *BOOM!* bits on the ceiling. (It would've been nice if they'd documented this in the 3.0 docs—I spent a week pounding sand trying to figure out what I was doing wrong.)

▢ You can determine what size icon is used by the current display driver with the `GetSystemMetrics()` call. The values SM_CXICON and SM_CYICON give you back the width and height, respectively.

▢ Any icon created in this fashion is a private icon resource and must be deleted using the `DestroyIcon()` call.

SEE ALSO:

DestroyIcon()

DestroyIcon()

BOOL DestroyIcon(HICON   hIcon)

WHAT IT DOES:

Destroys the icon specified by hIcon and frees the system resources used by it.

PARAMETER:

hIcon   Handle of the icon to be destroyed

WHAT IT RETURNS:

TRUE if the function is successful and FALSE otherwise.

THINGS TO WATCH FOR:

☐ This function is incorrectly referred to as DeleteIcon in the first chapter of Volume 1 of the Programmer's Reference Manual.

☐ If you're deleting an icon resource, don't forget to zero out any local copies of the handle you might have.

☐ You must use this function to destroy any icons you loaded from a private resource with the **LoadIcon()** call; however, you must not delete system icons that were loaded in such a fashion.

SEE ALSO:

CreateIcon()
LoadIcon()

DrawIcon()

```
BOOL DrawIcon(    HDC     hDC,
                  int     x,
                  int     y,
                  HICON   hIcon)
```

WHAT IT DOES:

Draws the icon specified by the hIcon parameter into the DC specified by hDC.

PARAMETERS:

hDC   Specifies the DC to draw the icon into

x   Specifies the x coordinate of the upper-left corner of the destination within the DC

y   Specifies the y coordinate of the upper-left corner of the destination within the DC

hIcon   Specifies the handle of the icon to draw

WHAT IT RETURNS:

TRUE if the function is successful, and FALSE if it isn't.

THINGS TO WATCH FOR:

The point specified by x and y is subject to the mapping mode of the specified DC. This means that if you don't use MM_TEXT, you might not be able to predict where a particular point is mapped into a DC. (Amusingly

enough, the docs for this function specify that MM_TEXT must be specified as the mapping mode before this function is called. If that's true, why all the blather about the mapping mode having an effect on the location in the DC?)

SEE ALSO:

```
LoadIcon()
CreateIcon()
```

LoadIcon()

```
HICON LoadIcon(    HANDLE    hInst,
                   LPSTR     icoName)
```

WHAT IT DOES:

Loads an icon resource from the module instance specified by the hInst parameter.

PARAMETERS:

> hInst   Handle to the module instance the icon is to be loaded from.
>
> icoName   Points to a NULL-terminated text string specifying the name of the icon resource. (It can also be a numerical value, which can be gotten with MAKEINTRESOURCE, for icons that have numeric IDs.)

WHAT IT RETURNS:

A handle to an icon if the function is successful and NULL otherwise.

THINGS TO WATCH FOR:

> ☐ Just as with other loadable resources, there's no reason you cannot load an icon from an instance of an application other than your own.
>
> ☐ This function actually loads an icon only if the icon hasn't been previously loaded. If it's already loaded, this function simply returns a handle to it.
>
> ☐ For privately loaded icon resources, you must use the **DestroyIcon()** call when you are done with an icon. However, you must not destroy system icons (listed next).

In addition to privately defined icons, Windows provides system icons that can be loaded. If you set the hInst parameter to NULL, the icoName parameter must be one of the following system icons:

IDI_APPLICATION	Default application icon
IDI_ASTERISK	Asterisk (used in informative messages)
IDI_EXCLAMATION	Exclamation point (used in warning messages)
IDI_HAND	Hand-shaped icon (used in serious warning messages)
IDI_QUESTION	Question mark (used in prompting messages)

SEE ALSO:

DrawIcon()

The Cursor Resource

Cursors are similar to icons, in that they can contain multiple images and have a very similar layout, consisting of a header structure, a series of information structures, and a series of images.

Topics covered in this chapter are

☐ The differences between cursors and icons

☐ The cursor resource structures

☐ Building a cursor by hand: the HandCursor App

☐ Loading a cursor from a resource

☐ Displaying cursors: the Happy Cursor App

There are two big differences between cursors and icons, at least as far as Windows is concerned:

☐ Cursors are monochrome only

☐ Cursors have something called a hotspot

The first difference, that cursors are monochrome only, actually limits your application to four colors, not two. The first two colors are obvious: black and white. The second two colors are *clear,* meaning whatever is under the cursor shows through, and *inverse,* meaning whatever is under the cursor is inverted. Still, it isn't as nice as under OS2/PM, in which cursors can be full color and aren't essentially any different from icons. Oh, well.

The second difference is that cursors have a *hotspot.* This is a point that defines the "hot" pixel of the current cursor. The hotspot is used by Windows to determine where the cursor is when a user clicks the mouse button or moves the cursor over an object. This important visual attribute of cursors is illustrated in Figure 6.1.

Figure 6.1.
Setting an
appropriate
hotspot.

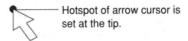

Hotspot of arrow cursor is
set at the tip.

The reason for setting the hotspot of the arrow cursor at its tip is quite simple: users expect that to be the tip of a real arrow. This means that when users move the arrow cursor around on-screen, they expect to be able to place the tip of the cursor on the objects they want to select and then single- or double-click to get a result. The *visual cue* being presented by the arrow cursor (that is, that the tip of the arrow is pointing to something) must match the hotspot of the cursor for users not to be confused.

If the hotspot of the arrow cursor were placed somewhere else (in the tail, for example), the visual cue presented by the cursor would conflict with the hotspot. The user would expect the tip of the arrow to be the "tip" of the cursor, whereas Windows would respond to the point underneath the tail. It's critically important that your application's cursors match their visual cues with their hotspots. It's such an important point that ICE/Works actually checks the hotspot of a cursor to see whether you've set it, and reminds you if you haven't.

The Cursor Resource File Format

A cursor resource file is composed of three pieces: the header, the cursor directory entries, and the cursor images. In this fashion, it's exactly the same as an icon resource file (which consists of an icon header, icon directories, and icon images), although the format of these headers is somewhat different. Take a look at each of them.

The CURSORHEADER Structure

```
typedef struct
    {
        WORD curReserved;        /* Reserved, must be 0 */
        WORD curResourceType;    /* Resource type, for cursors,
                                  * must be 2
                                  */
        WORD curResourceCount;   /* Number of images contained in file
                                  * equal to the number
                                  * of CURSORRCDESCRIPT
                                  * structures which follow it.
                                  */

    }    CURSORHEADER;
```

This header is straightforward enough. It has a reserved value (curReserved), which must be set to 0. That's followed by the curResourceType value, which for cursors must be set to 2. (Remember, this structure also occurs at the beginning of icon resource files, although not with the same names, and this value is used in determining what type of resources the file contains.) Finally, the value curResourceCount lets you know how many cursor images are in this file.

The CURSORRCDESCRIPT Structure

```
typedef struct
    {
        BYTE curWidth;      /* Width of image in pixels */
        BYTE curHeight;     /* Height of image in pixels */
        BYTE ColorCount;    /* Reserved, must be 0 */
        BYTE rByte;         /* Reserved, must be 0 */
        WORD curXHotspot;   /* Specifies in pixels the horz position
                             * of the hotspot.
                             */
        WORD curYHotspot;   /* Specifies in pixels the vertical
                             * position of the hotspot.
                             */
        DWORD curDIBSize;   /* Specifies in bytes size of pixel array
                             * for this form of the cursor image.
                             */
```

```
DWORD curDIBOffset;      /* Specifies the offset in bytes from the
                          * beginning of the file to the device
                          * independent bitmap for this form.
                          */

}      CURSORRCDESCRIPT;
```

This structure is a little more complex; it's a variant of the ICONRCDESCRIPT structure you saw in Chapter 5, "The Icon Resources." The curWidth and curHeight fields are the same, specifying the width and height of the cursor. Notice that unlike an icon, a cursor does not have to have a width or height that is an integer multiple of 16. The ColorCount field is also present, just as it is with an icon. Cursors are always monochrome, however, and for cursors this field must be set to 0.

Next is the rByte (reserved, set to 0). In the ICONRCDESCRIPT structure, it's followed by two reserved words. Here, however, it's followed by two words that specify the hotspot of the cursor: curXHotspot (specifying the horizontal position of the hotspot) and curYHotspot (specifying the vertical position of the hotspot). Now you see what those two reserved words were for!

The final two DWORDs, curDIBSize and curDIBOffset, are exactly the same as in the ICONRCDESCRIPT. They specify, respectively, the size in bytes of the image for this cursor, and the offset in bytes from the beginning of the file to the start of this cursor image.

The Cursor Image Structure

Cursor images are just DIBs, two of them, one right after the other. They are both monochrome images: the first image defines the background mask for the cursor, and the second image defines the foreground mask for the cursor image. The first mask is the XOR mask, and the second mask is the AND mask. Given a bit in each mask, there are four possible results:

AND Mask	OR Mask	Resulting Pixel
0	0	Black
0	1	White
1	0	Clear (see-through)
1	1	Inverted (inverse see-through)

Figure 6.2 serves as an example of two masks for an image.

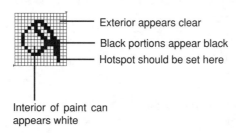

Exterior appears clear

Black portions appear black

Hotspot should be set here

Interior of paint can
appears white

Figure 6.2.
A simple black-
and-white cursor
image.

The center of this paint can is white, whereas the area outside the paint can is displayed as clear (that is, the background shows through when the paint can is moved). Black is displayed as black. Here's how the two masks work:

AND mask

```
1 1 1 1 1 1 1 1 1 1 1 1 1 1 1 1
1 1 1 1 1 1 1 1 1 1 1 1 1 1 1 1
1 1 1 1 1 1 0 0 0 1 1 1 1 1 1 1
1 1 1 1 1 0 0 0 0 0 1 1 1 1 1 1
1 1 1 1 0 0 0 0 0 0 0 1 1 1 1 1
1 1 1 0 0 0 0 0 0 0 0 0 1 1 1 1
1 1 0 0 0 0 0 0 0 0 0 0 1 1 1 1
1 1 0 0 0 0 0 0 0 0 0 0 0 1 1 1
1 1 0 0 0 0 0 0 0 0 0 0 0 1 1 1
1 1 0 0 0 0 0 0 0 0 0 0 0 1 1 1
1 1 1 0 0 0 0 0 0 1 1 0 0 1 1 1
1 1 1 1 0 0 0 0 1 1 1 0 0 1 1 1
1 1 1 1 1 0 0 0 1 1 1 0 0 1 1 1
1 1 1 1 1 1 1 1 1 1 1 1 0 1 1 1
1 1 1 1 1 1 1 1 1 1 1 1 0 1 1 1
1 1 1 1 1 1 1 1 1 1 1 1 1 1 1 1
```

XOR mask

```
0 0 0 0 0 0 0 0 0 0 0 0 0 0 0 0
0 0 0 0 0 0 0 0 0 0 0 0 0 0 0 0
0 0 0 0 0 0 0 0 0 0 0 0 0 0 0 0
0 0 0 0 0 0 0 1 0 0 0 0 0 0 0 0
0 0 0 0 0 1 0 1 1 0 0 0 0 0 0 0
0 0 0 0 1 1 0 0 1 1 0 0 0 0 0 0
0 0 0 1 1 1 1 0 0 1 1 0 0 0 0 0
0 0 0 1 1 1 1 1 0 0 1 0 0 0 0 0
0 0 0 1 1 1 1 1 1 0 0 0 0 0 0 0
0 0 0 1 1 1 1 1 1 0 0 0 0 0 0 0
0 0 0 0 1 1 1 1 0 0 0 0 0 0 0 0
0 0 0 0 0 1 1 0 0 0 0 0 0 0 0 0
0 0 0 0 0 0 0 0 0 0 0 0 0 0 0 0
0 0 0 0 0 0 0 0 0 0 0 0 0 0 0 0
0 0 0 0 0 0 0 0 0 0 0 0 0 0 0 0
0 0 0 0 0 0 0 0 0 0 0 0 0 0 0 0
```

There are a couple of interesting things to note here. First, in the AND mask, both the pixels that are going to appear white and the pixels that are going to appear black are zeroes. It's only when you get to the XOR mask that you can differentiate between the white and black pixels. Second, in the XOR masks, only the *white* pixels are ones. Everything else (both black and clear pixels) are zeroes. It's only by mapping the XOR and the AND masks together that you can see the results.

The other thing to note is that these images are right-side up. But remember that when they're stored in a cursor resource file, they're DIBs. Therefore, the images are upside down (relative to the Windows coordinate system, in which the upper-left corner of an image is (0,0)), because DIBs have as their origin point the lower-left corner. So when these images are stored in memory, they would look like this:

Cursorheader
CursorRCDescript
DIB of xor mask

    `BITMAPINFOHEADER`

    `RGBQUAD[2]` (the colors black and white)

    xor bits, in reverse order to that shown previously

DIB of and mask

    `BITMAPINFOHEADER`

    `RGBQUAD[2]` (black and white)

    and bits, in reverse order to that shown previously

As noted previously, cursors don't have the same limitations in size that icons do. That means if you want to create a really big cursor (like 128 by 128), you can. However, there are a couple of practical reasons why, in general, you don't want to do this. First, it's slow. The bigger you make the cursor, the more bits Windows has to push around. Furthermore, this isn't a linear progression, but a logarithmic one—a 32-by-32 cursor has 4 times as many pixels as a 16-by-16 cursor, a 64-by-64 cursor has 16 times as many pixels, and a 128-by-128 cursor has 64 times as many pixels! This way ruin lies.

The other reason you don't want to make your cursors bigger than 32 by 32 is that many video boards have hardware assist for small cursors. This means that for small cursors—under the limit of the hardware assist, which is usually 32 or 64 pixels on a side—the cursor is very fast, but over that limit, and the board has to fall back on the generalized drawing hardware to support the cursor. Depending on the board, this can be slower, even a lot slower. So stay with small cursors.

Using Cursors in Your Program

Having gone to all the trouble of figuring out the bits of the masks, you might as well take the next step and figure out the byte values. (This code might not work on all video drivers.)

```
unsigned char andMask[]={
/* Row 32 */ 0xFF, 0xFF, 0xFF, 0xFF,
/* Row 31 */ 0xFF, 0xFF, 0xFF, 0xFF,
/* Row 30 */ 0xFF, 0xFF, 0xFF, 0xFF,
/* Row 29 */ 0xFF, 0xFF, 0xFF, 0xFF,
/* Row 28 */ 0xFF, 0xC3, 0xFF, 0xFF,
/* Row 27 */ 0xFF, 0x81, 0xFF, 0xFF,
/* Row 26 */ 0xFF, 0x00, 0x7F, 0xFF,
/* Row 25 */ 0xFE, 0x00, 0x3F, 0xFF,
/* Row 24 */ 0xFC, 0x00, 0x1F, 0xFF,
/* Row 23 */ 0xF8, 0x00, 0x0F, 0xFF,
/* Row 22 */ 0xF0, 0x00, 0x07, 0xFF,
/* Row 21 */ 0xE0, 0x00, 0x03, 0xFF,
/* Row 20 */ 0xE0, 0x00, 0x01, 0xFF,
/* Row 19 */ 0xE0, 0x00, 0x01, 0xFF,
/* Row 18 */ 0xE0, 0x00, 0x60, 0xFF,
/* Row 17 */ 0xE0, 0x00, 0xF0, 0xFF,
/* Row 16 */ 0xF0, 0x01, 0xF8, 0xFF,
/* Row 15 */ 0xF0, 0x03, 0xFF, 0xFF,
/* Row 14 */ 0xF8, 0x07, 0xFF, 0xFF,
/* Row 13 */ 0xFE, 0x0F, 0xFF, 0xFF,
/* Row 12 */ 0xFF, 0xFF, 0xFF, 0xFF,
/* Row 11 */ 0xFF, 0xFF, 0xFF, 0xFF,
/* Row 10 */ 0xFF, 0xFF, 0xFF, 0xFF,
/* Row 09 */ 0xFF, 0xFF, 0xFF, 0xFF,
/* Row 08 */ 0xFF, 0xFF, 0xFF, 0xFF,
/* Row 07 */ 0xFF, 0xFF, 0xFF, 0xFF,
/* Row 06 */ 0xFF, 0xFF, 0xFF, 0xFF,
/* Row 05 */ 0xFF, 0xFF, 0xFF, 0xFF,
/* Row 04 */ 0xFF, 0xFF, 0xFF, 0xFF,
/* Row 03 */ 0xFF, 0xFF, 0xFF, 0xFF,
/* Row 02 */ 0xFF, 0xFF, 0xFF, 0xFF,
/* Row 01 */ 0xFF, 0xFF, 0xFF, 0xFF,
};

unsigned char orMask[]={
/* Row 32 */ 0x00, 0x00, 0x00, 0x00,
/* Row 31 */ 0x00, 0x00, 0x00, 0x00,
/* Row 30 */ 0x00, 0x00, 0x00, 0x00,
/* Row 29 */ 0x00, 0x00, 0x00, 0x00,
/* Row 28 */ 0x00, 0x00, 0x00, 0x00,
/* Row 27 */ 0x00, 0x0C, 0x00, 0x00,
/* Row 26 */ 0x00, 0x2E, 0x00, 0x00,
/* Row 25 */ 0x00, 0x2F, 0x00, 0x00,
/* Row 24 */ 0x00, 0xA7, 0x80, 0x00,
/* Row 23 */ 0x00, 0xB0, 0x00, 0x00,
```

```
/* Row 22 */ 0x02, 0x98, 0x00, 0x00,
/* Row 21 */ 0x06, 0xCC, 0x00, 0x00,
/* Row 20 */ 0x0E, 0x67, 0x00, 0x00,
/* Row 19 */ 0x0F, 0x30, 0x00, 0x00,
/* Row 18 */ 0x0F, 0x9E, 0x00, 0x00,
/* Row 17 */ 0x0F, 0xC0, 0x00, 0x00,
/* Row 16 */ 0x07, 0xF8, 0x00, 0x00,
/* Row 15 */ 0x03, 0xF0, 0x03, 0x00,
/* Row 14 */ 0x01, 0xE0, 0x01, 0x00,
/* Row 13 */ 0x00, 0x00, 0x00, 0x00,
/* Row 12 */ 0x00, 0x00, 0x01, 0x00,
/* Row 11 */ 0x00, 0x00, 0x00, 0x00,
/* Row 10 */ 0x00, 0x00, 0x00, 0x00,
/* Row 09 */ 0x00, 0x00, 0x00, 0x00,
/* Row 08 */ 0x00, 0x00, 0x00, 0x00,
/* Row 07 */ 0x00, 0x00, 0x00, 0x00,
/* Row 06 */ 0x00, 0x00, 0x00, 0x00,
/* Row 05 */ 0x00, 0x00, 0x00, 0x00,
/* Row 04 */ 0x00, 0x00, 0x00, 0x00,
/* Row 03 */ 0x00, 0x00, 0x00, 0x00,
/* Row 02 */ 0x00, 0x00, 0x00, 0x00,
/* Row 01 */ 0x00, 0x00, 0x00, 0x00,
};
```

Having gone that far, you might as well take the final step and actually build a cursor out of the byte values.

The HandCursor App: Building a Cursor by Hand

Here's the source code to an app that takes these two masks and builds the resulting cursor. The code to build a cursor is simple and occurs in response to the WM_CREATE message. Listings 6.1 through 6.7 show the actual implementation of the HandCursor App.

Listing 6.1. HANDCURS.C—source code to the HandCursor App.

```
//File name: HANDCURS.C
//"HANDCURS" Generated by WindowsMAKER Professional
//Author: Alex Leavens, for ShadowCat Technologies
```

```
#include <WINDOWS.H>
#include "HANDCURS.H"

WMPDEBUG
#include "HANDCURS.WMC"

//****************************************************************
//                         WinMain FUNCTION
//****************************************************************

    int PASCAL
WinMain(HINSTANCE hInstance,
        HINSTANCE hPrevInstance,
        LPSTR     lpCmdLine,
        int       nCmdShow)
{
    MSG msg;                    // Message

    hInst = hInstance;          // Saves the current instance

    if (!BLDInitApplication(hInstance,hPrevInstance,&nCmdShow,lpCmdLine))
        return FALSE;

    if (!hPrevInstance)         // Is there another instance of the task
        {
        if (!BLDRegisterClass(hInstance))
            return FALSE;       // Exits if unable to initialize
        }

    MainhWnd = BLDCreateWindow(hInstance);
    if (!MainhWnd)              // Check if the window is created
        return FALSE;

    ShowWindow(MainhWnd, nCmdShow);  // Show the window
    UpdateWindow(MainhWnd);          // Send WM_PAINT message to window

    BLDInitMainMenu(MainhWnd);  // Initialize main menu if necessary

    while (GetMessage(&msg,     // Message structure
                      0,        // Handle of window receiving the message
                      0,        // Lowest message to examine
                      0))       // Highest message to examine
```

continues

Listing 6.1. continued

```
        {
        if (BLDKeyTranslation(&msg)) // WindowsMAKER code for key translation
            continue;
        TranslateMessage(&msg); // Translates character keys
        DispatchMessage(&msg);  // Dispatches message to window
        }
    BLDExitApplication();        // Clean up if necessary
    return(msg.wParam);          // Returns the value from PostQuitMessage
}


//***************************************************************
//                WINDOW PROCEDURE FOR MAIN WINDOW
//***************************************************************


unsigned char andMask[]={
/* Row 32 */ 0xFF, 0xFF, 0xFF, 0xFF,
/* Row 31 */ 0xFF, 0xFF, 0xFF, 0xFF,
/* Row 30 */ 0xFF, 0xFF, 0xFF, 0xFF,
/* Row 29 */ 0xFF, 0xFF, 0xFF, 0xFF,
/* Row 28 */ 0xFF, 0xC3, 0xFF, 0xFF,
/* Row 27 */ 0xFF, 0x81, 0xFF, 0xFF,
/* Row 26 */ 0xFF, 0x00, 0x7F, 0xFF,
/* Row 25 */ 0xFE, 0x00, 0x3F, 0xFF,
/* Row 24 */ 0xFC, 0x00, 0x1F, 0xFF,
/* Row 23 */ 0xF8, 0x00, 0x0F, 0xFF,
/* Row 22 */ 0xF0, 0x00, 0x07, 0xFF,
/* Row 21 */ 0xE0, 0x00, 0x03, 0xFF,
/* Row 20 */ 0xE0, 0x00, 0x01, 0xFF,
/* Row 19 */ 0xE0, 0x00, 0x01, 0xFF,
/* Row 18 */ 0xE0, 0x00, 0x60, 0xFF,
/* Row 17 */ 0xE0, 0x00, 0xF0, 0xFF,
/* Row 16 */ 0xF0, 0x01, 0xF8, 0xFF,
/* Row 15 */ 0xF0, 0x03, 0xFF, 0xFF,
/* Row 14 */ 0xF8, 0x07, 0xFF, 0xFF,
/* Row 13 */ 0xFE, 0x0F, 0xFF, 0xFF,
/* Row 12 */ 0xFF, 0xFF, 0xFF, 0xFF,
/* Row 11 */ 0xFF, 0xFF, 0xFF, 0xFF,
/* Row 10 */ 0xFF, 0xFF, 0xFF, 0xFF,
/* Row 09 */ 0xFF, 0xFF, 0xFF, 0xFF,
/* Row 08 */ 0xFF, 0xFF, 0xFF, 0xFF,
/* Row 07 */ 0xFF, 0xFF, 0xFF, 0xFF,
/* Row 06 */ 0xFF, 0xFF, 0xFF, 0xFF,
/* Row 05 */ 0xFF, 0xFF, 0xFF, 0xFF,
/* Row 04 */ 0xFF, 0xFF, 0xFF, 0xFF,
```

```
/* Row 03 */ 0xFF, 0xFF, 0xFF, 0xFF,
/* Row 02 */ 0xFF, 0xFF, 0xFF, 0xFF,
/* Row 01 */ 0xFF, 0xFF, 0xFF, 0xFF,
};

unsigned char orMask[]={
/* Row 32 */ 0x00, 0x00, 0x00, 0x00,
/* Row 31 */ 0x00, 0x00, 0x00, 0x00,
/* Row 30 */ 0x00, 0x00, 0x00, 0x00,
/* Row 29 */ 0x00, 0x00, 0x00, 0x00,
/* Row 28 */ 0x00, 0x00, 0x00, 0x00,
/* Row 27 */ 0x00, 0x0C, 0x00, 0x00,
/* Row 26 */ 0x00, 0x2E, 0x00, 0x00,
/* Row 25 */ 0x00, 0x2F, 0x00, 0x00,
/* Row 24 */ 0x00, 0xA7, 0x80, 0x00,
/* Row 23 */ 0x00, 0xB0, 0x00, 0x00,
/* Row 22 */ 0x02, 0x98, 0x00, 0x00,
/* Row 21 */ 0x06, 0xCC, 0x00, 0x00,
/* Row 20 */ 0x0E, 0x67, 0x00, 0x00,
/* Row 19 */ 0x0F, 0x30, 0x00, 0x00,
/* Row 18 */ 0x0F, 0x9E, 0x00, 0x00,
/* Row 17 */ 0x0F, 0xC0, 0x00, 0x00,
/* Row 16 */ 0x07, 0xF8, 0x00, 0x00,
/* Row 15 */ 0x03, 0xF0, 0x03, 0x00,
/* Row 14 */ 0x01, 0xE0, 0x01, 0x00,
/* Row 13 */ 0x00, 0x00, 0x00, 0x00,
/* Row 12 */ 0x00, 0x00, 0x01, 0x00,
/* Row 11 */ 0x00, 0x00, 0x00, 0x00,
/* Row 10 */ 0x00, 0x00, 0x00, 0x00,
/* Row 09 */ 0x00, 0x00, 0x00, 0x00,
/* Row 08 */ 0x00, 0x00, 0x00, 0x00,
/* Row 07 */ 0x00, 0x00, 0x00, 0x00,
/* Row 06 */ 0x00, 0x00, 0x00, 0x00,
/* Row 05 */ 0x00, 0x00, 0x00, 0x00,
/* Row 04 */ 0x00, 0x00, 0x00, 0x00,
/* Row 03 */ 0x00, 0x00, 0x00, 0x00,
/* Row 02 */ 0x00, 0x00, 0x00, 0x00,
/* Row 01 */ 0x00, 0x00, 0x00, 0x00,
};

HCURSOR    testCursor;
HCURSOR    oldCursor;
```

continues

Listing 6.1. continued

```
    LONG FAR PASCAL
BLDMainWndProc(HWND  hWnd,
               UINT  message,
               UINT  wParam,
               LONG  lParam )
{

    switch (message)
    {

    case WM_CREATE:
        testCursor = CreateCursor ( hInst,     // Instance handle to our app
                                    23,        // X hotspot
                                    20,        // Y hotspot
                                    32,        // Width of cursor
                                    32,        // Height of cursor
                                    (LPSTR) andMask,
                                    (LPSTR) orMask );
        if ( testCursor != NULL )
        {
            oldCursor = SetCursor ( testCursor );
        }
        else
        {
            MessageBox(NULL,
                       "Cannot create cursor",
                       "",
                       MB_OK);
        }

        // Send to BLDDefWindowProc in (.WMC) for controls in main window
        return BLDDefWindowProc(hWnd, message, wParam, lParam);
        break;
    case WM_SETCURSOR:
        SetCursor ( testCursor );
        return TRUE;

    case WM_SETFOCUS:            // Window is notified of focus change
        // Send to BLDDefWindowProc in (.WMC) for controls in main window
        return BLDDefWindowProc(hWnd, message, wParam, lParam);
        break;

    case WM_DESTROY:            // Window being destroyed
        SetCursor ( oldCursor );
```

```
        DestroyCursor ( testCursor );
        PostQuitMessage(0);
        return BLDDefWindowProc(hWnd, message, wParam, lParam);
        break;

    case WM_COMMAND:              // Command from the main window
        if (BLDMenuCommand(hWnd, message, wParam, lParam))
            break;                // Processed by BLDMenuCommand.
        // Else default processing by BLDDefWindowProc.
    default:
        // Pass on message for default processing
        return BLDDefWindowProc(hWnd, message, wParam, lParam);
    }


    return FALSE;                 // Returns FALSE if processed
}
```

Listing 6.2. HANDCURS.WMC—special include file for the HANDCURS.C file.

```
//File name: HANDCURS.WMC
//"HANDCURS" Generated by WindowsMAKER Professional
//Author: Alex Leavens, for ShadowCat Technologies


//****************************************************************
//                    GLOBAL VARIABLES
//****************************************************************

HBRUSH      hMBrush = 0;         // Handle to brush for main window.
HINSTANCE   hInst   = 0;         // Handle to instance.
HWND        MainhWnd= 0;         // Handle to main window.
HWND        hClient = 0;         // Handle to window in client area.
FARPROC     lpClient= 0L;        // Function for window in client area.


//****************************************************************
//            PROCESSES KEYBOARD ACCELERATORS
//            AND MODELESS DIALOG BOX KEY INPUT
//****************************************************************

BOOL BLDKeyTranslation(MSG *pMsg)
    {
    return FALSE;                 // No special key input
    }
```

continues

Listing 6.2. continued

```
//***************************************************************
//           CUSTOM MESSAGE PROCESSING FOR MAIN WINDOW
//***************************************************************

LONG FAR PASCAL BLDDefWindowProc(HWND hWnd, UINT message, UINT wParam,
                          LONG lParam )

    {

    switch (message)
        {

          default:
        // Pass on message for default processing by Windows
        return DefWindowProc(hWnd, message, wParam, lParam);
        }
    return FALSE;                    // Returns FALSE if not processed by Windows
    }


//***************************************************************
//              PROCESSES ALL MENU ITEM SELECTIONS
//***************************************************************

BOOL BLDMenuCommand(HWND hWnd, UINT message, UINT wParam, LONG lParam )
{

    switch( LOWORD(wParam) )
        {

        // Processing of linked menu items in menu: HANDCURS

    default:
        return FALSE;                // Not processed by this function.
        }
    return TRUE;                     // Processed by this function.
    }


//***************************************************************
//    FUNCTIONS FOR INITIALIZATION AND EXIT OF APPLICATION
//***************************************************************

BOOL BLDInitApplication(HANDLE hInst, HANDLE hPrev, int *pCmdShow,
                    LPSTR lpCmd)
    {
    // No initialization necessary
```

```
    return TRUE;
    }


// Registers the class for the main window
BOOL BLDRegisterClass( HANDLE hInstance )
    {
    WNDCLASS WndClass;

    hMBrush=CreateSolidBrush(GetSysColor(COLOR_WINDOW));

    WndClass.style        = 0;
    WndClass.lpfnWndProc  = BLDMainWndProc;
    WndClass.cbClsExtra   = 0;
    WndClass.cbWndExtra   = 0;
    WndClass.hInstance    = hInstance;
    WndClass.hIcon        = LoadIcon(NULL,IDI_APPLICATION);
    WndClass.hCursor      = LoadCursor(NULL,IDC_ARROW);
    WndClass.hbrBackground = hMBrush;
    WndClass.lpszMenuName  = NULL;
    WndClass.lpszClassName = "HANDCURS";

    return RegisterClass(&WndClass);
    }


HWND BLDCreateWindow( HANDLE hInstance )   // Creates the main window
{
    HWND hWnd;                   // Window handle
    int coordinate[4];           // Coordinates of main window

    coordinate[0]=CW_USEDEFAULT;
    coordinate[1]=0;
    coordinate[2]=CW_USEDEFAULT;
    coordinate[3]=0;

    hWnd = CreateWindow("HANDCURS",  // Window class registered earlier
        "Cursor Example - by Alex Leavens",        // Window caption
      WS_OVERLAPPED¦WS_THICKFRAME¦WS_SYSMENU¦WS_MINIMIZEBOX¦WS_MAXIMIZEBOX,
                          // Window style
        coordinate[0],       // X position
        coordinate[1],       // Y position
        coordinate[2],       // Width
        coordinate[3],       // Height
        0,                   // Parent handle
        0,                   // Menu or child ID
```

continues

Listing 6.2. continued

```
                hInstance,          // Instance
                (LPSTR)NULL);       // Additional info

    return hWnd;
    }


// Called just before entering message loop
BOOL BLDInitMainMenu(HWND hWnd)
    {
    // No initialization necessary
    return TRUE;
    }


BOOL BLDExitApplication()       // Called just before exit of application
    {
    if (hMBrush)
        DeleteObject(hMBrush);
    return TRUE;
    }

//**********************************************************
// ERROR MESSAGE HANDLING (Definitions can be overruled.)
//**********************************************************

#ifndef ERRORCAPTION
#define ERRORCAPTION "Cursor Example - by Alex Leavens"
#endif

#ifndef LOADERROR
#define LOADERROR "Cannot load string."
#endif


int BLDDisplayMessage(HWND hWnd, unsigned uMsg, char *pContext, int iType)
    {
    int i, j;
    char Message[200+1];

    if (uMsg)
        {
        if (!LoadString(hInst,uMsg,Message,200))
```

```
                    {
                    MessageBox(hWnd,LOADERROR,ERRORCAPTION, MB_OK¦MB_SYSTEMMODAL¦
                                                            MB_ICONHAND);
                    return FALSE;
                    }
                }
        else
            Message[0]=0;

        if (pContext)
            {
            i = lstrlen(Message);
            j = lstrlen(pContext);
            if (i + j + 1 <= 200)
                {
                lstrcat(Message, " ");
                lstrcat(Message, pContext);
                }
            }

        return MessageBox(hWnd,Message,ERRORCAPTION,iType);
        }


//****************************************************************
//          FUNCTIONS FOR DRAWING GRAPHICS BUTTONS
//****************************************************************

BOOL BLDDrawIcon(LPDRAWITEMSTRUCT lpDrawItem, char *pIconName)
    {
    HICON hIcon;

    hIcon = LoadIcon(hInst,pIconName);
    if (!hIcon)
        {
        BLDDisplayMessage(GetActiveWindow(),BLD_CannotLoadIcon,pIconName, MB_OK¦
                        MB_ICONASTERISK);
        return FALSE;
        }

    SetMapMode(lpDrawItem->hDC,MM_TEXT);
    return DrawIcon(lpDrawItem->hDC,0,0,hIcon);
    }
```

continues

Listing 6.2. continued

```
BOOL BLDDrawBitmap(LPDRAWITEMSTRUCT lpDrawItem, char *pBitmapName,
                   BOOL bStretch)
    {
    HBITMAP hBitmap;
    HDC hMemDC;
    BITMAP Bitmap;
    int iRaster;

    iRaster = GetDeviceCaps(lpDrawItem->hDC,RASTERCAPS);
    if ((iRaster&RC_BITBLT)!=RC_BITBLT)
        return FALSE;                // Device cannot display bitmap

    hBitmap = LoadBitmap(hInst,pBitmapName);
    if (!hBitmap)
        {
        BLDDisplayMessage(GetActiveWindow(),BLD_CannotLoadBitmap,pBitmapName,
                          MB_OK | MB_ICONASTERISK);
        return FALSE;
        }

    if (!GetObject(hBitmap,sizeof(BITMAP),(LPSTR)&Bitmap))
        {
        DeleteObject(hBitmap);
        return FALSE;
        }
    hMemDC = CreateCompatibleDC(lpDrawItem->hDC);
    if (!hMemDC)
        {
        DeleteObject(hBitmap);
        return FALSE;
        }
    if (!SelectObject(hMemDC,hBitmap))
        {
        DeleteDC(hMemDC);
        DeleteObject(hBitmap);
        return FALSE;
        }

    if (bStretch)
        {
        StretchBlt(lpDrawItem->hDC,
                   lpDrawItem->rcItem.left,
                   lpDrawItem->rcItem.top,
```

326

```
                    lpDrawItem->rcItem.right-lpDrawItem->rcItem.left,
                    lpDrawItem->rcItem.bottom-lpDrawItem->rcItem.top,
                    hMemDC,
                    0,
                    0,
                    Bitmap.bmWidth,
                    Bitmap.bmHeight,
                    SRCCOPY);
        }
    else
        {
          BitBlt(lpDrawItem->hDC,
                    lpDrawItem->rcItem.left,
                    lpDrawItem->rcItem.top,
                    lpDrawItem->rcItem.right-lpDrawItem->rcItem.left,
                    lpDrawItem->rcItem.bottom-lpDrawItem->rcItem.top,
                    hMemDC,
                    0,
                    0,
                    SRCCOPY);
        }
    DeleteDC(hMemDC);
    DeleteObject(hBitmap);
    return TRUE;
    }


//**************************************************************
//        FUNCTION FOR CREATING CONTROLS IN MAIN WINDOW
//**************************************************************

// Startup procedure for window in client area
HWND BLDCreateClientControls(char *pTemplateName, FARPROC lpNew)
{
    RECT rClient,rMain,rDialog;
    int dxDialog,dyDialog,dyExtra,dtXold,dtYold;
    HANDLE hRes,hMem;
    LPBLD_DLGTEMPLATE lpDlg;
    unsigned long styleold,style;
    HWND hNew;

    if (!IsWindow(MainhWnd))
        return 0;
    if (IsZoomed(MainhWnd))
        ShowWindow(MainhWnd,SW_RESTORE);
```

continues

Listing 6.2. continued

```
if (IsWindow(hClient))
    DestroyWindow(hClient); // Destroy Previous window in client area

// Get access to data structure of dialog box containing layout of ctrls
hRes=FindResource(hInst,(LPSTR)pTemplateName,RT_DIALOG);
if (!hRes)
    return 0;
hMem=LoadResource(hInst,hRes);
if (!hMem)
    return 0;
lpDlg=(LPBLD_DLGTEMPLATE)LockResource(hMem);
if (!lpDlg)
    return 0;

// Change dialog box data structure so it can be used as a window
// in client area
styleold        = lpDlg->dtStyle;
style           = lpDlg->dtStyle&(CLIENTSTRIP);
lpDlg->dtStyle  = lpDlg->dtStyle^style;
lpDlg->dtStyle  = lpDlg->dtStyle | WS_CHILD | WS_CLIPSIBLINGS;
dtXold          = lpDlg->dtX;
dtYold          = lpDlg->dtY;
lpDlg->dtX      = 0;
lpDlg->dtY      = 0;

hNew = CreateDialogIndirect(hInst,(LPSTR)lpDlg, MainhWnd,lpNew);
if (!hNew)
    return 0;

// Restore dialog box data structure.
lpDlg->dtStyle = styleold;
lpDlg->dtX     = dtXold;
lpDlg->dtY     = dtYold;

UnlockResource(hMem);
FreeResource(hMem);

// Move and size window in client area and main window
GetClientRect(MainhWnd,&rClient);
GetWindowRect(MainhWnd,&rMain);
GetWindowRect(hNew,&rDialog);
dxDialog=(rDialog.right-rDialog.left)-(rClient.right-rClient.left);
dyDialog=(rDialog.bottom-rDialog.top)-(rClient.bottom-rClient.top);
BLDMoveWindow(MainhWnd,rMain.left,rMain.top,
```

```
                        (rMain.right-rMain.left)+dxDialog,
                            (rMain.bottom-rMain.top)+dyDialog,
                  TRUE);
      MoveWindow(hNew,0,0,
                            (rDialog.right-rDialog.left),
                            (rDialog.bottom-rDialog.top),
                            TRUE);
      GetClientRect(MainhWnd,&rClient);

      // Compensate size if menu bar is more than one line.
      if ((rDialog.bottom-rDialog.top)>(rClient.bottom-rClient.top))
          {
          dyExtra=(rDialog.bottom-rDialog.top)-(rClient.bottom-rClient.top);
          BLDMoveWindow(MainhWnd,rMain.left,rMain.top,
                      (rMain.right-rMain.left)+dxDialog,
                      (rMain.bottom-rMain.top)+dyDialog+dyExtra,
                      TRUE);
          }

      ShowWindow(hNew,SW_SHOW);
      hClient=hNew;
      lpClient=lpNew;
      return hClient;
      }


// Ensure that window is within screen.
void BLDMoveWindow(HWND hWnd, int x, int y,
        int nWidth, int nHeight, BOOL bRepaint)
      {
      int xMax,yMax,xNew,yNew;

      xMax = GetSystemMetrics(SM_CXSCREEN);
      yMax = GetSystemMetrics(SM_CYSCREEN);

      if ((nWidth<=xMax)&&(x+nWidth>xMax))
          xNew=xMax-nWidth;
      else
          xNew=x;

      if ((nHeight<=yMax)&&(y+nHeight>yMax))
          yNew=yMax-nHeight;
      else
          yNew=y;
```

continues

Listing 6.2. continued

```c
    MoveWindow(hWnd,xNew,yNew,nWidth,nHeight,bRepaint);
    return;
    }


//****************************************************************
//                 FUNCTION FOR SWITCHING MENU SET
//****************************************************************

BOOL BLDSwitchMenu(HWND hWnd, char *pTemplateName)
    {
    HMENU hMenu1,hMenu;
    DWORD style;

    style = GetWindowLong(hWnd,GWL_STYLE);
    if((style & WS_CHILD) == WS_CHILD)  // Called from control in main window?
        {
        hWnd=GetParent(hWnd);
        if (!hWnd)
            return FALSE;
        style = GetWindowLong(hWnd,GWL_STYLE);
        if((style & WS_CHILD) == WS_CHILD) // No menu in a WS_CHILD window.
            return FALSE;
        }
    if((style & WS_CAPTION) != WS_CAPTION) // No menu if no caption.
        return FALSE;

    hMenu1 = GetMenu(hWnd);
    hMenu = LoadMenu(hInst,pTemplateName);
    if (!hMenu)
        {
        BLDDisplayMessage(hWnd,BLD_CannotLoadMenu,pTemplateName,
                        MB_OK | MB_ICONASTERISK);
        return FALSE;
        }

    if (!SetMenu(hWnd,hMenu))
        return FALSE;
    if (hMenu1)
        DestroyMenu(hMenu1);

    DrawMenuBar(hWnd);
    return TRUE;
    }
```

Listing 6.3. HANDCURS.H—header file for the HandCursor App.

```
//File name: HANDCURS.H
//"HANDCURS" Generated by WindowsMAKER Professional
//Author: Alex Leavens, for ShadowCat Technologies

// These definitions are provided to support
// compilers with older versions of WINDOWS.H.
typedef unsigned int        UINT;
#ifndef WINAPI
typedef HANDLE              HINSTANCE;
#endif


#ifndef WM_SYSTEMERROR
#define WM_SYSTEMERROR          0x0017
#endif
#ifndef WM_QUEUESYNC
#define WM_QUEUESYNC            0x0023
#endif
#ifndef WM_COMMNOTIFY
#define WM_COMMNOTIFY           0x0044
#endif
#ifndef WM_WINDOWPOSCHANGING
#define WM_WINDOWPOSCHANGING    0x0046
#endif
#ifndef WM_WINDOWPOSCHANGED
#define WM_WINDOWPOSCHANGED     0x0047
#endif
#ifndef WM_POWER
#define WM_POWER                0x0048
#endif
#ifndef WM_DROPFILES
#define WM_DROPFILES            0x0233
#endif
#ifndef WM_PALETTEISCHANGING
#define WM_PALETTEISCHANGING    0x0310
#endif


// Give access to handles in all code modules
extern HINSTANCE hInst;
extern HWND      MainhWnd;

// Constants for error message strings
```

continues

Listing 6.3. continued

```c
#define BLD_CannotRun          4000
#define BLD_CannotCreate       4001
#define BLD_CannotLoadMenu     4002
#define BLD_CannotLoadIcon     4003
#define BLD_CannotLoadBitmap   4004


#if !defined(THISISBLDRC)


int  PASCAL WinMain( HINSTANCE hInstance, HINSTANCE hPrevInstance,
                     LPSTR lpCmdLine, int nCmdShow );
LONG FAR PASCAL BLDMainWndProc( HWND hWnd, UINT message, UINT wParam,
                                LONG lParam );
LONG FAR PASCAL BLDDefWindowProc( HWND hWnd, UINT message, UINT wParam,
                                  LONG lParam );
BOOL BLDKeyTranslation( MSG *pMsg );
BOOL BLDInitApplication( HANDLE hInst, HANDLE hPrev, int *pCmdShow,
                         LPSTR lpCmd );
BOOL BLDExitApplication( void );
HWND BLDCreateClientControls( char *pTemplateName, FARPROC lpNew );
BOOL BLDInitMainMenu( HWND hWnd );
BOOL BLDMenuCommand( HWND hWnd, UINT message, UINT wParam, LONG lParam );
BOOL BLDRegisterClass( HANDLE hInstance );
HWND BLDCreateWindow( HANDLE hInstance );
int  BLDDisplayMessage(HWND hWnd, unsigned uMsg, char *pContext, int iType );
BOOL BLDSwitchMenu( HWND hWnd, char *pTemplateName );
BOOL BLDDrawBitmap( LPDRAWITEMSTRUCT lpDrawItem, char *pBitmapName,
                    BOOL bStretch );
BOOL BLDDrawIcon( LPDRAWITEMSTRUCT lpDrawItem, char *pIconName );
void BLDMoveWindow( HWND hWnd, int x, int y, int nWidth, int nHeight,
                    BOOL bRepaint );


//****************************************************************
// Variables, types, and constants for controls in main window.
//****************************************************************


extern HWND    hClient;        // Handle to window in client area.
extern FARPROC lpClient;       // Function for window in client area.

#define CLIENTSTRIP
WS_MINIMIZE|WS_MAXIMIZE|WS_CAPTION|WS_BORDER|WS_DLGFRAME|WS_SYSMENU|WS_POPUP|
WS_THICKFRAME|DS_MODALFRAME

typedef struct
    {
```

```
        unsigned long dtStyle;
        BYTE dtItemCount;
        int dtX;
        int dtY;
        int dtCX;
        int dtCY;
        } BLD_DLGTEMPLATE;


typedef BLD_DLGTEMPLATE far              *LPBLD_DLGTEMPLATE;


#endif


#define WMPDEBUG



// User Defined ID Values



// WindowsMAKER Pro generated ID Values
```

Listing 6.4. HANDCURS.RC—resource file for the HandCursor App.

```
//File name: HANDCURS.RC
//"HANDCURS" Generated by WindowsMAKER Professional
//Author: Alex Leavens, for ShadowCat Technologies

#define THISISBLDRC

#include <WINDOWS.H>
#include "HANDCURS.H"


//********************************************************
//        Resource code for error message strings
//********************************************************

STRINGTABLE
    BEGIN
        BLD_CannotRun          "Cannot run "
        BLD_CannotCreate       "Cannot create dialog box "
        BLD_CannotLoadMenu     "Cannot load menu "
        BLD_CannotLoadIcon     "Cannot load icon "
        BLD_CannotLoadBitmap   "Cannot load bitmap "
    END
```

Listing 6.5. HANDCURS—the makefile for the HandCursor App.

```
#File name: HANDCURS
#"HANDCURS" Generated by WindowsMAKER Professional
#Author: Alex Leavens, for ShadowCat Technologies

comp= /c /AS /Os /Gsw /Zpe /D _WINDOWS /W2
cc=cl

HANDCURS.EXE : HANDCURS.OBJ HANDCURS.DEF HANDCURS.RES
    LINK @HANDCURS.LNK
    rc HANDCURS.RES

HANDCURS.RES : HANDCURS.RC HANDCURS.H
    rc -r HANDCURS.RC

HANDCURS.OBJ : HANDCURS.C HANDCURS.WMC HANDCURS.H
    $(cc) $(comp) HANDCURS.C
```

Listing 6.6. HANDCURS.LNK—link file for the HandCursor App.

```
HANDCURS ,HANDCURS.EXE ,/align:16 /NOD   , LIBW SLIBCEW, HANDCURS.DEF
```

Listing 6.7. HANDCURS.DEF—module definition file for the HandCursor App.

```
;File name: HANDCURS.DEF
;"HANDCURS" Generated by WindowsMAKER Professional
;Author: Alex Leavens, for ShadowCat Technologies

NAME         HANDCURS
DESCRIPTION  'HandCurs, a cursor by hand'
EXETYPE      WINDOWS
STUB         'WINSTUB.EXE'
DATA         MOVEABLE MULTIPLE
CODE         MOVEABLE DISCARDABLE PRELOAD
HEAPSIZE     1024
STACKSIZE    5120
EXPORTS

             BLDMainWndProc
```

The interesting things here occur in response to the WM_CREATE message. You take the masks you've defined and pass them to the **CreateCursor()** call, which turns the images into a cursor handle you can then use in the **SetCursor()** call. Note that before attempting to use the cursor handle that you've been passed back, you should check first to make sure that the handle isn't NULL — passing in a NULL handle to **SetCursor()** is yet another way to generate a UAE. (Under 3.1, UAEs don't exist—they're called GPFs instead, for general protection faults.)

Using System-Defined Cursors

If creating a cursor by hand strikes you as being a bit labor intensive (it's just like creating bitmaps by hand, only worse, because you have two images), you have a couple of alternatives. The first solution is to use one of the built-in Windows cursors, which you can access through the **LoadCursor()** API call.

Here's a list of the available system cursors (defined in windows.h):

Identifier	Description
IDC_ARROW	Standard arrow cursor
IDC_CROSS	Crosshair cursor
IDC_IBEAM	Text I-beam cursor
IDC_ICON	Empty icon (used for creating draggable icon cursors)
IDC_SIZE	Square with a smaller square inside its lower-right corner
IDC_SIZENESW	Double-pointed cursor with arrows pointing northeast and southwest
IDC_SIZENS	Double-pointed cursor with arrows pointing north and south
IDC_SIZENWSE	Double-pointed cursor with arrows pointing northwest and southeast
IDC_SIZEWE	Double-pointed cursor with arrows pointing west and east
IDC_UPARROW	Vertical arrow cursor
IDC_WAIT	Hourglass cursor

If you look closely at this list, you can see that most of the cursors listed are really very system-specific. For example, four cursors are used by Windows to indicate a sizeable window frame (that is, a window frame you can drag and make bigger or smaller). Do you really want to use one of these in your

application, when the user has planted firmly in mind the idea that these cursors mean "size me" and nothing else? Unless you have something to size in your application, it's probably not a good idea to use these cursors. Similarly, the I-beam cursor is representative of text selection or insertion. The hourglass cursor is symbolic of "busy," and so on. Unless you have a specific need for one of these cursors, you're going to want to build your own cursors.

Creating and Using Custom Cursors

The first thing you need to do to use a custom cursor in your application is build it. This certainly seems like a straightforward process. It pretty much is, if you use a cursor creation program, such as ICE/Works. You should keep in mind a couple of things when creating cursors, though:

- [ ] Make it big. Cursors have a funny way of looking a lot bigger in the editor than they do in your application. When you create a cursor, make sure you can see it! (ICE/Works has a special test area that lets you play with the cursor you're creating and see whether you like the results in action.) If you ran the HandCursor App, the first thing you noticed was that the cursor was tiny! A 16-by-16 cursor just doesn't show up at all.

- [ ] On the other hand, don't make it too big. Remember what I said about 128-by-128 cursors? Right. A good size is 32 by 32. Occasionally (very occasionally), you might need a 64-by-64 cursor.

- [ ] Make it relevant. Remember, the cursor is the user's alter-ego on the screen. In the best applications, it's an extension of the user's own self, so much so that the user isn't aware that he or she is interacting with an application, only that the work is getting done. This argues for cursors that provide useful feedback without overtly calling attention to themselves. For example, in ICE/Works, when you select Mirroring mode, the drawing cursor (pencil, paint brush, spray can) has appended to it a little mirror. (See Figure 6.3.)

  It's fairly subtle, but it works; when the user is in mirror mode, a simple visual cue indicates that what the user is drawing differs from the normal drawing mode (mirroring is on). To show you how important this kind of visual cueing is, I'll give you another example of an application that doesn't do it right—OK, I admit it, it's also ICE/Works. I blew this one; there's no way to differentiate between normal flood fill mode (the paint-can cursor) and special "magic replace fill" mode (again, the paint-can cursor). What these functions do is really quite different, and if the user wants one of them, it's a pretty safe bet that she doesn't want the other one. Yet there's no visual indicator of which kind of paint can you've got. You can do a paint operation expecting one thing and get something quite different. I've been meaning to fix it (I know, I know... <grin>), if only to prevent me from irritating *myself*. (Every time I use the darn thing in the wrong mode I feel like tweaking myself!) [Note: I finally fixed it in version 5.] In any case, though, this should give you an idea of why this kind of visual cueing is important and how to achieve it.

————————— Normal paint-brush cursor

Figure 6.3.
A different cursor can be used to give the user visual feedback.

————————— Paint-brush mirror cursor

Make it distinctive. If the user can't distinguish between your pencil cursor, your paint-brush cursor, and your eraser cursor, you've got a problem. (My favorite cursor comment is "Ewwww! What's *that?* It looks like an armadillo that's been hit by a truck!")

Including Cursors in Your App

Including cursors in your application is easy; it's just another resource, like an icon or a bitmap. In your .RC file, you have a line that looks something like

```
FOOCURSOR    CURSOR    FOO.CUR
```

in which FOOCURSOR is the name you use to reference the cursor. (See the next section.) The CURSOR statement indicates that this is (of course) a cursor resource, and it's followed by the name of the file that contains the resource, in this case FOO.CUR.

337

Loading Cursors from a Resource

After you've compiled a cursor into your program, you'll want to be able to access it for use. You're probably way ahead of me by now, so I'll just say that like bitmaps and icons, cursors have their own load routine, **LoadCursor()**. It takes two arguments, like so:

```
myCursor = LoadCursor ( hInst,              // Instance handle of the app
                                            // containing the cursor
                    "FOOCURSOR" );          // Name reference of the cursor
                                            // (note that it's a TEXT STRING,
                                            // and NOT a #define...
```

This returns a handle to your cursor resource, which you can then use in calls such as **SetCursor()**. (It can also return NULL, if Windows can't find the requested cursor—be sure to check the return value!)

Any *custom* cursor you load from a resource (as opposed to one of the standard Windows cursors) should be deleted when you're done with it. Use the **DestroyCursor()** call, like this:

```
DestroyCursor ( myCursor );
```

This applies to both cursors that you create by hand (with **CreateCursor()**) and cursors that you load from a resource (with **LoadCursor()**). In the HandCursor App, note that I destroy the cursor I created in the WM_DESTROY message handler. For cursors that you load via **LoadCursor()**, you must destroy only cursors that are your own, not system cursors.

> **Caution:** You must *not* attempt to delete system cursors. You have been warned! <grin>

Window Control: Specifying Custom Cursors by Window Handle

In the HandCursor App, you probably noticed that the cursor didn't change, even when you moved it into the nonclient area of the window. (Remember, the nonclient area is the stuff like the mover bar, the sizer frame, and so on.)

The cursor didn't change because the HandCursor App was being very dumb about how it responded to the WM_SETCURSOR message—it just blasted the handle of the paint-can cursor in there, regardless.

Most of the time, however, this isn't going to be what you want. Do you really want to have to deal with figuring out which part of the window frame the user is in, and displaying the right cursor (such as the left-right sizer bar when the user is on the left or right edge)? Probably not. For me, the answer is definitely not! <grin> Fortunately, there's a very easy way to intercept the cursor messages you're interested in and skip the ones you aren't interested in.

The Happy Cursor App— an Example

Any time I start a sentence "There's a very easy way to...," it's probably time for another example—and this time is no exception. Presented next is the Happy Cursor App. Not only does this app deal with things like passing along nonclient area cursor messages to `DefWndProc()`, but it also demonstrates some cute animation techniques—whenever you move the cursor, Mr. Happy's eyes look expectantly in the direction you're going. Listings 6.8 through 6.15 present the source for the Happy Cursor App.

Listing 6.8. HAPPYCUR.C—source code for the Happy Cursor App.

```
//File name: HAPPYCUR.C
//"HAPPYCUR" Generated by WindowsMAKER Professional
//Author: Alex Leavens, for ShadowCat Technologies

#include <WINDOWS.H>
#include "HAPPYCUR.H"

WMPDEBUG
#include "HAPPYCUR.WMC"

//****************************************************************
//                      WinMain FUNCTION
//****************************************************************
```

continues

Listing 6.8. continued

```
    int PASCAL
WinMain(HINSTANCE hInstance,
        HINSTANCE hPrevInstance,
        LPSTR     lpCmdLine,
        int       nCmdShow)
{

    MSG msg;                    // Message

    //---------------------------

    hInst = hInstance;          // Saves the current instance

    if (!BLDInitApplication(hInstance,hPrevInstance,&nCmdShow,lpCmdLine))
        return FALSE;

    if (!hPrevInstance)         // Is there another instance of the task
    {
        if (!BLDRegisterClass(hInstance))
            return FALSE;       // Exits if unable to initialize
    }

    MainhWnd = BLDCreateWindow(hInstance);
    if (!MainhWnd)              // Check if the window is created
        return FALSE;

    ShowWindow(MainhWnd, nCmdShow);  // Show the window
    UpdateWindow(MainhWnd);          // Send WM_PAINT message to window

    BLDInitMainMenu(MainhWnd);  // Initialize main menu if necessary

    while (GetMessage(&msg,     // Message structure
                      0,        // Handle of window receiving the message
                      0,        // Lowest message to examine
                      0))       // Highest message to examine
    {
        if (BLDKeyTranslation(&msg)) // WindowsMAKER code for key translation
            continue;
        TranslateMessage(&msg); // Translates character keys
        DispatchMessage(&msg);  // Dispatches message to window
    }
```

```
    BLDExitApplication();          // Clean up if necessary
    return(msg.wParam);            // Returns the value from PostQuitMessage
}


//***************************************************************
//              WINDOW PROCEDURE FOR MAIN WINDOW
//***************************************************************

WORD    mX = 0;             // Mouse X position
WORD    mY = 0;             // Mouse Y Position


//-------------------------

    LONG FAR PASCAL
BLDMainWndProc(HWND hWnd,
               UINT message,
               UINT wParam,
               LONG lParam )
{

    switch (message)
    {

    case WM_MOUSEMOVE:
    {
        WORD        newX = LOWORD ( lParam );
        WORD        newY = HIWORD ( lParam );

        WORD        cursorStatus = 0;

        //----------------------

        // First test to see if the mouse has moved relative
        // to its last x,y position.
        // First, check X...

        if (newX < mX )
        {
            cursorStatus |= CURSOR_LEFT;
            mX = newX;
        }
        else if (newX > mX)
        {
            cursorStatus |= CURSOR_RIGHT;
            mX - nowX;
```

continues

Listing 6.8. continued

```
        }

        // Now check Y position

        if (newY < mY )
        {
            cursorStatus |= CURSOR_UP;
            mY = newY;
        }
        else if (newY > mY)
        {
            cursorStatus |= CURSOR_DOWN;
            mY = newY;
        }

        // Now update the cursor...

        SetCursorImage ( cursorStatus );
    }
        break;


    case WM_SETCURSOR:
        return HandleCursorSet ( hWnd,
                                 message,
                                 wParam,
                                 lParam );
         break;

    case WM_CREATE:                // Window creation
        // Send to BLDDefWindowProc in (.WMC) for controls in main window
        return BLDDefWindowProc(hWnd, message, wParam, lParam);
        break;

    case WM_SETFOCUS:              // Window is notified of focus change
        // Send to BLDDefWindowProc in (.WMC) for controls in main window
        return BLDDefWindowProc(hWnd, message, wParam, lParam);
        break;

    case WM_DESTROY:               // Window being destroyed
        PostQuitMessage(0);
```

```
        return BLDDefWindowProc(hWnd, message, wParam, lParam);
        break;

    case WM_COMMAND:                // Command from the main window
        if (BLDMenuCommand(hWnd, message, wParam, lParam))
            break;                  // Processed by BLDMenuCommand.
        // Else default processing by BLDDefWindowProc.
    default:
        // Pass on message for default processing
        return BLDDefWindowProc(hWnd, message, wParam, lParam);
    }

    return FALSE;                   // Returns FALSE if processed
}
```

Listing 6.9. HAPPYCUR.WMC—special include file for the Happy Cursor App.

```
//File name: HAPPYCUR.WMC
//"HAPPYCUR" Generated by WindowsMAKER Professional
//Author: Alex Leavens, for ShadowCat Technologies


//**************************************************************
//                  GLOBAL VARIABLES
//**************************************************************

HBRUSH      hMBrush = 0;         // Handle to brush for main window.
HINSTANCE   hInst   = 0;         // Handle to instance.
HWND        MainhWnd= 0;         // Handle to main window.
HWND        hClient = 0;         // Handle to window in client area.
FARPROC     lpClient= 0L;        // Function for window in client area.


//**************************************************************
//              PROCESSES KEYBOARD ACCELERATORS
//              AND MODELESS DIALOG BOX KEY INPUT
//**************************************************************

BOOL BLDKeyTranslation(MSG *pMsg)
    {
    return FALSE;                // No special key input
    }
```

continues

Listing 6.9. continued

```
//****************************************************************
//          CUSTOM MESSAGE PROCESSING FOR MAIN WINDOW
//****************************************************************

LONG FAR PASCAL BLDDefWindowProc(HWND hWnd, UINT message, UINT wParam,
                                 LONG lParam )
    {

    switch (message)
        {

         default:
        // Pass on message for default processing by Windows
        return DefWindowProc(hWnd, message, wParam, lParam);
        }
    return FALSE;                  // Returns FALSE if not processed by Windows
    }



//****************************************************************
//             PROCESSES ALL MENU ITEM SELECTIONS
//****************************************************************

BOOL BLDMenuCommand(HWND hWnd, UINT message, UINT wParam, LONG lParam )
{

    switch( LOWORD(wParam) )
        {

        // Processing of linked menu items in menu: HAPPYCUR

    default:
        return FALSE;             // Not processed by this function.
        }
    return TRUE;                  // Processed by this function.
    }

//****************************************************************
//    FUNCTIONS FOR INITIALIZATION AND EXIT OF APPLICATION
//****************************************************************

BOOL BLDInitApplication(HANDLE hInst, HANDLE hPrev, int *pCmdShow,
```

```
                       LPSTR lpCmd)
    {
    // No initialization necessary
    return TRUE;
    }



// Registers the class for the main window
BOOL BLDRegisterClass( HANDLE hInstance )
    {
    WNDCLASS WndClass;

    hMBrush=CreateSolidBrush(GetSysColor(COLOR_WINDOW));

    WndClass.style          = 0;
    WndClass.lpfnWndProc    = BLDMainWndProc;
    WndClass.cbClsExtra     = 0;
    WndClass.cbWndExtra     = 0;
    WndClass.hInstance      = hInstance;
    WndClass.hIcon          = LoadIcon(NULL,IDI_APPLICATION);
    WndClass.hCursor        = LoadCursor(NULL,IDC_ARROW);
    WndClass.hbrBackground  = hMBrush;
    WndClass.lpszMenuName   = NULL;
    WndClass.lpszClassName  = "HAPPYCUR";

    return RegisterClass(&WndClass);
    }



HWND BLDCreateWindow( HANDLE hInstance )  // Creates the main window
{
    HWND hWnd;                  // Window handle
    int coordinate[4];          // Coordinates of main window

    coordinate[0]=CW_USEDEFAULT;
    coordinate[1]=0;
    coordinate[2]=CW_USEDEFAULT;
    coordinate[3]=0;

    hWnd = CreateWindow("HAPPYCUR",  // Window class registered earlier
            "Happy Cursor - by Alex Leavens",       // Window caption
        WS_OVERLAPPED¦WS_THICKFRAME¦WS_SYSMENU¦WS_MINIMIZEBOX¦WS_MAXIMIZEBOX,
                            // Window style
            coordinate[0],      // X position
            coordinate[1],      // Y position
```

continues

345

Listing 6.9. continued

```
            coordinate[2],       // Width
            coordinate[3],       // Height
            0,                   // Parent handle
            0,                   // Menu or child ID
            hInstance,           // Instance
            (LPSTR)NULL);        // Additional info

    return hWnd;
    }


// Called just before entering message loop
BOOL BLDInitMainMenu(HWND hWnd)
    {
    // No initialization necessary
    return TRUE;
    }


BOOL BLDExitApplication()        // Called just before exit of application
    {
    if (hMBrush)
        DeleteObject(hMBrush);
    return TRUE;
    }


//*********************************************************
// ERROR MESSAGE HANDLING (Definitions can be overruled.)
//*********************************************************

#ifndef ERRORCAPTION
#define ERRORCAPTION "Happy Cursor - by Alex Leavens"
#endif

#ifndef LOADERROR
#define LOADERROR "Cannot load string."
#endif


int BLDDisplayMessage(HWND hWnd, unsigned uMsg, char *pContext, int iType)
    {
    int i, j;
    char Message[200+1];
```

```
        if (uMsg)
            {
            if (!LoadString(hInst,uMsg,Message,200))
                {
                MessageBox(hWnd,LOADERROR,ERRORCAPTION, MB_OK¦MB_SYSTEMMODAL¦
                                            MB_ICONHAND);
                return FALSE;
                }
            }
        else
            Message[0]=0;

        if (pContext)
            {
            i = lstrlen(Message);
            j = lstrlen(pContext);
            if (i + j + 1 <= 200)
                {
                lstrcat(Message, " ");
                lstrcat(Message, pContext);
                }
            }

        return MessageBox(hWnd,Message,ERRORCAPTION,iType);
        }

//**************************************************************
//          FUNCTIONS FOR DRAWING GRAPHICS BUTTONS
//**************************************************************

BOOL BLDDrawIcon(LPDRAWITEMSTRUCT lpDrawItem, char *pIconName)
    {
    HICON hIcon;

    hIcon = LoadIcon(hInst,pIconName);
    if (!hIcon)
        {
        BLDDisplayMessage(GetActiveWindow(),BLD_CannotLoadIcon,pIconName,
                      MB_OK ¦ MB_ICONASTERISK);
        return FALSE;
        }

    SetMapMode(lpDrawItem->hDC,MM_TEXT);
    return DrawIcon(lpDrawItem->hDC,0,0,hIcon);
    }
```

continues

Listing 6.9. continued

```
BOOL BLDDrawBitmap(LPDRAWITEMSTRUCT lpDrawItem, char *pBitmapName, BOOL bStretch)
    {
    HBITMAP hBitmap;
    HDC hMemDC;
    BITMAP Bitmap;
    int iRaster;

    iRaster = GetDeviceCaps(lpDrawItem->hDC,RASTERCAPS);
    if ((iRaster&RC_BITBLT)!=RC_BITBLT)
        return FALSE;                 // Device cannot display bitmap

    hBitmap = LoadBitmap(hInst,pBitmapName);
    if (!hBitmap)
        {
        BLDDisplayMessage(GetActiveWindow(),BLD_CannotLoadBitmap,pBitmapName,
                        MB_OK | MB_ICONASTERISK);
        return FALSE;
        }

    if (!GetObject(hBitmap,sizeof(BITMAP),(LPSTR)&Bitmap))
        {
        DeleteObject(hBitmap);
        return FALSE;
        }
    hMemDC = CreateCompatibleDC(lpDrawItem->hDC);
    if (!hMemDC)
        {
        DeleteObject(hBitmap);
        return FALSE;
        }
    if (!SelectObject(hMemDC,hBitmap))
        {
        DeleteDC(hMemDC);
        DeleteObject(hBitmap);
        return FALSE;
        }

    if (bStretch)
        {
        StretchBlt(lpDrawItem->hDC,
                lpDrawItem->rcItem.left,
                lpDrawItem->rcItem.top,
```

```
                        lpDrawItem->rcItem.right-lpDrawItem->rcItem.left,
                        lpDrawItem->rcItem.bottom-lpDrawItem->rcItem.top,
                        hMemDC,
                        0,
                        0,
                        Bitmap.bmWidth,
                        Bitmap.bmHeight,
                        SRCCOPY);
        }
    else
        {
          BitBlt(lpDrawItem->hDC,
                    lpDrawItem->rcItem.left,
                    lpDrawItem->rcItem.top,
                    lpDrawItem->rcItem.right-lpDrawItem->rcItem.left,
                    lpDrawItem->rcItem.bottom-lpDrawItem->rcItem.top,
                    hMemDC,
                    0,
                    0,
                    SRCCOPY);
        }
    DeleteDC(hMemDC);
    DeleteObject(hBitmap);
    return TRUE;
    }


//**************************************************************
//       FUNCTION FOR CREATING CONTROLS IN MAIN WINDOW
//**************************************************************

// Startup procedure for window in client area
HWND BLDCreateClientControls(char *pTemplateName, FARPROC lpNew)
{
    RECT rClient,rMain,rDialog;
    int dxDialog,dyDialog,dyExtra,dtXold,dtYold;
    HANDLE hRes,hMem;
    LPBLD_DLGTEMPLATE lpDlg;
    unsigned long styleold,style;
    HWND hNew;

    if (!IsWindow(MainhWnd))
        return 0;
    if (IsZoomed(MainhWnd))
        ShowWindow(MainhWnd,SW_RESTORE);
```

continues

Listing 6.9. continued

```
if (IsWindow(hClient))
     DestroyWindow(hClient); // Destroy Previous window in client area

// Get access to data structure of dialog box containing layout of ctrls
hRes=FindResource(hInst,(LPSTR)pTemplateName,RT_DIALOG);
if (!hRes)
    return 0;
hMem=LoadResource(hInst,hRes);
if (!hMem)
    return 0;
lpDlg=(LPBLD_DLGTEMPLATE)LockResource(hMem);
if (!lpDlg)
    return 0;

// Change dialog box data structure so it can be used as a window
// in client area
styleold        = lpDlg->dtStyle;
style           = lpDlg->dtStyle&(CLIENTSTRIP);
lpDlg->dtStyle  = lpDlg->dtStyle^style;
lpDlg->dtStyle  = lpDlg->dtStyle | WS_CHILD | WS_CLIPSIBLINGS;
dtXold          = lpDlg->dtX;
dtYold          = lpDlg->dtY;
lpDlg->dtX      = 0;
lpDlg->dtY      = 0;

hNew = CreateDialogIndirect(hInst,(LPSTR)lpDlg, MainhWnd,lpNew);
if (!hNew)
    return 0;

// Restore dialog box data structure.
lpDlg->dtStyle = styleold;
lpDlg->dtX     = dtXold;
lpDlg->dtY     = dtYold;

UnlockResource(hMem);
FreeResource(hMem);

// Move and size window in client area and main window
GetClientRect(MainhWnd,&rClient);
GetWindowRect(MainhWnd,&rMain);
GetWindowRect(hNew,&rDialog);
dxDialog=(rDialog.right-rDialog.left)-(rClient.right-rClient.left);
dyDialog=(rDialog.bottom-rDialog.top)-(rClient.bottom-rClient.top);
```

```
        BLDMoveWindow(MainhWnd,rMain.left,rMain.top,
                (rMain.right-rMain.left)+dxDialog,
                        (rMain.bottom-rMain.top)+dyDialog,
                TRUE);
    MoveWindow(hNew,0,0,
                        (rDialog.right-rDialog.left),
                        (rDialog.bottom-rDialog.top),
                        TRUE);
    GetClientRect(MainhWnd,&rClient);

    // Compensate size if menu bar is more than one line.
    if ((rDialog.bottom-rDialog.top)>(rClient.bottom-rClient.top))
        {
        dyExtra=(rDialog.bottom-rDialog.top)-(rClient.bottom-rClient.top);
        BLDMoveWindow(MainhWnd,rMain.left,rMain.top,
                (rMain.right-rMain.left)+dxDialog,
                (rMain.bottom-rMain.top)+dyDialog+dyExtra,
                TRUE);
        }

    ShowWindow(hNew,SW_SHOW);
    hClient=hNew;
    lpClient=lpNew;
    return hClient;
    }


// Ensure that window is within screen.
void BLDMoveWindow(HWND hWnd, int x, int y,
        int nWidth, int nHeight, BOOL bRepaint)
    {
    int xMax,yMax,xNew,yNew;

    xMax = GetSystemMetrics(SM_CXSCREEN);
    yMax = GetSystemMetrics(SM_CYSCREEN);

    if ((nWidth<=xMax)&&(x+nWidth>xMax))
        xNew=xMax-nWidth;
    else
        xNew=x;

    if ((nHeight<=yMax)&&(y+nHeight>yMax))
        yNew=yMax-nHeight;
    else
        yNew=y;
```

continues

Listing 6.9. continued

```c
    MoveWindow(hWnd,xNew,yNew,nWidth,nHeight,bRepaint);
    return;
    }


//*************************************************************
//                FUNCTION FOR SWITCHING MENU SET
//*************************************************************

BOOL BLDSwitchMenu(HWND hWnd, char *pTemplateName)
    {
    HMENU hMenu1,hMenu;
    DWORD style;

    style = GetWindowLong(hWnd,GWL_STYLE);
    if((style & WS_CHILD) == WS_CHILD)  // Called from control in main window?
        {
        hWnd=GetParent(hWnd);
        if (!hWnd)
            return FALSE;
        style = GetWindowLong(hWnd,GWL_STYLE);
        if((style & WS_CHILD) == WS_CHILD) // No menu in a WS_CHILD window.
            return FALSE;
        }
    if((style & WS_CAPTION) != WS_CAPTION) // No menu if no caption.
        return FALSE;

    hMenu1 = GetMenu(hWnd);
    hMenu = LoadMenu(hInst,pTemplateName);
    if (!hMenu)
        {
        BLDDisplayMessage(hWnd,BLD_CannotLoadMenu,pTemplateName,
                        MB_OK | MB_ICONASTERISK);
        return FALSE;
        }

    if (!SetMenu(hWnd,hMenu))
        return FALSE;
    if (hMenu1)
        DestroyMenu(hMenu1);

    DrawMenuBar(hWnd);
    return TRUE;
    }
```

Listing 6.10. HAPPYCUR.H—include file for the Happy Cursor App.

```
//File name: HAPPYCUR.H
//"HAPPYCUR" Generated by WindowsMAKER Professional
//Author: Alex Leavens, for ShadowCat Technologies

// These definitions are provided to support
// compilers with older versions of WINDOWS.H.
typedef unsigned int        UINT;
#ifndef WINAPI
typedef HANDLE              HINSTANCE;
#endif

#ifndef WM_SYSTEMERROR
#define WM_SYSTEMERROR       0x0017
#endif
#ifndef WM_QUEUESYNC
#define WM_QUEUESYNC         0x0023
#endif
#ifndef WM_COMMNOTIFY
#define WM_COMMNOTIFY        0x0044
#endif
#ifndef WM_WINDOWPOSCHANGING
#define WM_WINDOWPOSCHANGING 0x0046
#endif
#ifndef WM_WINDOWPOSCHANGED
#define WM_WINDOWPOSCHANGED  0x0047
#endif
#ifndef WM_POWER
#define WM_POWER             0x0048
#endif
#ifndef WM_DROPFILES
#define WM_DROPFILES         0x0233
#endif
#ifndef WM_PALETTEISCHANGING
#define WM_PALETTEISCHANGING 0x0310
#endif


// Give access to handles in all code modules
extern HINSTANCE hInst;
extern HWND      MainhWnd;

// Constants for error message strings
```

continues

Listing 6.10. continued

```
#define BLD_CannotRun          4000
#define BLD_CannotCreate       4001
#define BLD_CannotLoadMenu     4002
#define BLD_CannotLoadIcon     4003
#define BLD_CannotLoadBitmap   4004


#if !defined(THISISBLDRC)


int  PASCAL WinMain( HINSTANCE hInstance,
                     HINSTANCE hPrevInstance, LPSTR lpCmdLine, int nCmdShow );
LONG FAR PASCAL BLDMainWndProc( HWND hWnd,
                               UINT message, UINT wParam, LONG lParam );
LONG FAR PASCAL BLDDefWindowProc( HWND hWnd,
                                 UINT message, UINT wParam, LONG lParam );
BOOL BLDKeyTranslation( MSG *pMsg );
BOOL BLDInitApplication( HANDLE hInst,
                         HANDLE hPrev, int *pCmdShow, LPSTR lpCmd );
BOOL BLDExitApplication( void );
HWND BLDCreateClientControls( char *pTemplateName, FARPROC lpNew );
BOOL BLDInitMainMenu( HWND hWnd );
BOOL BLDMenuCommand( HWND hWnd, UINT message, UINT wParam, LONG lParam );
BOOL BLDRegisterClass( HANDLE hInstance );
HWND BLDCreateWindow( HANDLE hInstance );
int  BLDDisplayMessage(HWND hWnd, unsigned uMsg, char *pContext, int iType );
BOOL BLDSwitchMenu( HWND hWnd, char *pTemplateName );
BOOL BLDDrawBitmap( LPDRAWITEMSTRUCT lpDrawItem,
                    char *pBitmapName, BOOL bStretch );
BOOL BLDDrawIcon( LPDRAWITEMSTRUCT lpDrawItem, char *pIconName );
void BLDMoveWindow( HWND hWnd, int x, int y,
                    int nWidth, int nHeight, BOOL bRepaint );
long FAR PASCAL HandleCursorSet(HWND hWnd,
                                unsigned message,
                                WORD     wParam,
                                LONG     lParam);


void FAR PASCAL SetCursorImage(WORD curDirection);


//****************************************************************
// Variables, types, and constants for controls in main window.
//****************************************************************
```

```
extern HWND      hClient;        // Handle to window in client area.
extern FARPROC   lpClient;       // Function for window in client area.

#define CLIENTSTRIP WS_MINIMIZE¦WS_MAXIMIZE¦WS_CAPTION¦WS_BORDER¦WS_DLGFRAME¦
WS_SYSMENU¦WS_POPUP¦WS_THICKFRAME¦DS_MODALFRAME

typedef struct
    {
    unsigned long dtStyle;
    BYTE dtItemCount;
    int dtX;
    int dtY;
    int dtCX;
    int dtCY;
    } BLD_DLGTEMPLATE;

typedef BLD_DLGTEMPLATE far        *LPBLD_DLGTEMPLATE;

#endif

#define WMPDEBUG


#define  CURSOR_UP              0x01
#define CURSOR_DOWN             0x02
#define  CURSOR_LEFT            0x04
#define  CURSOR_RIGHT           0x08

#define CURSOR_UP_LEFT          0x05
#define CURSOR_UP_RIGHT         0x09
#define CURSOR_DOWN_LEFT    0x06
#define CURSOR_DOWN_RIGHT   0x0A

#define CURSOR_ANIMATE          0x10

// User Defined ID Values


// WindowsMAKER Pro generated ID Values
```

Listing 6.11. CURSUTIL.C—cursor utilities for the Happy Cursor App.

```c
// CURSUTIL.C
//
// Utility routines for the happy cursor app
//
// Written by Alex Leavens, for ShadowCat Technologies


#include <WINDOWS.H>
#include "HAPPYCUR.H"

/*----------------------- Local variables ---------------------*/

BOOL    whirling;                   /* Cursor spinning or not */
WORD    whichWatch;                 /* Current watch value */

WORD    speed;                      /* How fast to go... */

//------------ Function prototypes

void FAR PASCAL SetCursorBusy(WORD  curDirection);

/***********************************
 * HandleCursorSet()
 *     Handles the message when Windows wants to set the cursor.
 *
 * Arguments:
 *     hWnd - Handle to the window that the message is destined for
 *     message - What the message is
 *     wParam - Points to the window handle that contains the cursor
 *     lParam - In the loword: hit test code
 *              In the hiword: mouse message number
 *
 * Returns:
 *     TRUE if you processed the event
 *     The return from DefWindowProc() if Windows handled the event
 */

    long FAR PASCAL
HandleCursorSet(HWND        hWnd,
                unsigned message,
                    WORD        wParam,
                    LONG        lParam)
{
```

```
    int hitTest;

    /*-----------------------*/

    if (wParam != MainhWnd)          /* If not your window, then don't change */
         return DefWindowProc(hWnd, message, wParam, lParam);

    hitTest = LOWORD(lParam);        /* Get cursor position within window */

    if (hitTest != HTCLIENT)         /* If not in client area, let
                                      * Windows handle it.
                                      */
         return DefWindowProc(hWnd, message, wParam, lParam);

    // Well, the cursor is within your client window. Since you've
    // gotten this message in response to your setting the cursor for
    // yourself, you don't need to do any more--you've already set the
    // cursor. The only thing you have to do here is prevent Windows
    // from un-setting it.


    return TRUE;

}


/********************
 * SetCursorImage()
 *
 * Sets the image of the cursor to one of eight possible directions,
 * or to the animation, if the cursor isn't moving...
 */

    void FAR PASCAL
SetCursorImage(WORD          curDirection)
{
    HCURSOR        loadCur;

    /*---------------------------*/

    // Check and see if the cursor is animated...

    if ( curDirection & CURSOR_ANIMATE )
    {
        curDirection ^= CURSOR_ANIMATE;
```

continues

Listing 6.11. continued

```
        switch ( curDirection )
        {
            case 0:
            case 1:
                break;
        }
    }

    switch ( curDirection )
    {
        case CURSOR_UP:
            loadCur = LoadCursor(hInst,"HAPPYUP");
            if (loadCur !- NULL)
                SetCursor(loadCur);
            break;

        case CURSOR_DOWN:
            loadCur = LoadCursor(hInst,"HAPPYDN");
            if (loadCur != NULL)
                SetCursor(loadCur);
            break;

        case CURSOR_LEFT:
            loadCur = LoadCursor(hInst,"HAPPYLF");
            if (loadCur != NULL)
                SetCursor(loadCur);
            break;

        case CURSOR_RIGHT:
            loadCur = LoadCursor(hInst,"HAPPYRT");
            if (loadCur != NULL)
                SetCursor(loadCur);
            break;

        case CURSOR_UP_LEFT:
            loadCur = LoadCursor(hInst,"HAPPYUL");
            if (loadCur != NULL)
                SetCursor(loadCur);
            break;

        case CURSOR_UP_RIGHT:
            loadCur = LoadCursor(hInst,"HAPPYUR");
            if (loadCur != NULL)
```

```
          SetCursor(loadCur);
      break;

  case CURSOR_DOWN_LEFT:
     loadCur = LoadCursor(hInst,"HAPPYDL");
      if (loadCur != NULL)
          SetCursor(loadCur);
      break;

  case CURSOR_DOWN_RIGHT:
     loadCur = LoadCursor(hInst,"HAPPYDR");
      if (loadCur != NULL)
          SetCursor(loadCur);
      break;

  default:
      break;
  }
}
```

Listing 6.12. HAPPYCUR.RC—resource file for the Happy Cursor App.

```
//File name: HAPPYCUR.RC
//"HAPPYCUR" Generated by WindowsMAKER Professional
//Author: Alex Leavens, for ShadowCat Technologies

#define THISISBLDRC

#include <WINDOWS.H>
#include "HAPPYCUR.H"

HAPPY CURSOR HAPPY.CUR
HAPPYDL CURSOR HAPPYDL.CUR
HAPPYDN CURSOR HAPPYDN.CUR
HAPPYDR CURSOR HAPPYDR.CUR
HAPPYLF CURSOR HAPPYLF.CUR
HAPPYRT CURSOR HAPPYRT.CUR
HAPPYUL CURSOR HAPPYUL.CUR
HAPPYUP CURSOR HAPPYUP.CUR
HAPPYUR CURSOR HAPPYUR.CUR
```

continues

Listing 6.12. continued

```
//*********************************************************
//      Resource code for error message strings
//*********************************************************

STRINGTABLE
    BEGIN
        BLD_CannotRun          "Cannot run "
        BLD_CannotCreate       "Cannot create dialog box "
        BLD_CannotLoadMenu     "Cannot load menu "
        BLD_CannotLoadIcon     "Cannot load icon "
        BLD_CannotLoadBitmap   "Cannot load bitmap "
    END
```

Listing 6.13. HAPPYCUR.DEF—module definition file for the Happy Cursor App.

```
;File name: HAPPYCUR.DEF
;"HAPPYCUR" Generated by WindowsMAKER Professional
;Author: Alex Leavens, for ShadowCat Technologies

NAME          HAPPYCUR
DESCRIPTION   'Happy Cursor - by Alex Leavens'
EXETYPE       WINDOWS
STUB          'WINSTUB.EXE'
DATA          MOVEABLE MULTIPLE
CODE          MOVEABLE DISCARDABLE PRELOAD
HEAPSIZE      1024
STACKSIZE     5120
EXPORTS

              BLDMainWndProc
```

Listing 6.14. HAPPYCUR.LNK—link file for the Happy Cursor App.

```
HAPPYCUR CURSUTIL ,HAPPYCUR.EXE ,/align:16 /NOD  , LIBW SLIBCEW, HAPPYCUR.DEF
```

Listing 6.15. HAPPYCUR—makefile for the Happy Cursor App.

```
#File name: HAPPYCUR
#"HAPPYCUR" Generated by WindowsMAKER Professional
#Author: Alex Leavens, for ShadowCat Technologies


comp= /c /AS /Os /Gsw /Zpe /D _WINDOWS /W2 /DWINVER=0x300
cc=cl

HAPPYCUR.EXE : HAPPYCUR.OBJ CURSUTIL.OBJ HAPPYCUR.DEF HAPPYCUR.RES
    LINK @HAPPYCUR.LNK
    rc HAPPYCUR.RES


HAPPYCUR.RES : HAPPYCUR.RC HAPPYCUR.H HAPPY.CUR HAPPYDL.CUR HAPPYDN.CUR \
         HAPPYDR.CUR HAPPYLF.CUR HAPPYRT.CUR HAPPYUL.CUR HAPPYUP.CUR \
         HAPPYUR.CUR
    rc -r HAPPYCUR.RC

HAPPYCUR.OBJ : HAPPYCUR.C HAPPYCUR.WMC HAPPYCUR.H
    $(cc) $(comp) HAPPYCUR.C

CURSUTIL.OBJ : CURSUTIL.C HAPPYCUR.H
    $(cc) $(comp) CURSUTIL.C
```

In Figure 6.4 you can see the eight positions of the happy face cursor images used in the Happy Cursor App:

 Happydl, looking left and down

 Happydn, looking only down

 Happydr, looking down and right

 Happylf, looking only left

Happyrt, looking only right

 Happyul, looking up and left

 Happyup, looking only up

 Happyur, looking up and right

When the mouse moves in one of the indicated eight directions, the cursor changes to the corresponding image. Note the position of the eyes in each picture. The last two letters of each cursor name designate the direction that the eyes are looking in; for example, Happydl is looking *d*own and *l*eft.

Examining the Happy Cursor App

The really interesting things about this app are how to track the cursor, how to intercept the **SetCursor()** messages, and why to use **SetCursor()**. You use it when you want to change the visual state of the cursor. In this case, because you're tracking the mouse, you want to change the visual state every time the mouse is moved to reflect the new direction of travel. First, look at how you track the cursor.

Tracking the cursor is actually simple: you hook the WM_MOUSEMOVE message. In the code that handles this message, you crack the new x,y position of the mouse out of lParam, using LOWORD and HIWORD (x is the low word, and y the high word). Next, you compare this new position against your old position, which is kept in mX and mY. If the new value is less than the old value, the mouse has moved either up or to the left; if the value is greater, the mouse has moved down or to the right. (Note that the mouse can have moved such that in one direction the new position is less, and in the other direction the new position is greater.)

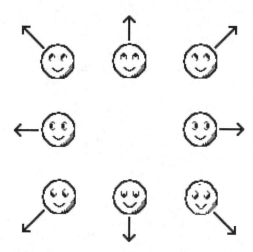

Figure 6.4.
The eight positions of the happy face cursor.

Set a flag for each direction, and then OR those values together. This gives you the final flag value, which you pass to the SetCursorImage() routine, in cursutil.c.

The other thing you do is hook the WM_SETCURSOR routine. This call is handled by the HandleCursorSet() function in cursutil.c. What it does is this:

1. If the window setting the cursor isn't your window, let **DefWindowProc()** handle it.

2. If the cursor isn't in the client area of your window, let **DefWindowProc()** handle it.

3. If the cursor is in the client area, and your window is doing the cursor setting, then do nothing. Do nothing? Right. Do nothing except return TRUE.

This definitely seems counterintuitive. Why, if the cursor is in your client area, and it is your window doing the setting, don't you do anything? The answer lies in the way Windows deals with cursors.

If, when you create the window class for your application, you specify a default cursor for the window class, Windows attempts to set the cursor to that default cursor image every time the cursor is in the client area of your window. I mean, *every time.* Even when you've just set the cursor to something else.

This drove me bananas the first time I tried setting a cursor in an application. I would set the cursor using the **SetCursor()** call, and nothing would happen. I finally figured out that my cursor *was* being displayed, albeit very briefly, because when I did a **SetCursor()** call to set my cursor, it generated a WM_SETCURSOR message, whereupon Windows would cheerfully set the default cursor.

363

This was not the answer I was looking for. The next thing I tried was setting my application's default cursor (the one specified by the WNDCLASS structure) to be NULL. This worked all right—it worked too well. Now Windows *never* set my cursor—even when I wanted it to, like in the nonclient area of my window. I didn't want to have to be responsible for handling that stuff.

Worse, I found that every time I moved the mouse, I got a WM_SETCURSOR message in addition to the mouse move message. Because I told Windows not to set the cursor, that I was going to, it was making sure I always got the messages I needed, just in case the mouse moved into a nonclient area or something. I was drowning in WM_SETCURSOR messages!

> **Note:** Incidentally, because of the tons of WM_SETCURSOR messages, the SetCursor() routine is documented as being "very fast" in the Windows documentation, "when you set the same cursor." It bloody well has to be, considering that you're going to be calling it about a thousand times a second! Furthermore, this method of setting the cursor required me to keep track of what state I wanted the mouse cursor to be in and to then be able to set it as requested. Well, forget that. I'd already set the thing in response to the user pressing a button (which is why I got the WM_SETCURSOR message in the first place). I didn't want to have to set it again and do a big switch statement to figure out what I should set it to. Yuck! (This is probably why more applications don't have lots of custom cursors.)

What you really want is a way to have Windows handle most of the cursor housekeeping (the sizer cursors and that kind of stuff), while at the same time being able to dynamically set the cursor as needed, without it getting yanked out from under your feet. This is exactly the method I described previously. You give your application a default cursor and hook the WM_SETCURSOR message. Checking the window handle means that you're going to set the cursor to something custom for only your window—other windows get their normal behavior.

Checking to make sure the cursor is in the client area of the window means that Windows also handles all the grungy stuff of the sizer cursors, the mover cursors, and so on.

Returning TRUE in response to the WM_SETCURSOR message, as you do if it's your window handle and the cursor is in the client area, means that further processing of the WM_SETCURSOR message is halted—which effectively prevents

Windows from swapping out the cursor you just swapped in (because the reason you're getting a `WM_SETCURSOR` message is due to your using the `SetCursor()` function).

> **Tip:** By checking the window handle to see whether it's yours or a child window of yours, you can also prevent child windows of yours from changing the cursor on you. (If you've got a bunch of text buttons, having a "dancing cursor" as it moves off and on the buttons can be *very* disconcerting.)

Summary

The cursor is an important resource for your application. You can give the user visual feedback, as well as information on what actions can be taken, or should be taken, by intelligent use of cursors.

Building cursors can be done in various ways. You can build them by hand, although such a process is difficult and time-consuming. An easier method of using cursors is to build them using a graphics resource editor and include them in your program's resource. You can then load them using the `LoadCursor()` call and display them using the `SetCursor()` call.

Cursors can be updated on a very active basis, as shown in the Happy Cursor App, which demonstrates a technique of animating the cursor in response to the user's mouse movements. Other techniques include animated busy cursors to show activity, and animated system cursors to show the next action to perform.

Function Reference

What follows is a list of the functions that deal directly with loading and creating cursors within running programs.

ClipCursor()

```
void ClipCursor(    LPRECT    lprc)
```

WHAT IT DOES:

Confines the cursor to a rectangle on-screen. Subsequent calls to **SetCursorPos()** and mouse movements are adjusted by Windows to lie within this rectangle (that is, the user cannot move the cursor outside the rectangle, nor can calls to **SetCursorPos()**).

PARAMETER:

lprc   Pointer to a RECT struct that contains the bounding rectangle the cursor is constrained within. If the parameter is NULL, the cursor is free to move about the entire screen.

WHAT IT RETURNS:

Nothing.

THINGS TO WATCH FOR:

Because there's only one system cursor, it's generally not a good idea to constrain the mouse cursor to a particular area.

SEE ALSO:

```
GetClipCursor()
GetCursorPos()
SetCursorPos()
```

CreateCursor()

```
HCURSOR CreateCursor(    HINSTANCE    hinst,
                         int          xHotSpot,
                         int          yHotSpot,
                         int          nWidth,
                         int          nHeight,
                         LPSTR        lpAndBits,
                         LPSTR        lpOrBits)
```

WHAT IT DOES:

Creates a cursor out of the two sets of image bits. The cursor is created with the requested width and height, and with the requested hotspot.

PARAMETERS:

hInst	Instance handle of the application creating the cursor
xHotSpot	X position for the cursor's hotspot
yHotSpot	Y position for the cursor's hotspot
nWidth	Width in pixels of the cursor
nHeight	Height in pixels of the cursor
lpAndBits	Pointer to the array of bytes defining the AND mask of the cursor
lpOrBits	Pointer to the array of bytes defining the XOR mask of the cursor

WHAT IT RETURNS:

A handle to the created cursor, or NULL if the function fails.

THINGS TO WATCH FOR:

☐ nWidth and nHeight must be values that are supported by the current display driver. You can get these values with the **GetSystemMetrics()** call, using SM_CXCURSOR for the width and SM_CYCURSOR for the height.

☐ Before your program finishes, it must call **DestroyCursor()** to free the cursor created by this function.

SEE ALSO:

CreateIcon()
DestroyCursor()
SetCursor()

DestroyCursor()

BOOL DestroyCursor(HCURSOR   hCurs)

WHAT IT DOES:

Destroys the cursor associated with the handle and frees the system resources used by the cursor.

PARAMETER:

hCurs   Handle of the cursor to be destroyed

WHAT IT RETURNS:

TRUE if the function is successful and FALSE if it isn't.

THINGS TO WATCH FOR:

This call works for cursors created with **CreateCursor()**. It also works for *private* cursors that were loaded from a resource with **LoadCursor()**. You must not destroy a system cursor gotten with **LoadCursor()**.

SEE ALSO:

CreateCursor()
LoadCursor()

GetClipCursor()

void **GetClipCursor**(LPRECT   lprc)

WHAT IT DOES:

The **GetClipCursor()** function returns the screen coordinates of the current cursor clipping rectangle, which was set by the **ClipCursor()** function. If the cursor isn't clipped to a rectangle, the coordinates retrieved are the dimensions of the screen.

PARAMETER:

lprc   Pointer to a RECT structure, into which the bounding rectangle is returned

WHAT IT RETURNS:

Nothing.

SEE ALSO:

ClipCursor()
GetCursorPos()

GetCursorPos()

void **GetCursorPos**(LPPOINT   lpPnt)

WHAT IT DOES:

Retrieves the cursor's current position, in screen (not client) coordinates.

PARAMETER:

lpPnt   Pointer to a POINT structure, which receives the cursor coordinates

WHAT IT RETURNS:

Nothing.

THINGS TO WATCH FOR:

☐ The cursor position is always given in screen, not client (that is, window), coordinates.

☐ The current mapping mode has no effect on this function.

SEE ALSO:

ClipCursor()
SetCursorPos()

LoadCursor()

```
HCURSOR LoadCursor(    HINSTANCE    hInst,
                       LPSTR        lpCurName)
```

WHAT IT DOES:

Loads the cursor resource specified by the lpCurName parameter from the instance of the application specified by hInst and returns a handle to the cursor. If the resource has already been loaded, this function merely returns the handle to it.

PARAMETERS:

hInst   Instance handle of the application or library to load the cursor resource from.

lpCurName   Name of the cursor resource, as a string. If you've numbered your cursor resources, you can use the number of the resource here by using the MAKEINTRESOURCE macro on the numerical value and passing that in. If hInst is NULL, you can also use one of the values shown in Table 6.1, in which case a handle to a system cursor is provided.

369

WHAT IT RETURNS:

A handle to the cursor resource. If the function is unsuccessful, it returns a NULL.

THINGS TO WATCH FOR:

☐ This function works properly only if you've specified a cursor resource to load. It's possible, for example, to specify an icon resource here—in this case, the function does not return a NULL value, but the handle it returns is not valid (and causes UAEs if you try to use it for anything).

☐ You can use the values shown in Table 6.1 to load a predefined Windows cursor.

Table 6.1. Windows cursors.

Cursor	Description
IDC_ARROW	Standard arrow cursor
IDC_CROSS	Crosshair cursor
IDC_IBEAM	Text I-beam cursor
IDC_ICON	Empty icon (used for dragging)
IDC_SIZE	Square with a smaller square inside its lower-right corner
IDC_SIZENESW	Double-pointed cursor with arrows pointing northeast and southwest
IDC_SIZENS	Double-pointed cursor with arrows pointing north and south
IDC_SIZENWSE	Double-pointed cursor with arrows pointing northwest and southeast
IDC_SIZEWE	Double-pointed cursor with arrows pointing west and east
IDC_UPARROW	Vertical arrow cursor
IDC_WAIT	Hourglass cursor

SEE ALSO:

SetCursor()
ShowCursor()

SetCursor()

HCURSOR SetCursor(HCURSOR   hCurs)

WHAT IT DOES:

Sets the cursor to the handle of the cursor that's been passed in.

PARAMETER:

>   hCurs   Handle to the cursor that is the new cursor image

WHAT IT RETURNS:

The handle to the previously selected cursor image.

THINGS TO WATCH FOR:

- ☐ The handle to the cursor can be gotten through either the **LoadCursor()** or the **CreateCursor()** function.

- ☐ If the handle passed into this function is NULL, the cursor is turned off (made invisible).

- ☐ The cursor is changed only if the new cursor is different from the old one; otherwise, the function returns immediately.

- ☐ Any application that needs to set the cursor while it is in a window must make sure the class cursor for the given window's class is set to NULL. If the class cursor is not NULL, the system restores the previous shape each time the mouse is moved. If you don't want to set the cursor for your window class to NULL, you can hook the **WM_SETCURSOR** message, like so:

```
case WM_SETCURSOR:
if (wParam != MainhWnd)              /* If not your window,
                                        then don't change */
return DefWindowProc(hWnd, message, wParam, lParam);

hitTest = LOWORD(lParam);            /* Get cursor position
                                        within window */

if (hitTest != HTCLIENT)             /* If not in client area, let
                                      * Windows handle it.
                                      */
```

371

```
        return DefWindowProc(hWnd, message, wParam, lParam);

        // Well, the cursor is within your client window. Since you've
        // gotten this message in response to your setting the cursor for
        // yourselves, you don't need to do any more--you've already set the
        // cursor. The only thing you have to do here is prevent Windows
        // from un-setting it.


            return TRUE;
```

SEE ALSO:

GetCursor()
LoadCursor()
ShowCursor()

SetCursorPos()

```
void SetCursorPos(    int    x,
                      int    y)
```

WHAT IT DOES:

Sets the cursor position to the requested location. The position is specified in screen coordinates. Further, if the position is outside the current cursor clipping rectangle (set by ClipCursor()), Windows adjusts the position so that it remains within the clipping rectangle.

PARAMETERS:

x   New x position for the cursor

y   New y position for the cursor

WHAT IT RETURNS:

Nothing.

THINGS TO WATCH FOR:

Applications should be careful not to cause the cursor to "warp" to a different part of the screen, because this causes a loss of visual continuity on the user's part.

SEE ALSO:

```
ClipCursor()
GetCursorPos()
```

ShowCursor()

```
int ShowCursor( BOOL     fShow)
```

WHAT IT DOES:

Shows or hides the mouse cursor. Windows keeps an internal count of how many times this function has been called. For hides (fShow == FALSE), Windows decrements the internal count; for shows (fShow == TRUE), Windows increments the count. The mouse cursor is visible if the count is greater than or equal to zero.

PARAMETER:

fShow   Flag that indicates whether to show or hide the cursor. TRUE means show (increment the count), and FALSE means hide (decrement the count).

WHAT IT RETURNS:

The new value of the display counter.

THINGS TO WATCH FOR:

The following example forces the cursor to be shown:

```
while ( ShowCursor ( TRUE ) < 0 )
{
   // Dummy statement
}
```

SEE ALSO:

```
SetCursor()
```

Bitmap Buttons

In the previous several chapters, you looked at the fundamental graphics primitives of Windows: icons, cursors, and bitmaps. Now it's time to look at something that isn't a graphics primitive but probably should be: the *bitmap button*.

A bitmap button isn't fundamentally any different from a text button—it's just a button with a graphics (that is, a bitmap) in it, rather than a text string. But although there's lots of support for text buttons (they're easy to build; just do a `CreateWindow()` with a class name of `BUTTON`), for bitmap buttons it's a little more difficult. All right, it's a lot more difficult—or at least, it was. The whole purpose of this chapter is to provide you with a cookbook approach to building bitmap buttons. By the time you're done, you should be able to build your own bitmap buttons with ease.

I even introduce a bitmap button object class, BmButton, which takes more of the work off you and really lets you concentrate on building the functionality of the buttons, rather than the buttons themselves.

Topics covered in this chapter are

Text Buttons and using them in an application

Text Button App, a sample program using text buttons

Bitmap buttons and their differences from text buttons

Bitmap Button App, a sample program using bitmap buttons

BmButton, a bitmap button class for C++

Understanding Buttons

The first step in understanding how graphics buttons work is simply understanding in general how buttons work. In principle, a *button* is an area of an application window that is "hot" and that responds in some fashion when the user single- or double-clicks it.

How a Button Works

You're probably thinking that this definition of a button is too simplistic; what about the button pressing down, and all of that? Really, that's cosmetics. Mind you, it's very important cosmetics, but it has nothing to do with the underlying metaphor: the user clicks a space on the screen, and something happens.

It's true, though, that the interface cosmetics of the button are very important. Think about elevator buttons, for instance. Press the down button, and the button lights up, indicating that you've pressed it. This feedback enables you (and others) to know that the elevator has already been called.

Ever pushed an elevator button on which the bulb was burned out? You push it. The next person who comes along pushes it. The next person who comes along pushes it. The person after that pushes it, and so on, ad infinitum (or at least until the elevator comes).

The burned-out bulb removes the feedback element from the interaction, so it's impossible to tell that someone else has pushed the button. Pedestrian crosswalk buttons are missing this critical element of feedback—ever notice how every person who comes to a pedestrian crosswalk pushes the button to cross, even if half a dozen people are already there? No feedback.

Obviously, then, although the visual feedback provided by a button isn't an integral part of its resultant action, it is an integral part of providing good feedback to the user. To understand the complete visual behavior of a button, examine what happens under various circumstances. Look at Figure 7.1.

Figure 7.1 demonstrates the standard behavior of a text button. A user moves the mouse cursor over the button, clicks, and releases, and an action is generated. In response to the user's down-click (also known as a *mouse down*), the button changes its image to that of a "depressed" button, a button that has been pushed in.

This image change gives the user the visual feedback necessary to let the user know that he has actually selected the button, in a fashion similar to the feedback a real button gives when you push it with the tip of your finger. Note that this example also demonstrates the importance of having the hotspot of the current cursor match the visual attribute of that cursor—the user expects the tip of the arrow to be the "touch" point.

From your application's standpoint, nothing happens until the user releases the mouse button (known as a *mouse up*) over the Foo button. This is important—the entire behavior of changing the Foo button image in response to the user's actions is handled by the BUTTON class (in this case, the particular instantiation of the BUTTON class represented by the Foo button). Your application is informed of a mouse up action only if the mouse cursor was over the button at the time the mouse up occurred.

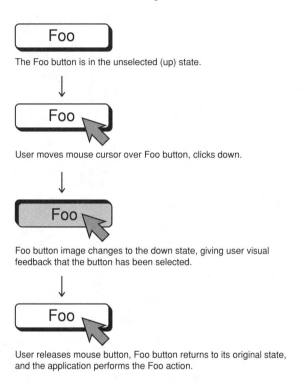

The Foo button is in the unselected (up) state.

User moves mouse cursor over Foo button, clicks down.

Foo button image changes to the down state, giving user visual feedback that the button has been selected.

User releases mouse button, Foo button returns to its original state, and the application performs the Foo action.

Figure 7.1.
Visual behavior of a single-clicked button.

This notification comes in the form of a WM_COMMAND message, which contains (in the wParam parameter) the ID of the button clicked. This ID is the value you set when you create the window, with the **CreateWindow()** call. The following section gives you an example of how this works.

A Text Button Example

As you can see from Figure 7.2, the Text Button App posts a window with two buttons in it: Eat Me and Drink Me. Clicking either button produces an appropriately amusing result, shown in Figure 7.3 and Figure 7.4.

Listings 7.1 through 7.8 give you all the source code to the Text Button App.

Figure 7.2.
The Text Button
App in action.

Figure 7.3.
The results of
clicking the Eat
Me button.

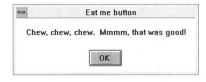

Figure 7.4.
The results of
clicking the
Drink Me
button.

Listing 7.1. TEXTBUTN.C—C source code for the Text Button App.

```
//File name: TEXTBUTN.C
//"TEXTBUTN" Generated by WindowsMAKER Professional
//Author: Alex Leavens, for ShadowCat Technologies

#include <WINDOWS.H>
#include "TEXTBUTN.H"

#include "TEXTBUTN.WMC"

BOOL    CreateButtonControls(HWND);


//***************************************************************
//                    WinMain FUNCTION
//***************************************************************
```

```
int PASCAL WinMain(HINSTANCE hInstance, HINSTANCE hPrevInstance,
                LPSTR lpCmdLine, int nCmdShow)
    {
    MSG msg;                      // Message
    hInst = hInstance;            // Saves the current instance

    if (!BLDInitApplication(hInstance,hPrevInstance,&nCmdShow,lpCmdLine))
        return FALSE;

    if (!hPrevInstance)           // Is there another instance of the task
        {
        if (!BLDRegisterClass(hInstance))
            return FALSE;         // Exits if unable to initialize
        }

    MainhWnd = BLDCreateWindow(hInstance);
    if (!MainhWnd)                // Check if the window is created
        return FALSE;

    ShowWindow(MainhWnd, nCmdShow);  // Show the window
    UpdateWindow(MainhWnd);          // Send WM_PAINT message to window

    BLDInitMainMenu(MainhWnd);  // Initialize main menu if necessary

    while (GetMessage(&msg,       // Message structure
                    0,            // Handle of window receiving the message
                    0,            // Lowest message to examine
                    0))           // Highest message to examine
        {
        if (BLDKeyTranslation(&msg)) // WindowsMAKER code for key translation
            continue;
        TranslateMessage(&msg); // Translates character keys
        DispatchMessage(&msg);  // Dispatches message to window
        }
    BLDExitApplication();       // Clean up if necessary
    return(msg.wParam);         // Returns the value from PostQuitMessage
}


//**************************************************************
//            WINDOW PROCEDURE FOR MAIN WINDOW
//**************************************************************

    LONG FAR PASCAL
BLDMainWndProc(HWND hWnd,
```

continues

Listing 7.1. continued

```c
                    UINT message,
                    UINT wParam,
                    LONG lParam )
{

    switch (message)
    {

    case WM_CREATE:              // Window creation
        CreateButtonControls ( hWnd );      // Create child text buttons
        // Send to BLDDefWindowProc in (.WMC) for controls in main window
        return BLDDefWindowProc(hWnd, message, wParam, lParam);
        break;

    case WM_SETFOCUS:            // Window is notified of focus change
        // Send to BLDDefWindowProc in (.WMC) for controls in main window
        return BLDDefWindowProc(hWnd, message, wParam, lParam);
        break;

    case WM_DESTROY:             // Window being destroyed
        PostQuitMessage(0);
        return BLDDefWindowProc(hWnd, message, wParam, lParam);
        break;

    case WM_COMMAND:                 // Command from the main window
        switch ( wParam )
        {
            case ID_EAT_ME_BTN:
                MessageBox ( hWnd,
                        "Chew, chew, chew. Mmmm, that was good!",
                        "Eat me button",
                        MB_OK );
                    return FALSE;

            case ID_DRINK_ME_BTN:
                MessageBox ( hWnd,
                        "Slurrrrrp!  Boy, that really hit the spot.",
                        "Drink me button",
                        MB_OK );
                    return FALSE;

            default:
                break;
        }
```

```
        if (BLDMenuCommand(hWnd, message, wParam, lParam))
            break;              // Processed by BLDMenuCommand.
        // Else default processing by BLDDefWindowProc.
    default:
        // Pass on message for default processing
        return BLDDefWindowProc(hWnd, message, wParam, lParam);
    }


    return FALSE;               // Returns FALSE if processed
}
```

Listing 7.2. TEXTBUTN.WMC—special include file for the Text Button App.

```
//File name: TEXTBUTN.WMC
//"TEXTBUTN" Generated by WindowsMAKER Professional
//Author: Alex Leavens, for ShadowCat Technologies


//****************************************************************
//                    GLOBAL VARIABLES
//****************************************************************


HBRUSH      hMBrush = 0;       // Handle to brush for main window.
HINSTANCE   hInst   = 0;       // Handle to instance.
HWND        MainhWnd= 0;       // Handle to main window.
HWND        hClient = 0;       // Handle to window in client area.
FARPROC     lpClient= 0L;      // Function for window in client area.


//****************************************************************
//              PROCESSES KEYBOARD ACCELERATORS
//              AND MODELESS DIALOG BOX KEY INPUT
//****************************************************************


BOOL BLDKeyTranslation(MSG *pMsg)
    {
    return FALSE;              // No special key input
    }


//****************************************************************
//          CUSTOM MESSAGE PROCESSING FOR MAIN WINDOW
//****************************************************************
```

continues

Listing 7.2. continued

```
LONG FAR PASCAL BLDDefWindowProc(HWND hWnd, UINT message, UINT wParam,
                                 LONG lParam )
    {

    switch (message)
        {

         default:
        // Pass on message for default processing by Windows
        return DefWindowProc(hWnd, message, wParam, lParam);
        }
    return FALSE;                    // Returns FALSE if not processed by Windows
    }


//**************************************************************
//           PROCESSES ALL MENU ITEM SELECTIONS
//**************************************************************

BOOL BLDMenuCommand(HWND hWnd, UINT message, UINT wParam, LONG lParam )
{

    switch( LOWORD(wParam) )
        {

        // Processing of linked menu items in menu: TEXTBUTN

    default:
        return FALSE;            // Not processed by this function.
        }
    return TRUE;                 // Processed by this function.
    }


//**************************************************************
//    FUNCTIONS FOR INITIALIZATION AND EXIT OF APPLICATION
//**************************************************************

BOOL BLDInitApplication(HANDLE hInst, HANDLE hPrev, int *pCmdShow,
                        LPSTR lpCmd)
    {
    // No initialization necessary
    return TRUE;
    }
```

```
// Registers the class for the main window
BOOL BLDRegisterClass( HANDLE hInstance )
    {
    WNDCLASS WndClass;

    hMBrush=CreateSolidBrush(GetSysColor(COLOR_WINDOW));

    WndClass.style        = 0;
    WndClass.lpfnWndProc  = BLDMainWndProc;
    WndClass.cbClsExtra   = 0;
    WndClass.cbWndExtra   = 0;
    WndClass.hInstance    = hInstance;
    WndClass.hIcon        = LoadIcon(NULL,IDI_APPLICATION);
    WndClass.hCursor      = LoadCursor(NULL,IDC_ARROW);
    WndClass.hbrBackground = hMBrush;
    WndClass.lpszMenuName  = NULL;
    WndClass.lpszClassName = "TEXTBUTN";

    return RegisterClass(&WndClass);
    }


HWND BLDCreateWindow( HANDLE hInstance )  // Creates the main window
{
    HWND hWnd;                 // Window handle
    int coordinate[4];         // Coordinates of main window

    coordinate[0]=CW_USEDEFAULT;
    coordinate[1]=0;
    coordinate[2]=CW_USEDEFAULT;
    coordinate[3]=0;

    hWnd = CreateWindow("TEXTBUTN",  // Window class registered earlier
        "Text Button Example",           // Window caption
      WS_OVERLAPPED|WS_THICKFRAME|WS_SYSMENU|WS_MINIMIZEBOX|WS_MAXIMIZEBOX,
                            // Window style
        coordinate[0],      // X position
        coordinate[1],      // Y position
        coordinate[2],      // Width
        coordinate[3],      // Height
        0,                  // Parent handle
        0,                  // Menu or child ID
        hInstance,          // Instance
        (LPSTR)NULL);       // Additional info
```

continues

Listing 7.2. continued

```
        return hWnd;
        }


// Called just before entering message loop
BOOL BLDInitMainMenu(HWND hWnd)
    {
    // No initialization necessary
    return TRUE;
    }


BOOL BLDExitApplication()         // Called just before exit of application
    {
    if (hMBrush)
        DeleteObject(hMBrush);
    return TRUE;
    }

//*********************************************************
// ERROR MESSAGE HANDLING (Definitions can be overruled.)
//*********************************************************

#ifndef ERRORCAPTION
#define ERRORCAPTION "Text Button Example"
#endif

#ifndef LOADERROR
#define LOADERROR "Cannot load string."
#endif


int BLDDisplayMessage(HWND hWnd, unsigned uMsg, char *pContext, int iType)
    {
    int i, j;
    char Message[200+1];

    if (uMsg)
        {
        if (!LoadString(hInst,uMsg,Message,200))
            {
            MessageBox(hWnd,LOADERROR,ERRORCAPTION, MB_OK¦MB_SYSTEMMODAL¦
                                                MB_ICONHAND);
```

```
                    return FALSE;
                    }
                }
        else
            Message[0]=0;

        if (pContext)
            {
            i = lstrlen(Message);
            j = lstrlen(pContext);
            if (i + j + 1 <= 200)
                {
                lstrcat(Message, " ");
                lstrcat(Message, pContext);
                }
            }

    return MessageBox(hWnd,Message,ERRORCAPTION,iType);
    }


//****************************************************************
//          FUNCTIONS FOR DRAWING GRAPHICS BUTTONS
//****************************************************************

BOOL BLDDrawIcon(LPDRAWITEMSTRUCT lpDrawItem, char *pIconName)
    {
    HICON hIcon;

    hIcon = LoadIcon(hInst,pIconName);
    if (!hIcon)
        {
        BLDDisplayMessage(GetActiveWindow(),BLD_CannotLoadIcon,pIconName,
                        MB_OK | MB_ICONASTERISK);
        return FALSE;
        }

    SetMapMode(lpDrawItem->hDC,MM_TEXT);
    return DrawIcon(lpDrawItem->hDC,0,0,hIcon);
    }



BOOL BLDDrawBitmap(LPDRAWITEMSTRUCT lpDrawItem, char *pBitmapName,
                    BOOL bStretch)
    {
    HBITMAP hBitmap;
```

continues

Listing 7.2. continued

```
HDC hMemDC;
BITMAP Bitmap;
int iRaster;

iRaster = GetDeviceCaps(lpDrawItem->hDC,RASTERCAPS);
if ((iRaster&RC_BITBLT)!=RC_BITBLT)
    return FALSE;              // Device cannot display bitmap

hBitmap = LoadBitmap(hInst,pBitmapName);
if (!hBitmap)
    {
    BLDDisplayMessage(GetActiveWindow(),BLD_CannotLoadBitmap,pBitmapName,
                      MB_OK | MB_ICONASTERISK);
    return FALSE;
    }

if (!GetObject(hBitmap,sizeof(BITMAP),(LPSTR)&Bitmap))
    {
    DeleteObject(hBitmap);
    return FALSE;
    }
hMemDC = CreateCompatibleDC(lpDrawItem->hDC);
if (!hMemDC)
    {
    DeleteObject(hBitmap);
    return FALSE;
    }
if (!SelectObject(hMemDC,hBitmap))
    {
    DeleteDC(hMemDC);
    DeleteObject(hBitmap);
    return FALSE;
    }

if (bStretch)
    {
    StretchBlt(lpDrawItem->hDC,
              lpDrawItem->rcItem.left,
              lpDrawItem->rcItem.top,
              lpDrawItem->rcItem.right-lpDrawItem->rcItem.left,
              lpDrawItem->rcItem.bottom-lpDrawItem->rcItem.top,
              hMemDC,
              0,
```

```
                        0,
                        Bitmap.bmWidth,
                        Bitmap.bmHeight,
                        SRCCOPY);
            }
        else
            {
            BitBlt(lpDrawItem->hDC,
                        lpDrawItem->rcItem.left,
                        lpDrawItem->rcItem.top,
                        lpDrawItem->rcItem.right-lpDrawItem->rcItem.left,
                        lpDrawItem->rcItem.bottom-lpDrawItem->rcItem.top,
                        hMemDC,
                        0,
                        0,
                        SRCCOPY);
            }
        DeleteDC(hMemDC);
        DeleteObject(hBitmap);
        return TRUE;
        }


//***************************************************************
//          FUNCTION FOR CREATING CONTROLS IN MAIN WINDOW
//***************************************************************

// Startup procedure for window in client area
HWND BLDCreateClientControls(char *pTemplateName, FARPROC lpNew)
{
    RECT rClient,rMain,rDialog;
    int dxDialog,dyDialog,dyExtra,dtXold,dtYold;
    HANDLE hRes,hMem;
    LPBLD_DLGTEMPLATE lpDlg;
    unsigned long styleold,style;
    HWND hNew;

    if (!IsWindow(MainhWnd))
        return 0;
    if (IsZoomed(MainhWnd))
        ShowWindow(MainhWnd,SW_RESTORE);

    if (IsWindow(hClient))
        DestroyWindow(hClient); // Destroy Previous window in client area
```

continues

387

Listing 7.2. continued

```
// Get access to data structure of dialog box containing layout of ctrls
hRes=FindResource(hInst,(LPSTR)pTemplateName,RT_DIALOG);
if (!hRes)
    return 0;
hMem=LoadResource(hInst,hRes);
if (!hMem)
    return 0;
lpDlg=(LPBLD_DLGTEMPLATE)LockResource(hMem);
if (!lpDlg)
    return 0;

// Change dialog box data structure so it can be used as a window
// in client area
styleold        = lpDlg->dtStyle;
style           = lpDlg->dtStyle&(CLIENTSTRIP);
lpDlg->dtStyle  = lpDlg->dtStyle^style;
lpDlg->dtStyle  = lpDlg->dtStyle | WS_CHILD | WS_CLIPSIBLINGS;
dtXold          = lpDlg->dtX;
dtYold          = lpDlg->dtY;
lpDlg->dtX      = 0;
lpDlg->dtY      = 0;

hNew = CreateDialogIndirect(hInst,(LPSTR)lpDlg, MainhWnd,lpNew);
if (!hNew)
    return 0;

// Restore dialog box data structure.
lpDlg->dtStyle = styleold;
lpDlg->dtX     = dtXold;
lpDlg->dtY     = dtYold;

UnlockResource(hMem);
FreeResource(hMem);

// Move and size window in client area and main window
GetClientRect(MainhWnd,&rClient);
GetWindowRect(MainhWnd,&rMain);
GetWindowRect(hNew,&rDialog);
dxDialog=(rDialog.right-rDialog.left)-(rClient.right-rClient.left);
dyDialog=(rDialog.bottom-rDialog.top)-(rClient.bottom-rClient.top);
BLDMoveWindow(MainhWnd,rMain.left,rMain.top,
            (rMain.right-rMain.left)+dxDialog,
                        (rMain.bottom-rMain.top)+dyDialog,
```

```
                    TRUE);
    MoveWindow(hNew,0,0,
                        (rDialog.right-rDialog.left),
                        (rDialog.bottom-rDialog.top),
                        TRUE);
    GetClientRect(MainhWnd,&rClient);

    // Compensate size if menu bar is more than one line.
    if ((rDialog.bottom-rDialog.top)>(rClient.bottom-rClient.top))
        {
        dyExtra=(rDialog.bottom-rDialog.top)-(rClient.bottom-rClient.top);
        BLDMoveWindow(MainhWnd,rMain.left,rMain.top,
                (rMain.right-rMain.left)+dxDialog,
                (rMain.bottom-rMain.top)+dyDialog+dyExtra,
                TRUE);
        }

    ShowWindow(hNew,SW_SHOW);
    hClient=hNew;
    lpClient=lpNew;
    return hClient;
    }


// Ensure that window is within screen.
void BLDMoveWindow(HWND hWnd, int x, int y,
        int nWidth, int nHeight, BOOL bRepaint)
    {
    int xMax,yMax,xNew,yNew;

    xMax = GetSystemMetrics(SM_CXSCREEN);
    yMax = GetSystemMetrics(SM_CYSCREEN);

    if ((nWidth<=xMax)&&(x+nWidth>xMax))
        xNew=xMax-nWidth;
    else
        xNew=x;

    if ((nHeight<=yMax)&&(y+nHeight>yMax))
        yNew=yMax-nHeight;
    else
        yNew=y;

    MoveWindow(hWnd,xNew,yNew,nWidth,nHeight,bRepaint);
    return;
    }
```

continues

Listing 7.2. continued

```c
//****************************************************************
//                  FUNCTION FOR SWITCHING MENU SET
//****************************************************************

BOOL BLDSwitchMenu(HWND hWnd, char *pTemplateName)
    {
    HMENU hMenu1,hMenu;
    DWORD style;

    style = GetWindowLong(hWnd,GWL_STYLE);
    if((style & WS_CHILD) == WS_CHILD)  // Called from control in main window?
        {
        hWnd=GetParent(hWnd);
        if (!hWnd)
            return FALSE;
        style = GetWindowLong(hWnd,GWL_STYLE);
        if((style & WS_CHILD) == WS_CHILD) // No menu in a WS_CHILD window.
            return FALSE;
        }
    if((style & WS_CAPTION) != WS_CAPTION) // No menu if no caption.
        return FALSE;

    hMenu1 = GetMenu(hWnd);
    hMenu = LoadMenu(hInst,pTemplateName);
    if (!hMenu)
        {
        BLDDisplayMessage(hWnd,BLD_CannotLoadMenu,pTemplateName,
                          MB_OK | MB_ICONASTERISK);
        return FALSE;
        }

    if (!SetMenu(hWnd,hMenu))
        return FALSE;
    if (hMenu1)
        DestroyMenu(hMenu1);

    DrawMenuBar(hWnd);
    return TRUE;
    }
```

Listing 7.3. TEXTBUTN.H—include file for the Text Button App.

```
//File name: TEXTBUTN.H
//"TEXTBUTN" Generated by WindowsMAKER Professional
//Author: Alex Leavens, for ShadowCat Technologies


// These definitions are provided to support
// compilers with older versions of WINDOWS.H.
typedef unsigned int          UINT;
#ifndef WINAPI
typedef HANDLE                HINSTANCE;
#endif


#ifndef WM_SYSTEMERROR
#define WM_SYSTEMERROR         0x0017
#endif
#ifndef WM_QUEUESYNC
#define WM_QUEUESYNC           0x0023
#endif
#ifndef WM_COMMNOTIFY
#define WM_COMMNOTIFY          0x0044
#endif
#ifndef WM_WINDOWPOSCHANGING
#define WM_WINDOWPOSCHANGING   0x0046
#endif
#ifndef WM_WINDOWPOSCHANGED
#define WM_WINDOWPOSCHANGED    0x0047
#endif
#ifndef WM_POWER
#define WM_POWER               0x0048
#endif
#ifndef WM_DROPFILES
#define WM_DROPFILES           0x0233
#endif
#ifndef WM_PALETTEISCHANGING
#define WM_PALETTEISCHANGING   0x0310
#endif


// Give access to handles in all code modules
extern HINSTANCE hInst;
extern HWND      MainhWnd;
```

continues

Listing 7.3. continued

```
// Constants for error message strings
#define BLD_CannotRun          4000
#define BLD_CannotCreate       4001
#define BLD_CannotLoadMenu     4002
#define BLD_CannotLoadIcon     4003
#define BLD_CannotLoadBitmap   4004


#if !defined(THISISBLDRC)


int  PASCAL WinMain( HINSTANCE hInstance, HINSTANCE hPrevInstance,
                     LPSTR lpCmdLine, int nCmdShow );
LONG FAR PASCAL BLDMainWndProc( HWND hWnd, UINT message,
                                UINT wParam, LONG lParam );
LONG FAR PASCAL BLDDefWindowProc( HWND hWnd, UINT message,
                                  UINT wParam, LONG lParam );
BOOL BLDKeyTranslation( MSG *pMsg );
BOOL BLDInitApplication( HANDLE hInst, HANDLE hPrev,
                         int *pCmdShow, LPSTR lpCmd );
BOOL BLDExitApplication( void );
HWND BLDCreateClientControls( char *pTemplateName, FARPROC lpNew );
BOOL BLDInitMainMenu( HWND hWnd );
BOOL BLDMenuCommand( HWND hWnd, UINT message, UINT wParam, LONG lParam );
BOOL BLDRegisterClass( HANDLE hInstance );
HWND BLDCreateWindow( HANDLE hInstance );
int  BLDDisplayMessage(HWND hWnd, unsigned uMsg, char *pContext, int iType );
BOOL BLDSwitchMenu( HWND hWnd, char *pTemplateName );
BOOL BLDDrawBitmap( LPDRAWITEMSTRUCT lpDrawItem, char *pBitmapName,
                    BOOL bStretch );
BOOL BLDDrawIcon( LPDRAWITEMSTRUCT lpDrawItem, char *pIconName );
void BLDMoveWindow( HWND hWnd, int x, int y, int nWidth, int nHeight,
                    BOOL bRepaint );



//*************************************************************
// Variables, types, and constants for controls in main window.
//*************************************************************


extern HWND     hClient;        // Handle to window in client area.
extern FARPROC  lpClient;       // Function for window in client area.


#define CLIENTSTRIP WS_MINIMIZE¦WS_MAXIMIZE¦WS_CAPTION¦WS_BORDER¦WS_DLGFRAME¦
```

```
WS_SYSMENU¦WS_POPUP¦WS_THICKFRAME¦DS_MODALFRAME

typedef struct
    {
    unsigned long dtStyle;
    BYTE dtItemCount;
    int dtX;
    int dtY;
    int dtCX;
    int dtCY;
    } BLD_DLGTEMPLATE;

typedef BLD_DLGTEMPLATE far          *LPBLD_DLGTEMPLATE;

#endif

#define WMPDEBUG


// User Defined ID Values

#define ID_EAT_ME_BTN                        8000
#define ID_DRINK_ME_BTN                      8001

// WindowsMAKER Pro generated ID Values
```

Listing 7.4. USERCODE.C—source code supporting creation of the text buttons, for the Text Button App.

```
//File name: USERCODE.C
//"TEXTBUTN" Generated by WindowsMAKER Professional
//Author: Alex Leavens, for ShadowCat Technologies

#include <WINDOWS.H>
#include "TEXTBUTN.H"

HWND      btnHand[2];

BOOL      CreateButtonControls(HWND);

/************************************
 * CreateButtonControls()
 *
```

continues

Listing 7.4. continued

```
 * Creates a text button control in the main
 * window of your application.
 */

    BOOL
CreateButtonControls(HWND hWnd)
{
    int  xOffset[] = { 50, 50 };
    int  yOffset[] = { 50, 200 };

    int  i;

    int          buttonHeight;

    HWND         deskhWnd;
    HDC          deskhDC;

    char         *btnText[]={
                        "EAT ME",
                        "DRINK ME"
                 };

    int          btnIDVals[]={
                        ID_EAT_ME_BTN,
                        ID_DRINK_ME_BTN
    };

    TEXTMETRIC   sysText;

    int          gl_hchar;       /* Height of an average character cell */
    int          gl_wchar;       /* Width of an average character cell */

    /*-----------------*/

    // In order to ensure that your buttons are properly sized,
    // regardless of the default font that's installed, you
    // need to retrieve the average size of a text cell.
    // First, you get the desktop window, and a DC to that...

    deskhWnd = GetDesktopWindow();
    deskhDC = GetDC(deskhWnd);

    // Now get the size of a character cell...
```

```
GetTextMetrics(deskhDC, (LPTEXTMETRIC)&sysText);

gl_wchar = sysText.tmAveCharWidth;    /* Width of average cell */
gl_hchar = sysText.tmHeight;          /* Height of average cell */

// Give the DC back...

ReleaseDC(deskhWnd, deskhDC);


// Calculate a button height that will hold the text fully

buttonHeight = gl_hchar + gl_hchar / 3 + 1;

for (i = 0; i <= 1; i++)
{
    btnHand[i] = CreateWindow(

            "BUTTON",               // Standard text button class
            (LPSTR)btnText[i],      // String to display in button
            BS_PUSHBUTTON |         // Standard pushbutton type,
               WS_CHILD | WS_VISIBLE, // child window, visible at
                                    // creation time
            xOffset[i],             // X position of the button
            yOffset[i],             // Y position of the button
            14 * gl_wchar,          // Width of the button
            buttonHeight,           // Height of the button
            hWnd,                   // Parent window
            btnIDVals[i],           // ID of the button
            hInst,                  // Instance of app creating
                                    // button
            NULL);                  // No extra data

    if (!btnHand[i])
    {
        DestroyWindow(hWnd);
        return FALSE;
    }
}
return TRUE;
}
```

Listing 7.5. TEXTBUTN—makefile for the Text Button App.

```
#File name: TEXTBUTN
#"TEXTBUTN" Generated by WindowsMAKER Professional
#Author: Alex Leavens, for ShadowCat Technologies

comp= /c /AS /Os /Gsw /Zpe /D _WINDOWS /W2
cc=cl

TEXTBUTN.EXE : TEXTBUTN.OBJ USERCODE.OBJ TEXTBUTN.DEF TEXTBUTN.RES
    LINK @TEXTBUTN.LNK
    rc TEXTBUTN.RES

TEXTBUTN.RES : TEXTBUTN.RC TEXTBUTN.H
    rc -r TEXTBUTN.RC

TEXTBUTN.OBJ : TEXTBUTN.C TEXTBUTN.WMC TEXTBUTN.H
    $(cc) $(comp) TEXTBUTN.C

USERCODE.OBJ : USERCODE.C TEXTBUTN.H
    $(cc) $(comp) USERCODE.C
```

Listing 7.6. TEXTBUTN.LNK—link file for the Text Button App.

```
TEXTBUTN USERCODE ,TEXTBUTN.EXE ,/align:16 /NOD  , LIBW SLIBCEW, TEXTBUTN.DEF
```

Listing 7.7. TEXTBUTN.DEF—module definition file for the Text Button App.

```
;File name: TEXTBUTN.DEF
;"TEXTBUTN" Generated by WindowsMAKER Professional
;Author: Alex Leavens, for ShadowCat Technologies

NAME        TEXTBUTN
DESCRIPTION 'TEXTBUTN generated by WindowsMAKER Professional'
EXETYPE     WINDOWS
STUB        'WINSTUB.EXE'
DATA        MOVEABLE MULTIPLE
CODE        MOVEABLE DISCARDABLE PRELOAD
HEAPSIZE    1024
STACKSIZE   5120
EXPORTS

        BLDMainWndProc
```

Listing 7.8. TEXTBUTN.RC—resource file for the Text Button App.

```
//File name: TEXTBUTN.RC
//"TEXTBUTN" Generated by WindowsMAKER Professional
//Author: Alex Leavens, for ShadowCat Technologies

#define THISISBLDRC

#include <WINDOWS.H>
#include "TEXTBUTN.H"

//*******************************************************
//      Resource code for error message strings
//*******************************************************

STRINGTABLE
   BEGIN
       BLD_CannotRun            "Cannot run "
       BLD_CannotCreate         "Cannot create dialog box "
       BLD_CannotLoadMenu       "Cannot load menu "
       BLD_CannotLoadIcon       "Cannot load icon "
       BLD_CannotLoadBitmap     "Cannot load bitmap "
   END
```

Examining the Text Button Example

Most of this program is a fairly standard Windows application. The pieces significant to you in this case are the `CreateWindow()` call and the WM_COMMAND message processing section. First, the window creation:

```
btnHand[i] = CreateWindow(

   "BUTTON",                    // Standard text button class
   (LPSTR)btnText[i],           // String to display in the button
   BS_PUSHBUTTON |              // Standard pushbutton type,
      WS_CHILD | WS_VISIBLE,    // child window, visible at
                                // creation time
            xOffset[i],         // X position of the button
            yOffset[i],         // Y position of the button
            14 * gl_wchar,      // Width of the button
            buttonHeight,       // Height of the button
            hWnd,               // Parent window
            btnIDVals[i],       // ID of the button
```

397

```
        hInst,                     // Instance of app creating
                                   // the button
        NULL);                     // No extra data
```

The first question you probably ask is Why create a window? Under Windows, all text buttons are child windows. Not only is creating them straightforward, but in doing so, you make message processing a snap. Further, by making them windows, you get to take advantage of all the support for windows that's built into the Windows OS. (I'll show you what I mean in a minute.)

Here's what the parameters mean in your window creation. First, you specify the class of window you're creating. This is important because it defines the type of behavior you want the window to have. You could create several types of windows: BUTTON, COMBOBOX, EDIT, LISTBOX, MDICLIENT, SCROLLBAR, and STATIC. As you can see, these are the names of most of the visual elements of Windows. In this case, you're creating an object with button behavior, so naturally you create a window of type BUTTON.

The second parameter you pass in is a pointer to the text string you want the button to have. Not all window classes use this field, but buttons do—it's the text displayed inside the button when the button is drawn on-screen.

The third parameter you pass in is the *type* of button you want to create, along with any additional styles you want to have. There are several basic button types you can create: pushbuttons (the type created here), radio buttons, and check boxes. You're probably familiar with radio buttons and check boxes—although they have different appearances, and quite distinct behavior, they are all flavors of the basic button class.

Additionally, you can create a *default* pushbutton, which is the kind of pushbutton that has a thick black line around it. When the user hits the Enter key in response to something, the default pushbutton is the one that gets the response. In this case, however, you simply want a standard pushbutton, hence the BS_PUSHBUTTON style.

Because you want your parent window to receive notification messages from this pushbutton, you create the button with the additional style of WS_CHILD—this means create the window as a child window of the main parent window. You also create it with the style of WS_VISIBLE; this causes the button to be shown when you show the main window. You could create the button without this style, which would mean that the button would be created but not visible until you sent a ShowWindow() message to it. (This can be useful if you want to create a button but not have it appear until you're ready for it.) The additional control styles are OR'd together.

398

The next two parameters, xOffset[i] and yOffset[i], define the x and y locations for the initial position of the window. Unless you explicitly change the position of the window later (with the MoveWindow() function), the window appears at and remains at this position. Like most things in Windows, this (x,y) location defines the upper-left corner of the window.

The next two parameters, 14 * gl_wchar and buttonHeight, define the width and height of the button image, respectively. Notice that before creating the window, you determine the size of an average character cell with the GetSystemMetrics() function, which returns a variety of information about system parameters. In this case, you want to make sure the text string you put into the button fits, regardless of the size and style of the font the user has installed as the default. Determining the size of the font and then using that width to size the button ensures that this is the case. You use the value of 14 in the multiplication to give yourself a little extra room on both edges of the button. Simply using the length of the longest string means the text goes right up to the edge of the button, giving it a crowded look. You determine the height of the button by taking the average height of a character and multiplying it by $3/2$. This gives you $1/4$ of a character height both above and below the text string in the button, which again gives you an attractive appearance and avoids crowding.

The next parameter, hWnd, defines the parent window for this button. It's possible to create button windows that are children of a window that is a child window of the main window. There's no reason the button window has to be the child of the top-level window. One of the reasons you might want to create a button window that's the child of a child window is that the child window might have its own window message loop, separate from the main, top-level window. In this case, the messages of the button (which is a child of the child) would be passed to the child window's message loop and not to the top-level window's message loop. If you pass in a NULL value here, you create a window that has no parent, which means that you also have to provide a message loop if you want to process any messages from the button. (Actually, the button window has a parent window. It's just that the parent window is the desktop, and because your application doesn't receive desktop messages, it's effectively the same as the button window not having a parent.)

After the parent window parameter comes a very important parameter: the *ID of this window*. This is the value passed back to your program in the wParam parameter under the WM_COMMAND message when an action occurs for this button window. This is how you identify this button window versus other button window controls you might have. You must have a unique ID for each button window you create, or your application won't be able to tell the button windows apart!

399

You can address the problem of unique identifiers in one of a couple of ways. You can create a base ID and then increment it once per window creation, like so:

```
for ( i = 0; i < 10; i++)
{
      CreateWindow(....., BASE_ID + i....)
}
```

This method gives all your windows ascending IDs. A second way to create IDs is to build a set of defines by hand, like so:

```
#define         ID_PAINT_BUTTON         1001
#define         ID_PENCIL_BUTTON        1002
```

Then you would create a table of those values in your program and access the table. I prefer the second method of window creation, because it means I can reference the buttons with identifiers that indicate exactly which button I'm talking about. This makes reading the source code easier and more obvious, as opposed to simply using a base ID value and an offset. However, it's more work to make a table like this, and you also have to be careful not to duplicate numbers (skipping them is OK). For me, however, the additional work is worth it.

The following parameter, hInst, is the instance handle of your application—it defines that the button is being created by this instance of your application. This enables Windows to distinguish between multiple buttons that have the same ID (even multiple instances of the same application), and it ensures that your application gets messages only from your button.

The final parameter is NULL; this parameter is also used to pass in extra data (in particular, when creating multiple document interface, or MDI, windows, this value is used). However, in your case, you can ignore it.

Although this certainly seems like a lot of information, it's really all straightforward. You're creating a window with a particular set of styles, of a particular size, and in a particular location. You've assigned it an ID and informed Windows of who the owner (your application) is.

After you've created this window, the question then becomes How do I use it?

Using the Button

Using your button is even easier than creating it. When you created it, you had to worry about such things as what size the button was going to be, and where, and what ID it would have. By contrast, to respond to a button, all you have to do is add a `WM_COMMAND` message handler in your application's main message loop, like this:

```
case WM_COMMAND:
    switch ( wParam )
    {
        case ID_BUTTON:
            // Do button action here...
            break;
    }
```

By switching off the `wParam` parameter, you can determine which button was pressed and what action to take. In the test application, you simply post a message box indicating which button was pressed—in your application, of course, you probably want something a bit more complex.

Building Bitmap Buttons

Now that you've got the basics of button manipulation down with a simple text button, you can move on to dealing with a much more complex object: the graphics button.

From a user's standpoint, graphics buttons are simply buttons that have an image in them, as opposed to text. From your perspective, however, graphics buttons are quite a bit more involved. Although Windows provides support for creating graphics buttons, all the real work is up to you. If you run the graphics button example (the source for which is given next), you notice that the buttons behave pretty much the way you'd expect. The buttons move down and up in the same way text buttons do. The big difference is that with text buttons, all the button behavior is free—with graphics buttons, it's not.

You can examine the source code to see where the differences lie.

A Graphics Button Example

The Happy Button App source code is given in Listings 7.9 through 7.16. This application, like the previous one, shows two buttons for the user to press. Rather than displaying text buttons, however, the Happy Button App displays two graphics buttons, which the user can then press. Note in particular how the face on the Sad button changes when the user clicks it. Figure 7.5 shows the main window of the Happy Button application. Figures 7.6 and 7.7 show the results of pressing the two buttons.

Figure 7.5.
The Happy
Button App in
action.

Figure 7.6.
The results of
pressing the
happy face
button.

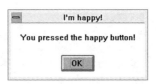

Figure 7.7.
The results of
pressing the sad
face button.

Listing 7.9. GRAPHBTN.C—source code for the main module of the Happy Button App.

```
//File name: GRAPHBTN.C
//"GRAPHBTN" Generated by WindowsMAKER Professional
//Author: Alex Leavens, for ShadowCat Technologies

#include <WINDOWS.H>
#include "GRAPHBTN.H"

WMPDEBUG
#include "GRAPHBTN.WMC"


//------------ Function prototypes ------------------

BOOL      CreateGraphicButtons ( HWND );
void FAR PASCAL    SetGraphicButtonToUnselected ( HWND, WORD, WORD );
void      DrawButtonTools(HWND, UINT, UINT, LONG );


//****************************************************************
//                    WinMain FUNCTION
//****************************************************************
```

```
        int PASCAL
WinMain(HINSTANCE hInstance,
        HINSTANCE        hPrevInstance,
        LPSTR            lpCmdLine,
        int              nCmdShow)
{
    MSG msg;                     // Message

    hInst = hInstance;           // Saves the current instance

    if (!BLDInitApplication(hInstance,hPrevInstance,&nCmdShow,lpCmdLine))
        return FALSE;

    if (!hPrevInstance)          // Is there another instance of the task
        {
        if (!BLDRegisterClass(hInstance))
            return FALSE;        // Exits if unable to initialize
        }

    MainhWnd = BLDCreateWindow(hInstance);
    if (!MainhWnd)               // Check if the window is created
        return FALSE;

    ShowWindow(MainhWnd, nCmdShow);  // Show the window
    UpdateWindow(MainhWnd);          // Send WM_PAINT message to window

    BLDInitMainMenu(MainhWnd);   // Initialize main menu if necessary

    while (GetMessage(&msg,      // Message structure
                      0,         // Handle of window receiving the message
                      0,         // Lowest message to examine
                      0))        // Highest message to examine
    {
        if (BLDKeyTranslation(&msg)) // WindowsMAKER code for key translation
            continue;
        TranslateMessage(&msg); // Translates character keys
        DispatchMessage(&msg);  // Dispatches message to window
    }

    BLDExitApplication();        // Clean up if necessary
    return(msg.wParam);          // Returns the value from PostQuitMessage
}


//**************************************************************
//               WINDOW PROCEDURE FOR MAIN WINDOW
//**************************************************************
```

continues

Listing 7.9. continued

```
    LONG FAR PASCAL
BLDMainWndProc(HWND hWnd,
               UINT message,
               UINT wParam,
               LONG lParam )
{

    switch (message)
    {

    case WM_DRAWITEM:                // If an owner-draw tool, you draw it.
        DrawButtonTools ( hWnd,
                          message,
                          wParam,
                          lParam );
        break;

    case WM_CREATE:              // Window creation

        // Create owner-draw button windows

        CreateGraphicButtons ( hWnd );

        // Send to BLDDefWindowProc in (.WMC) for controls in main window
        return BLDDefWindowProc(hWnd, message, wParam, lParam);
        break;

    case WM_SETFOCUS:            // Window is notified of focus change
        // Send to BLDDefWindowProc in (.WMC) for controls in main window
        return BLDDefWindowProc(hWnd, message, wParam, lParam);
        break;

    case WM_DESTROY:             // Window being destroyed
        PostQuitMessage(0);
        return BLDDefWindowProc(hWnd, message, wParam, lParam);
        break;

    case WM_COMMAND:             // Command from the main window

        // Now check to see if either of the buttons has
        // been pressed...
```

```
    switch ( wParam )
    {
        case ID_HAPPY_BUTTON:

                // Post a message showing which button was pressed...

            MessageBox ( hWnd,
                    "You pressed the happy button!",
                    "I'm happy!",
                    MB_OK );
                return FALSE;
                break;

        case ID_SAD_BUTTON:
            MessageBox ( hWnd,
                        "You pressed the sad button!",
                        "I'm really blue...",
                        MB_OK );
                return FALSE;
                break;
        }

    if (BLDMenuCommand(hWnd, message, wParam, lParam))
        break;                  // Processed by BLDMenuCommand.
    // Else default processing by BLDDefWindowProc.

default:
    // Pass on message for default processing
    return BLDDefWindowProc(hWnd, message, wParam, lParam);

}

return FALSE;                   // Returns FALSE if processed
}
```

Listing 7.10. GRAPHBTN.WMC—special include file for the Happy Button App.

```
//File name: GRAPHBTN.WMC
//"GRAPHBTN" Generated by WindowsMAKER Professional
//Author: Alex Leavens, for ShadowCat Technologies
```

continues

405

Listing 7.10. continued

```
//*************************************************************
//                    GLOBAL VARIABLES
//*************************************************************

HBRUSH      hMBrush = 0;        // Handle to brush for main window.
HINSTANCE   hInst   = 0;        // Handle to instance.
HWND        MainhWnd= 0;        // Handle to main window.
HWND        hClient = 0;        // Handle to window in client area.
FARPROC     lpClient= 0L;       // Function for window in client area.


//*************************************************************
//             PROCESSES KEYBOARD ACCELERATORS
//             AND MODELESS DIALOG BOX KEY INPUT
//*************************************************************

BOOL BLDKeyTranslation(MSG *pMsg)
    {
    return FALSE;               // No special key input
    }


//*************************************************************
//         CUSTOM MESSAGE PROCESSING FOR MAIN WINDOW
//*************************************************************

LONG FAR PASCAL BLDDefWindowProc(HWND hWnd,UINT message,UINT wParam,
LONG lParam )
    {

    switch (message)
        {

        default:
        // Pass on message for default processing by Windows
        return DefWindowProc(hWnd, message, wParam, lParam);
        }
    return FALSE;               // Returns FALSE if not processed by Windows
    }


//*************************************************************
//             PROCESSES ALL MENU ITEM SELECTIONS
//*************************************************************

BOOL BLDMenuCommand(HWND hWnd, UINT message, UINT wParam, LONG lParam )
{
```

```
        switch( LOWORD(wParam) )
            {

            // Processing of linked menu items in menu: GRAPHBTN

        default:
            return FALSE;           // Not processed by this function.
            }
        return TRUE;                // Processed by this function.
        }


//**********************************************************
//    FUNCTIONS FOR INITIALIZATION AND EXIT OF APPLICATION
//**********************************************************

BOOL BLDInitApplication(HANDLE hInst, HANDLE hPrev, int *pCmdShow,
                        LPSTR lpCmd)
    {
    // No initialization necessary
    return TRUE;
    }



// Registers the class for the main window
BOOL BLDRegisterClass( HANDLE hInstance )
    {
    WNDCLASS WndClass;

    hMBrush=CreateSolidBrush(GetSysColor(COLOR_WINDOW));

    WndClass.style          = 0;
    WndClass.lpfnWndProc    = BLDMainWndProc;
    WndClass.cbClsExtra     = 0;
    WndClass.cbWndExtra     = 0;
    WndClass.hInstance      = hInstance;
    WndClass.hIcon          = LoadIcon(NULL,IDI_APPLICATION);
    WndClass.hCursor        = LoadCursor(NULL,IDC_ARROW);
    WndClass.hbrBackground  = hMBrush;
    WndClass.lpszMenuName   = NULL;
    WndClass.lpszClassName  = "GRAPHBTN";

    return RegisterClass(&WndClass);
    }
```

continues

Listing 7.10. continued

```
HWND BLDCreateWindow( HANDLE hInstance )   // Creates the main window
{
    HWND hWnd;                      // Window handle
    int coordinate[4];              // Coordinates of main window

    coordinate[0]=CW_USEDEFAULT;
    coordinate[1]=0;
    coordinate[2]=CW_USEDEFAULT;
    coordinate[3]=0;

    hWnd = CreateWindow("GRAPHBTN",  // Window class registered earlier
            "The Happy Button App",            // Window caption
          WS_OVERLAPPED¦WS_THICKFRAME¦WS_SYSMENU¦WS_MINIMIZEBOX¦WS_MAXIMIZEBOX,
                                   // Window style
            coordinate[0],         // X position
            coordinate[1],         // Y position
            coordinate[2],         // Width
            coordinate[3],         // Height
            0,                     // Parent handle
            0,                     // Menu or child ID
            hInstance,             // Instance
            (LPSTR)NULL);          // Additional info

    return hWnd;
    }


// Called just before entering message loop
BOOL BLDInitMainMenu(HWND hWnd)
    {
    // No initialization necessary
    return TRUE;
    }


BOOL BLDExitApplication()        // Called just before exit of application
    {
    if (hMBrush)
        DeleteObject(hMBrush);
    return TRUE;
    }
```

```
//*********************************************************
// ERROR MESSAGE HANDLING (Definitions can be overruled.)
//*********************************************************

#ifndef ERRORCAPTION
#define ERRORCAPTION "The Happy Button App"
#endif

#ifndef LOADERROR
#define LOADERROR "Cannot load string."
#endif


int BLDDisplayMessage(HWND hWnd, unsigned uMsg, char *pContext, int iType)
    {
    int i, j;
    char Message[200+1];

    if (uMsg)
        {
        if (!LoadString(hInst,uMsg,Message,200))
            {
            MessageBox(hWnd,LOADERROR,ERRORCAPTION, MB_OK|MB_SYSTEMMODAL|
                                                    MB_ICONHAND);
            return FALSE;
            }
        }
    else
        Message[0]=0;

    if (pContext)
        {
        i = lstrlen(Message);
        j = lstrlen(pContext);
        if (i + j + 1 <= 200)
            {
            lstrcat(Message, " ");
            lstrcat(Message, pContext);
            }
        }

    return MessageBox(hWnd,Message,ERRORCAPTION,iType);
    }
```

continues

Listing 7.10. continued

```c
//******************************************************************
//           FUNCTIONS FOR DRAWING GRAPHICS BUTTONS
//******************************************************************

BOOL BLDDrawIcon(LPDRAWITEMSTRUCT lpDrawItem, char *pIconName)
    {
    HICON hIcon;

    hIcon = LoadIcon(hInst,pIconName);
    if (!hIcon)
        {
        BLDDisplayMessage(GetActiveWindow(),BLD_CannotLoadIcon,pIconName,
                        MB_OK | MB_ICONASTERISK);
        return FALSE;
        }

    SetMapMode(lpDrawItem->hDC,MM_TEXT);
    return DrawIcon(lpDrawItem->hDC,0,0,hIcon);
    }


BOOL BLDDrawBitmap(LPDRAWITEMSTRUCT lpDrawItem, char *pBitmapName,
                BOOL bStretch)
    {
    HBITMAP hBitmap;
    HDC hMemDC;
    BITMAP Bitmap;
    int iRaster;

    iRaster = GetDeviceCaps(lpDrawItem->hDC,RASTERCAPS);
    if ((iRaster&RC_BITBLT)!=RC_BITBLT)
        return FALSE;              // Device cannot display bitmap

    hBitmap = LoadBitmap(hInst,pBitmapName);
    if (!hBitmap)
        {
        BLDDisplayMessage(GetActiveWindow(),BLD_CannotLoadBitmap,pBitmapName,
                        MB_OK | MB_ICONASTERISK);
        return FALSE;
        }

    if (!GetObject(hBitmap,sizeof(BITMAP),(LPSTR)&Bitmap))
        {
```

```
        DeleteObject(hBitmap);
        return FALSE;
        }
hMemDC = CreateCompatibleDC(lpDrawItem->hDC);
if (!hMemDC)
        {
        DeleteObject(hBitmap);
        return FALSE;
        }
if (!SelectObject(hMemDC,hBitmap))
        {
        DeleteDC(hMemDC);
        DeleteObject(hBitmap);
        return FALSE;
        }


if (bStretch)
        {
        StretchBlt(lpDrawItem->hDC,
                lpDrawItem->rcItem.left,
                lpDrawItem->rcItem.top,
                lpDrawItem->rcItem.right-lpDrawItem->rcItem.left,
                lpDrawItem->rcItem.bottom-lpDrawItem->rcItem.top,
                hMemDC,
                0,
                0,
                Bitmap.bmWidth,
                Bitmap.bmHeight,
                SRCCOPY);
        }
else
        {
        BitBlt(lpDrawItem->hDC,
                lpDrawItem->rcItem.left,
                lpDrawItem->rcItem.top,
                lpDrawItem->rcItem.right-lpDrawItem->rcItem.left,
                lpDrawItem->rcItem.bottom-lpDrawItem->rcItem.top,
                hMemDC,
                0,
                0,
                SRCCOPY);
        }
DeleteDC(hMemDC);
DeleteObject(hBitmap);
```

continues

411

Listing 7.10. continued

```
    return TRUE;
    }

//*****************************************************************
//          FUNCTION FOR CREATING CONTROLS IN MAIN WINDOW
//*****************************************************************

// Startup procedure for window in client area
HWND BLDCreateClientControls(char *pTemplateName, FARPROC lpNew)
{
    RECT rClient,rMain,rDialog;
    int dxDialog,dyDialog,dyExtra,dtXold,dtYold;
    HANDLE hRes,hMem;
    LPBLD_DLGTEMPLATE lpDlg;
    unsigned long styleold,style;
    HWND hNew;

    if (!IsWindow(MainhWnd))
        return 0;
    if (IsZoomed(MainhWnd))
        ShowWindow(MainhWnd,SW_RESTORE);

    if (IsWindow(hClient))
        DestroyWindow(hClient); // Destroy Previous window in client area

    // Get access to data structure of dialog box containing layout of ctrls
    hRes=FindResource(hInst,(LPSTR)pTemplateName,RT_DIALOG);
    if (!hRes)
        return 0;
    hMem=LoadResource(hInst,hRes);
    if (!hMem)
        return 0;
    lpDlg=(LPBLD_DLGTEMPLATE)LockResource(hMem);
    if (!lpDlg)
        return 0;

    // Change dialog box data structure so it can be used as a window
    // in client area
    styleold         = lpDlg->dtStyle;
    style            = lpDlg->dtStyle&(CLIENTSTRIP);
    lpDlg->dtStyle   = lpDlg->dtStyle^style;
    lpDlg->dtStyle   = lpDlg->dtStyle | WS_CHILD | WS_CLIPSIBLINGS;
    dtXold           = lpDlg->dtX;
```

```
dtYold          = lpDlg->dtY;
lpDlg->dtX      = 0;
lpDlg->dtY      = 0;

hNew = CreateDialogIndirect(hInst,(LPSTR)lpDlg, MainhWnd,lpNew);
if (!hNew)
    return 0;

// Restore dialog box data structure.
lpDlg->dtStyle  = styleold;
lpDlg->dtX      = dtXold;
lpDlg->dtY      = dtYold;

UnlockResource(hMem);
FreeResource(hMem);

// Move and size window in client area and main window
GetClientRect(MainhWnd,&rClient);
GetWindowRect(MainhWnd,&rMain);
GetWindowRect(hNew,&rDialog);
dxDialog=(rDialog.right-rDialog.left)-(rClient.right-rClient.left);
dyDialog=(rDialog.bottom-rDialog.top)-(rClient.bottom-rClient.top);
BLDMoveWindow(MainhWnd,rMain.left,rMain.top,
          (rMain.right-rMain.left)+dxDialog,
                    (rMain.bottom-rMain.top)+dyDialog,
              TRUE);
MoveWindow(hNew,0,0,
                    (rDialog.right-rDialog.left),
                    (rDialog.bottom-rDialog.top),
                    TRUE);
GetClientRect(MainhWnd,&rClient);

// Compensate size if menu bar is more than one line.
if ((rDialog.bottom-rDialog.top)>(rClient.bottom-rClient.top))
    {
    dyExtra=(rDialog.bottom-rDialog.top)-(rClient.bottom-rClient.top);
    BLDMoveWindow(MainhWnd,rMain.left,rMain.top,
              (rMain.right-rMain.left)+dxDialog,
              (rMain.bottom-rMain.top)+dyDialog+dyExtra,
              TRUE);
    }

ShowWindow(hNew,SW_SHOW);
hClient=hNew;
```

continues

413

Listing 7.10. continued

```
        lpClient=lpNew;
        return hClient;
        }


// Ensure that window is within screen.
void BLDMoveWindow(HWND hWnd, int x, int y,
        int nWidth, int nHeight, BOOL bRepaint)
    {
    int xMax,yMax,xNew,yNew;

    xMax = GetSystemMetrics(SM_CXSCREEN);
    yMax = GetSystemMetrics(SM_CYSCREEN);

    if ((nWidth<=xMax)&&(x+nWidth>xMax))
        xNew=xMax-nWidth;
    else
        xNew=x;

    if ((nHeight<=yMax)&&(y+nHeight>yMax))
        yNew=yMax-nHeight;
    else
        yNew=y;

    MoveWindow(hWnd,xNew,yNew,nWidth,nHeight,bRepaint);
    return;
    }

//**************************************************************
//              FUNCTION FOR SWITCHING MENU SET
//**************************************************************

BOOL BLDSwitchMenu(HWND hWnd, char *pTemplateName)
    {
    HMENU hMenu1,hMenu;
    DWORD style;

    style = GetWindowLong(hWnd,GWL_STYLE);
    if((style & WS_CHILD) == WS_CHILD)  // Called from control in main window?
        {
        hWnd=GetParent(hWnd);
        if (!hWnd)
            return FALSE;
```

```
            style = GetWindowLong(hWnd,GWL_STYLE);
            if((style & WS_CHILD) == WS_CHILD) // No menu in a WS_CHILD window.
                return FALSE;
            }
    if((style & WS_CAPTION) != WS_CAPTION) // No menu if no caption.
        return FALSE;

    hMenu1 = GetMenu(hWnd);
    hMenu = LoadMenu(hInst,pTemplateName);
    if (!hMenu)
        {
        BLDDisplayMessage(hWnd,BLD_CannotLoadMenu,pTemplateName,
                          MB_OK | MB_ICONASTERISK);
        return FALSE;
        }

    if (!SetMenu(hWnd,hMenu))
        return FALSE;
    if (hMenu1)
        DestroyMenu(hMenu1);

    DrawMenuBar(hWnd);
    return TRUE;
    }
```

Listing 7.11. GRAPHBTN.H—include file for the Happy Button App.

```
//File name: GRAPHBTN.H
//"GRAPHBTN" Generated by WindowsMAKER Professional
//Author: Alex Leavens, for ShadowCat Technologies

// These definitions are provided to support
// compilers with older versions of WINDOWS.H.
typedef unsigned int        UINT;
#ifndef WINAPI
typedef HANDLE              HINSTANCE;
#endif

#ifndef WM_SYSTEMERROR
#define WM_SYSTEMERROR         0x0017
#endif
#ifndef WM_QUEUESYNC
```

continues

415

Listing 7.11. continued

```
#define WM_QUEUESYNC            0x0023
#endif
#ifndef WM_COMMNOTIFY
#define WM_COMMNOTIFY           0x0044
#endif
#ifndef WM_WINDOWPOSCHANGING
#define WM_WINDOWPOSCHANGING    0x0046
#endif
#ifndef WM_WINDOWPOSCHANGED
#define WM_WINDOWPOSCHANGED     0x0047
#endif
#ifndef WM_POWER
#define WM_POWER                0x0048
#endif
#ifndef WM_DROPFILES
#define WM_DROPFILES            0x0233
#endif
#ifndef WM_PALETTEISCHANGING
#define WM_PALETTEISCHANGING    0x0310
#endif


// Give access to handles in all code modules
extern HINSTANCE hInst;
extern HWND      MainhWnd;

// Constants for error message strings
#define BLD_CannotRun         4000
#define BLD_CannotCreate      4001
#define BLD_CannotLoadMenu    4002
#define BLD_CannotLoadIcon    4003
#define BLD_CannotLoadBitmap  4004

#if !defined(THISISBLDRC)

int  PASCAL WinMain( HINSTANCE hInstance,
                     HINSTANCE hPrevInstance, LPSTR lpCmdLine, int nCmdShow );
LONG FAR PASCAL BLDMainWndProc( HWND hWnd, UINT message,
                                UINT wParam, LONG lParam );
LONG FAR PASCAL BLDDefWindowProc( HWND hWnd, UINT message,
                                  UINT wParam, LONG lParam );
BOOL BLDKeyTranslation( MSG *pMsg );
```

```
BOOL BLDInitApplication( HANDLE hInst, HANDLE hPrev,
                         int *pCmdShow, LPSTR lpCmd );
BOOL BLDExitApplication( void );
HWND BLDCreateClientControls( char *pTemplateName, FARPROC lpNew );
BOOL BLDInitMainMenu( HWND hWnd );
BOOL BLDMenuCommand( HWND hWnd, UINT message, UINT wParam, LONG lParam );
BOOL BLDRegisterClass( HANDLE hInstance );
HWND BLDCreateWindow( HANDLE hInstance );
int  BLDDisplayMessage(HWND hWnd, unsigned uMsg, char *pContext, int iType );
BOOL BLDSwitchMenu( HWND hWnd, char *pTemplateName );
BOOL BLDDrawBitmap( LPDRAWITEMSTRUCT lpDrawItem,
                    char *pBitmapName, BOOL bStretch );
BOOL BLDDrawIcon( LPDRAWITEMSTRUCT lpDrawItem, char *pIconName );
void BLDMoveWindow( HWND hWnd, int x, int y,
                    int nWidth, int nHeight, BOOL bRepaint );


//****************************************************************
// Variables, types, and constants for controls in main window.
//****************************************************************


extern HWND     hClient;        // Handle to window in client area.
extern FARPROC  lpClient;       // Function for window in client area.


#define CLIENTSTRIP WS_MINIMIZE¦WS_MAXIMIZE¦WS_CAPTION¦WS_BORDER¦WS_DLGFRAME¦
WS_SYSMENU¦WS_POPUP¦WS_THICKFRAME¦DS_MODALFRAME


typedef struct
    {
    unsigned long dtStyle;
    BYTE dtItemCount;
    int dtX;
    int dtY;
    int dtCX;
    int dtCY;
    } BLD_DLGTEMPLATE;


typedef BLD_DLGTEMPLATE far          *LPBLD_DLGTEMPLATE;


#endif


#define WMPDEBUG



// User Defined ID Values
```

continues

```
#define ID_HAPPY_BUTTON                       8000
#define ID_SAD_BUTTON                         8001

// WindowsMAKER Pro generated ID Values
```

Listing 7.12. USERCODE.C—support routines for the Happy Button App.

```
//File name: USERCODE.C
//"GRAPHBTN" Generated by WindowsMAKER Professional
//Author: Alex Leavens, for ShadowCat Technologies

#include <WINDOWS.H>
#include "GRAPHBTN.H"

// Defines how many tool buttons you create
// (You can change this to create more in your own applications)

#define   NUM_TOOLBUTTONS           2

// Placeholders for your graphics button window handles

HWND      btnHand[2];

// This is stuff that you use to handle user-drawn buttons...


#define          NOFOCUS_NOFLAGS          0
#define          FOCUS_NOFLAGS            1
#define          FOCUS_FOCUS              2
#define          DRAWALL                  4
#define          SELECT_NOFLAGS           8
#define          SELECT_SELECT            0x10
#define          SELECT_FOCUS             0x20
#define          SELECT_FOCUS_SELECT      0x30
#define          ALL_NOFLAGS              0x40
#define          ALL_FOCUS                0x80
#define          ALL_SELECT               0x100
#define          ALL_FOCUS_SELECT         0x180

//------------ Function prototypes ------------------

BOOL      CreateGraphicButtons ( HWND );
```

```
void FAR PASCAL   SetGraphicButtonToUnselected ( HWND, WORD, WORD );
void      DrawButtonTools(HWND, UINT, UINT, LONG );
BOOL      DrawBitmap (HDC, int, int, HBITMAP, DWORD );
WORD FAR PASCAL GetDesiredButtonState(HWND, WORD, WORD );


/********************************
 * CreateGraphicButtons()
 *    Creates an owner-draw button which is used to
 *    draw graphics buttons.
 *
 * Params:
 *    hWnd - Parent window handle
 *
 * Returns:
 *    TRUE - Window was created successfully
 *    FALSE - Failure...
 */


    BOOL
CreateGraphicButtons ( HWND          hWnd )
{
    // Create some positions for your buttons here.
    // You can hard-code these values at creation time,
    // or use an algorithm which calculates their position
    // based on the size of the window.

    int  xOffset[]={ 25, 75 };
    int  yOffset[]={ 25, 25 };

    int  i;


    WORD buttonID[] = { ID_HAPPY_BUTTON,
                              ID_SAD_BUTTON };

    /*------------------*/

    // Create a pair of owner-draw buttons here. Owner-draw
    // buttons must be used in order for you to draw your own buttons.

    for (i = 0; i < NUM_TOOLBUTTONS; i++)
    {
```

continues

Listing 7.12. continued

```
                btnHand [ i ] = CreateWindow(
                            "BUTTON",           // Button class
                            NULL,               // No text string in button
                            BS_OWNERDRAW |      // Ownerdraw means you draw it,
                                                // child window, and visible
                                                // at creation time
                              WS_CHILD | WS_VISIBLE,
                            xOffset [ i ],      // X position of button
                            yOffset [ i ],      // Y position of button
                            32,                 // Width of button in pixels
                            32,                 // Height of button in pixels
                            hWnd,               // Parent window
                              buttonID [ i ],   // ID of button
                            hInst,              // Instance of app
                            NULL);              // Additional data (none)

        // If button window failed to create, then
        // punt the main app.

        if ( !btnHand [ i ] )
        {
            DestroyWindow(hWnd);
            return FALSE;
        }
    }
    return TRUE;
}


/*******************************
 * SetGraphicButtonToUnselected()
 *    Causes an owner-draw button to be redrawn in the up position.
 *
 * Params:
 *    hWnd - Parent window handle
 *    buttonID - ID of the button to draw as unselected
 *    bHandle - Index into the handle table of the button
 *
 * Returns:
 *    Nada.
 *
 * Assumptions:
 *    This routine assumes a button size of 32x32
 */
```

```
        void FAR PASCAL
SetGraphicButtonToUnselected(HWND    hWnd,
                                WORD            buttonID,
                                WORD            bHandle)
{
    HDC                     hDC;        // DC for owner-draw button to use

    DRAWITEMSTRUCT          dwI;        // Draw item information for the button

    /*--------------------*/

    // First, you need to create a DC for the owner-draw button to draw
    // into. Do this by getting the DC of the window handle of
    // the owner-draw button in question.

    hDC = GetDC((HWND)btnHand[bHandle]);

    // Now you need to fill in all the information that's needed
    // for drawing an owner-draw button in a DRAWITEMSTRUCT

    dwI.CtlType = ODT_BUTTON;        // This is an owner-draw button
    dwI.CtlID = buttonID;  // ID of the button to render
    dwI.itemAction = ODA_DRAWENTIRE; // Draw all of the button
    dwI.itemState = NULL;  // No state specified
    dwI.hDC = hDC;                   // DC to draw into
    dwI.rcItem.left = 0;   // Upper-left corner of position to
    dwI.rcItem.top = 0;              // draw into
    dwI.rcItem.right = 33;           // Size of the button
    dwI.rcItem.bottom = 33;

    // Now, by sending yourself a message, you cause your own
    // owner-draw code to process this message, and thereby redraw
    // your button in the up state. Note the double cast in the
    // last parameter, first to a Long pointer to a DRAWITEMSTRUCT,
    // and then to a DWORD.

    SendMessage(MainhWnd,
                WM_DRAWITEM,
                (WORD)0,
                (DWORD)((LPDRAWITEMSTRUCT)&dwI));

    // Now that you're done with the DC for the button, give it
    // back.
```

continues

421

Listing 7.12. continued

```
    ReleaseDC((HWND)btnHand[bHandle], hDC);

}


/***************************
 * DrawButtonTools()
 *    Draws an owner-draw button into the DC that's been passed int.
 *
 * Returns:
 *    Nothing
 */

    void
DrawButtonTools(HWND        hWnd,
                UINT        message,
                UINT        wParam,
                LONG        lParam)
{
    LPDRAWITEMSTRUCT        lpDis;              // Drawitem information
    HDC                     hDC;                // HDC to draw into

    WORD         flags;               // Flags containing draw info

    HBITMAP                 hBM;                 // Bitmap to draw...

    WORD         left;               // Upper-left corner...
    WORD         top;                // Upper-left corner

    /*------------------------------*/

    // Get the pointer to the owner-draw information here

    lpDis = (LPDRAWITEMSTRUCT)lParam;

    /* If control is not the right type, punt.
     * (This should never happen, right?)
     */

    if (lpDis->CtlType != ODT_BUTTON)
        return;

    // Get the DC that you're going to draw into
```

```
hDC = lpDis->hDC;

left = lpDis->rcItem.left;
top  = lpDis->rcItem.top;

// Find out how you're supposed to be drawing the button...

flags = GetDesiredButtonState(hWnd,
                                  lpDis->itemAction,
                                  lpDis->itemState);

// The ID of the button determines what image you're
// going to need to draw...

switch ( lpDis->CtlID )
{
    case ID_HAPPY_BUTTON:
        switch(flags)
        {
            case ALL_SELECT:
            case ALL_FOCUS_SELECT:
            case SELECT_SELECT:
            case SELECT_FOCUS_SELECT:
                hBM = LoadBitmap ( hInst,
                                        "DHAPPY" );
                 break;

            default:
                hBM = LoadBitmap ( hInst,
                                        "UHAPPY" );
                break;
        }

        // If bitmap was successfully loaded, then
        // draw it; otherwise, post an error message

        if ( hBM != NULL )
        {
            DrawBitmap ( hDC,
                         left,
                         top,
                         hBM,
                         SRCCOPY );
            DeleteObject ( hBM );
        }
```

continues

423

Listing 7.12. continued

```
            else
            {
                MessageBox ( hWnd,
                             "Cannot load bitmap for drawing",
                             "No bitmap!",
                             MB_OK );
            }
            break;

        case ID_SAD_BUTTON:
            switch(flags)
            {
                case ALL_SELECT:
                case ALL_FOCUS_SELECT:
                case SELECT_SELECT:
                case SELECT_FOCUS_SELECT:
                    hBM = LoadBitmap ( hInst,
                                       "DSAD" );
                    break;

                default:
                    hBM = LoadBitmap ( hInst,
                                       "USAD" );
                    break;
            }

            // If bitmap was successfully loaded, then
            // draw it; otherwise, post an error message

            if ( hBM != NULL )
            {
                DrawBitmap ( hDC,
                             left,
                             top,
                             hBM,
                             SRCCOPY );
                DeleteObject ( hBM );
            }
            else
            {
                MessageBox ( hWnd,
                             "Cannot load bitmap for drawing",
                             "No bitmap!",
                             MB_OK );
```

```
                }
                break;

            default:
                break;
        }
    }


/***************************
 * GetDesiredButtonState()
 *    Returns a value which indicates the desired end result
 *    of a button press on an owner-drawn button.
 *
 * Params:
 *    hWnd - Window handle
 *    itemAction - Action taken
 *    itemState - Desired end state
 *
 * Returns:
 *    Flag setting
 *
 * Assumptions:
 *    None
 */

    WORD FAR PASCAL
GetDesiredButtonState(HWND        hWnd,
                      WORD        itemAction,
                      WORD        itemState)
{
    WORD lFlags;            /* Local flag value */

    /*--------------------*/

    lFlags = NOFOCUS_NOFLAGS;

    if (itemAction & ODA_FOCUS)
    {
        if (itemState & ODS_FOCUS)
            lFlags = FOCUS_FOCUS;
        else
            lFlags = FOCUS_NOFLAGS;
    }
```

continues

425

Listing 7.12. continued

```
    if (itemAction & ODA_SELECT)
    {
        if (itemState & ODS_FOCUS)
            lFlags |= SELECT_FOCUS;
        if (itemState & ODS_SELECTED)
            lFlags |= SELECT_SELECT;
    }

    if (itemAction & ODA_DRAWENTIRE)
    {
        lFlags = ALL_NOFLAGS;

        if (itemState & ODS_FOCUS)
            lFlags |= ALL_FOCUS;
        if (itemState & ODS_SELECTED)
            lFlags |= ALL_SELECT;
    }

    return (lFlags);
}


/***********************************
 * DrawBitmap()
 *    Draws a bitmap into the requested DC at the requested
 *    location using the requested raster operation.
 *
 * Returns:
 *    TRUE - you drew the bitmap
 *    FALSE - you didn't
 */

    BOOL
DrawBitmap (HDC        hDC,              /* Destination DC */
            int        x,                /* x-offset */
            int        y,                /* y-offset */
            HBITMAP    hbm,              /* Handle to source bitmap */
            DWORD      rop)              /* Raster OP to perform */
{
    HDC        hMemoryDC;
    BITMAP     bm;
    BOOL       f;
    HBITMAP    bmHand;
```

```
/*-------------------------*/

if (!hDC ¦¦ !hbm)       /* If either handle is bad, punt */
    return FALSE;

/* Before you can blit the bitmap, it has to be selected into a device
 * context compatible with the destination. So first, you need
 * to create the compatible DC.
 */

hMemoryDC = CreateCompatibleDC(hDC);

/* Select desired bitmap into the memory DC you just created.
 * Also remember the old bitmap handle that used to be in the
 * DC so that you can restore it after you're done.
 */

bmHand = SelectObject(hMemoryDC,
                          hbm);

/* Get information about the bitmap so that you can blit it
 * properly.
 */

GetObject(hbm,
            sizeof(BITMAP),
            (LPSTR)&bm);

/* Everything's set up--you can now blit the image into the destination
 * DC.
 */

f = BitBlt(hDC,                 /* Destination DC */
            x,                  /* Destination x offset (if any) */
            y,                  /* Destination y offset (if any) */
            bm.bmWidth,         /* Width of source bitmap */
            bm.bmHeight,        /* Height of source bitmap */
            hMemoryDC,          /* Source DC */
            0,                  /* Source x offset (none) */
            0,                  /* Source y offset (none) */
            SRCCOPY);   /* Copy the bitmap... */

/* Now select the old bitmap handle back into the memory DC.
 * (Failure to do this causes a small piece of Windows resource
 * to be lost until reboot time.)
 */
```

continues

Listing 7.12. continued

```
SelectObject(hMemoryDC,
             bmHand);

/* Delete the memory DC so that you're not using up system resources. */

DeleteDC(hMemoryDC);

/* Return status of the BitBlt() call. */

return TRUE;
}
```

Listing 7.13. GRAPHBTN—makefile for the Happy Button App.

```
#File name: GRAPHBTN
#"GRAPHBTN" Generated by WindowsMAKER Professional
#Author: Alex Leavens, for ShadowCat Technologies

comp= /c /AS /Os /Gsw /Zpe /D _WINDOWS /W2
cc=cl

GRAPHBTN.EXE : GRAPHBTN.OBJ USERCODE.OBJ GRAPHBTN.DEF GRAPHBTN.RES
    LINK @GRAPHBTN.LNK
    rc GRAPHBTN.RES

GRAPHBTN.RES : GRAPHBTN.RC GRAPHBTN.H DHAPPY.BMP UHAPPY.BMP \
         DSAD.BMP USAD.BMP
    rc -r GRAPHBTN.RC

GRAPHBTN.OBJ : GRAPHBTN.C GRAPHBTN.WMC GRAPHBTN.H
    $(cc) $(comp) GRAPHBTN.C

USERCODE.OBJ : USERCODE.C GRAPHBTN.H
    $(cc) $(comp) USERCODE.C
```

Listing 7.14. GRAPHBTN.DEF—module definition file for the Happy Button App.

```
;File name: GRAPHBTN.DEF
;"GRAPHBTN" Generated by WindowsMAKER Professional
;Author: Alex Leavens, for ShadowCat Technologies

NAME          GRAPHBTN
DESCRIPTION   'GRAPHBTN generated by WindowsMAKER Professional'
EXETYPE       WINDOWS
STUB          'WINSTUB.EXE'
DATA          MOVEABLE MULTIPLE
CODE          MOVEABLE DISCARDABLE PRELOAD
HEAPSIZE      1024
STACKSIZE     5120
EXPORTS

              BLDMainWndProc
```

Listing 7.15. GRAPHBTN.LNK—link file for the Happy Button App.

```
GRAPHBTN USERCODE ,GRAPHBTN.EXE ,/align:16 /NOD  , LIBW SLIBCEW, GRAPHBTN.DEF
```

Listing 7.16. GRAPHBTN.RC—resource file for the Happy Button App.

```
//File name: GRAPHBTN.RC
//"GRAPHBTN" Generated by WindowsMAKER Professional
//Author: Alex Leavens, for ShadowCat Technologies

#define THISISBLDRC

#include <WINDOWS.H>
#include "GRAPHBTN.H"

DHAPPY BITMAP DHAPPY.BMP
UHAPPY BITMAP UHAPPY.BMP
DSAD BITMAP DSAD.BMP
USAD BITMAP USAD.BMP
```

continues

429

Listing 7.16. continued

```
//**********************************************************
//        Resource code for error message strings
//**********************************************************

STRINGTABLE
   BEGIN
      BLD_CannotRun          "Cannot run "
      BLD_CannotCreate       "Cannot create dialog box "
      BLD_CannotLoadMenu      "Cannot load menu "
      BLD_CannotLoadIcon      "Cannot load icon "
      BLD_CannotLoadBitmap    "Cannot load bitmap "
   END
```

Bitmaps for the Happy Button App

Following are all the bitmaps for the Happy Button App:

 UHAPPY.BMP—Up (unselected) image for the happy button. This image is displayed when the user is not pressing the happy button.

 DHAPPY.BMP—Down (selected) image for the happy button. This image is displayed when the user is pressing the happy button.

 USAD.BMP—Up (unselected) image for the sad button. This image is displayed when the user is not pressing the sad button.

 DSAD.BMP—Down (selected) image for the sad button. This image is displayed when the user is pressing the sad button.

Examining the Graphics Button Example

There's a great deal more going on here than in the text button application—that much is clear just from the size of the source code. What may be less clear is exactly what is going on and why. To get a better handle on what's going on, I break the process down into three areas:

- Window creation
- Internal message processing for the graphics button
- Command message processing by your application

Window Creation

You handle the creation of your graphics buttons in the WM_CREATE message handler, just as you do for text buttons. (The creation of the buttons is handled by the routine CreateGraphicButtons().) The window creation procedure for your graphics buttons is actually much like that of your text buttons, but with one very important difference. Instead of creating a BS_PUSHBUTTON class window, you create a BS_OWNERDRAW window. This change tells Windows to create a window for you that has the attributes of a button window, but to let you take care of drawing it. By doing this, you assume total responsibility for the display of this button. If you don't draw it, it won't get drawn.

The rest of the window creation parameters are virtually the same. Again, you're creating a window of a specific size, and at a specific position, with a specific ID. In this case, you don't size the window to the text string of the window, because you put an image, rather than text, into the window. (This is also why you pass a NULL parameter for the text string of the window—because bitmap buttons don't have a text string in them.) Because you know in advance how big your graphics images are going to be, you size the window accordingly. Doing this is cheating, just a little. To make this routine truly general purpose, you'd find the size of the bitmap you were going to use, and then create the window that size. In fact, this is what the bitmap button class (coming up) does.

The Messages a Graphics Button Receives

This is where the big differences lie. The window creation of your graphics button (described previously) and the external processing that your main

application performs (described next) are pretty similar to the text button application. This middle step, however, is completely new—it's also quite complex.

First, you have to have your application respond to a new message: the WM_DRAWITEM message. This message informs your main application that one of your child windows needs drawing. Your application receives this message only for objects created with the OWNERDRAW attribute. (These objects can be more than buttons; for example, you can create or modify a menu so that it has the MF_OWNERDRAW attribute, which means you're responsible for drawing that menu item. I discuss this feature in more detail in Chapter 8, "Menu Resources.")

In your case, because the processing for owner-draw objects is necessarily complex, you pass it to the source file DrawButtonTools(), which is in the source file USERCODE.C. Examine the routine in detail.

The first thing you do is get the pointer to the DRAWITEMSTRUCT structure that defines the information about how to draw this object.

```
// Get the pointer to the owner-draw information here

lpDis = (LPDRAWITEMSTRUCT)lParam;
```

This enables you to get at the information you need in order to draw the object. Here's what the DRAWITEMSTRUCT looks like:

```
typedef struct tagDRAWITEMSTRUCT
  {
          WORD    CtlType;        // Type of item to be drawn
          WORD    CtlID;          // ID of item to be drawn
          WORD    itemAction;     // What kind of drawing action to perform
          WORD    itemState;      // What the new state of the object is
          HWND    hWndItem;       // Window handle for certain objects
          HDC     hDC;            // DC to draw into
          RECT    rcItem;         // Defines boundary of object
          DWORD   itemData;       // Other information
  };
```

This structure is defined in more detail in the reference at the end of the chapter. However, there are a couple of important fields to touch on now:

dwID   This defines the ID of the control that needs to be drawn. This is the ID you passed to the **CreateWindow()** call.

itemAction   Specifies what kind of drawing is to take place. You can determine from this field whether the entire control is being redrawn in its current state, or whether the control is changing from one position to another.

hDC This is a very important field—it defines the DC you must use in all of your drawing operations regarding this control. Unlike with normal drawing operations in your main window (where you do a `GetDC()` or `BeginPaint()`), you use the DC already provided. This is for a couple of reasons, but the primary one is that this DC has been set up with a bunch of default attributes set to "reasonable" values.

Look at how you use these fields in the drawing routine.

```
// Get the DC that you're going to draw into

hDC = lpDis->hDC;

left = lpDis->rcItem.left;
top  = lpDis->rcItem.top;
```

The first thing you do is get the DC that you use for your drawing operations. You also get the upper-left corner of where you're supposed to draw into. The RECT structure in the DRAWITEMSTRUCT defines for you the upper-left and lower-right corners of the area you're supposed to draw into. Although these can be (0,0) (and usually are), they don't have to be. For example, you could create a window that's larger than your 32 x 32 image size, so you could draw a focus rect around the entire image. In that case, you want to center the image in the rectangle, which would mean using an offset into it, which you could put here. (See the `SetGraphicButtonToUnselected()` function, which isn't used in this version of the application, but which demonstrates how to cause an owner-draw button to respond to a message generated by your application.)

Next, use the `itemAction` and `itemState` fields to determine how to draw the image. This is accomplished by the routine `GetDesiredButtonState()`, which returns a flag value that indicates in what form the image should be drawn.

```
// Find out how you're supposed to be drawing the button...

flags = GetDesiredButtonState(hWnd,
                              lpDis->itemAction,
                              lpDis->itemState);
```

Now that you know how to draw the image, you have to determine what image to draw. This is accomplished by switching off the CtlID field of the DRAWITEMSTRUCT. This is the ID you created the control window with.

```
// The ID of the button determines what image you
// draw...
```

```
switch ( lpDis->CtlID )
{
...
```

I'm just going to examine what you do in the case of ID_HAPPY_BUTTON, the ID of the button with the happy face on it. The case for the sad button (ID_SAD_BUTTON) is similar; it doesn't need to be discussed here.

First, you switch off the flags value you got back from the GetDesiredButtonState() routine. In cases in which the button has been selected, or has the selection and focus, the button is in the "depressed" state (that is, the user is clicking it with the mouse or hitting the space bar), and you should draw the down image. In any other case, you draw the up image, which means the button is not being clicked.

To draw the image, you load the appropriate bitmap from your program's resource table and use the DrawBitmap() routine (which you saw in Chapter 4, "Device Independent Bitmaps") to display it on-screen. Notice that the DC used for drawing the bitmap is the one you retrieved from the DRAWITEMSTRUCT.

You also provide the appropriate error trapping routines for cases in which you weren't able to load the bitmap from disk, as well as making sure to delete the bitmap when you're done with it. This approach (loading the bitmap resource immediately before use and then deleting it immediately afterward) means a slight delay in displaying your images. However, it means a decrease in the amount of GDI resources you're using at any given time. The other approach (which I use in the bitmap button class) is to preload all the resources before use and then display them when requested to do so. The first case makes the trade-off of speed for size (load each time), whereas the second case makes the trade-off of size for speed (preload and display). I've demonstrated both approaches so that you can decide for yourself which is more applicable for your applications.

```
case ID_HAPPY_BUTTON:
  switch(flags)
  {
    case ALL_SELECT:
     case ALL_FOCUS_SELECT:
     case SELECT_SELECT:
     case SELECT_FOCUS_SELECT:
         hBM = LoadBitmap ( hInst,
                            "DHAPPY" );
```

```
        break;

    default:
        hBM = LoadBitmap ( hInst,
                            "UHAPPY" );
        break;
}

// If bitmap was successfully loaded, then
// draw it; otherwise, post an error message

if ( hBM != NULL )
{
  DrawBitmap ( hDC,
               left,
               top,
               hBM,
               SRCCOPY );

  DeleteObject ( hBM );

}
else
{
  MessageBox ( hWnd,
               "Cannot load bitmap for drawing",
               "No bitmap!",
               MB_OK );
}
break;
```

The Messages Your Application Receives

Your handling of messages from owner-draw buttons is virtually indistinguishable from that of text buttons. You switch off the wParam value, which gives you the ID of the button pressed. Just as with your text application, you post a silly message in a message box. In a more substantial application, you would obviously do a bit more processing than this!

A Bitmap Button Object Class

Now that you've seen how to create and support a bitmap button, you're probably eager to build a couple of your own. Before you do, I need to make a couple of important points. Most of them have to do with the exponential increase in difficulty you're likely to encounter when building, say, 20 graphics buttons rather than only 1 or 2.

The reason it's much harder to build and support many buttons as opposed to just a couple stems from all the bureaucratic things you have to do to support a large number of buttons.

If you notice in the sample app, I've cheated in lots of little ways—I included the `define` statements for the number of tool buttons, and the various selection states in the beginning of the Usercode.c module. In a full and robust app, these are, of course, in a .h file somewhere. Similarly, I've created a small array to hold the window handles of the various buttons you create. In a large app, you need to create a much bigger array and manage it as well. Further, if you look at the `DrawButtonTools()` routine, you can see that it's already getting pretty big, and it's supporting only two buttons, with two images each. Of course, for a full application, I wouldn't duplicate code the way I have; I'd simply have a `switch` that loaded the appropriate bitmap, and a single drawing routine at the end.

This is what I did for ICE/Works, and I ended up with a five-page `switch` statement, just to load the bitmaps for all the different buttons. And that was only for the up button images. I had another five-page `switch` statement to load the down button images. And I wanted to add about 20 buttons to the interface. To make things worse, when I wanted to add a button, I had to change about five different source modules, as well as a couple of .h files and the resource file, and—you get the picture. Not fun.

The Source Code for the BmButton Object Class

About this time I decided that a bitmap button class would be an excellent idea. I wanted one that would remove most of the drudgery of building bitmap buttons and yet be flexible and easy to use. Here, then, in Listings 7.17 and 7.18, are the header file and C++ file for the BmButton object class.

Listing 7.17. BmButton.h—define file for the BmButton object class.

```
/* BMBUTTON.H
 *
 * Defines the class for a bitmap button, which
 * knows how to do all sorts of buttony things.
 *
 * Written by Alex Leavens, for ShadowCat Technologies
 */

#ifndef __BMBUTTON_H

#define __BMBUTTON_H

#include <windows.h>

#include "boolean.h"

#include "pmorph.h"

#include "compatdc.h"

#include "bitmap.h"

#ifdef __cplusplus

//-------------------------------------------------------------


/*****************************
 * Class: BmButton
 *
 * Bitmap button class, which uses the ResBitmap class
 * to build its objects with.
 */

    class

BmButton
{

    // ---------------- PROTECTED ------------------

    protected:
```

Listing 7.17. continued

```
int             xSavePos;           // Desired x position (used for
                                    // deferred button creation)
int             ySavePos;

Boolean         internalsBuilt;

HANDLE          saveInst;

Boolean         btEnabled;          // Will button respond to actions?

//-------------------------

// BuildInternals() sets up all the internal stuff
// that you need to have happen in order for a button
// to work.

    void
BuildInternals(HANDLE           hInst,
               HMENU            windID,
               int              xPos,
               int              yPos,
               LPSTR            upName,
               LPSTR            dnName,
               LPSTR            greyName,
               LPSTR            selectName,
               PMorphCall  sCall,
               PMorphCall  dCall);

//-------------------------------------------

ResBitmap       imageUp;        // Up image
ResBitmap       imageDown;      // Down image
ResBitmap       imageGrey;      // Imagestate if tool is unavailable
ResBitmap       imageSelect;    // Button pressed, but not released

BtnState btnState;              // Current setting of the button image

HWND            btnWnd;             // Window handle of button

HMENU           selfID;             // ID of object

PMorphCall      singleClick;        // Single-click callback for
                                    // the button
```

```
        PMorphCall          doubleClick;        // Double-click callback

// --------------- PUBLIC -------------------

public:

    /*------------------------
     *
     * BmButton() - DEFAULT constructor
     */

    BmButton( void );

    /*-----------------------
     *
     * BmButton() - Constructor
     */

    BmButton(HANDLE         hInst,         // Instance of application
             HWND           hWnd,          // Parent window handle
             HMENU          windID,        // ID for the button
             int            xPos,          // X position for button
             int            yPos,          // Y position for button
             LPSTR          upName,        // Name of up image
             LPSTR          dnName,        // Name of down image
             LPSTR          greyName,      // Name of grey image
             LPSTR          selectName,    // Name of selected image
             PMorphCall     sCall,         // Single-click callback
             PMorphCall     dCall);        // Double-click callback

    /*------------------------
     *
     * ~BmButton() - Destructor
     */

    ~BmButton( void );

    //----------------------------------------------------------
    //----------------- Information retrieval routines --------
    //----------------------------------------------------------

    /*--------------------------
     *
     * GetWndHand() returns the window handle
```

continues

Listing 7.17. continued

```
    * of the button image.
    */

    HWND
GetWndHand( void )
{
    return btnWnd;
}

/*-------------------------
 *
 * GetButtonState() returns the current state
 * of the button image.
 */

    BtnState
GetButtonState( void )
{
    return btnState;
}

/*-------------------------
 *
 * GetID() returns the value of the ID associated with
 * this button control's window.
 */

    HMENU
GetID( void )
{
    return selfID;
}

/*------------------
 *
 * GetButtonSize()
 *
 * Returns the size of the button image
 * (based on the up image).
 */

    POINT
GetButtonSize ( void )
```

```
{
    return imageUp.GetSize();
}

//---------------------------
//
// DetermineRequestedDisplayState()
//
// Determines the display state that the button is being
// asked to be drawn in, but does not change any of the
// internal states of the button itself.

    virtual BtnState
DetermineRequestedDisplayState ( LPDRAWITEMSTRUCT      lpDis );

/*---------------------------
 *
 * MatchSelfID()
 *
 * This routine returns a boolean, indicating
 * whether the ID passed in matches the ID
 * of this control.
 */

    Boolean
MatchSelfID ( HMENU        testID )
{
    if (testID == GetID())
        return true;
    else
        return false;
}

/*----------------------------
 *
 * MatchSelfWindow()
 *
 * Same idea as MatchSelfID, this routine returns a
 * boolean, indicating whether the Window handle
 * passed in matches the window handle of this control.
 */

    Boolean
MatchSelfWindow ( HWND     testWnd )
{
```

continues

Listing 7.17. continued

```
        if ( testWnd == GetWndHand() )
            return true;
        else
            return false;
    }

    /*-----------------------------
     *
     * ButtonEnabled()
     *
     * Returns the state of the enabled flag:
     *     true - button is active
     *     false - button is inactive
     */

        Boolean
    ButtonEnabled ( void ) { return     btEnabled; }

    //**************************************************

    //----------------------------------------------------------
    //----------------- Data alteration routines ------
    //----------------------------------------------------------

    /*------------------------
     *
     * EnableButton()
     *
     * Enables or disables the button
     */

        void

    EnableButton ( HWND        parentWnd,
                   Boolean     enState );


    /*------------------------
     *
     * SetButtonState() sets the button state.
     */

    SetButtonState( BtnState newState )
    {
```

```
        btnState = newState;
        return NULL;
    }


    //****************************************************


    //-----------------------------------------------------------
    //----------------- Construction routines ------
    //-----------------------------------------------------------


    //-----------------------------------
    //
    // BuildButtonWindow() actually creates the button's window for
    // you. This call can be made immediately after the BuildInternals()
    // call (as in the case of BuildSelf()), or it can occur at a later
    // time (as in the case of BuildSelfDeferred()). IT MUST OCCUR
    // AFTER a call to BuildInternals().

        void
    BuildButtonWindow(HWND              hWnd);

    /*----------------------------------
     *
     * BmButton::BuildSelfDeferred()
     *
     * Creates a bitmap button, BUT WITHOUT CREATING THE WINDOW FOR IT.
     * This enables you to come back at a later point in time, and
     * perform a CreateWindow() call on the button, at which point it
     * creates itself in a window.
     */

        void
    BuildSelfDeferred(HANDLE    hInst,             // Instance of application
                      HMENU         windID,  // ID for the button
                      int           xPos,    // X position for button
                      int           yPos,    // Y position for button
                      LPSTR         upName,  // Up name
                      LPSTR         dnName,  // Down name
                      LPSTR         greyName,   // Grey name
                      LPSTR         selectName, // Selected name
                      PMorphCall    sCall,   // Single-click callback
                      PMorphCall    dCall);

    /*----------------------
     *
     * BuildSelf()
```

continues

Listing 7.17. continued

```
         *
         * Does the same thing as the constructor
         */

             void
         BuildSelf(HANDLE  hInst,
                     HWND          hWnd,            // Parent window handle
                     HMENU         windID,          // ID for the button
                     int           xPos,            // X position for button
                     int           yPos,            // Y position for button
                     LPSTR         upName,          // Name of up image
                     LPSTR         dnName,          // Name of down image
                     LPSTR         greyName,        // Name of grey image
                     LPSTR         selectName,      // Name of selected image
                     PMorphCall    sCall,           // Single-click callback
                     PMorphCall    dCall);          // Double-click callback


         /*-------------------------
          *
          * RenderSelfIfID()
          *
          * Causes the button to check and see
          * if the control ID being passed in
          * matches its own ID. If it does,
          * then it displays itself in its window
          * in its current state.
          */

             virtual Boolean
         RenderSelfIfID( HMENU       testID,
                         LONG     lParam );


         /*-------------------------
          *
          * RenderSelfInWindow()
          *
          * Causes the button to render itself into its
          * own window.
          */

             virtual
         RenderSelfInWindow( void );
```

```
//------------------------
//
// RenderSelfAsDialogControl()
//
// This function assumes that the bitmap button is a child window
// control of some parent window (typically a toolbar or toolpalette)
// and renders itself in its current state into that parent window.

    virtual
RenderSelfAsDialogControl ( HWND     parentWnd );

/*------------------------
 *
 * RenderSelf() causes the button to
 * display itself in its current state in the
 * requested DC.
 */

    virtual void
RenderSelf(HDC            hDC,
           short x,
           short y);

/*------------------------
 *
 * RenderSelfRequested()
 *
 * Renders the button in the requested state
 */

    virtual void
RenderSelfRequested(BtnState        requestState,
                    HDC             hDC,
                    short           x,
                    short           y);

/*------------------------
 *
 * DetermineDisplayState()
 *
 * Determines if the button is up or down, according
 * to the itemState field of the DrawItemStruct that is
 * passed in.
 */
```

continues

445

Listing 7.17. continued

```
        virtual BtnState
DetermineDisplayState(LPDRAWITEMSTRUCT        lpDis);

/*--------------------------
 *
 * SingleClickAction()
 *
 * Performs the function associated with this button
 * (which is a user-supplied routine that must be passed in
 * at creation time).
 */

    void
SingleClickAction(HWND            hWnd,
                  unsigned        message,
                  WORD            wParam,
                  LONG            lParam);


/*--------------------------
 *
 * DoubleClickAction()
 *
 * Performs the function associated with this button
 * (which is a user-supplied routine that must be passed in
 * at creation time).
 */

    void
DoubleClickAction(HWND            hWnd,
                  unsigned        message,
                  WORD            wParam,
                  LONG            lParam);

/*--------------------------
 *
 * PerformActionIfID()
 *
 * Checks to see if the ID passed in matches
 * the ID of the control (which is a value supplied
 * by the user), and if it is, executes the
 * callback function for this tool.
 */
```

```
        Boolean
    PerformActionIfID(HMENU          testID,
                      HWND           hWnd,
                      unsigned       message,
                      WORD           wParam,
                      LONG           lParam);

};


//------------------------------------------------------------

#endif // __cplusplus

#endif // __BMBUTTON_H
```

Listing 7.18. BmButton.cpp—C++ source code for the BmButton object class.

```
/* BMBUTTON.CPP
 *
 * Routines for handling bitmap button class
 *
 * Written by Alex Leavens, for ShadowCat Technologies
 */

#include <WINDOWS.H>

#include "boolean.h"

#include "pmorph.h"

#include "compatdc.h"

#include "bitmap.h"

#include "bmbutton.h"

#define _EXPORT _export

//---------------------------
//
// BuildInternals() sets up all the internal stuff
```

continues

Listing 7.18. continued

```
// that you need to have happen in order for a button
// to work.

    void
BmButton::BuildInternals(HANDLE        hInst,       // Instance of app
                         HMENU         windID,      // ID of parent
                         int           xPos,        // X position
                         int           yPos,        // Y position
                         LPSTR         upName,      // String for up image
                         LPSTR         dnName,      // String for down image
                         LPSTR         greyName,    // String for grey image
                         LPSTR         selectName,  // String for press image
                         PMorphCall    sCall,       // Single-click callback
                         PMorphCall    dCall)       // Double-click callback
{

    /*----------------------------*/

    internalsBuilt = true;

    saveInst = hInst;

    imageUp.LoadSelf ( hInst,               // Load up image
                       upName );

    imageDown.LoadSelf ( hInst,
                         dnName );          // Load down image

    imageGrey.LoadSelf ( hInst,
                         greyName );        // Load grey image (if there)

    imageSelect.LoadSelf ( hInst,   // Load selected image ( if there )
                           selectName );

    singleClick = sCall;            // Set callback routines
    doubleClick = dCall;

    xSavePos = xPos;                        // X position of button in parent
    ySavePos = yPos;                        // Y position of button in parent

    btnState = invalid;                     // Set initial button state

    btEnabled = true;                       // Button initially enabled
```

```
    btnWnd = NULL;                          // No button window handle

    selfID = windID;                        // ID of button when created
}

//---------------------------------
//
// BuildButtonWindow() actually creates the button's window
// for you. This call can be made immediately after the BuildInternals()
// call (as in the case of BuildSelf()), or it can occur at a later time,
// (as in the case of BuildSelfDeferred()).
//
// >>>> DANGER DANGER DANGER <<<<
//
// This call MUST OCCUR __AFTER__ a call to BuildInternals().

    void
BmButton::BuildButtonWindow(HWND     hWnd)
{
    POINT           ptSize;                 // Size of bitmap image

    /*----------------------------*/

    // If you haven't already built the window, build it

    if (btnWnd == NULL && internalsBuilt == true)
    {
        ptSize = imageUp.GetSize();             // Get image size

        btnWnd = CreateWindow("BUTTON",    // Button class
                              NULL,             // No text string
                              BS_OWNERDRAW | WS_CHILD |
                              WS_VISIBLE,       // styles
                              xSavePos,   // X position of button
                              ySavePos,   // Y position of button,
                              ptSize.x,   // Image size, x
                              ptSize.y,   // Image size, y
                              hWnd,       // Parent window handle
                              selfID,     // Child window ID
                              saveInst,   // Module instance
                              NULL);      // Extra data
    }

    // If you've already built the window, just show it.
```

continues

449

Listing 7.18. continued

```
    else if (btnWnd && internalsBuilt == true)
    {
        ShowWindow(btnWnd,
                    SW_SHOW);
    }
}

/*-----------------------------
 *
 * BmButton::BmButton() - DEFAULT Constructor
 *
 * For creating BmButton classes inside other classes.
 */

BmButton::BmButton(void)
{
    /*-----------------*/

    internalsBuilt = false;
}

/*---------------------------------
 *
 * BmButton::BuildSelfDeferred()
 *
 * Creates a bitmap button, BUT WITHOUT CREATING THE WINDOW FOR IT.
 * This enables you to come back at a later point in time and
 * perform a CreateWindow() call on the button, at which point it
 * creates itself in a window.
 */

    void
BmButton::BuildSelfDeferred(HANDLE      hInst,      // Instance of application
                            HMENU       windID,     // ID for the button
                            int         xPos,       // X position for button
                            int         yPos,       // Y position for button
                            LPSTR       upName,     // Up name
                            LPSTR       dnName,     // Down name
                            LPSTR       greyName,   // Grey name
                            LPSTR       selectName, // selected name
                            PMorphCall  sCall,      // Single-click callback
                            PMorphCall  dCall)
{
    /*-----------------------*/
```

```
     BuildInternals(hInst,
                     windID,        // Build internal structures that
                     xPos,          // don't rely on having a window
                     yPos,          // built.
                     upName,
                     dnName,
                     greyName,
                     selectName,
                     sCall,
                     dCall);
}


/*---------------------------------
 *
 * BmButton::BuildSelf()
 *
 * Builds itself. Wrapper function so that you
 * can initialize arrays of BmButton types.
 *
 * This function simply calls BuildInternals(), which does all the
 * real work of _constructing_ the button, and then calls BuildButtonWindow()
 * which actually causes the thing to blossom...
 */

     void
BmButton::BuildSelf(HANDLE       hInst,       // Instance of application
                    HWND         hWnd,        // Parent window handle
                    HMENU        windID,      // ID for the button
                    int          xPos,        // X position for button
                    int          yPos,        // Y position for button
                    LPSTR        upName,      // Up name
                    LPSTR        dnName,      // Down name
                    LPSTR        greyName,    // Grey name
                    LPSTR        selectName,  // Selected name
                    PMorphCall   sCall,       // Single-click callback
                    PMorphCall   dCall)
{
     BuildInternals(hInst,
                     windID,        // Build internal structures that
                     xPos,          // don't rely on having a window
                     yPos,          // built.
                     upName,
                     dnName,
```

continues

451

Listing 7.18. continued

```
                        greyName,
                        selectName,
                        sCall,
                        dCall);

    BuildButtonWindow(hWnd);
}

/*-------------------
 *
 * BmButton::BmButton() - Constructor
 *
 * Returns: Nothing
 *
 * Points to the BuildSelf() routine
 */

BmButton::BmButton(HANDLE      hInst,        // Instance of application
                   HWND        hWnd,         // Parent window handle
                   HMENU       windID,       // ID for the button
                   int         xPos,         // X position for button
                   int         yPos,         // Y position for button
                   LPSTR       upName,       // Up name
                   LPSTR       dnName,       // Down name
                   LPSTR       greyName,     // Greyed image
                   LPSTR       selectName,   // Selected image
                   PMorphCall  sCall,        // Single-click callback
                   PMorphCall  dCall)
{
    BuildSelf(hInst,
              hWnd,
              windID,
              xPos,
              yPos,
              upName,
              dnName,
              greyName,
              selectName,
              sCall,
              dCall);
}

/*-----------------------
 *
 * ~BmButton() - Destructor
```

```
 *
 * Makes sure that all the resource bitmaps for
 * the buttons get deleted. Overkill, really, because
 * the destructor routines for them would get automagically
 * called anyway.
 */

BmButton::~BmButton( void )
{
    /*--------------------*/

    imageUp.DeleteSelf();
    imageDown.DeleteSelf();
    imageGrey.DeleteSelf();
    imageSelect.DeleteSelf();
}


/*-------------------------
 *
 * RenderSelfIfID()
 *
 * Causes the button to check and see
 * if the control ID being passed in
 * matches its own ID. If it does,
 * then it displays itself in its window
 * in its current state.
 */

    Boolean
BmButton::RenderSelfIfID( HMENU     testID,
                          LONG   lParam)
{
    BtnState              cState;

    LPDRAWITEMSTRUCT      lpDis;

    /*--------------*/

    if ( testID == GetID() )
    {
        lpDis = (LPDRAWITEMSTRUCT)lParam;

        // Figure out requested button state
        cState = DetermineDisplayState(lpDis);
```

continues

Listing 7.18. continued

```
            switch(cState)
            {
                case up:
                case down:
                case grey:
                case selected:

                        RenderSelfRequested(cState,
                                                lpDis->hDC,    // hDC to draw into...
                                                0,
                                                0);
                        break;

                case invalid:
                default:
                    return false;
            }

            return true;
        }
        else
            return false;
}


/*------------------------
 *
 * RenderSelfInWindow()
 *
 * Causes the button to render itself into its
 * own window.
 */

BmButton::RenderSelfInWindow( void )
{
    HDC   hDC;

    /*-------------------*/

    hDC = GetDC(btnWnd);

    if (hDC)
    {
        RenderSelf(hDC,
```

```
                        0,
                        0);

            ReleaseDC(btnWnd,
                        hDC);
    }


    return NULL;
}
//-----------------------
//
// RenderSelfAsDialogControl()
//
// This function assumes that the bitmap button is a child window
// control of some parent window (typically a toolbar or toolpalette),
// and will render itself in its current state into that parent window.

BmButton::RenderSelfAsDialogControl ( HWND    parentWnd )
{
    HWND toolWnd; // Window handle of this button as a child control

    HDC             toolDC;

    //----------------

    toolWnd = GetDlgItem ( parentWnd,        // Window handle of parent(dialog)
                            (int)selfID );

    if ( toolWnd )
    {
        toolDC = GetDC ( toolWnd );

        if ( toolDC )
        {
            RenderSelf ( toolDC,
                            0,
                            0 );

            ReleaseDC ( toolWnd,
                        toolDC );
        }
    }

    return NULL;
}
```

continues

Listing 7.18. continued

```
/*----------------------
 *
 * RenderSelfRequested()
 *
 * Renders the button in the requested state
 */

    void
BmButton::RenderSelfRequested(BtnState        requestState,
                              HDC             hDC,
                              short           x,
                              short           y)
{
    /*----------------*/

    switch(requestState)
    {
        case down:
            imageDown.DisplaySelf(hDC,
                                    x,
                                    y);
            break;

        case grey:
            imageGrey.DisplaySelf(hDC,
                                    x,
                                    y);
            break;

        case selected:

            if ( imageSelect.GetBitmapHandle() )
            {
                imageSelect.DisplaySelf ( hDC,
                                            x,
                                            y );
            }
            else
            {
                imageDown.DisplaySelf ( hDC,
                                            x,
                                            y );
            }
            break;
```

```
            case up:
            case focus:
            default:

                imageUp.DisplaySelf(hDC,
                                        0,
                                        0);
                break;
        }
    }


/*-------------------------
 *
 * RenderSelf() causes the button to
 * display itself in its current state.
 */

    void
BmButton::RenderSelf(HDC     hDC,
                        short       x,
                        short       y)
{
    BtnState        currentState;

    /*----------------*/

    currentState = GetButtonState();

    RenderSelfRequested(currentState,
                        hDC,
                        x,
                        y);
}


//-----------------------------------------
//
// DetermineRequestedDisplayState()
//
//      itemAction        itemState         Action
//      -------------------------------------------
//      ODA_SELECT        ODS_FOCUS         Mouse down, moved OFF of button
//      ODA_SELECT        FOCUS | SELECT    Mouse down, moved ON to button,
//                                          or new mouse down on button
//      ODA_FOCUS         ODS_SELECT        Mouse up while on button
```

continues

Listing 7.18. continued

```
    BtnState

BmButton::DetermineRequestedDisplayState ( LPDRAWITEMSTRUCT    lpDis )
{

    // If not an owner-draw button, punt.

    if ( lpDis->CtlType != ODT_BUTTON )
        return invalid;

    // If button disabled, the only thing it can be is grey.

    if ( ButtonEnabled() != true )
        return grey;

    // If drawing the entire button, and the button state is valid, go
    // ahead and return current button state.

    if ( lpDis->itemAction & ODA_DRAWENTIRE )
    {
        switch ( GetButtonState() )
        {
            case down:
            case grey:
                return GetButtonState();
                break;

            default:
                break;
        }
    }

    // Only a portion of the button is being redrawn
    // (due to some form of state change). Do that...

    if (lpDis->itemState & ODS_SELECTED)      // Button down
    {
        if ( lpDis->itemAction & ODA_SELECT )
            return selected;
        else
            return down;
    }
    else if (lpDis->itemState & ODS_DISABLED)
```

```
        {
            return grey;
        }
        else
        {
            return up;
        }

        return invalid;        // Should never reach here.
    }

/*---------------------------
 *
 * DetermineDisplayState()
 *
 * Determines if the button is up or down, according
 * to the itemState field of the DrawItemStruct that is
 * passed in.
 */

    BtnState
BmButton::DetermineDisplayState(LPDRAWITEMSTRUCT        lpDis)
{
    BtnState        requestedState;

    /*-----------------*/

    requestedState = DetermineRequestedDisplayState ( lpDis );

    switch ( requestedState )
    {
        case down:
        case grey:
        case up:
        case selected:

            SetButtonState ( requestedState );
            return requestedState;
            break;

        case invalid:
        default:
            return requestedState;
            break;
```

continues

Listing 7.18. continued

```
    }

    return invalid;

}

/*--------------------------
 *
 * SingleClickAction()
 *
 * Performs the function associated with this button
 * (which is a user-supplied routine that must be passed in
 * at creation time).
 */

    void
BmButton::SingleClickAction(HWND     hWnd,
                            unsigned      message,
                            WORD wParam,
                            LONG lParam)
{
    /*--------------*/

    if ( ( singleClick != NULL ) && ( ButtonEnabled() == true ) )
    {
        (*singleClick)(hWnd,
                       message,
                       wParam,
                       lParam);
    }
}

/*--------------------------
 *
 * DoubleClickAction()
 *
 * Performs the function associated with this button
 * (which is a user-supplied routine that must be passed in
 * at creation time).
 */

    void
BmButton::DoubleClickAction(HWND     hWnd,
```

```
                                        unsigned        message,
                                        WORD wParam,
                                        LONG lParam)
{
    /*--------------*/

    if ( ( doubleClick != NULL ) && ( ButtonEnabled() == true ) )
    {
        (*doubleClick)(hWnd,
                             message,
                             wParam,
                             lParam);
    }
}


/*--------------------------
 *
 * PerformActionIfID()
 *
 * Checks to see if the ID passed in matches
 * the ID of the control (which is a value supplied
 * by the user), and if it is, executes the
 * callback function for this tool.
 */

    Boolean

BmButton::PerformActionIfID(HMENU    testID,
                                HWND hWnd,
                                unsigned        message,
                                WORD wParam,
                                LONG lParam)
{
    WORD noteCode = HIWORD (lParam);          // Double-click code

    /*---------------*/

    if ( testID == GetID() )
    {
        switch ( noteCode )
        {
            case BN_DOUBLECLICKED:

                DoubleClickAction(hWnd,
```

continues

Listing 7.18. continued

```
                              message,
                              wParam,
                              lParam);
                break;

            default:

                SingleClickAction(hWnd,
                          message,
                          wParam,
                          lParam);
                break;

    }
    return true;
}

    return false;
}


/*-------------------------
 *
 * EnableButton()
 *
 * Enables or disables the button
 */

    void

BmButton::EnableButton ( HWND                parentWnd,
                          Boolean            enState )
{
    //------------------

    // If requested new state is the same as the current
    // one, then you're done, so return.

    if ( btEnabled == enState )
        return;

    // Set new window state...

    btEnabled = enState;   // Set new window state
```

```
    // Set the new button image according to the desired button state...

    switch ( enState )
    {
        case true:

            SetButtonState ( up );

            break;

        case false:

            SetButtonState ( grey );

            break;
    }

    RenderSelfAsDialogControl ( parentWnd );          // Redraw self
}
```

Using the BmButton Object Class

I won't try to cover all the details of all the internals of the BmButton object class. Many of the smaller routines simply give you access to various important bits inside the object, such as the window handle of the button.

What I am going to cover is how you can use the BmButton object class to create graphics buttons. It has a number of major routines and a number of supporting routines, all designed for this end.

Constructor Routines

There are two constructor routines. One, the default constructor (which takes no arguments), simply marks the flag `internalsBuilt` as being false. This flag is important because it defines for the object whether to perform a **CreateWindow()** call. More on that in a moment.

The other constructor routine takes a whole raft of arguments. Take a look:

```
BmButton(HANDLE        hInst,       // Instance of application
         HWND          hWnd,        // Parent window handle
         HMENU         windID,      // ID for the button
         int           xPos,        // X position for button
         int           yPos,        // Y position for button
         LPSTR         upName,      // Name of up image
         LPSTR         dnName,      // Name of down image
         LPSTR         greyName,    // Name of grey image
         LPSTR         selectName,  // Name of selected image
         PMorphCall    sCall,       // Single-click callback
         PMorphCall    dCall);      // Double-click callback
```

The `hInst` parameter is fairly obvious—because you're going to create a window for this button, you're going to need to know what the instance of the application doing the creating is. The next two parameters also derive directly from the needs of the **CreateWindow()** call. `hWnd` is the window of the parent of the button, and `windID` is the ID of the button being created.

The next two parameters, `xPos` and `yPos`, define the position of the button in the parent window's client area.

The next four parameters, `upName`, `dnName`, `greyName`, and `selectName`, are all strings that define the name of the resources that should be used for, respectively, the up button image, the down button image, the grey (that is, disabled) button image, and the selected (that is, pressed but not released) button image. These resources must exist in the application that's using the bitmap button object—no resource DLLs, sorry.

The final two parameters, `sCall` and `dCall`, are (at least to my mind) two of the most useful pieces of the BmButton class. These two parameters define the action a button should take when the user single-clicks (`sCall`) and double-clicks (`dCall`) the button. In other words, BmButton objects are smart—they know what to do when you click them!

Destructor Routines

Like most of my destructor routines, the one for the BmButton class simply deletes or frees all the system resources used by the particular instantiation of an object. It takes no parameters.

Utility Routines

There are several utility routines in the BmButton class that enable you to manipulate the class in various ways.

Information Retrieval Routines

The first class of utility routine is the information retrieval routine. Not too surprisingly, these routines return various kinds of information about the class.

- GetWndHand()—Returns the window handle of this particular instantiation of a BmButton object.

- GetButtonState()—Returns the current state of the button, which can be one of the following values:

State	Description
up	Button image is up
down	Button image is down
grey	Button has been set to unavailable
focus	Button has the focus
selected	Button has been pressed but not released (radio buttons only)
invalid	State is undefined

- GetID()—Returns the ID of the button. (This is the value passed into the button at creation time.)

- GetButtonSize()—Returns the size of the bitmap used to draw the up image of the button. Although the class assumes that all button images are the same size, there's no checking to ensure that this is actually the case.

- DetermineRequestedDisplayState()—Takes a DRAWITEMSTRUCT and, based on the information in that structure, figures out how the button should be drawn. It then returns that value. (The value is one of the values in the table listed under the GetButtonState() call.) It does not actually change the button state itself.

- MatchSelfID()—Returns a Boolean (true/false), which indicates whether the ID passed to this routine is the same as the button's ID. This is basically a way of asking the button, "Is this you?"

465

■ MatchSelfWindow()—Returns a Boolean (true/false), which indicates whether the window handle passed to this routine is the same as this button's window handle. This is another way of asking the button "Is this you?" this time based on the window handle.

■ ButtonEnabled()—Returns a Boolean (true/false), which indicates whether the button is currently active. This is the logical equivalent of a text button's being enabled or disabled.

Data Alteration Routines

Data alteration routines enable you to manipulate the button in various ways.

■ EnableButton()—Lets you enable or disable the button. Passing in true enables the button window, and passing in false disables it.

■ SetButtonState()—Sets the button state to the new value requested. The value can be one of the settings previously documented under the GetButtonState() call.

Button Creation Routines

Button creation routines are responsible for the actual creation of the window for the button, the loading of the bitmaps, and so on.

■ BuildButtonWindow()—Actually creates the window for the button. It can occur immediately after a call to the BuildInternals() member function (as in the case of BuildSelf()), or it can occur later (as in the case of BuildSelfDeferred()). However, it must occur after a call to BuildInternals().

■ BuildSelfDeferred()—Takes the same parameter list as the second constructor routine, so I'm not going to document it again. The purpose of this routine is to enable you to specify all the pieces for creating a button window, but it doesn't actually build the window—it saves all the pieces for you. At some later point you can call the BuildButtonWindow() member function, and the button is created. (This is primarily useful for toolbars, which I talk about next.)

■ BuildSelf()—Does the same thing as the second constructor routine.

Test and Display Routines

Test and display routines enable a program to ask the button to do various things based on the results of different kinds of tests.

- `RenderSelfIfID()`—Tests to see whether the ID being passed in is the same as the button's. If it is, the button displays itself in its own window, based on its own internal window handle.

- `RenderSelfInWindow()`—Causes the button to display itself in its own window.

- `RenderSelfAsDialogControl()`—Assumes that the bitmap button is a child window control of some parent window (typically a toolbar or toolpalette) and renders itself in its current state into that parent window.

- `RenderSelf()`—Causes the button to display itself in the requested DC at the requested point.

- `RenderSelfRequested()`—Causes the button to render itself in the requested state (see `GetButtonState()` for a list of valid states) into the requested DC at the requested point.

- `DetermineDisplayState()`—Determines the display state according to the information in a `DRAWITEMSTRUCT` that's passed in, and sets the button state accordingly.

Miscellaneous Routines

These routines govern the actions a button takes, and under what circumstances it takes them.

- `SingleClickAction()`—Calls the associated single-click callback routine (if one was provided) for this button.

- `DoubleClickAction()`—Calls the associated double-click callback routine (if one was provided) for this button.

- `PerformActionIfID()`—Tests to see whether the ID passed in matches the ID of this button. If it does, it calls the appropriate callback routine. Returns `true` if the IDs matched, and `false` if they did not.

467

Understanding the BmButton Class

Although there's a great deal going on in the BmButton class, it's all fund-amentally simple stuff. Display of the button is handled by the underlying ResBitmap object class. Although the BmButton class isn't derived from the ResBitmap class, it has four ResBitmap objects in it, one for each of the four images it can have (up, down, grey, and select). All the displaying of images ultimately resolves down to one of these four objects being asked to display itself. (Isn't reusable code great? <grin>)

The BmButton class itself is mainly concerned with hiding the details of window creation and testing. Your program won't have to do any of these things, because the class does it all for you. The only moderately difficult thing the class is doing is in `DetermineRequestedDisplayState()`, which figures out (based on a `DRAWITEMSTRUCT`) what the state of the button should be.

Although the BmButton class clearly relieves you of a lot of the drudgery of creating and maintaining bitmap buttons, there's clearly a lot of work still involved in using them. Better than the BmButton class is a higher-level class, one that enables you to group buttons by functionality (or whatever other criteria you want to use) and have all the individual button processing dealt with by this meta class.

You asked for it, you got it. Here's the Toolbar class. A *toolbar* is a floating set of buttons that are selectable at any time by the user of an application. I'm going to give you the source code to the Toolbar object class first, and then I'm going to give you the complete source code to a sample application that uses a toolbar and some bitmap buttons to create a powerful application with just a few lines of code. (Maybe I should make that a *potentially* powerful applica-tion—as it stands now, all it does is post some silly message boxes! <grin>)

The Toolbar Class: A Class Object for Holding Buttons

Like the BmButton class, the Toolbar class doesn't derive directly from its antecedent—rather, it encapsulates a variable number of BmButton objects and does intelligent things with them. Listings 7.19 and 7.20 give you the header file and the source file for the Toolbar class.

Listing 7.19. TOOLBAR.H—header file for the Toolbar object class.

```
/* TOOLBAR.H
 *
 * Class definitions for a toolbar class.
 *
 * Written by Alex Leavens, for ShadowCat Technologies
 */

#ifndef __TOOLBAR_H

#define __TOOLBAR_H

#include <windows.h>

#include "boolean.h"

#include "pmorph.h"

#include "bitmap.h"

#include "bmbutton.h"

#ifdef __cplusplus

//-------------------------------------------------------

// Toolbar styles

#define  TB_VERTICAL            0x01      // Vertical toolbar
#define TB_HORIZONTAL           0x02      // Horizontal toolbar
#define  TB_RECTANGULAR         0x04      // Rectangular toolbar

#define TB_DISPLAY_STYLES  0x07


#define TB_RADIOBUTTON     0x10      // Radio button style toolbar:
                                     // One button down, all the others up;
                                     // pressing on a new button pops old one
                                     // up.

#define TB_PUSHBUTTON      0x20      // Pushbutton-style toolbar:
                                     // All buttons up, current button press
                                     // only slays down momentarily.
```

continues

Listing 7.19. continued

```
#define TB_BUTTON_STYLE    0x30


/************************************
 *
 * Class:  ToolBar
 *
 * ToolBar class, which builds a toolbar-like object
 * and knows how to display it.
 */

    class

ToolBar
{

    //----------------- PROTECTED --------------

    protected:

    // Private routines for toolbars; these routines handle various
    // window messages that the modeless dialog for a toolbar receives
            virtual BOOL WINAPI
        InitMessage(HWND  hWnd);                // WM_INITDIALOG

            virtual BOOL WINAPI
        CommandMessage(HWND          hWnd,
                       unsigned      message,
                       WORD          wParam,
                       LONG          lParam); // WM_COMMAND

            virtual BOOL WINAPI
        SizeMessage(HWND  hWnd);                // WM_SIZE

            virtual BOOL WINAPI
        MoveMessage(HWND  hWnd);                // WM_MOVE

            virtual BOOL WINAPI
        DrawItemMessage(HWND          hWnd,
                        WORD          wParam,
                        LONG          lParam); // WM_DRAWITEM

            virtual BOOL WINAPI
```

```
        CloseMessage( void ) { HideSelf(); return TRUE; }      // WM_CLOSE

//-------------------------------------------------

// Protected data members of the toolbar class.

        FARPROC              winCallback;       // User-supplied callback.

        HWND                 toolWnd; // Window handle of this toolbar

        BmButton *toolBtn;            // Tool button controls

        WORD                 numToolBtns;       // Number of created tools

        WORD                 tbToolIndex;       // Used at startup time

        WORD                 tbSpacing;         // # of pixels between tools

        WORD                 tbWidthSize;       // Horizontal size, in tools

        WORD                 tbHeightSize;      // Vertical size, in tools

        POINT                initToolPos;       // Initial tool position

        POINT                nextToolPos;       // Next tool position

        POINT                tbPosition;        // Position of toolbar
                                                // (relative to parent)

        POINT                tbSize;            // Toolbar size

        WORD                 tbStyle;           // Style of toolbar

        POINT                toolSize;          // Size of tools in pixels

        HANDLE               sInst;

        Boolean              forceBMSize;       // Force size of 1st bitmap
                                                // If this flag is true,
                                                // the window creation routine
                                                // uses the size of firstBMSize
                                                // to scale the dialogbox instead
                                                // of using the actual size of the
                                                // first bitmap.
```

continues

471

Listing 7.19. continued

```
        POINT              firstBMSize;      // Size if bitmap forced

        Boolean            winMoved;         // Window moved?

        Boolean            visible; // Toolbar visible?

//----------------- PUBLIC -----------------

public:

    /*-----------------------------
     *
     * ToolBarWinCallBack()
     *
     * Callback routine for this toolbar.
     * This routine must handle all the standard
     * behaviors for a window...
     */

        BOOL WINAPI

    ToolBarWinCallBack(HWND          hWnd,
                       unsigned      message,
                       WORD          wParam,
                       LONG          lParam);

    // Base constructor and destructor types.

    ToolBar ( void )
    {
        InitToolBar();
    }

    // Base initialization routine, which sets up all sorts of
    // nice default behavior. Basically, the default behavior
    // is that you haven't done anything yet...

    InitToolBar ( void )
    {
        toolWnd = NULL;
        numToolBtns = 0;
        tbToolIndex = 0;
```

```
        forceBMSize = false;

        winMoved = false;

        visible = false;

        POINT           tPst;

        tPst.x = 0;
        tPst.y = 0;

        SetToolBarPosition ( tPst );

        return NULL;
}

// Destructor routines

~ToolBar ( void )
{
        DestroyToolBar();
}

DestroyToolBar ( void )
{
        // Delete the tool buttons here.

        if ( numToolBtns )
        {
            delete [] toolBtn;

            numToolBtns = 0;
        }

        return NULL;
}

//-----------------------------------------------------------
//----------------- Information retrieval routines ------
//-----------------------------------------------------------

// GetBarHandle retrieves the window handle of the toolbar

    HWND
GetBarHandle ( void ) { return toolWnd; }
```

continues

Listing 7.19. continued

```
            // GetBarPosition returns current position of tool

                POINT
            GetBarPosition ( void ) { return tbPosition; }

            // GetBarSize returns current size of toolbar

                POINT
            GetBarSize ( void ) { return tbSize; }

            // GetDisplayState() - Returns current visibility state of window

                Boolean
            GetDisplayState ( void ) { return visible; }

            // ToolBarMoved returns whether or not the bar's been
            // moved.

                Boolean
            ToolBarMoved ( void ) { return winMoved; }

            // GetNumButtons() tells you how many buttons there
            // are in the toolbar.

                WORD
            GetNumButtons ( void ) { return numToolBtns; }


            // MatchChildWindows() takes a window handle and returns
            // a boolean, indicating if the window handle matches any of
            // the buttons in the toolbar, or the toolbar window itself.

                BOOL
            MatchChildWindows( HWND     parentWnd );

            //--------------------------------------------------------
            //-------------- Button Control Routines ----------------
            //--------------------------------------------------------

            // SendToolMessage() - Dispatches the requested message, and
            // parameters to the requested tool button.
```

```
    void
SendToolMessage ( HMENU           buttonID,
                   unsigned        message,
                   WORD            wParam,
                   LONG            lParam );

// EnableTool() - Causes a WM_ENABLE message to be sent to the
// appropriate tool button, and sets the tool grey

    void
EnableTool ( HMENU           buttonID,
             BOOL            enableState );

//
//---------------------------------------------------------
//---------------- Data alteration routines ------
//---------------------------------------------------------
// SetToolBarSize() - Sets the size of the toolbar (in pixels)

SetToolBarSize ( POINT nSize ) { tbSize = nSize; return NULL; }

// SetDisplayState() - Sets the current visibility state

SetDisplayState ( Boolean nState ) { visible = nState; return NULL; }

// SetToolBarPosition() - Sets the position on-screen of the toolbar

SetToolBarPosition ( POINT           pnt )
{
    tbPosition = pnt;
    return NULL;
}

// SaveToIniFile() - Saves the toolbar settings to the .ini file

SaveToIniFile ( LPSTR       iniFile,
                LPSTR       sectionTag );

// RestoreFromIniFile() - Restores the toolbar settings from
// the .ini file

RestoreFromIniFile ( LPSTR           iniFile,
                     LPSTR           sectionTag );
```

continues

Listing 7.19. continued

```
//----------------------------------------------------------
//----------------- Construction routines ------
//----------------------------------------------------------


//-------------------------------
//
// CreateToolBar() causes the toolbar to fire up...

    void
CreateToolBar ( HWND        parentWnd,
                LPSTR       toolTitle );


//-------------------------------
//
// AddTool()

    void
AddTool(HMENU             windID,         // ID for the button
        WORD              xPos,
        WORD              yPos,
        LPSTR             upName,         // Name of up image
        LPSTR             dnName,         // Name of down image
        LPSTR             greyName,       // Name of grey image
        LPSTR             selectName,     // Name of selected image
        PMorphCall        sCall,          // Single-click callback
        PMorphCall        dCall);         // Double-click callback


//-------------------------------
//
// InitToolBar()
//
// Creates some important things that you need
// in order to successfully build a toolbar.

    void
InitToolBar ( WORD    toolStyle,    // Toolbar style
              WORD    toolBarWidth, // Width of toolbar, in tools
                                    //  --For vertical toolbars, this
                                    //      is how wide the bar is
                                    //  --For horizontal toolbars, this
                                    //      is how tall the bar is
                                    //  --For rectangular toolbars, this
                                    //      is both width and height
```

```
         WORD     toolSpacing,  // How many pixels between tools
         WORD     toolCount,    // Number of tools in toolbar

         WORD     xPos,         // X position of 1st tool
         WORD     yPos,         // Y position of 1st tool

         POINT    barPos,       // Initial bar position

         HANDLE   hInst,        // Instance handle
         FARPROC callHandle );  // Callback handle for callback

//------------------------------
//
// Same as InitToolBar, above, but forces the
// dialog box to size itself using the size given
// in the last parameter, instead of scaling itself
// according to the bitmap being loaded.

    void
InitToolBarForce (
         WORD toolStyle,        // Toolbar style
         WORD toolBarWidth,     // Width of toolbar, in tools
                           //   --For vertical toolbars, this
                           //       is how wide the bar is
                           //   --For horizontal toolbars, this
                           //       is how tall the bar is
                           //   --For rectangular toolbars, this
                           //       is both width and height
         WORD toolSpacing,      // How many pixels between tools
         WORD toolCount,        // Number of tools in toolbar

         WORD     xPos,         // X position of 1st tool
         WORD     yPos,         // Y position of 1st tool

         POINT    barPos,       // Initial bar position

         HANDLE   hInst,        // Instance handle
         FARPROC  callHandle,   // Callback handle
                                // for callback
         POINT    sizeBM );     // Size of forced BM

// SizeSelf() - Causes the window to resize itself.
```

continues

Listing 7.19. continued

```
SizeSelf ( void ) {
                      SendSelfMessage ( WM_SIZE,
                                          NULL,
                                          NULL );
                      return NULL;
                  }

// SendSelfMessage() - If the window exists, sends a passed-in
//     message to itself.

SendSelfMessage ( unsigned msg,
                  WORD       wParam,
                  LONG       lParam )
                {
                    if ( toolWnd )
                    {
                          SendMessage ( toolWnd,
                                          msg,
                                          wParam,
                                          lParam );
                    }
                    return NULL;
                }

// HideSelf() - If window exists, window hides itself.

HideSelf ( void ) { if ( toolWnd )
                    {
                          ShowWindow ( toolWnd, SW_HIDE );

                          SetDisplayState ( false );
                    }
                    return NULL;
                }

// ShowSelf() - If window exists, window shows itself.

ShowSelf ( void ) { if ( toolWnd )
                    {
                          ShowWindow ( toolWnd, SW_SHOW );

                          SetDisplayState ( true );
                    }
```

```
                              return NULL;
                          }

         // IconifySelf() - If window exists, window hides itself, and
         // remembers its current display setting (hidden or visible)

         IconifySelf ( void ) { if ( toolWnd )
                              {
                                   ShowWindow ( toolWnd, SW_HIDE );
                              }
                              return NULL;
                          }

         // RestoreSelf() - Restores the window to its previous display state

         RestoreSelf ( void ) { if ( toolWnd )
                              {
                              if ( visible == true )
                                 {
                                      ShowWindow ( toolWnd,
                                                SW_SHOW );
                                 }
                              }
                              return NULL;
                          }
};


//----------------------------------------------------

#endif // __cplusplus

#endif // __TOOLPAL_H
```

Listing 7.20. TOOLBAR.CPP—C++ source for the Toolbar object class.

```
/* TOOLBAR.CPP
 *
 * Routines that implement a toolbar object class
 *
 * Written by Alex Leavens, for ShadowCat Technologies
 */
```

continues

Listing 7.20. continued

```
#include <WINDOWS.H>

#include "boolean.h"

#include "pmorph.h"

#include "compatdc.h"

#include "bitmap.h"

#include "bmbutton.h"

#include "toolbar.h"

#include "btexampl.h"  // Include the stuff for your sample application

#define _EXPORT   _export

//-----------------------
//
// InitMessage()
//
// Routine handles the WM_INITDIALOG message for default toolbar
// behavior.

    BOOL WINAPI
ToolBar::InitMessage(HWND   hWnd)
{
    int  i;

    //---------------------
    // Build all tool buttons here

    for (i = 0; i < numToolBtns; i++)
    {
        toolBtn[i].BuildButtonWindow(hWnd);
    }

    // Resize the dialog window...

    WORD xSize;
```

```
WORD ySize;

POINT          btnSize;

WORD captionSize;

//-----------------------------

captionSize = GetSystemMetrics(SM_CYCAPTION);

if ( forceBMSize == true )
{
    btnSize = firstBMSize;
}
else
{
    btnSize = toolBtn[0].GetButtonSize();
}

switch ( tbStyle & TB_DISPLAY_STYLES )
{
    case TB_VERTICAL:

        xSize = ( btnSize.x + tbSpacing ) * tbWidthSize + 4;

        ySize = ( btnSize.y + tbSpacing ) *
                    (numToolBtns / tbWidthSize +
                     numToolBtns % tbWidthSize) + 4 + captionSize;
        break;

    case TB_HORIZONTAL:

        ySize = ( btnSize.y + tbSpacing ) * tbHeightSize +
                    4 + captionSize;

        xSize = ( btnSize.x + tbSpacing ) *
                    (numToolBtns / tbHeightSize +
                     numToolBtns % tbHeightSize) + 4;
        break;

    case TB_RECTANGULAR:
    default:

        xSize = ( btnSize.x + tbSpacing ) * tbWidthSize + 4;
```

continues

481

Listing 7.20. continued

```
                        ySize = ( btnSize.y + tbSpacing ) * tbHeightSize + 4
                                              + captionSize;
                    break;
        }

        tbSize.x = xSize;
        tbSize.y = ySize;

        MoveWindow ( hWnd,
                        tbPosition.x,
                        tbPosition.y,
                        tbSize.x,
                        tbSize.y,
                        TRUE );

        return 0;                    // Return 0 to indicate you processed this one

    }


    //---------------------------
    //
    // CommandMessage()
    //
    // Handles the WM_COMMAND message for toolbars.

        BOOL WINAPI
    ToolBar::CommandMessage(HWND                    hWnd,
                            unsigned    message,
                            WORD                    wParam,
                            LONG                    lParam)  // WM_COMMAND
    {
        int  i;

        //----------------------

        switch ( wParam )
        {
            default:

                for (i = 0; i < numToolBtns; i++)
                {
                    if ( toolBtn[i].GetID() == (HMENU) wParam )
                    {
```

```
                        // Set parent window back in focus

                        SetActiveWindow ( MainhWnd );
                        SetFocus ( MainhWnd );

                        toolBtn[i].PerformActionIfID ( (HMENU) wParam,
                                                       hWnd,
                                                       message,
                                                       wParam,
                                                       lParam );
                    return TRUE;
                }
            }
        }

    return FALSE;

}
//--------------------------------
//
// SizeMessage()
//
// Handles the WM_SIZE message for a toolbar window

    BOOL WINAPI
ToolBar::SizeMessage ( HWND        hWnd )
{
    //-----------------------

    MoveWindow ( hWnd,
                 tbPosition.x,
                 tbPosition.y,
                 tbSize.x,
                 tbSize.y,
                 TRUE );

    return TRUE;
}

//--------------------------------
//
// MoveMessage()
//
// Handles the WM_MOVE message for toolbars
```

continues

Listing 7.20. continued

```
    BOOL WINAPI
ToolBar::MoveMessage ( HWND          hWnd )
{
    RECT wRect;

    //----------------------

    if ( hWnd == toolWnd )              // Is this your window?
    {
        GetWindowRect ( toolWnd,
                        (LPRECT)&wRect );

        tbPosition.x = wRect.left;
        tbPosition.y = wRect.top;

        winMoved = true;

        return TRUE;
    }

    return FALSE;
}

//-------------------------------
//
// DrawItemMessage()
//
// Handles the WM_DRAWITEM message for toolbars

    BOOL WINAPI
ToolBar::DrawItemMessage ( HWND      hWnd,
                           WORD      wParam,
                           LONG      lParam )
{
    int   i;

    //----------------------

    for ( i = 0; i < numToolBtns; i++)
    {
        if (toolBtn[i].RenderSelfIfID((HMENU) wParam,
                                                    lParam))
```

```
            {
                return TRUE;
            }
        }

    return FALSE;

}

/*--------------------------------
 *
 * ToolBarWinCallBack()
 *
 * Callback routine for a toolbar...
 */

    BOOL WINAPI

ToolBar::ToolBarWinCallBack(HWND    hWnd,
                            unsigned       message,
                            WORD wParam,
                            LONG lParam)
{
    //----------------------------

    switch ( message )
    {
        case WM_INITDIALOG:

            return InitMessage ( hWnd );
            break;

        case WM_COMMAND:

            return CommandMessage ( hWnd,
                                    message,
                                    wParam,
                                    lParam );
            break;

        case WM_SIZE:

            return SizeMessage ( hWnd );
            break;
```

continues

Listing 7.20. continued

```
                case WM_MOVE:

                    return MoveMessage ( hWnd );
                    break;

                case WM_DRAWITEM:

                    return DrawItemMessage ( hWnd,
                                                    wParam,
                                                    lParam );
                    break;

                case WM_CLOSE:

                    return CloseMessage();
                    break;

                default:
                    return FALSE;
                    break;
        }

    return TRUE;
}


//-----------------------------
//
// CreateToolBar()
//
// This routine causes a previously created toolbar
// with loaded tools to be displayed.

    void

ToolBar::CreateToolBar ( HWND      parentWnd,
                            LPSTR    toolTitle )
{
    /*-------------------*/

    if (toolWnd && IsWindow ( toolWnd ) )
    {
        if ( IsWindowVisible ( toolWnd ) )
```

```
        {
            SetFocus ( toolWnd );
        }
        else
        {
            ShowSelf();              // Window makes itself visible
        }
        return;
    }


    toolWnd = CreateDialog ( sInst,
                             (LPSTR)"DIALOG_1",
                             parentWnd,
                             winCallback );

    if ( toolWnd == 0 )
    {
        MessageBox ( NULL,
                     "Cannot create toolbar",
                     "Uh-oh...",
                     MB_OK );

    }
    else
    {
        SetWindowText(toolWnd, toolTitle);

        ShowSelf();                  // Make window visible
    }

}

//----------------------------
//
// SendToolMessage()
//
// Sends the requested message and parameters to the requested tool.

    void
ToolBar::SendToolMessage ( HMENU      buttonID,
                           unsigned      message,
                           WORD          wParam,
                           LONG          lParam )
{
```

continues

487

Listing 7.20. continued

```
    int  i;

    //--------------------

    for ( i = 0; i < numToolBtns; i++)
    {
        if ( toolBtn[i].MatchSelfID ( buttonID ) )
        {
            SendMessage ( GetDlgItem ( toolWnd,
                                              buttonID ),
                            message,
                            wParam,
                            lParam );
            break;
        }
    }
}


//---------------------------------------------
//
// EnableTool()
//
// Causes a WM_ENABLE message to be sent to the
// appropriate tool button, and sets the tool grey

    void
ToolBar::EnableTool ( HMENU         buttonID,
                      BOOL          enableState )
{
    int  i;

    //--------------------

    for ( i = 0; i < numToolBtns; i++)
    {
        if ( toolBtn[i].MatchSelfID( buttonID ) )
        {
            if ( enableState )                // TRUE == ENABLE
            {
                toolBtn[i].EnableButton ( toolWnd,
                                              true );
            }
            else                   // FALSE == DISABLE
```

```
                {
                    toolBtn[i].EnableButton ( toolWnd,
                                                    false );
                }
            }
        }
}


//-----------------------------
//
// AddTool()
//
// This routine adds a tool to the toolbar.

    void
ToolBar::AddTool(HMENU              windID,        // ID for the button
                 WORD               xPos,          // X position for the tool
                 WORD               yPos,          // Y position for the tool
                 LPSTR              upName,         // Name of up image
                 LPSTR              dnName,         // Name of down image
                 LPSTR              greyName,       // Name of grey image
                 LPSTR              selectName,     // Name of selected image
                 PMorphCall         sCall,          // Single-click callback
                 PMorphCall         dCall)          // Double-click callback
{
    /*-------------------------------*/

    if ( tbToolIndex < numToolBtns )
    {
        toolBtn[tbToolIndex].BuildSelfDeferred(sInst,
                                        windID,
                                        initToolPos.x + xPos + tbSpacing,
                                        initToolPos.y + yPos + tbSpacing,
                                        upName,
                                        dnName,
                                        greyName,
                                        selectName,
                                        sCall,
                                        dCall);
        if ( tbToolIndex == 0 )
        {
            toolSize = toolBtn[0].GetButtonSize();
        }
```

continues

489

Listing 7.20. continued

```
        tbToolIndex++;
    }

}

//--------------------------------
//
// InitToolBar()
//
// Creates some important things that you need
// in order to successfully build a toolbar.
//
// This routine is called before a toolbar can be
// displayed.

    void

ToolBar::InitToolBar ( WORD     toolStyle,     // Toolbar style

                WORD    toolBarWidth, // Width of toolbar, in tools
                                      // --For vertical toolbars, this
                                      //    is how wide the bar is
                                      // --For horizontal toolbars, this
                                      //    is how tall the bar is
                                      // --For rectangular toolbars, this
                                      //    is both width and height
                WORD    toolSpacing,  // How many pixels between tools

                WORD    toolCount,    // Number of tools in toolbar

                WORD    xPos,         // X position of 1st tool
                WORD    yPos,         // Y position of 1st tool

                POINT   barPos,       // Initial bar position

                HANDLE  hInst,        // Instance handle

                FARPROC callHandle)   // Callback handle for callback
{
    /*-------------------*/

    if ( tbPosition.x == 0 &&
         tbPosition.y == 0 )
```

```
    {
         tbPosition = barPos;         // Initial bar position
    }

    initToolPos.x = xPos;            // X position of 1st tool

    initToolPos.y = yPos;            // Y Position of 1st tool

    nextToolPos = initToolPos;       // Get next position, too

    tbWidthSize = toolBarWidth;      // Width in tools of toolbar
    tbHeightSize = toolBarWidth;     // Height in tools of toolbar

    tbSpacing = toolSpacing;         // # of pixels between tools

    tbStyle = toolStyle;             // Toolbar style

    sInst = hInst;                   // Instance handle

    toolBtn = new BmButton[toolCount];   // Bitmap button handles

    numToolBtns = toolCount;             // # of tools

    winCallback = callHandle;            // Save callback handle for later...
}

//-----------------------------
//
// Same as InitToolBar, above, but will force the
// dialog box to size itself using the size given
// in the last parameter, instead of scaling itself
// according to the bitmap being loaded.

    void
ToolBar::InitToolBarForce (
                 WORD     toolStyle,     // Toolbar style
                 WORD     toolBarWidth,  // Width of toolbar, in tools
                                         //  --For vertical toolbars, this
                                         //      is how wide the bar is
                                         //  --For horizontal toolbars, this
                                         //      is how tall the bar is
                                         //  --For rectangular toolbars, this
                                         //      is both width and height
                 WORD     toolSpacing,   // How many pixels between tools
                 WORD     toolCount,     // Number of tools in toolbar
```

continues

Listing 7.20. continued

```
                    WORD     xPos,        // X position of 1st tool
                    WORD     yPos,        // Y position of 1st tool

                    POINT    barPos,      // Initial bar position

                    HANDLE   hInst,       // Instance handle
                    FARPROC  callHandle,  // Callback handle for callback
                    POINT    sizeBM )     // Size of forced BM
{
    forceBMSize = true;

    firstBMSize = sizeBM;

    InitToolBar(toolStyle,
                toolBarWidth,
                toolSpacing,
                toolCount,
                xPos,
                yPos,
                barPos,
                hInst,
                callHandle);
}

// MatchChildWindows() takes a window handle and returns
// a boolean, indicating if the window handle matches any of
// the buttons in the toolbar, or the toolbar window itself.

    BOOL
ToolBar::MatchChildWindows( HWND     parentWnd )
{
    int  i;

    //------------------

    if ( parentWnd == GetBarHandle() )
    {
        return TRUE;
    }

    for ( i = 0; i < GetNumButtons(); i++)
    {
        if ( toolBtn[i].MatchSelfWindow ( parentWnd ) == true )
```

```
        {
            return TRUE;
        }
    }

    return FALSE;
}

//----------------------------------------
//
// SaveToIniFile() - Saves the toolbar settings to the .ini file

ToolBar::SaveToIniFile ( LPSTR      iniFile,
                         LPSTR   sectionTag )
{
    char outBuff[12];       // String buffer for output stuff

    //----------------------------------------------------

    // If the toolbar's been moved, then save it out.

    if ( ToolBarMoved() )
    {
        POINT    pos;

        pos = GetBarPosition();

        outBuff[0] = '0' + (pos.x / 100);
        outBuff[1] = '0' + ((pos.x % 100) / 10);
        outBuff[2] = '0' + ((pos.x % 100) % 10);

        WritePrivateProfileString ( sectionTag,      // Header for the section
                                    (LPSTR)"XP",     // X position
                                    (LPSTR)&outBuff[0], // Value of position
                                    iniFile );       // Ini file name

        outBuff[0] = '0' + (pos.y / 100);
        outBuff[1] = '0' + ((pos.y % 100) / 10);
        outBuff[2] = '0' + ((pos.y % 100) % 10);

        WritePrivateProfileString ( sectionTag,      // Header for the section
                                    (LPSTR)"YP",            // Y position
                                    (LPSTR)&outBuff[0],  // Value of position
                                    iniFile );              // Ini file name
```

continues

493

Listing 7.20. continued

```
    }
}

//-----------------------------------------
//
// RestoreFromIniFile() - Restores the toolbar settings to the .ini file

ToolBar::RestoreFromIniFile ( LPSTR          iniFile,
                              LPSTR          sectionTag )
{
    POINT         tbP;              // Toolbar position

    //--------------------

    tbP.x = GetPrivateProfileInt( sectionTag,
                                  (LPSTR)"XP",
                                  0,
                                  iniFile );

    tbP.y = GetPrivateProfileInt( sectionTag,
                                  (LPSTR)"YP",
                                  0,
                                  iniFile );

    SetToolBarPosition ( tbP );

}
```

Using the Toolbar Object Class

The best way for you to understand how the Toolbar object class works is for me to give an example of it in action. It's incredibly powerful and almost transparent in use (after you've gotten it set up). There are, however, a few caveats you should know about using it.

The biggest warning is that every toolbar you create (you aren't limited in how many you can create) must have a Windows callback stub routine in your application code, like so:

```
     Toolbar          myToolBar;


   WINAPI
MyToolBarWindowCallback ( HWND          hWnd,
                          unsigned      message,
                          WORD          wParam,
                          LONG          lParam)
{
  myToolBar.ToolbarWinCallback ( hWnd,
                                 message,
                                 wParam,
                                 lParam);

}
```

The callback function is to get around a problem with Windows—it doesn't pass the "this" pointer in its callbacks. That means that you can't do a **MAKEPROCINSTANCE** on the ToolbarWinCallback member function. Remember, the member function isn't defining code for an instance of an app, it's only prototyping what the code is for when an instance *is* generated. Hence this ugly hack of having Windows call your application, which promptly turns around and calls the instance of the toolbar you want. I know, I know—there's just gotta be a better way!

Given the ugly hack just mentioned, this point is relatively minor: toolbars require that you have an empty dialog box, titled DIALOG_1, as a resource in your application. This dialog box *must be modeless*. Toolbars also require you to have a global variable, MainhWnd, which holds the handle to your application's main window.

Using the Toolbar Object Class: A Sample Application

As I mentioned, by far the best way to see how to use a Toolbar is to see one in action. Here's a complete sample application that displays a toolbar with three graphics buttons in it. (The only source pieces not listed here are the BmButton and Toolbar classes, which were listed previously.) Each button generates a different action when clicked, and probably the most amazing thing is that it's virtually transparent in doing so. Figure 7.8 demonstrates the use of the Toolbar object class.

Figure 7.8.
The Button App
in action.

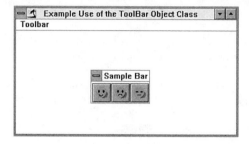

Listings 7.21 through 7.28 give you the source code for a complete sample application that uses the toolbar.

Listing 7.21. BTEXAMPL.CPP—C++ source module to the Button toolbar example.

```
// BTEXAMPL.CPP
//
// "BTEXAMPL" Generated by WindowsMAKER Professional
// Author: Alex Leavens, for ShadowCat Technologies

#include <WINDOWS.H>

#include "boolean.h"

#include "pmorph.h"

#include "compatdc.h"

#include "bitmap.h"

#include "bmbutton.h"

#include "toolbar.h"

#include "BTEXAMPL.H"

#include "BTEXAMPL.WMC"

ToolBar          sampleTB;          // Sample toolbar...

     BOOL WINAPI
```

```
SampleBarCallBack ( HWND      hWnd,
                       unsigned      message,
                    WORD wParam,
                    LONG lParam );
    PMorphRoutine
HappyAction ( HWND          hWnd,
              unsigned    message,
              WORD        wParam,
              LONG        lParam );


    PMorphRoutine
SadAction ( HWND   hWnd,
            unsigned      message,
            WORD wParam,
            LONG lParam );


    PMorphRoutine
DullAction ( HWND hWnd,
            unsigned      message,
            WORD wParam,
            LONG lParam );


#define ID_HAPPY_BUTTON    8000
#define ID_SAD_BUTTON      8001
#define ID_DULL_BUTTON     8002


//***************************************************************
//                    WinMain FUNCTION
//***************************************************************

    int PASCAL
WinMain(HANDLE    hInstance,
        HANDLE    hPrevInstance,
        LPSTR     lpCmdLine,
        int       nCmdShow)
{
    MSG msg;                    // Message

    hInst = hInstance;          // Saves the current instance

    if (!BLDInitApplication(hInstance,hPrevInstance,&nCmdShow,lpCmdLine))
        return FALSE;

    if (!hPrevInstance)         // Is there another instance of the task
```

continues

Listing 7.21. continued

```
        {
        if (!BLDRegisterClass(hInstance))
            return FALSE;         // Exits if unable to initialize
        }

    MainhWnd = BLDCreateWindow(hInstance);
    if (!MainhWnd)                // Check if the window is created
        return FALSE;

    ShowWindow(MainhWnd, nCmdShow);  // Show the window
    UpdateWindow(MainhWnd);          // Send WM_PAINT message to window

    BLDInitMainMenu(MainhWnd);   // Initialize main menu if necessary

    while (GetMessage(&msg,      // Message structure
                    0,           // Handle of window receiving the message
                    0,           // Lowest message to examine
                    0))          // Highest message to examine
        {
        if (BLDKeyTranslation(&msg)) // WindowsMAKER code for key translation
            continue;
        TranslateMessage(&msg); // Translates character keys
        DispatchMessage(&msg);  // Dispatches message to window
        }
    BLDExitApplication();        // Clean up if necessary
    return(msg.wParam);          // Returns the value from PostQuitMessage
}


//***************************************************************
//              WINDOW PROCEDURE FOR MAIN WINDOW
//***************************************************************

    LONG FAR PASCAL
BLDMainWndProc(HWND hWnd,
              UINT message,
              UINT wParam,
              LONG lParam )
{

    switch (message)
        {
```

```
case WM_SIZE:
     switch (wParam)
     {
         case SIZEICONIC:
             sampleTB.IconifySelf();
             break;

         default:
             sampleTB.RestoreSelf();
             break;
     }
     break;

case WM_CREATE:               // Window creation

     // Now create sample toolbar...

     POINT    where;   // Place to put toolbar

     where.x = 50;     // Just choose a place...
     where.y = 50;

     // Instantiate your toolbar first. This sets up all the
     // housekeeping stuff that your toolbar needs

     sampleTB.InitToolBar ( TB_HORIZONTAL,    // Toolbar style
                            1,                // # of tools (vertically)
                            1,                // # of pixels between tools
                            3,                // # of tools
                            0,                // X position of 1st tool
                            1,                // Y position of 1st tool
                            where,            // Place toolbar 1st appears
                            hInst,            // Instance handle...

                         MakeProcInstance ( (FARPROC) SampleBarCallBack,
                                            hInst) );

     // Add a tool to your toolbar

     sampleTB.AddTool ( ID_HAPPY_BUTTON,          // ID of tool
                        1,                        // X position
                        1,                        // Y position
                        "UHAPPY",                 // Up image
                        "DHAPPY",                 // Down image
                        NULL,          // Grey image (none)
```

continues

Listing 7.21. continued

```
                                NULL,             // Selected image (none)
                                HappyAction,            // Single-click action
                                NULL );                 // Double-click action

        // Add another tool to your toolbar

        sampleTB.AddTool ( ID_SAD_BUTTON,   // ID of tool
                                34,                     // X position
                                1,                      // Y position
                                "USAD",                 // Up image
                                "DSAD",                 // Down image
                                NULL,         // Grey image (none)
                                NULL,         // Selected image (none)
                                SadAction,              // Single-click action
                                NULL );                 // Double-click action

        // Add still another tool to your toolbar

        sampleTB.AddTool ( ID_DULL_BUTTON,  // ID of tool
                                67,                     // X position
                                1,                      // Y position
                                "UDULL",                // Up image
                                "DDULL",                // Down image
                                NULL,         // Grey image (none)
                                NULL,         // Selected image (none)
                                DullAction,             // Single-click action
                                NULL );                 // Double-click action

        // Now actually create and display your toolbar

        sampleTB.CreateToolBar ( hWnd,
                                "Sample Bar" );

    // Send to BLDDefWindowProc in (.WMC) for controls in main window
    return BLDDefWindowProc(hWnd, message, wParam, lParam);
    break;

case WM_INITMENU:

    // Here, you're going to set up the proper menu
    // states just before the menus are displayed.
    // This bit of code determines if a check mark
    // should be placed next to the toolbar entry;
```

```
            // if the toolbar is currently visible, then a check
            // mark is placed; otherwise, it isn't.

            HMENU      hMenu = GetMenu ( hWnd );   // Get menu handle

            if ( sampleTB.GetDisplayState() == true )
            {
                CheckMenuItem ( hMenu,
                                IDM_SampleToolbar,
                                MF_CHECKED );
            }
            else
            {
                CheckMenuItem ( hMenu,
                                IDM_SampleToolbar,
                                MF_UNCHECKED );
            }
            break;

    case WM_SETFOCUS:           // Window is notified of focus change
        // Send to BLDDefWindowProc in (.WMC) for controls in main window
        return BLDDefWindowProc(hWnd, message, wParam, lParam);
        break;

    case WM_DESTROY:            // Window being destroyed
        PostQuitMessage(0);
        return BLDDefWindowProc(hWnd, message, wParam, lParam);
        break;

    case WM_COMMAND:            // Command from the main window

        switch ( wParam )
        {
            case IDM_SampleToolbar:
                if ( sampleTB.GetDisplayState() == true )
                {
                    SendMessage ( sampleTB.GetBarHandle(),
                                  WM_CLOSE,
                                  (WORD)NULL,
                                  NULL);
                }
                else
                {
                    sampleTB.CreateToolBar ( MainhWnd,
                                             "Sample" );
```

continues

Listing 7.21. continued

```
                }
                return FALSE;
                break;
        }

        if (BLDMenuCommand(hWnd, message, wParam, lParam))
            break;                  // Processed by BLDMenuCommand.
        // Else default processing by BLDDefWindowProc.
    default:
        // Pass on message for default processing
        return BLDDefWindowProc(hWnd, message, wParam, lParam);
    }
    return FALSE;                   // Returns FALSE if processed
}

//--------------------------
//
// SampleBarCallBack()
//
// Silly way of providing callbacks for
// each toolbar dialog window.

    BOOL WINAPI

SampleBarCallBack ( HWND    hWnd,
                    unsigned     message,
                    WORD wParam,
                    LONG lParam )
{
    //--------------

    return sampleTB.ToolBarWinCallBack ( hWnd,
                                         message,
                                         wParam,
                                         lParam );
}

//--------------------------
//
// HappyAction()
//
```

```
// Callback action for the Happy Face button

    PMorphRoutine
HappyAction ( HWND        hWnd,
              unsigned    message,
              WORD        wParam,
              LONG        lParam )
{
    MessageBox ( hWnd,
           "Hello, this is the happy single-click action response routine!",
           "I'm singly happy!",
           MB_OK );
}



//--------------------------
//
// SadAction()
//
// Callback action for the Sad Face button

    PMorphRoutine
SadAction ( HWND   hWnd,
            unsigned      message,
            WORD wParam,
            LONG lParam )
{
    MessageBox ( hWnd,
                 "Hello, this is the Sad callback (boo-hoo)",
                 "I'm totally bummed...",
                 MB_OK );
}




//--------------------------
//
// SadAction()
//
// Callback action for the Sad Face button

    PMorphRoutine
DullAction ( HWND hWnd,
             unsigned      message,
             WORD wParam,
             LONG lParam )
```

continues

Listing 7.21. continued

```
{
    MessageBox ( hWnd,
                "This is the dull callback. Dull, isn't it?",
                "zzzzzzzz....",
                MB_OK );
}
```

Listing 7.22. BTEXAMPL.WMC—special include file for Btexampl.cpp.

```
//File name: BTEXAMPL.WMC
//"BTEXAMPL" Generated by WindowsMAKER Professional
//Author: Alex Leavens, for ShadowCat Technologies


//***************************************************************
//                   GLOBAL VARIABLES
//***************************************************************


HBRUSH     hMBrush = 0;      // Handle to brush for main window.
HANDLE     hInst   = 0;      // Handle to instance.
HWND       MainhWnd= 0;      // Handle to main window.
HWND       hClient = 0;      // Handle to window in client area.
FARPROC    lpClient= 0L;     // Function for window in client area.


//***************************************************************
//            PROCESSES KEYBOARD ACCELERATORS
//            AND MODELESS DIALOG BOX KEY INPUT
//***************************************************************


BOOL BLDKeyTranslation(MSG *pMsg)
    {
    return FALSE;            // No special key input
    }


//***************************************************************
//        CUSTOM MESSAGE PROCESSING FOR MAIN WINDOW
//***************************************************************


LONG FAR PASCAL BLDDefWindowProc(HWND hWnd, UINT message, UINT wParam,
                        LONG lParam )
    {
```

```
    switch (message)
        {

          default:
        // Pass on message for default processing by Windows
        return DefWindowProc(hWnd, message, wParam, lParam);
        }
    return FALSE;                   // Returns FALSE if not processed by Windows
    }


//****************************************************************
//              PROCESSES ALL MENU ITEM SELECTIONS
//****************************************************************

BOOL BLDMenuCommand(HWND hWnd, UINT message, UINT wParam, LONG lParam )
{

    switch( LOWORD(wParam) )
        {

        // Processing of linked menu items in menu: BTEXAMPL

    default:
        return FALSE;              // Not processed by this function.
        }
    return TRUE;                   // Processed by this function.
    }


//****************************************************************
//    FUNCTIONS FOR INITIALIZATION AND EXIT OF APPLICATION
//****************************************************************

BOOL BLDInitApplication(HANDLE hInst, HANDLE hPrev, int *pCmdShow,
                        LPSTR lpCmd)
    {
    // No initialization necessary
    return TRUE;
    }



// Registers the class for the main window
BOOL BLDRegisterClass( HANDLE hInstance )
    {
    WNDCLASS WndClass;
```

continues

505

Listing 7.22. continued

```
        hMBrush=CreateSolidBrush(GetSysColor(COLOR_WINDOW));

        WndClass.style          = 0;
        WndClass.lpfnWndProc    = BLDMainWndProc;
        WndClass.cbClsExtra     = 0;
        WndClass.cbWndExtra     = 0;
        WndClass.hInstance      = hInstance;
        WndClass.hIcon          = LoadIcon(NULL,IDI_APPLICATION);
        WndClass.hCursor        = LoadCursor(NULL,IDC_ARROW);
        WndClass.hbrBackground = hMBrush;
        WndClass.lpszMenuName  = "BTEXAMPL";
        WndClass.lpszClassName = "BTEXAMPL";

        return RegisterClass(&WndClass);
        }


HWND BLDCreateWindow( HANDLE hInstance )  // Creates the main window
{
    HWND hWnd;                   // Window handle
    int coordinate[4];           // Coordinates of main window

    coordinate[0]=CW_USEDEFAULT;
    coordinate[1]=0;
    coordinate[2]=CW_USEDEFAULT;
    coordinate[3]=0;

    hWnd = CreateWindow("BTEXAMPL",  // Window class registered earlier
            "Example Use of the ToolBar Object Class",      // Window caption
        WS_OVERLAPPED¦WS_THICKFRAME¦WS_SYSMENU¦WS_MINIMIZEBOX¦WS_MAXIMIZEBOX,
                            // Window style
            coordinate[0],       // X position
            coordinate[1],       // Y position
            coordinate[2],       // Width
            coordinate[3],       // Height
            0,                   // Parent handle
            0,                   // Menu or child ID
            hInstance,           // Instance
            (LPSTR)NULL);        // Additional info

    return hWnd;
    }
```

```
// Called just before entering message loop
BOOL BLDInitMainMenu(HWND hWnd)
    {
    // No initialization necessary
    return TRUE;
    }


BOOL BLDExitApplication()        // Called just before exit of application
    {
    if (hMBrush)
        DeleteObject(hMBrush);
    return TRUE;
    }


//**********************************************************
// ERROR MESSAGE HANDLING (Definitions can be overruled.)
//**********************************************************

#ifndef ERRORCAPTION
#define ERRORCAPTION "Example Use of the ToolBar Object Class"
#endif

#ifndef LOADERROR
#define LOADERROR "Cannot load string."
#endif


int BLDDisplayMessage(HWND hWnd, unsigned uMsg, char *pContext, int iType)
    {
    int i, j;
    char Message[200+1];

    if (uMsg)
        {
        if (!LoadString(hInst,uMsg,Message,200))
            {
            MessageBox(hWnd,LOADERROR,ERRORCAPTION, MB_OK¦MB_SYSTEMMODAL¦
                                                    MB_ICONHAND);
            return FALSE;
            }
        }
    else
        Message[0]=0;
```

continues

Listing 7.22. continued

```
        if (pContext)
            {
            i = lstrlen(Message);
            j = lstrlen(pContext);
            if (i + j + 1 <= 200)
                {
                lstrcat(Message, " ");
                lstrcat(Message, pContext);
                }
            }

        return MessageBox(hWnd,Message,ERRORCAPTION,iType);
        }


//*****************************************************************
//            FUNCTIONS FOR DRAWING GRAPHICS BUTTONS
//*****************************************************************

BOOL BLDDrawIcon(LPDRAWITEMSTRUCT lpDrawItem, char *pIconName)
    {
    HICON hIcon;

    hIcon = LoadIcon(hInst,pIconName);
    if (!hIcon)
        {
        BLDDisplayMessage(GetActiveWindow(),BLD_CannotLoadIcon,pIconName,
                        MB_OK | MB_ICONASTERISK);
        return FALSE;
        }

    SetMapMode(lpDrawItem->hDC,MM_TEXT);
    return DrawIcon(lpDrawItem->hDC,0,0,hIcon);
    }


BOOL BLDDrawBitmap(LPDRAWITEMSTRUCT lpDrawItem, char *pBitmapName,
                    BOOL bStretch)
    {
    HBITMAP hBitmap;
    HDC hMemDC;
    BITMAP Bitmap;
    int iRaster;
```

```
iRaster = GetDeviceCaps(lpDrawItem->hDC,RASTERCAPS);
if ((iRaster&RC_BITBLT)!=RC_BITBLT)
    return FALSE;              // Device cannot display bitmap

hBitmap = LoadBitmap(hInst,pBitmapName);
if (!hBitmap)
    {
    BLDDisplayMessage(GetActiveWindow(),BLD_CannotLoadBitmap,pBitmapName,
                    MB_OK ¦ MB_ICONASTERISK);
    return FALSE;
    }

if (!GetObject(hBitmap,sizeof(BITMAP),(LPSTR)&Bitmap))
    {
    DeleteObject(hBitmap);
    return FALSE;
    }
hMemDC = CreateCompatibleDC(lpDrawItem->hDC);
if (!hMemDC)
    {
    DeleteObject(hBitmap);
    return FALSE;
    }
if (!SelectObject(hMemDC,hBitmap))
    {
    DeleteDC(hMemDC);
    DeleteObject(hBitmap);
    return FALSE;
    }

if (bStretch)
    {
    StretchBlt(lpDrawItem->hDC,
            lpDrawItem->rcItem.left,
            lpDrawItem->rcItem.top,
            lpDrawItem->rcItem.right-lpDrawItem->rcItem.left,
            lpDrawItem->rcItem.bottom-lpDrawItem->rcItem.top,
            hMemDC,
            0,
            0,
            Bitmap.bmWidth,
            Bitmap.bmHeight,
            SRCCOPY);
    }
else
```

continues

509

Listing 7.22. continued

```
        {
          BitBlt(lpDrawItem->hDC,
                     lpDrawItem->rcItem.left,
                     lpDrawItem->rcItem.top,
                     lpDrawItem->rcItem.right-lpDrawItem->rcItem.left,
                     lpDrawItem->rcItem.bottom-lpDrawItem->rcItem.top,
                     hMemDC,
                     0,
                     0,
                     SRCCOPY);
        }
    DeleteDC(hMemDC);
    DeleteObject(hBitmap);
    return TRUE;
    }


//***************************************************************
//          FUNCTION FOR CREATING CONTROLS IN MAIN WINDOW
//***************************************************************


// Startup procedure for window in client area
HWND BLDCreateClientControls(char *pTemplateName, FARPROC lpNew)
{
    RECT rClient,rMain,rDialog;
    int dxDialog,dyDialog,dyExtra,dtXold,dtYold;
    HANDLE hRes,hMem;
    LPBLD_DLGTEMPLATE lpDlg;
    unsigned long styleold,style;
    HWND hNew;

    if (!IsWindow(MainhWnd))
        return 0;
    if (IsZoomed(MainhWnd))
        ShowWindow(MainhWnd,SW_RESTORE);

    if (IsWindow(hClient))
        DestroyWindow(hClient); // Destroy previous window in client area

    // Get access to data structure of dialog box containing layout of ctrls
    hRes=FindResource(hInst,(LPSTR)pTemplateName,RT_DIALOG);
    if (!hRes)
        return 0;
    hMem=LoadResource(hInst,hRes);
```

```
if (!hMem)
    return 0;
lpDlg=(LPBLD_DLGTEMPLATE)LockResource(hMem);
if (!lpDlg)
    return 0;


// Change dialog box data structure so it can be used as a window
// in client area
styleold        = lpDlg->dtStyle;
style           = lpDlg->dtStyle&(CLIENTSTRIP);
lpDlg->dtStyle  = lpDlg->dtStyle^style;
lpDlg->dtStyle  = lpDlg->dtStyle ¦ WS_CHILD ¦ WS_CLIPSIBLINGS;
dtXold          = lpDlg->dtX;
dtYold          = lpDlg->dtY;
lpDlg->dtX      = 0;
lpDlg->dtY      = 0;


hNew = CreateDialogIndirect(hInst,(LPSTR)lpDlg, MainhWnd,lpNew);
if (!hNew)
    return 0;


// Restore dialog box data structure.
lpDlg->dtStyle  = styleold;
lpDlg->dtX      = dtXold;
lpDlg->dtY      = dtYold;


UnlockResource(hMem);
FreeResource(hMem);


// Move and size window in client area and main window
GetClientRect(MainhWnd,&rClient);
GetWindowRect(MainhWnd,&rMain);
GetWindowRect(hNew,&rDialog);
dxDialog=(rDialog.right-rDialog.left)-(rClient.right-rClient.left);
dyDialog=(rDialog.bottom-rDialog.top)-(rClient.bottom-rClient.top);
BLDMoveWindow(MainhWnd,rMain.left,rMain.top,
          (rMain.right-rMain.left)+dxDialog,
                      (rMain.bottom-rMain.top)+dyDialog,
              TRUE);
MoveWindow(hNew,0,0,
                      (rDialog.right-rDialog.left),
                      (rDialog.bottom-rDialog.top),
                      TRUE);
GetClientRect(MainhWnd,&rClient);
```

continues

Listing 7.22. continued

```
    // Compensate size if menu bar is more than one line.
    if ((rDialog.bottom-rDialog.top)>(rClient.bottom-rClient.top))
        {
        dyExtra=(rDialog.bottom-rDialog.top)-(rClient.bottom-rClient.top);
        BLDMoveWindow(MainhWnd,rMain.left,rMain.top,
                    (rMain.right-rMain.left)+dxDialog,
                    (rMain.bottom-rMain.top)+dyDialog+dyExtra,
                    TRUE);
        }

    ShowWindow(hNew,SW_SHOW);
    hClient=hNew;
    lpClient=lpNew;
    return hClient;
    }


// Ensure that window is within screen.
void BLDMoveWindow(HWND hWnd, int x, int y,
        int nWidth, int nHeight, BOOL bRepaint)
    {
    int xMax,yMax,xNew,yNew;

    xMax = GetSystemMetrics(SM_CXSCREEN);
    yMax = GetSystemMetrics(SM_CYSCREEN);

    if ((nWidth<=xMax)&&(x+nWidth>xMax))
        xNew=xMax-nWidth;
    else
        xNew=x;

    if ((nHeight<=yMax)&&(y+nHeight>yMax))
        yNew=yMax-nHeight;
    else
        yNew=y;

    MoveWindow(hWnd,xNew,yNew,nWidth,nHeight,bRepaint);
    return;
    }

//*************************************************************
//                 FUNCTION FOR SWITCHING MENU SET
//*************************************************************
```

```
BOOL BLDSwitchMenu(HWND hWnd, char *pTemplateName)
    {
    HMENU hMenu1,hMenu;
    DWORD style;

    style = GetWindowLong(hWnd,GWL_STYLE);
    if((style & WS_CHILD) == WS_CHILD)  // Called from control in main window?
        {
        hWnd=GetParent(hWnd);
        if (!hWnd)
            return FALSE;
        style = GetWindowLong(hWnd,GWL_STYLE);
        if((style & WS_CHILD) == WS_CHILD) // No menu in a WS_CHILD window.
            return FALSE;
        }
    if((style & WS_CAPTION) != WS_CAPTION) // No menu if no caption.
        return FALSE;

    hMenu1 = GetMenu(hWnd);
    hMenu = LoadMenu(hInst,pTemplateName);
    if (!hMenu)
        {
        BLDDisplayMessage(hWnd,BLD_CannotLoadMenu,pTemplateName,
                        MB_OK | MB_ICONASTERISK);
        return FALSE;
        }

    if (!SetMenu(hWnd,hMenu))
        return FALSE;
    if (hMenu1)
        DestroyMenu(hMenu1);

    DrawMenuBar(hWnd);
    return TRUE;
    }
```

Listing 7.23. BTEXAMPL.H—header file for Btexampl.cpp.

```
//File name: BTEXAMPL.H
//"BTEXAMPL" Generated by WindowsMAKER Professional
//Author: Alex Leavens, for ShadowCat Technologies
```

continues

Listing 7.23. continued

```c
// Give access to handles in all code modules
extern HANDLE hInst;
extern HWND    MainhWnd;

// Constants for error message strings
#define BLD_CannotRun        4000
#define BLD_CannotCreate     4001
#define BLD_CannotLoadMenu   4002
#define BLD_CannotLoadIcon   4003
#define BLD_CannotLoadBitmap 4004


#if !defined(THISISBLDRC)

#ifdef __cplusplus
extern "C"
{
#endif


int  PASCAL WinMain( HANDLE hInstance, HANDLE hPrevInstance,
                     LPSTR lpCmdLine, int nCmdShow );
LONG FAR PASCAL BLDMainWndProc( HWND hWnd, UINT message,
                                UINT wParam, LONG lParam );
LONG FAR PASCAL BLDDefWindowProc( HWND hWnd, UINT message,
                                  UINT wParam, LONG lParam );
BOOL BLDKeyTranslation( MSG *pMsg );
BOOL BLDInitApplication( HANDLE hInst, HANDLE hPrev,
                         int *pCmdShow, LPSTR lpCmd );
BOOL BLDExitApplication( void );
HWND BLDCreateClientControls( char *pTemplateName, FARPROC lpNew );
BOOL BLDInitMainMenu( HWND hWnd );
BOOL BLDMenuCommand( HWND hWnd, UINT message, UINT wParam, LONG lParam );
BOOL BLDRegisterClass( HANDLE hInstance );
HWND BLDCreateWindow( HANDLE hInstance );
int  BLDDisplayMessage(HWND hWnd, unsigned uMsg, char *pContext, int iType );
BOOL BLDSwitchMenu( HWND hWnd, char *pTemplateName );
BOOL BLDDrawBitmap( LPDRAWITEMSTRUCT lpDrawItem,
                    char *pBitmapName, BOOL bStretch );
BOOL BLDDrawIcon( LPDRAWITEMSTRUCT lpDrawItem, char *pIconName );
void BLDMoveWindow( HWND hWnd, int x, int y, int nWidth,
                    int nHeight, BOOL bRepaint );
```

```
#ifdef __cplusplus
}
#endif

//***************************************************************
// Variables, types, and constants for controls in main window.
//***************************************************************

extern HWND      hClient;        // Handle to window in client area.
extern FARPROC   lpClient;       // Function for window in client area.

#define CLIENTSTRIP WS_MINIMIZE|WS_MAXIMIZE|WS_CAPTION|WS_BORDER|
WS_DLGFRAME|WS_SYSMENU|WS_POPUP|WS_THICKFRAME|DS_MODALFRAME

typedef struct
    {
    unsigned long dtStyle;
    BYTE dtItemCount;
    int dtX;
    int dtY;
    int dtCX;
    int dtCY;
    } BLD_DLGTEMPLATE;

typedef BLD_DLGTEMPLATE far          *LPBLD_DLGTEMPLATE;

#endif

#define WMPDEBUG


// User Defined ID Values


// WindowsMAKER Pro generated ID Values


#define IDM_SampleToolbar                    15000
```

Listing 7.24. BOOLEAN.H—additional header file needed for the Button example.

```
/* BOOLEAN.H
 *
 * Enumerated true/false type, and other enumerated types
 *
 * Written by Alex Leavens, for ShadowCat Technologies
 */

#ifndef  __BOOLEAN_H

#define  __BOOLEAN_H

/* Logical true/false category that's really limited to true/false */

enum    Boolean  {false, true};              // false == 0, true == 1

/* Possible states of displayed buttons
 *
 *    up        - button image is up
 *    down      - button image is down
 *    grey      - button has been set to unavailable
 *    focus     - button has the focus
 *    selected  - (radio buttons only) button has been pressed but not released
 *    invalid   - state is undefined
 */

enum    BtnState {up, down, grey, focus, selected, invalid};

#endif   // __BOOLEAN_H
```

Listing 7.25. PMORPH.H—additional header file.

```
// PMORPH.H
//
// Define file containing definitions for handling
// your polymorphic callback routines...

#ifndef __PMORPH_CALL

#define __PMORPH_CALL
```

```
#include <windows.h>

//----------------------------------------

/* Polymorphic callback prototype */

#define PMorphRoutine              void FAR

typedef  void FAR (*PMorphCall)(HWND, unsigned, WORD, LONG);



//----------------------------------------

#endif
```

Listing 7.26. BTEXAMPL.RC—resource file for the Button example.

```
//File name: BTEXAMPL.RC
//"BTEXAMPL" Generated by WindowsMAKER Professional
//Author: Alex Leavens, for ShadowCat Technologies

#define THISISBLDRC

#include <WINDOWS.H>
#include "BTEXAMPL.H"


UHAPPY    BITMAP    UHAPPY.BMP
DHAPPY    BITMAP    DHAPPY.BMP
USAD      BITMAP    USAD.BMP
DSAD      BITMAP    DSAD.BMP
UDULL     BITMAP    UDULL.BMP
DDULL     BITMAP    DDULL.BMP


//*****************************************************
//                 Resource code for menus
//*****************************************************

BTEXAMPL MENU
    BEGIN
    POPUP "Toolbar"
```

continues

Listing 7.26. continued

```
        BEGIN
            MENUITEM  "Sample Toolbar", IDM_SampleToolbar
        END
    END


//*******************************************************
//      Resource code for error message strings
//*******************************************************

STRINGTABLE
    BEGIN
        BLD_CannotRun          "Cannot run "
        BLD_CannotCreate       "Cannot create dialog box "
        BLD_CannotLoadMenu     "Cannot load menu "
        BLD_CannotLoadIcon     "Cannot load icon "
        BLD_CannotLoadBitmap   "Cannot load bitmap "
    END

DIALOG_1 DIALOG 18, 18, 142, 92
CAPTION "DIALOG_1"
STYLE WS_POPUP | WS_CAPTION | WS_SYSMENU
BEGIN
END
```

Listing 7.27. BUTTON.MAK—makefile for the Button example.

```
.AUTODEPEND

#                 *Translator Definitions*
CC = bcc +BUTTON.CFG
TASM = tasm
TLIB = tlib
TLINK = tlink
LIBPATH = D:\BRC\LIB
INCLUDEPATH = D:\BRC\INCLUDE;E:\WBDEV\INCLUDE;D:\BRC\INCLUDE;E:\ICE5\CLASS


#                 *Implicit Rules*
.c.obj:
  $(CC) -c {$< }
```

```
.cpp.obj:
  $(CC) -c {$< }

.rc.res:
  rc -r {$< }
#                  *List Macros*


EXE_dependencies =  \
 compatdc.obj \
 btexampl.obj \
 bmbutton.obj \
 toolbar.obj \
 btexampl.res \
 bitmap.obj

#                *Explicit Rules*
button.exe: button.cfg $(EXE_dependencies)
  $(TLINK) /x/c/P-/Twe/L$(LIBPATH) @&&¦
c0ws.obj+
compatdc.obj+
btexampl.obj+
bmbutton.obj+
toolbar.obj+
bitmap.obj
button
                  # no map file
mathws.lib+
import.lib+
cws.lib

¦
¦
    rc btexampl.res button.exe


#                *Individual File Dependencies*
compatdc.obj: button.cfg compatdc.cpp

btexampl.obj: button.cfg btexampl.cpp

bmbutton.obj: button.cfg bmbutton.cpp

toolbar.obj: button.cfg toolbar.cpp
```

continues

519

Listing 7.27. continued

```
bitmap.obj: button.cfg bitmap.cpp

#                    *Compiler Configuration File*
button.cfg: button.mak
  copy &&¦
-R
-2
-v
-WS
-vi-
-w-ret
-w-nci
-w-inl
-wpin
-wamb
-wamp
-w-par
-wasm
-wcln
-w-cpt
-wdef
-w-dup
-w-pia
-wsig
-wnod
-w-ill
-w-sus
-wstv
-wucp
-wuse
-w-ext
-w-ias
-w-ibc
-w-pre
-w-nst
-I$(INCLUDEPATH)
-L$(LIBPATH)
¦ button.cfg
```

Listing 7.28. BUTTON.CFG—configuration file for the Button example.

```
-R
-2
-v
-WS
-vi-
-w-ret
-w-nci
-w-inl
-wpin
-wamb
-wamp
-w-par
-wasm
-wcln
-w-cpt
-wdef
-w-dup
-w-pia
-wsig
-wnod
-w-ill
-w-sus
-wstv
-wucp
-wuse
-w-ext
-w-ias
-w-ibc
-w-pre
-w-nst
-ID:\BRC\INCLUDE;E:\WBDEV\INCLUDE;D:\BRC\INCLUDE;E:\ICE5\CLASS
-LD:\BRC\LIB
```

Note several things about the files: This program was developed and compiled under Borland C++ 3.0 and tested under Borland C++ 3.1; the last two files, BUTTON.MAK and BUTTON.CFG, are used by the Borland command line compiler. Also on your disk are the .PRJ and .DSK files necessary to compile this application under the Borland Windows-hosted IDE (which is how I

developed it). You should not use the same include and library paths I use—obviously, yours should be different. If you use the IDE, these paths are easy enough to change; if you use the .MAK file and the command line compiler, be sure to change both the .MAK file and the .CFG file to point to the right places.

Bitmaps for the Button Application

Following are the images for each of the buttons in the sample button application:

 UHAPPY.BMP—The up image for the happy button.

 DHAPPY.BMP—The down image for the happy button.

 USAD.BMP—The up image for the sad button.

 DSAD.BMP—The down image for the sad button.

 UDULL.BMP—The up image for the dull button.

 DDULL.BMP—The down image for the dull button. Perhaps it's waking up?

Understanding the Button Sample App

There are some fairly fundamental pieces of magic that go into using the toolbar. The first major piece is creating it. You create the toolbar in response to the WM_CREATE message for your main window. (In fact, all the messages that drive the toolbar come from here.) The first thing you do is initialize the toolbar; *this must always come first.*

You initialize several important pieces of the toolbar: what kind it is (horizontal, vertical, or rectangular), how many tools it has, how many pixels appear between the tools, where the toolbar first appears, and its callback. Here's the function call:

```
InitToolBar (WORD      toolStyle,      // Toolbar style
            WORD      toolBarWidth,   // Width of toolbar, in tools
                                      //  --For vertical toolbars, this
                                      //      is how wide the bar is
                                      //  --For horizontal toolbars,
                                      //      this is how tall the bar is
                                      //  --For rectangular toolbars,
                                      //      this is both width and height
            WORD     toolSpacing,    // How many pixels between tools
            WORD     toolCount,      // Number of tools in toolbar

            WORD     xPos,           // X position of 1st tool
            WORD     yPos,           // Y position of 1st tool

            POINT         barPos, // Initial bar position

            HANDLE        hInst,         // Instance handle
            FARPROC       callHandle );  // Windows callback
                                         // handle for callback
```

The only really tricky thing here is the second parameter, toolBarWidth. It's counterintuitive, because it's the opposite measurement from the style of toolbar being created. That is, if you're creating a horizontal toolbar, toolBarWidth specifies how many tools you want to have stacked *vertically*. This enables you to create toolbars of all different sizes. For example, you can create a vertical strip toolbar that's only one tool wide (toolBarWidth = 1), and all the buttons in the toolbar will appear in a vertical line. If you make the same toolbar two tools wide (toolBarWidth = 2), you still have a vertical toolbar, except it has two

523

columns of tools. Don't worry if the number of tools doesn't work out properly; the Toolbar class takes care of dealing with odd numbers of tools (that is, orphan tools).

After you've set up the initial parameters of your toolbar, you need to add a few tools. You do this with the `AddTool()` member function. Here's what the `AddTool()` call looks like:

```
AddTool(HMENU     windID,        // ID for the button
        WORD      xPos,          // X position of tool in toolbar
        WORD      yPos,          // y position of tool in toolbar
        LPSTR     upName,        // Name of up image
        LPSTR     dnName,        // Name of down image
        LPSTR     greyName,      // Name of grey image
        LPSTR     selectName,    // Name of selected image
        PMorphCall sCall,        // Single-click callback
        PMorphCall dCall);       // Double-click callback
```

If the parameters to the `AddTool()` call look familiar, they should—they're the parameters to the BmButton class creation routine, and they work the same way.

After you've added a few tools to your toolbar, it's time to actually create the thing, with the `CreateToolBar()` call. Although this function takes only two parameters (the parent window handle, and the title you want displayed in the title of the toolbar), it causes an enormous amount of activity to be fired off—buttons get created, windows get created, windows get shown, the toolbar window callback gets called.

That last bit of information points up the reason that toolbars are so powerful (and so transparent): they have their own window callback routine, which handles all the appropriate message processing for the objects in the toolbar. After you create a toolbar with buttons, you never have to worry about it again—well, all right, you have to worry about it a little. But not much. This is because toolbars take the BmButton class and add to it—the button class handles all the worrisome aspects of actually displaying buttons and generating actions in response to being clicked. Toolbars, in turn, act as a sort of nanny for a set of buttons, chivying them about and asking them to draw themselves or perform actions ("Timmy! Timmy! Are these *your* galoshes? Well, don't just stand there; put them on!"). This separation of functionality works out very well—toolbars don't know (or care) how the buttons display themselves or perform actions; they just know how to ask the buttons to do that. The buttons, in turn, simply know there's some sort of supervisor object floating above them, constantly prodding them with requests for IDs and window handles and asking them whether this ID happens to match their own, and if it does, to please do something about it.

There are really only a couple of pieces left. When you get a WM_SIZE message, you determine whether the main window is hiding (iconifying) itself. If it is, the toolbar hides as well; otherwise, it shows itself.

The toolbar menu entry enables you to show and hide the toolbar as well. You process that in the WM_COMMAND message, which looks to see whether it's the ID of your menu entry. If it is, you toggle the current visibility state of the toolbar and tell it to either show or hide itself, as appropriate.

Finally, you process the WM_INITMENU message. This doesn't actually do anything to the toolbar, but you check the toolbar's visibility state here to determine whether to put a check mark next to the menu entry of your main window.

I haven't demonstrated the Toolbar class' full power here. Another important feature of toolbars is their capability to save and restore themselves from an .ini file. If you use this feature, your application automatically gets "sticky" toolbars that remember the last place they were positioned and then automatically reposition themselves there again the next time the app is run.

Further, because of the open design of the Toolbar class, I'm sure you can extend it in ways I haven't thought of. That, after all, is the whole purpose.

Summary

Buttons are a powerful method of enabling a user of an application to interact directly with that application. The easiest form of buttons to create are text buttons, because they are simply a standard Windows object.

Bitmap buttons have the added appeal of graphics but have the great drawback of being a nonstandard object. If you want a bitmap button, you have to create it yourself. The example I showed demonstrates how to build and support your own graphics buttons.

I also showed you the BmButton class, which is an object class that wraps much of the complexity of building bitmap buttons. It provides powerful additional capability and an easy method of creating and using bitmaps inside buttons.

Finally, I took the next step and created a button container meta-object, the Toolbar class, which functions much the same way as toolbars in many commercial apps. The Toolbar class I introduced has a high level of flexibility and virtually transparent operation.

Reference Section

Because bitmap buttons and toolbars are a C++ extension to Windows, there isn't a function reference for this chapter. Instead, here's a reference section on the DRAWITEMSTRUCT, which is a fundamentally important concept to understand for dealing with owner-draw objects.

tagDRAWITEMSTRUCT

```
typedef struct tagDRAWITEMSTRUCT
    {
        WORD    CtlType;      // Type of item to be drawn
        WORD    CtlID;        // ID of item to be drawn
        WORD    ItemID        // Unused for buttons; can be overloaded
        WORD    itemAction;   // What kind of drawing action to perform
        WORD    itemState;    // What the new state of the object is
        HWND    hWndItem;     // Window handle for certain objects
        HDC     hDC;          // DC to draw into
        RECT    rcItem;       // Defines boundary of object
        DWORD   itemData;     // Other information
    };
```

This structure provides all the information your application needs in order to draw an image in a button control created with the _OWNERDRAW style. When your application receives the WM_DRAWITEM message, the lParam of the message contains a pointer to this structure.

CtlType　　Specifies the type of owner-draw object in question. It can be any of the following types:

ODT_BUTTON　　　Owner-draw button

ODT_COMBOBOX　　Owner-draw combo box

ODT_LISTBOX　　　Owner-draw list box

ODT_MENU　　　　Owner-draw menu

CtlID　　Is the control ID for a combo box, list box, or button (the ID that was passed in during the creation of the object). For menus, this value is unused (and may be safely overloaded).

itemID   Specifies the menu-item ID (for menus) or the index to an item (for list boxes and combo boxes). It is unused for buttons. For an empty list box or combo box, this member can be −1, which enables your application to draw a focus rect (specified by the coordinates in the rcItem member) even if there are no items in the list or combo box.

itemAction   Specifies the necessary drawing action. It's one or more of the following bits (although for both Windows 3.0 and Windows 3.1 it appears that your application always receives messages containing only a single one of these bits set, at least for owner-draw buttons).

ODA_DRAWENTIRE—Draw the entire object in whatever state is specified by the next parameter.

ODA_FOCUS—You get this bit set whenever a control gets or loses the focus (it's a toggle). The itemState field contains the information about the new state of the object.

ODA_SELECT—You get this bit only when the selection state of the object has changed (that is, the user has moved on or off the control with the mouse and mouse button down). Again, the itemState field contains the information about the new state of the object.

itemState   Specifies the new visual state of the item—in other words, how the control should be drawn after this message has taken place. These are the possible states:

ODS_CHECKED (menus only)—This bit is set if the menu item is to be checked.

ODS_DISABLED—This bit is set if the item is to be drawn as disabled.

ODS_FOCUS—This bit is set if the item has input focus.

ODS_GRAYED (menus only)—This bit is set if the item is to be grayed.

ODS_SELECTED—This bit is set if the item's status is selected.

hwndItem   For combo boxes, list boxes, and buttons, specifies the window handle of the control. For menus, it contains the handle of the menu (HMENU) containing the item.

hDC   Identifies a device context to draw into. This device context must be used when performing drawing operations on the control.

rcItem   Gives the rectangle in the DC specified by the hDC member that defines the boundaries of the control to be drawn. Windows automatically clips anything the owner draws in the device context for combo boxes, list boxes, and buttons, but it does not clip menu items. When drawing menu items, the owner must ensure that the owner does not draw outside the boundaries of the rectangle defined by rcItem.

itemData   Is undefined for buttons.

Menu
Resources

Next to bitmaps, menus are probably the most used and least understood of all Windows resources. Although it's fairly easy to get your application up and running with menu basics, most applications don't go beyond the basics to exploit the full power of menus that's provided for in the Windows API. This chapter is designed to help correct that shortcoming. Topics covered in this chapter are

☐ Menu basics

☐ MenuDIL, a sample application demonstrating the use of a display information line (DIL)

☐ Advanced menuing: bitmaps, custom check marks, owner-draw menus, and tear-offs

☐ MenuDraw, a sample application demonstrating advanced menuing capabilities

Menu Basics

First I'll define a few terms. The Microsoft documentation makes numerous references to "tear-offs" and "pop-ups," without ever giving you a clear picture of what those are. Here's an attempt to remedy that situation—look at Figure 8.1.

To help you better understand what you're looking at, a few terms are defined here.

A *menu* is an object that contains things. The things a menu contains are either *menu entries* (defined later) or more menus. Menus can have a text string, a bitmap, or an owner-draw status associated with them. In addition, each object within the menu generates a WM_COMMAND message when the user clicks it. An application can add, change, or delete items in the menu, as well as create, modify, and delete the menu itself. All menus in Windows are *pop-up menus*.

Figure 8.1.
An illustration
of some of the
elements of
menus.

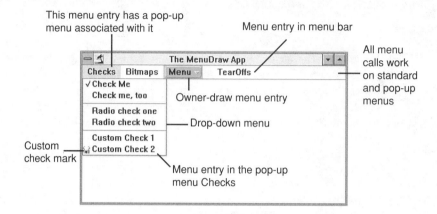

A *menu entry* is an object contained in a menu, but it is not itself a menu. A menu entry has several properties. It generates a WM_COMMAND message when the user clicks it. A menu entry can contain either text or one of several flavors of graphics images. A menu entry can be created, changed, and deleted—note that altering a menu entry does not alter the menu that contains it, except inasmuch as the menu reflects the new state of the menu entry. (That is, deleting a menu entry from a menu is not the same as deleting the menu itself.)

Figure 8.2 gives another illustration of the relationship between menus and menu entries.

A top-level menu in Windows is a menu bar. Although it appears quite different from the drop-down menus below it, the only real difference is how Windows displays it. A menu bar is created using the `CreateMenu()` call and is displayed as a series of horizontal entries. A drop-down or drag-right menu is created with the `CreatePopupMenu()` call and is displayed as a vertical list of one or more columns.

As you can see in Figure 8.2, a menu can have a mixture of menu entries and pop-up menus in it. A menu bar typically has nothing but pop-up menus in it, because each of these pop-up menus typically has menu entries beneath it. For example, the menu bar might have two pop-ups in it, File and Options. Each of these pop-ups might have several entries in it; the File pop-up would probably have Open, Save, and Quit in it.

Figure 8.2 also demonstrates the different ways in which Windows treats regular and pop-up menus. Here's a breakdown:

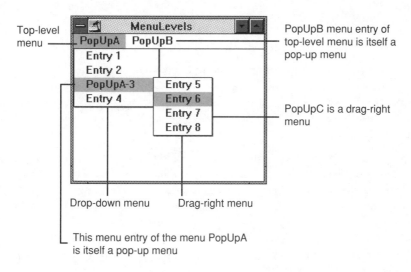

Figure 8.2.
Menus and
menu entries.

□ The top-level *menu bar* is a standard menu created using `CreateMenu()`. All the menu functions operate on a standard menu object. As with pop-ups, a standard menu does not have an ID.

□ If a pop-up menu is a second-level menu attached to the menu bar of a window, it is displayed as a *drop-down menu*. In Figure 8.2, PopUpA is a drop-down menu.

□ If a pop-up menu is a third-level or higher menu (that is, fourth-level, fifth-level, and so on) attached to a pop-up menu above it, it is displayed as a *drag-right menu*. In Figure 8.2, PopUpC is a drag-right menu.

You should note one other important thing about menus and menu entries: although menu entries have IDs associated with them (just as buttons and bitmap buttons do), menus (both standard and pop-up) do *not*. This means you must rely on several other techniques for determining which menu entry the user is over if that menu entry happens to be a pop-up menu and not just a plain menu entry.

Creating Menus

There are two ways of getting a menu to work with. One way is to create the menu by hand in your application at execution time. To create and use a menu, you need to do a couple of things:

1. Create an empty pop-up menu.

2. Fill the newly created pop-up with some menu entries.

The first step—creating an empty pop-up menu—is performed with the `CreatePopupMenu()` call. (The one exception to this is if you need to create a menu bar; in that case, you must use `CreateMenu()` instead.) This is a very easy function to use—it takes no parameters and if successful returns a handle to your new pop-up menu.

After you create the pop-up menu, you next need to put some entries into it; after all, an empty menu isn't really much good! To add entries to an empty menu, use `AppendMenu()` or `InsertMenu()`. `AppendMenu()` tacks the new entry onto the end of the list of entries; in contrast, `InsertMenu()` takes the menu entry and inserts it into the desired spot, moving all the other menu entries down a position. Both functions, however, define the type of menu entry that you insert into the menu, and how that menu entry appears. Look at an example:

```
AppendMenu(  hMenu,
             MF_STRING,
             ID_NewMenuID,
             "This is a menu entry" );
```

The first parameter, hMenu, is the handle to the menu you want to insert an item into. In this case you pass in the handle of the menu you just created. This is then followed by a flag value, which specifies what kind of menu entry you want to create, as well as how you want that entry initially to appear. Although there is a plethora of possibilities for this field (many of which I discuss under the section "Advanced Menuing"), stick to the simple case right now. You want to create a text menu entry, so you specify the value MF_STRING. Next, specify the ID you want this menu entry to have. This is very important! This value is passed back to your application in wParam with the WM_COMMAND message. Without a unique value here, you are unable to distinguish a mouse-click on this menu entry from others. Finally, you pass in the string you want to appear in the menu entry. The contents of this string are governed by the needs of your application.

Now that you've stuck a couple of entries into the menu, it's time to display it. To do this, you need to attach your menu to an already-existing menu bar, with `ModifyMenu()`. If you've created a top-level menu bar, you can replace the current menu bar with your new one with the `SetMenu()` call. Alternatively, you can use `AppendMenu()` or `InsertMenu()` to tack your new pop-up menu onto an already existing menu. In this sense, pop-ups are no different from "regular" menu entries, which means you can attach them to a higher-level menu just as you would a menu entry into a pop-up.

After you've attached your new pop-up menu to the system (by putting it into either a menu bar or a parent pop-up), you have to let Windows know that it needs to redraw your menu bar. You do this using the `DrawMenuBar()` call, which causes Windows to update the menu bar display for your window.

Creating menus by hand is one way of building a menu set for your application. The other method is to use a menu editor or generator (such as Borland's Resource Workshop, or WindowsMaker Professional), include the menu in your resource file, and load it at runtime.

Loading Menus

Of the two approaches—creating by hand and loading from a resource —the latter is by far the easier. In fact, if your application is going to have only one menu set during execution, it's virtually transparent. All you have to do is

1. Create the menu using the appropriate tool.

2. During your application's class registration, make sure you have lines similar to these:

```
WNDCLASS     wndClass;

// Fill in the various parameters here.
// The one you're concerned about right now is the
// menu name parameter. If this is not null, then when
// your application is started, it looks for a menu with the
// name "name"; if it finds the menu, it is automatically
// attached to your main window.
//
wndClass.lpszMenuName = "MYMENU";
```

If you've created a menu named MYMENU using a menu editing tool and compiled it into your application, you're done. At start-up time, Windows checks the `lpszMenuName` field of your window class. If this field is non-NULL, Windows attempts to load the specified menu from your application's resource table. If it can do so, it hooks the menu to your main window. At this point, all you have to do is respond to WM_COMMAND messages, and you have fully operational menus.

If you want to get a little fancier, you can put your menu into a resource-only DLL (a menu's just another resource, after all). To get access to it in this

fashion, you use the **LoadMenu()** call, which bears a not-too-surprising resemblance to the other **Load...()** resource calls you've seen. Like the other calls, it takes an instance handle (specifying where to get the resource from) and a name (specifying what menu to load).

You can then take this menu handle and insert it into your main window, using the **SetMenu()** call:

```
SetMenu (    myhWnd,
         LoadMenu (    hInst,
                    "MyMenu" ) );
```

This loads the menu MyMenu from the specified application instance and inserts it into the window myhWnd.

Using Menus

Now that you've loaded your menus, how do you use them? It's actually pretty easy. To respond to a menu command (that is, when the user clicks a menu entry with the mouse), you need to add an entry to the WM_COMMAND switch. Each menu entry generates a WM_COMMAND message when clicked. This brings up an important point about menu IDs.

Distinguishing Between Menu Entries and Buttons

Because the WM_COMMAND message is also where you respond to messages you receive from controls (such as buttons), a question naturally arises: How do you distinguish between buttons and menu entries? There are two ways: one is to use unique IDs across all menus and buttons (which makes it easy), and the other is to use the LOWORD of lParam, which for menus is zero and for buttons is not. This method is more difficult, however, and requires additional tests to determine whether the entry is a menu or button. With unique IDs, you can simply ignore the problem.

The situation isn't quite as bad for menu entries by themselves, but it's close. You can have menu entries that are in different menus with the same ID, if you really want. In this case, you have to distinguish between them based on the pop-up menu handle of the menu entry; these are different. (Having two menu entries in the same menu with the same ID is out.)

In any case, there's a compelling reason to use unique IDs across all menus (aside from the fact that it's bloody difficult when you don't): Windows walks all child menus when performing a menu manipulation call such as `CheckMenuItem()`. If you have unique identifiers for all your menu entries, it's trivially easy to use the menu manipulation functions. Simply perform a `GetMenu()` on the window handle, and then do a `CheckMenuItem()` (or whatever call you're going to be doing) using that menu handle and the ID of the menu entry you want to manipulate. In this case, because all the menu-entry IDs are unique, Windows treats the entire menu structure as essentially one vast flat space—it looks through *all* the menu IDs to try to find the one you've specified. If you don't have unique menu-entry IDs, this won't work—you need to get the handle of the pop-up menu that has the menu entry you want to manipulate. This isn't a lot more work, but because it's easier the other way, why bother?

Checking a Menu Entry

To make this clearer, here's an example. Suppose you want to check a menu entry, how (assuming unique menu-entry IDs) do you do so?

```
HMENU    hMenu;

hMenu = GetMenu ( hWnd );

CheckMenuItem (    hMenu,
                   ID_MenuEntryToCheck,
                   MF_BYCOMMAND | MF_CHECKED );
```

Done, and done. You get the menu handle of the window, with `GetMenu()`. Then you call `CheckMenuItem()` with that menu handle, the ID of the item you want to check, and the state you want the item to get—in this case, MF_CHECKED, meaning check the menu item. The only slightly tricky thing here is the MF_BYCOMMAND flag, which specifies *how* you are specifying your menu entry.

MF_BYCOMMAND specifies that the ID you're passing in is, in fact, an ID—this tells Windows to search through all the menu entries to find one with the matching ID. The other possibility for this field is MF_BYPOSITION. This specifies that you're going to pass in an absolute index, rather than an ID. Here's an example of this style:

```
CheckMenuItem (    hMenu,
                   3,
                   MF_BYPOSITION | MF_CHECKED );
```

This does the same thing as the previous command, except instead of setting the menu entry that has the ID ID_MenuEntryToCheck, you set the fourth menu entry, absolute. (Indexes into menu entries are zero based.)

Why on earth would you want to do this? It's much easier to specify a menu entry by ID than by position. In addition, if the menu entry changes position (say you add a couple of new menu entries), an ID-based system won't be affected, whereas one based on absolute positioning breaks. Most of the time, you won't want to use absolute positioning. There is one case, however, in which you not only want to, you have to. Remember what I said about pop-up menus not having IDs? Right. When you want to manipulate a pop-up menu (gray it out, put a check mark next to it, whatever), you must use MF_BYPOSITION— there simply isn't any ID for you to key off of.

Besides putting a check mark next to a menu entry (or removing it), there are a couple of other things you probably want to do with menus.

Enabling and Disabling a Menu Entry

The first thing you might want to do is to enable or disable (or gray) a menu entry. This, like setting a check mark on a menu entry, is quite straightforward. You use the **EnableMenuItem()** call. It takes virtually identical parameters to **CheckMenuItem()**.

```
HMENU    hMenu = GetMenu ( hWnd );

EnableMenuItem (  hMenu,
                  ID_MenuEntry,
                  newState );
```

The first two parameters are identical—the menu handle and the menu-entry ID. The third parameter is a flag representing one of three states the menu entry can be set to: MF_ENABLED (normal, selectable, generates WM_COMMAND messages), MF_GRAYED (gray text, unselectable, doesn't generate WM_COMMAND messages), and MF_DISABLED, which is slightly wonky. Although an MF_DISABLED entry appears in the same form as an entry that's been MF_ENABLED (that is, black, apparently selectable text), it in fact does nothing. (Your application never receives any messages from a control that's been MF_DISABLED.) Applications typically gray out menu entries in response to actions that don't make sense at the time— saving a file to disk, for example, when the file hasn't yet been touched.

Determining Responsibility for Menus

How and when should your application change a menu state? There are two rather different answers.

The first answer is that the piece of code responsible for the action in question (whatever it might be) is also responsible for setting the menu states. For example, if you have a File Open menu entry, it might be the responsibility of the piece of code that loads a file from disk to also set the Save menu entry to gray (which would prevent the user from immediately saving a file that hasn't changed). Then, when the user does something that causes the file in memory to change, the piece of code that does the changing would be responsible for setting the Save menu entry to black (that is, MF_ENABLED).

This approach works well for menus that only have limited spheres of influence. In the example I just discussed, however, there might be many things that could change the status of the file in memory. Do you really want to have lots of different areas in your program that either have the code in them to set the menu or have to make a function call to set the menu entry?

If you stop and think about it, there's no real reason you must set the menu entry immediately. After all, unless the menu is being displayed, setting the menu entry won't have any effect—it won't be seen until the next time the menu is displayed.

Looked at this way, it's clear that a better way of dealing with the menus is to have one piece of code that handles the display of the menus. Just before a menu is to be displayed, this code interrogates the application, finds out what the state of a menu should be, and sets it appropriately. In fact, this is what the WM_INITMENU message is useful for.

Your application receives the WM_INITMENU message just before a menu is displayed. Knowing this, you can build your code so that it sets the menus properly before they're displayed. For example, you could build a routine that sets the state of the Save menu, based on whether a file in memory has been touched:

```
WORD        enableStyle;          // Style which you're going to set
HMENU hMenu = GetMenu ( hWnd );   // Get the menu handle of your
                                  // app
if ( touched == TRUE )  // Global flag indicating whether
{                       // the memory file has changed
     enableStyle = MF_ENABLED;
}
else
```

```
{
        enableStyle = MF_GRAYED;
}


EnableMenuItem (   hMenu,
                   ID_SaveFile,
                   enableStyle | MF_BYCOMMAND );
```

Writing the code this way puts the responsibility for the display of the menu entry squarely on the menu entry itself. This makes menu entries semi-autonomous objects that interrogate the other parts of the application to determine how to display themselves. Although this approach can be a little more expensive up front, it has the great advantage of disconnecting the internals of the application (what the app is doing) from how that information is displayed (how the app appears to the user). This can also prevent the problem of code migration. If there are many places that have to set a menu entry, it's much easier to miss one or two spots.

Changing the Text of a Menu Entry

The final thing you want to be able to do with menus is change the text inside them. For example, you might want to change an Undo menu entry to Redo, if the user had undone something and could now redo it. To change the text in a menu entry, use the **ModifyMenu()** function. Here's an example of how the call might look:

```
ModifyMenu (     hMenu,          // Menu handle that contains
                                 // the item to modify
                 itemID,         // ID of item to be changed
                 mFlags,         // Specifies how to change the menu
                 newItemID,      // New ID of item
                 lpNewItem );    // Data for the new item
```

The first two parameters are the handle to the menu you want to modify, and the item ID of the item to be modified. mFlags, the next parameter, governs not only how you want to change the menu entry, but also how the itemID field is interpreted. Just as with the other menu calls, it can be either MF_BYCOMMAND, which means that itemID is the ID of a menu entry, or MF_BYPOSITION, in which case itemID is an absolute index into the menu entries. Again, you primarily use MF_BYPOSITION for dealing with pop-up menus, because they don't have IDs.

Following the mFlags field is newItemID, which is the new ID for your menu entry. You might be wondering why you would want to change the ID of your menu entry—the short answer is that you don't. For the simple case in which you're merely changing the text inside a menu entry, you can pass in the same ID value (assuming you're using MF_BYCOMMAND) as you do in itemID. This causes the menu entry to retain its current ID value.

Next comes the lpNewItem field. In this case, this field is a pointer to a text string that defines the new text for your menu entry. Here's an example of an Undo/Redo pair, based on a flag setting:

```
// Variable "canUndo" defines whether you can currently undo
// (if you can't undo you can redo).

HMENU    hMenu = GetMenu ( hWnd );

if ( canUndo )
{
     ModifyMenu (     hMenu,
                      ID_UndoEntry,
                      MF_BYCOMMAND | MF_STRING,
                      ID_UndoEntry,
                      "Undo" );
}
else
{
     ModifyMenu (     hMenu,
                      ID_UndoEntry,
                      MF_BYCOMMAND | MF_STRING,
                      ID_UndoEntry,
                      "Redo" );
}
```

Responding to Menu Messages

Now that you can manipulate menus, you need to be able to respond to them. As I mentioned earlier, it's a simple process. You need only add an entry in your WM_COMMAND message handler. Take a look at how this works. Suppose you have a menu entry with an ID of ID_FooMenu:

```
case WM_COMMAND:              // Command message handler
     switch ( wParam )
     {
          case ID_FooMenu:
               MessageBox (      hWnd,
                                 "Foo menu clicked",
                                 "",
```

```
                              MB_OK );
                   break;


          default:
                   break;
     }
     break;
```

This WM_COMMAND message handler responds to the ID_FooMenu entry being clicked (in fact, that's the only thing it responds to!) by posting a message box.

As you can see in the preceding example, the WM_COMMAND message makes no distinction between menu command messages and messages from, say, buttons you have in your main window. As you might remember from Chapter 7, "Bitmap Buttons," button messages are processed in the same way. This means, of course, that it's critical not only to have each menu-entry ID unique, but to have them unique across the buttons (and other command objects) as well. You can, of course, use the lParam of the WM_COMMAND message to determine what kind of object sent you the message, but it's much simpler to just create everything with a unique ID.

The MenuDIL App—a Display Information Line

Many applications sport an item known as a *display information line,* or DIL. This is a status line at the bottom of an application's main window that provides immediate online feedback for various user actions. In your case, you'd like it to provide feedback to the user on the menu entries of your application. Here, then, is MenuDIL, a sample application that shows you how to build and use a simple DIL. Figure 8.3 shows the application in action.

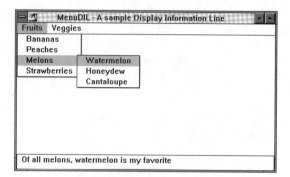

Figure 8.3.
The MenuDIL
App in action.

Looking at the Source Code for MenuDIL

Listings 8.1 through 8.8 give the source code for the MenuDIL application.

Listing 8.1. MENUDIL.C—C source for the MenuDIL application.

```
//File name: MENUDIL.C
//"MENUDIL" Generated by WindowsMAKER Professional
//Author: Alex Leavens

#include <WINDOWS.H>
#include "MENUDIL.H"

WMPDEBUG
#include "MENUDIL.WMC"


//----------------- Global variables ---------------


HWND        hwndDIL = 0;       // Handle to DIL Window


//****************************************************************
//                    WinMain FUNCTION
//****************************************************************

     int PASCAL
WinMain(HINSTANCE hInstance,
        HINSTANCE hPrevInstance,
        LPSTR     lpCmdLine,
        int       nCmdShow)
```

continues

Listing 8.1. continued

```
{
  MSG msg;                         // message

  hInst = hInstance;               // Saves the current instance

  if (!BLDInitApplication(hInstance,hPrevInstance,&nCmdShow,lpCmdLine))
      return FALSE;

  if (!hPrevInstance)              // Is there another instance of the task
      {
      if (!BLDRegisterClass(hInstance))
          return FALSE;            // Exits if unable to initialize
      }

  MainhWnd = BLDCreateWindow(hInstance);
  if (!MainhWnd)                   // Check if the window is created
      return FALSE;

  ShowWindow(MainhWnd, nCmdShow);  // Show the window
  UpdateWindow(MainhWnd);          // Send WM_PAINT message to window

  BLDInitMainMenu(MainhWnd);       // Initialize main menu if necessary

  while (GetMessage(&msg,          // message structure
                    0,             // handle of window receiving the message
                    0,             // lowest message to examine
                    0))            // highest message to examine
      {
      if (BLDKeyTranslation(&msg)) // WindowsMAKER code for key translation
          continue;
      TranslateMessage(&msg);      // Translates character keys
      DispatchMessage(&msg);       // Dispatches message to window
      }
  BLDExitApplication();            // Clean up if necessary
  return(msg.wParam);              // Returns the value from PostQuitMessage
}


//***************************************************************
//          WINDOW PROCEDURE FOR MAIN WINDOW
//***************************************************************

    LONG FAR PASCAL
BLDMainWndProc(   HWND hWnd,
```

```
                UINT message,
                UINT wParam,
                LONG lParam )
    {

    switch (message)
    {

    case WM_CREATE:             // window creation

        InitDILWindow ( hWnd,
                        hInst );    // Set up the DIL

        // Send to BLDDefWindowProc in (.WMC) for controls in main window
        return BLDDefWindowProc(hWnd, message, wParam, lParam);
        break;

    case WM_SETFOCUS:           // window is notified of focus change
        // Send to BLDDefWindowProc in (.WMC) for controls in main window
        return BLDDefWindowProc(hWnd, message, wParam, lParam);
        break;

    case WM_DESTROY:            // window being destroyed
     PostQuitMessage(0);
        return BLDDefWindowProc(hWnd, message, wParam, lParam);
        break;

    case WM_MENUSELECT:         // Menu's been selected, show the DIL info

        ShowDILInfo ( hWnd,
                      wParam,
                      lParam );

        return DefWindowProc ( hWnd,
                               message,
                               wParam,
                               lParam );

        break;

    case WM_SIZE:       // Need to move the DIL window here so that it
                        // stays anchored to the parent window.
        MoveWindow ( hwndDIL,
                     0,
                     HIWORD ( lParam ) - 25,
```

continues

545

Listing 8.1. continued

```
                        LOWORD ( lParam ),
                        26,
                        TRUE );

            return DefWindowProc ( hWnd,
                                   message,
                                   wParam,
                                   lParam );

            break;

    case WM_COMMAND:   // command from the main window
        if (BLDMenuCommand(hWnd, message, wParam, lParam))
            break;       // Processed by BLDMenuCommand.
        // else default processing by BLDDefWindowProc.
    default:
        // Pass on message for default processing
        return BLDDefWindowProc(hWnd, message, wParam, lParam);
    }
    return FALSE;        // Returns FALSE if processed
}
```

Listing 8.2. MENUDIL.H—header file for the MenuDIL application.

```
//File name: MENUDIL.H
//"MENUDIL" Generated by WindowsMAKER Professional
//Author: Alex Leavens

// These definitions are provided to support
// compilers with older versions of WINDOWS.H.
typedef unsigned int            UINT;
#ifndef WINAPI
typedef HANDLE                  HINSTANCE;
#endif

#ifndef WM_SYSTEMERROR
#define WM_SYSTEMERROR          0x0017
#endif
#ifndef WM_QUEUESYNC
#define WM_QUEUESYNC            0x0023
#endif
```

```
#ifndef WM_COMMNOTIFY
#define WM_COMMNOTIFY          0x0044
#endif
#ifndef WM_WINDOWPOSCHANGING
#define WM_WINDOWPOSCHANGING   0x0046
#endif
#ifndef WM_WINDOWPOSCHANGED
#define WM_WINDOWPOSCHANGED    0x0047
#endif
#ifndef WM_POWER
#define WM_POWER               0x0048
#endif
#ifndef WM_DROPFILES
#define WM_DROPFILES           0x0233
#endif
#ifndef WM_PALETTEISCHANGING
#define WM_PALETTEISCHANGING   0x0310
#endif


// Give access to handles in all code modules
extern HINSTANCE hInst;
extern HWND      MainhWnd;
extern HWND      hwndDIL;

// Constants for error message strings
#define BLD_CannotRun          4000
#define BLD_CannotCreate       4001
#define BLD_CannotLoadMenu     4002
#define BLD_CannotLoadIcon     4003
#define BLD_CannotLoadBitmap   4004

#if !defined(THISISBLDRC)

int  PASCAL WinMain( HINSTANCE hInstance,
                     HINSTANCE hPrevInstance, LPSTR lpCmdLine, int nCmdShow );
LONG FAR PASCAL BLDMainWndProc( HWND hWnd, UINT message,
                                UINT wParam, LONG lParam );
LONG FAR PASCAL BLDDefWindowProc( HWND hWnd, UINT message,
                                  UINT wParam, LONG lParam );
BOOL BLDKeyTranslation( MSG *pMsg );
BOOL BLDInitApplication( HANDLE hInst, HANDLE hPrev,
                         int *pCmdShow, LPSTR lpCmd );
BOOL BLDExitApplication( void );
HWND BLDCreateClientControls( char *pTemplateName, FARPROC lpNew );
```

continues

Listing 8.2. continued

```
BOOL BLDInitMainMenu( HWND hWnd );
BOOL BLDMenuCommand( HWND hWnd, UINT message, UINT wParam, LONG lParam );
BOOL BLDRegisterClass( HANDLE hInstance );
HWND BLDCreateWindow( HANDLE hInstance );
int  BLDDisplayMessage(HWND hWnd, unsigned uMsg, char *pContext, int iType );
BOOL BLDSwitchMenu( HWND hWnd, char *pTemplateName );
BOOL BLDDrawBitmap( LPDRAWITEMSTRUCT lpDrawItem,
                    char *pBitmapName, BOOL bStretch );
BOOL BLDDrawIcon( LPDRAWITEMSTRUCT lpDrawItem, char *pIconName );
void BLDMoveWindow( HWND hWnd, int x, int y, int nWidth,
                    int nHeight, BOOL bRepaint );
void WINAPI InitDILWindow( HWND hWnd, HANDLE hLInst );
void ShowDILInfo ( HWND, WORD, LONG );
int  GetDILIndex ( WORD );


//****************************************************************
// Variables, types, and constants for controls in main window.
//****************************************************************


extern HWND     hClient;        // Handle to window in client area.
extern FARPROC  lpClient;       // Function for window in client area.


#define CLIENTSTRIP WS_MINIMIZE¦WS_MAXIMIZE¦WS_CAPTION¦WS_BORDER¦
WS_DLGFRAME¦WS_SYSMENU¦WS_POPUP¦WS_THICKFRAME¦DS_MODALFRAME


typedef struct
    {
    unsigned long dtStyle;
    BYTE dtItemCount;
    int dtX;
    int dtY;
    int dtCX;
    int dtCY;
    } BLD_DLGTEMPLATE;


typedef BLD_DLGTEMPLATE far     *LPBLD_DLGTEMPLATE;


#endif


#define WMPDEBUG void static WMPDebugDummy(){}


// User Defined ID Values


// WindowsMAKER Pro generated ID Values
```

```
#define IDM_Bananas                    15000
#define IDM_Peaches                    15001
#define IDM_Watermelon                 15002
#define IDM_Honeydew                   15003
#define IDM_Cantaloupe                 15004
#define IDM_Strawberries               15005
#define IDM_Peas                       15006
#define IDM_GreenBeans                 15007
#define IDM_Artichokes                 15008
#define IDM_Asparagus                  15009
#define IDM_Melons                     15010
```

Listing 8.3. MENUDIL.WMC—special include file MenuDIL.

```
//File name: MENUDIL.WMC
//"MENUDIL" Generated by WindowsMAKER Professional
//Author: Alex Leavens


//****************************************************************
//                    GLOBAL VARIABLES
//****************************************************************


HBRUSH      hMBrush = 0;        // Handle to brush for main window.
HINSTANCE   hInst   = 0;        // Handle to instance.
HWND        MainhWnd= 0;        // Handle to main window.
HWND        hClient = 0;        // Handle to window in client area.
FARPROC     lpClient= 0L;       // Function for window in client area.


//****************************************************************
//          PROCESSES KEYBOARD ACCELERATORS
//          AND MODELESS DIALOG BOX KEY INPUT
//****************************************************************


BOOL BLDKeyTranslation(MSG *pMsg)
    {
    return FALSE;               // No special key input
    }


//****************************************************************
//        CUSTOM MESSAGE PROCESSING FOR MAIN WINDOW
//****************************************************************
```

continues

Listing 8.3. continued

```c
LONG FAR PASCAL BLDDefWindowProc(HWND hWnd, UINT message, UINT wParam,
                                  LONG lParam )
    {

    switch (message)
        {

        default:
        // Pass on message for default processing by Windows
        return DefWindowProc(hWnd, message, wParam, lParam);
        }
    return FALSE;                    // Returns FALSE if not processed by Windows
    }


//****************************************************************
//              PROCESSES ALL MENU ITEM SELECTIONS
//****************************************************************

BOOL BLDMenuCommand(HWND hWnd, UINT message, UINT wParam, LONG lParam )
{

    switch( LOWORD(wParam) )
        {

        // Processing of linked menu items in menu: MENUDIL

        default:
            return FALSE;            // Not processed by this function.
            }
        return TRUE;                 // Processed by this function.
        }


//****************************************************************
//    FUNCTIONS FOR INITIALIZATION AND EXIT OF APPLICATION
//****************************************************************

BOOL BLDInitApplication(HANDLE hInst, HANDLE hPrev,
                        int *pCmdShow, LPSTR lpCmd)
    {
    // No initialization necessary
    return TRUE;
    }
```

```
// Registers the class for the main window
BOOL BLDRegisterClass( HANDLE hInstance )
    {
    WNDCLASS WndClass;

    hMBrush=CreateSolidBrush(GetSysColor(COLOR_WINDOW));

    WndClass.style          = 0;
    WndClass.lpfnWndProc    = BLDMainWndProc;
    WndClass.cbClsExtra     = 0;
    WndClass.cbWndExtra     = 0;
    WndClass.hInstance      = hInstance;
    WndClass.hIcon          = LoadIcon(NULL,IDI_APPLICATION);
    WndClass.hCursor        = LoadCursor(NULL,IDC_ARROW);
    WndClass.hbrBackground  = hMBrush;
    WndClass.lpszMenuName   = "MENUDIL";
    WndClass.lpszClassName  = "MENUDIL";

    return RegisterClass(&WndClass);
    }


HWND BLDCreateWindow( HANDLE hInstance )  // Creates the main window
    {
    HWND hWnd;                    // window handle
    int coordinate[4];            // Coordinates of main window

    coordinate[0]=CW_USEDEFAULT;
    coordinate[1]=0;
    coordinate[2]=CW_USEDEFAULT;
    coordinate[3]=0;

    hWnd = CreateWindow("MENUDIL",  // window class registered earlier
          "MenuDIL - A sample Display Information Line",   // window caption
        WS_OVERLAPPED|WS_THICKFRAME|WS_SYSMENU|WS_MINIMIZEBOX|WS_MAXIMIZEBOX,
                              // window style
            coordinate[0],        // x position
            coordinate[1],        // y position
            coordinate[2],        // width
            coordinate[3],        // height
            0,                    // parent handle
            0,                    // menu or child ID
            hInstance,            // instance
            (LPSTR)NULL);         // additional info
```

continues

Listing 8.3. continued

```
        return hWnd;
        }


// Called just before entering message loop
BOOL BLDInitMainMenu(HWND hWnd)
    {
    // No initialization necessary
    return TRUE;
    }


BOOL BLDExitApplication()         // Called just before exit of application
    {
    if (hMBrush)
        DeleteObject(hMBrush);
    return TRUE;
    }

//***********************************************************
// ERROR MESSAGE HANDLING (Definitions can be overruled.)
//***********************************************************

#ifndef ERRORCAPTION
#define ERRORCAPTION "MenuDIL - A sample Display Information Line"
#endif

#ifndef LOADERROR
#define LOADERROR "Cannot load string."
#endif


int BLDDisplayMessage(HWND hWnd, unsigned uMsg, char *pContext, int iType)
    {
    int i, j;
    char Message[200+1];

    if (uMsg)
        {
        if (!LoadString(hInst,uMsg,Message,200))
            {
            MessageBox(hWnd,LOADERROR,ERRORCAPTION,
                    MB_OK¦MB_SYSTEMMODAL¦MB_ICONHAND);
```

```
                    return FALSE;
                    }
                }
        else
            Message[0]=0;

        if (pContext)
            {
            i = lstrlen(Message);
            j = lstrlen(pContext);
            if (i + j + 1 <= 200)
                {
                lstrcat(Message, " ");
                lstrcat(Message, pContext);
                }
            }

        return MessageBox(hWnd,Message,ERRORCAPTION,iType);
        }



//*****************************************************************
//          FUNCTIONS FOR DRAWING GRAPHICS BUTTONS
//*****************************************************************

BOOL BLDDrawIcon(LPDRAWITEMSTRUCT lpDrawItem, char *pIconName)
    {
    HICON hIcon;

    hIcon = LoadIcon(hInst,pIconName);
    if (!hIcon)
        {
        BLDDisplayMessage(GetActiveWindow(),BLD_CannotLoadIcon,
                        pIconName, MB_OK | MB_ICONASTERISK);
        return FALSE;
        }

    SetMapMode(lpDrawItem->hDC,MM_TEXT);
    return DrawIcon(lpDrawItem->hDC,0,0,hIcon);
    }



BOOL BLDDrawBitmap(LPDRAWITEMSTRUCT lpDrawItem,
                char *pBitmapName, BOOL bStretch)
```

continues

Listing 8.3. continued

```
{
HBITMAP hBitmap;
HDC hMemDC;
BITMAP Bitmap;
int iRaster;

iRaster = GetDeviceCaps(lpDrawItem->hDC,RASTERCAPS);
if ((iRaster&RC_BITBLT)!=RC_BITBLT)
    return FALSE;                // Device cannot display bitmap

hBitmap = LoadBitmap(hInst,pBitmapName);
if (!hBitmap)
    {
    BLDDisplayMessage(GetActiveWindow(),BLD_CannotLoadBitmap,pBitmapName,
                    MB_OK ¦ MB_ICONASTERISK);
    return FALSE;
    }

if (!GetObject(hBitmap,sizeof(BITMAP),(LPSTR)&Bitmap))
    {
    DeleteObject(hBitmap);
    return FALSE;
    }
hMemDC = CreateCompatibleDC(lpDrawItem->hDC);
if (!hMemDC)
    {
    DeleteObject(hBitmap);
    return FALSE;
    }
if (!SelectObject(hMemDC,hBitmap))
    {
    DeleteDC(hMemDC);
    DeleteObject(hBitmap);
    return FALSE;
    }

if (bStretch)
    {
    StretchBlt(lpDrawItem->hDC,
                lpDrawItem->rcItem.left,
                lpDrawItem->rcItem.top,
                lpDrawItem->rcItem.right-lpDrawItem->rcItem.left,
                lpDrawItem->rcItem.bottom-lpDrawItem->rcItem.top,
                hMemDC,
```

```
                            0,
                            0,
                            Bitmap.bmWidth,
                            Bitmap.bmHeight,
                            SRCCOPY);
            }
        else
            {
            BitBlt(lpDrawItem->hDC,
                    lpDrawItem->rcItem.left,
                    lpDrawItem->rcItem.top,
                    lpDrawItem->rcItem.right-lpDrawItem->rcItem.left,
                    lpDrawItem->rcItem.bottom-lpDrawItem->rcItem.top,
                    hMemDC,
                    0,
                    0,
                    SRCCOPY);
            }
        DeleteDC(hMemDC);
        DeleteObject(hBitmap);
        return TRUE;
        }


//**************************************************************
//          FUNCTION FOR CREATING CONTROLS IN MAIN WINDOW
//**************************************************************

// Startup procedure for window in client area
HWND BLDCreateClientControls(char *pTemplateName, FARPROC lpNew)
{
    RECT rClient,rMain,rDialog;
    int dxDialog,dyDialog,dyExtra,dtXold,dtYold;
    HANDLE hRes,hMem;
    LPBLD_DLGTEMPLATE lpDlg;
    unsigned long styleold,style;
    HWND hNew;

    if (!IsWindow(MainhWnd))
        return 0;
    if (IsZoomed(MainhWnd))
        ShowWindow(MainhWnd,SW_RESTORE);

    if (IsWindow(hClient))
        DestroyWindow(hClient); // Destroy Previous window in client area
```

continues

Listing 8.3. continued

```
// Get access to data structure of dialog box containing layout of ctrls
hRes=FindResource(hInst,(LPSTR)pTemplateName,RT_DIALOG);
if (!hRes)
    return 0;
hMem=LoadResource(hInst,hRes);
if (!hMem)
    return 0;
lpDlg=(LPBLD_DLGTEMPLATE)LockResource(hMem);
if (!lpDlg)
    return 0;

// Change dialog box data structure so it can be used as a window
// in client area
styleold        = lpDlg->dtStyle;
style           = lpDlg->dtStyle&(CLIENTSTRIP);
lpDlg->dtStyle  = lpDlg->dtStyle^style;
lpDlg->dtStyle  = lpDlg->dtStyle ¦ WS_CHILD ¦ WS_CLIPSIBLINGS;
dtXold          = lpDlg->dtX;
dtYold          = lpDlg->dtY;
lpDlg->dtX      = 0;
lpDlg->dtY      = 0;

hNew = CreateDialogIndirect(hInst,(LPSTR)lpDlg, MainhWnd,lpNew);
if (!hNew)
    return 0;

// Restore dialog box data structure.
lpDlg->dtStyle = styleold;
lpDlg->dtX     = dtXold;
lpDlg->dtY     = dtYold;

UnlockResource(hMem);
FreeResource(hMem);

// Move and size window in client area and main window
GetClientRect(MainhWnd,&rClient);
GetWindowRect(MainhWnd,&rMain);
GetWindowRect(hNew,&rDialog);
dxDialog=(rDialog.right-rDialog.left)-(rClient.right-rClient.left);
dyDialog=(rDialog.bottom-rDialog.top)-(rClient.bottom-rClient.top);
BLDMoveWindow(MainhWnd,rMain.left,rMain.top,
            (rMain.right-rMain.left)+dxDialog,
```

```
                         (rMain.bottom-rMain.top)+dyDialog,
                   TRUE);
         MoveWindow(hNew,0,0,
                            (rDialog.right-rDialog.left),
                            (rDialog.bottom-rDialog.top),
                            TRUE);
         GetClientRect(MainhWnd,&rClient);

         // Compensate size if menu bar is more than one line.
         if ((rDialog.bottom-rDialog.top)>(rClient.bottom-rClient.top))
             {
             dyExtra=(rDialog.bottom-rDialog.top)-(rClient.bottom-rClient.top);
             BLDMoveWindow(MainhWnd,rMain.left,rMain.top,
                       (rMain.right-rMain.left)+dxDialog,
                       (rMain.bottom-rMain.top)+dyDialog+dyExtra,
                       TRUE);
             }

         ShowWindow(hNew,SW_SHOW);
         hClient=hNew;
         lpClient=lpNew;
         return hClient;
         }


// Ensure that window is within screen.
void BLDMoveWindow(HWND hWnd, int x, int y,
        int nWidth, int nHeight, BOOL bRepaint)
    {
    int xMax,yMax,xNew,yNew;

    xMax = GetSystemMetrics(SM_CXSCREEN);
    yMax = GetSystemMetrics(SM_CYSCREEN);

    if ((nWidth<=xMax)&&(x+nWidth>xMax))
        xNew=xMax-nWidth;
    else
        xNew=x;

    if ((nHeight<=yMax)&&(y+nHeight>yMax))
        yNew=yMax-nHeight;
    else
        yNew=y;

    MoveWindow(hWnd,xNew,yNew,nWidth,nHeight,bRepaint);
```

continues

Listing 8.3. continued

```
    return;
    }


//****************************************************************
//                 FUNCTION FOR SWITCHING MENU SET
//****************************************************************

BOOL BLDSwitchMenu(HWND hWnd, char *pTemplateName)
    {
    HMENU hMenu1,hMenu;
    DWORD style;

    style = GetWindowLong(hWnd,GWL_STYLE);
    if((style & WS_CHILD) == WS_CHILD) // Called from control in main window?
        {
        hWnd=GetParent(hWnd);
        if (!hWnd)
            return FALSE;
        style = GetWindowLong(hWnd,GWL_STYLE);
        if((style & WS_CHILD) == WS_CHILD) // No menu in a WS_CHILD window.
            return FALSE;
        }
    if((style & WS_CAPTION) != WS_CAPTION) // No menu if no caption.
        return FALSE;

    hMenu1 = GetMenu(hWnd);
    hMenu = LoadMenu(hInst,pTemplateName);
    if (!hMenu)
        {
        BLDDisplayMessage(hWnd,BLD_CannotLoadMenu,pTemplateName,
                        MB_OK | MB_ICONASTERISK);
        return FALSE;
        }

    if (!SetMenu(hWnd,hMenu))
        return FALSE;
    if (hMenu1)
        DestroyMenu(hMenu1);

    DrawMenuBar(hWnd);
    return TRUE;
    }
```

Listing 8.4. DIL.C—C source support routines for MenuDIL.

```c
/* DIL.C
 *
 * Code support for DIL windows
 *
 * Written by Alex Leavens, for ShadowCat Technologies
 */


#include <WINDOWS.H>
#include "menudil.h"


//----------------- DIL been created yet? ------

BOOL    createdDIL;

extern WORD     dilIDs[];
extern char *   dilStrings[];


/********************************
 * InitDILWindow()
 *    Builds the DIL window for displaying information to
 *    the user.
 *
 * Parameters:
 *    lInst - handle to this instance of the program
 *
 * Returns:
 *    nothing.
 *
 * Assumptions:
 *    The global variable "hwndDIL" will be set to the window handle
 *    of the child window (if you could create it).
 *
 *    The global variable "createdDIL" defines whether the
 *    DIL can be used. (TRUE - yes, FALSE - no)
 */

    void WINAPI
InitDILWindow(HWND      hWnd,          /* Window handle      */
              HANDLE    hLInst)        /* Instance of the app */

{
    /*---------------------------*/

    createdDIL = FALSE;
```

continues

Listing 8.4. continued

```
        hwndDIL = CreateWindow("STATIC",    /* Class name                  */
                               "",          /* Window Name                 */
                               WS_BORDER | WS_CHILD | WS_VISIBLE,   /* styles */
                               0,           /* upper-left corner of window */
                               0,           /* in parent client area       */
                               10,          /* width of window             */
                               25,          /* Height of window            */
                               hWnd,        /* parent window handle        */
                               1,           /* child window ID             */
                               hLInst,      /* Instance of the app         */
                               NULL);       /* extra info                  */

    if (hwndDIL != NULL)
        createdDIL = TRUE;

}


/***********************************
 * ShowDILInfo()
 *     Shows information in the DIL line
 *
 * Parameters:
 *     hWnd - Window handle to child window
 *     wParam - menu ID of current menu selection
 */

    void
ShowDILInfo(HWND        hWnd,            /* Window handle    */
            WORD        wParam,          /* Word parameter   */
            LONG        lParam )         /* Long parameter   */
{
    int         i;                      /* Loop counter     */
    WORD        mID;                    /* Id of pop-up...  */

    /*-----------------------------*/

    // First, check to see if the menu entry being
    // passed in is a pop-up. If it is, there isn't
    // a valid ID to key off of, so you have to key off
    // of the first entry in the pop-up's table.

    if (LOWORD(lParam) & MF_POPUP)
    {
```

```
/* Prevent bad pop-up handles from hosing the system. */

if ((LOWORD(lParam)) == -1 ||
    (HIWORD(lParam)) == 0)
{
    SetWindowText ( hwndDIL,
                    " " );

    InvalidateRect ( hwndDIL,
                     NULL,
                     FALSE );

    UpdateWindow ( hwndDIL );
    return;
}

// Now, get the menu item ID of the menu entry

mID = GetMenuItemID ( wParam,
                      0 );

/* Now test which sub-menu entry you found--this defines
 * what the main pop-up is...
 */

switch ( mID )
{
    case IDM_Watermelon:
        i = GetDILIndex(IDM_Melons);    // Melons
        break;

    default:
        SetWindowText ( hwndDIL,
                        "          " );
        InvalidateRect ( hwndDIL,
                         NULL,
                         FALSE);

        UpdateWindow ( hwndDIL );
        return;
}

// If the index was OK, then load and display
// that string; otherwise, blank out the DIL
```

continues

Listing 8.4. continued

```
        if (i != -1)
        {
            SetWindowText ( hwndDIL,
                            dilStrings[i] );
        }
        else
        {
            SetWindowText ( hwndDIL,
                            "               ");
        }

        InvalidateRect ( hwndDIL,
                         NULL,
                         FALSE );

        UpdateWindow ( hwndDIL );
    }
    else
    {
        // Get the DIL index of the menu entry

        i = GetDILIndex(wParam);

        // If the index is valid, then display that
        // string in the DIL; otherwise, just blank the
        // DIL out.

        if (i != -1)
        {
            SetWindowText ( hwndDIL,
                            dilStrings[i] );
        }
        else
        {
            SetWindowText ( hwndDIL,
                            "                    " );
        }

        // Update the window rectangle immediately, so that
        // the DIL line gets displayed
```

```
        InvalidateRect ( hwndDIL,
                         NULL,
                         FALSE );

        UpdateWindow ( hwndDIL );
    }
}


/********************************
 * GetDILIndex()
 *    Returns the index into the text array that
 *    gives you the proper DIL line
 *
 * Returns:
 *    0 - n  :  index into text array
 *    -1     :  no item found
 */

    int
GetDILIndex(WORD id)
{
    unsigned int i;

    /*-------------------------*/

    for(i = 0; i < 100; i++)
    {
        if (id == dilIDs[i])
        {
            return i;
        }
        else if (dilIDs[i] == NULL)
        {
            return -1;
        }
    }

    return -1;
}

WORD    dilIDs[]=
        {
            IDM_Bananas,
            IDM_Peaches,
```

continues

Listing 8.4. continued

```
            IDM_Watermelon,
            IDM_Honeydew,
            IDM_Cantaloupe,
            IDM_Strawberries,
            IDM_Peas,
            IDM_GreenBeans,
            IDM_Artichokes,
            IDM_Asparagus,
            IDM_Melons
        };

char    *dilStrings[] =
        {
            "  High in potassium, no fat",
            "  Juicy peaches are tasty",
            "  Of all melons, watermelon is my favorite",
            "  Firm, orange flesh, a nice breakfast treat",
            "  Firm, green flesh, not too sweet",
            "  I love 'em!",
            "  English peas, fresh out of the shell, yum!",
            "  Lightly steamed with garlic",
            "  Boiled artichoke hearts are a favorite",
            "  Grows fresh along country lanes",
            "  A variety of melons"
        };
```

Listing 8.5. MENUDIL.DEF—module definition file for MenuDIL.

```
;File name: MENUDIL.DEF
;"MENUDIL" Generated by WindowsMAKER Professional
;Author: Alex Leavens


NAME            MENUDIL
DESCRIPTION     'MENUDIL generated by WindowsMAKER Professional'
EXETYPE         WINDOWS
STUB            'WINSTUB.EXE'
DATA            MOVEABLE MULTIPLE
CODE            MOVEABLE DISCARDABLE PRELOAD
HEAPSIZE        1024
STACKSIZE       5120
EXPORTS

                BLDMainWndProc
```

Listing 8.6. MENUDIL.RC—resource file for MenuDIL.

```
//File name: MENUDIL.RC
//"MENUDIL" Generated by WindowsMAKER Professional
//Author: Alex Leavens

#define THISISBLDRC

#include <WINDOWS.H>
#include "MENUDIL.H"

//*******************************************************
//              Resource code for menus
//*******************************************************

MENUDIL MENU
    BEGIN
    POPUP "Fruits"
        BEGIN
            MENUITEM   "Bananas", IDM_Bananas
            MENUITEM   "Peaches", IDM_Peaches
            POPUP "Melons"
                BEGIN
                    MENUITEM   "Watermelon", IDM_Watermelon
                    MENUITEM   "Honeydew", IDM_Honeydew
                    MENUITEM   "Cantaloupe", IDM_Cantaloupe
                END
            MENUITEM   "Strawberries", IDM_Strawberries
        END
    POPUP "Veggies"
        BEGIN
            MENUITEM   "Peas", IDM_Peas
            MENUITEM   "Green Beans", IDM_GreenBeans
            MENUITEM   "Artichokes", IDM_Artichokes
            MENUITEM   "Asparagus", IDM_Asparagus
        END
    END

//*******************************************************
//      Resource code for error message strings
//*******************************************************

STRINGTABLE
    BEGIN
        BLD_CannotRun         "Cannot run "
        BLD_CannotCreate      "Cannot create dialog box "
```

continues

Listing 8.6. continued

```
        BLD_CannotLoadMenu      "Cannot load menu "
        BLD_CannotLoadIcon      "Cannot load icon "
        BLD_CannotLoadBitmap    "Cannot load bitmap "
   END
```

Listing 8.7. MENUDIL.LNK—link file for MenuDIL.

```
/align:16 /NOD /co MENUDIL DIL ,MENUDIL.EXE ,, LIBW SLIBCEW, MENUDIL.DEF
```

Listing 8.8. MENUDIL—makefile for the MenuDIL application.

```
#File name: MENUDIL
#"MENUDIL" Generated by WindowsMAKER Professional
#Author: Alex Leavens

comp=/c /AS /W3 /GA /Gy /GEf /Zip /BATCH /f /Od /D_DEBUG /DWINVER=300
cc=cl

ALL : MENUDIL.EXE

MENUDIL.RES : MENUDIL.RC MENUDIL.H
    rc.exe -r MENUDIL.RC

MENUDIL.OBJ : MENUDIL.C MENUDIL.WMC MENUDIL.H
    $(cc) $(comp) MENUDIL.C

DIL.OBJ: DIL.C MENUDIL.WMC MENUDIL.H
    $(cc) $(comp) DIL.C

MENUDIL.EXE : MENUDIL.OBJ DIL.OBJ MENUDIL.DEF MENUDIL.RES
    link.exe @MENUDIL.LNK
    rc.exe menudil.res menudil.exe
```

Understanding the MenuDIL Code

There are a couple of interesting things about the MenuDIL app. First, you respond to the WM_CREATE message to create the DIL. You call the InitDILWindow() routine, which simply creates a static child window of the main window. You create a static child window because a static window displays text in it when you write text with the **SetWindowText()** call.

The other two messages you need to be concerned with in your main message loop are WM_SIZE and WM_MENUSELECT. To anchor the DIL at the bottom of your main window, you need to move the DIL window in response to a WM_SIZE message. Because you get the new size and position of the main window in lParam, you can easily adjust the DIL window's position to keep it at the bottom of the parent.

WM_MENUSELECT is a message you receive when a menu entry in a menu has been highlighted (but not actually clicked). wParam contains the ID of the menu entry (assuming it has one, and remember, pop-up menus don't). This is really where all the interesting stuff happens. Take a closer look at the ShowDILInfo() routine.

The first thing the routine does is check to see whether the menu entry is a pop-up menu. If it isn't, the routine is pretty straightforward. You take the ID of the menu item and match it against a list of all your menu entries. When you get a match (assuming you do), you get back an index. You then use this index to get a string from a string table (in a large application, it makes more sense to load these strings from a resource table rather than have them as static data). The only tricky thing here is to make sure the list of your menu-entry IDs and the list of the strings match up—if they don't match, the wrong message ends up displayed for a menu entry.

Anyway, you get the index back, and you use the **SetWindowText()** call to set the text of your DIL window to the string associated with the menu entry. You also immediately invalidate the rest of the DIL window and update it so that the new string is visible.

If you've selected a pop-up menu entry (as is the case for a drag-right menu), things are a little more complex. The first thing you need to do is make sure you haven't gotten a bad pop-up handle passed to you. It's possible (when dealing with the system menu) to get a pop-up handle that generates a UAE when you pass it to the **GetMenuItemID()** call. This is most assuredly not what you want. To prevent this, check the LOWORD of lParam for − 1, or the HIWORD of lParam for 0. If either of these two conditions is true, you simply blank out the DIL line and return. How did I arrive at these values? Completely empirically. I have no idea what the values mean; I just know they work.

If you do have a valid pop-up menu handle, the first thing you do is get the ID of the first menu entry *in* that pop-up. This is a clever bit of sleight of hand, because it enables you to get a unique ID for the pop-up menu. After all, the ID of the first menu entry for a pop-up is going to be different for each pop-up (assuming that you have globally unique menu IDs, and here's another reason to do so). Based on the unique ID of the first element of a pop-up, you can figure out which pop-up you're talking to. This enables you to display a DIL line for drag-right menus (in your case, you're showing a DIL line for the drag-right "Melons"), even though the drag-right itself doesn't have an ID you can use.

Now that you have a fairly simple menuing example under your belt, look at some of the more complex possibilities that menuing provides.

Advanced Menuing

Given the relatively few applications that take full advantage of menus, you would tend to think that there aren't too many things you can do with menus. Surprisingly, this isn't the case—menus are almost as flexible and powerful as bitmap buttons are. In some ways, they're even more powerful. Take a look at some of the more sophisticated things you can do with menus.

Custom Check Boxes

The first thing you might want to do is jazz up the check boxes that get put next to checked menu entries. Sure, a simple black check mark is functional, but does it have pizazz? Nah—put something better in there!

Changing the check mark of a menu entry is quite easy; the function you use is `SetMenuItemBitmaps()`. As you might guess from the name, this function sets the check-mark bitmaps on an individual menu-entry basis. This means you can set the check-mark bitmaps to be one thing for one menu entry and another thing for another menu entry. Although this is nice if you want to be able to have multiple styles of check marks for different menu entries, it's kind of a hassle if you want to globally set the check-mark bitmaps to something different.

Here's an example of how you would use the `SetMenuItemBitmaps()` call:

```
SetMenuItemBitmaps (    hMenu,
                        ID_MenuEntry,
```

```
                    MF_BYCOMMAND,
                    NULL,
                    hBmCheckMark );
```

Nothing too surprising here. hMenu is the handle to the menu that contains the menu entry you want to change, and ID_MenuEntry is the ID of the menu entry (assuming that the next parameter is MF_BYCOMMAND; if it is MF_BYPOSITION, ID_MenuEntry is an absolute offset).

The next two parameters are the handles to the bitmaps of the unchecked and the checked images, respectively. You might wonder why you'd need an unchecked image—after all, it's just the lack of a check mark, right? Well, other possibilities for a check mark include a radio button, a lock that's open or closed, or just about anything else you can think up. So having the capability to have two bitmaps is quite useful indeed.

> **Note:** An interesting point here is that if one of the bitmap handles is NULL, Windows won't display anything for that state. If both handles are NULL, however, Windows reverts to its default behavior of showing the standard check mark. This is an example of deliberate bulletproofing in Windows—if your application cannot load the bitmaps for the check marks, the system doesn't die, it simply reverts to default behavior. Pretty nice!

Bitmaps in Menus

The next neat thing you can do with a menu entry is put a bitmap into it. This is useful, for example, if you're going to put in an obvious menu entry that you want to get some immediate attention.

Bitmap menus are quite easy to make. First, you need to modify the menu entry so it handles a bitmap, rather than a text string. Second, you need to specify the bitmap you want displayed. You can achieve both of these steps with a single function call:

```
ModifyMenu (    hMenu,
                ID_BitmapEntry,
                MF_BYCOMMAND | MF_BITMAP,
                ID_BitmapEntry,
                MAKELONG ( hBitmap, 0 ) );
```

This is the same `ModifyMenu()` call you saw earlier. The first two entries specify the menu that has the entry to modify, and the entry itself. The first new bit is in the third parameter, where MF_BITMAP has joined MF_BYCOMMAND. MF_BITMAP specifies that you want the menu entry to be a bitmap. (The other two possibilities are MF_STRING—a standard text menu, already discussed—and MF_OWNERDRAW—an owner-draw menu, and that's next.) Following that is the new ID you want, and again, you can just specify the same ID as before. Finally, the last parameter is where you pass in the handle of the bitmap you want to go in the menu entry.

So far, this all seems pretty straightforward, and really it is. There's a reason for that, however: bitmap menus, although novel, don't really provide you with much flexibility. For one thing, when a bitmap menu is inverted, the results can range from merely unappealing to downright horrid. Color bitmaps, in particular, tend to look awful. This is because Windows simply inverts the image in the menu without regard to what the color scheme of the bitmap is.

To really get good-looking results from an image in a menu, you can't use a bitmap menu. You have to bite the bullet and take the next step, to an owner-draw menu.

Owner-Draw Menus

OK, here's where it gets interesting. You thought bitmap *buttons* were hard? Heh-heh. Actually it's not that bad—there are just complications that can arise due to the nature of menus, and some of the things that can go on with them.

First, look at the basics. How do you make a menu entry owner-draw? The same way you make one a bitmap, by using the `ModifyMenu()` call.

```
ModifyMenu (    hMenu,
                2,
                MF_BYPOSITION ¦ MF_OWNERDRAW ¦ MF_POPUP,
                hPopUp,
                MAKEINTRESOURCE ( newID ) );
```

Like the previous versions of `ModifyMenu()`, this version starts out with the menu handle you want to modify. The next parameter, however, is different—instead of being a menu-entry ID, it's an absolute position (as indicated by the MF_BYPOSITION flag in the third param). You're doing jt this way because you're altering a pop-up menu handle and not just a menu entry. A standard menu entry could, of course, use the MF_BYCOMMAND flag with a menu-entry ID.

The third parameter also specifies that you want this to be an owner-draw item (MF_OWNERDRAW) and a pop-up menu (MF_POPUP). The fourth parameter is the handle of the new pop-up menu you want to use—this must be created with the `CreatePopupMenu()` call.

The last parameter is somewhat of a puzzle until you examine the definition of what it is. For an owner-draw menu item, this value enables you to provide a 32-bit quantity that you want associated with the menu entry. Now, when you receive the WM_DRAWITEM message for this menu entry, you receive the 32-bit value in the itemData field. One thing you could use this for is a pointer to a data structure you created; another thing you could use it for is to hold an ID for this menu entry if the menu entry is a pop-up. That's what I did—no longer do pop-ups fail to have an ID!

Now that you've created an owner-draw menu entry, how do you use it? Really, it's just about the same as an owner-draw button. When the menu entry needs to be redrawn, you receive a WM_DRAWITEM message, just as you do with owner-draw buttons. Here's a code fragment that shows how to respond:

```
LPDRAWITEMSTRUCT  lpDIS;

lpDIS = (LPDRAWITEMSTRUCT)lParam;

switch ( lpDIS -> itemID )
{
    case ID_OurMenuEntry:
            if ( lpDIS->itemState & ODS_SELECTED )
            {
                    BLDDrawBitmap (  lpDIS,
                                     (char *)"DownImage",
                                     FALSE );
            }
            else
            {
                    BLDDrawBitmap (  lpDIS,
                                     (char *)"UpImage",
                                     FALSE );
            }
            break;
```

When the ODS_SELECTED flag is set, you need to draw the menu in the selected state; otherwise you need to draw it unselected.

The other message you need to respond to is WM_MEASUREITEM. This message is sent to you before the first time Windows is going to draw the item. It asks you to define how big the item is you're going to draw, in terms of the width and height of your bitmap.

There's an interesting gotcha at work here. When you return the size of your bitmap, Windows adds the size of a check mark to it. This means that when you display your bitmap in the menu, there's a chunk of whitespace on the left edge, where the bitmap for the check mark can go (if you have any owner-draw menu items checked, the check mark appears there). If you don't mind the whitespace, fine—but part of the reason that I chose to use owner-draw menu items was that I wanted full control of menu drawing, not just partial control.

One way around this whitespace issue is to cheat. In the code that responds to the WM_MEASUREITEM message, you return the width of your bitmap. Well, when you return this size, *lie*—tell it that your bitmap is smaller than it really is. Specifically, do a GetMenuCheckMarkDimensions(), which gives you the width and height of the check-mark bitmap, and then *subtract* the width of the check mark from the width of your bitmap. Return this value, and when the menu is drawn, that ugly whitespace won't be there. Of course, you won't be able to use the default check mark (that is, CheckMenuItem()), because it draws the check-mark bitmap on top of yours.

Another visual gotcha in owner-draw menus is what I refer to as the "drag-right arrow." This is the little arrow displayed on the right edge of a pop-up menu entry indicating that there's a child menu off to the right.

Well, if you create an owner-draw pop-up menu, Windows adds space to the right edge of the menu so that it can have space to draw this little arrow. Unlike with the check mark, whose dimensions you can retrieve as shown previously, with the arrow there's no API call that enables you to get its size—even GetSystemMetrics() doesn't do it. Sure, you can use ICE/Works to open up the driver file and find out how big the physical bitmap is. However, that's not quite what you want, because that's a machine-specific value—it's going to be different for different video boards and different display resolutions.

You can fake it, using the trick previously described, of subtracting the size out of the width of the bitmap you're creating in the WM_MEASUREITEM call. That works, but now the problem becomes that Windows cheerfully draws the little drag-right arrow on top of your bitmap. Naturally, this doesn't look very good. The worst part is that there appears to be no way to shut the little thing off, despite the fact that you're supposedly an owner-draw object. (If I'm an owner-draw menu item, what's Windows doing drawing something there for me?)

There is a way around this little hassle, but like most everything else, it's going to require additional work. The solution I'm speaking of is doing away with pop-up menus in your menu bar. Instead, you're going to use your own variant of a pop-up, known as a *tear-off menu*.

Tear-off Menus

Tear-off menus are probably the least-used aspect of menuing. I've seen a lot of Windows apps, but I've never seen anybody use tear-offs. A tear-off menu is a free-floating pop-up menu. It can appear anywhere on the screen, and it behaves just like a menu.

The really nice thing about tear-offs is that they're a breeze under Windows. If you have the code to support your regular menus, you already have everything you need to support tear-offs. The only thing you need to do is actually display the tear-off, which you do with the following call:

```
TrackPopupMen (    hMenu,
                   mFlags,
                   xAppear,
                   yAppear,
                   nReserved,
                   hWnd,
                   lpRect );
```

This call displays a pop-up menu and *tracks* it; that is, it interacts with the user the way an ordinary menu would. The menu tracked is specified by the hMenu parameter—this is the handle to the menu that you want to have appear. It can be any valid pop-up menu handle, whether it's one that you create in a resource editor or at runtime.

The next parameter, mFlags, specifies how you want the pop-up to be aligned with the x and y position specified by xAppear and yAppear. For Windows 3.0, the xAppear and yAppear parameters specify the top-left corner of the point where you want the menu to appear; for Windows 3.1, mFlags lets you specify whether you want the menu to appear to centered, left-justified, or right-justified with respect to the xAppear parameter.

For Windows 3.1 only, mFlags also lets you specify whether you want to track the left or the right mouse button. For Windows 3.0, you always track the left mouse button.

nReserved is just what it appears to be—reserved. It should be set to 0. Following that comes the hWnd parameter, which is the handle of the window that owns the pop-up menu to be displayed. This is important, because this window handle is the one that's going to receive the messages generated by this menu (in particular, the WM_COMMAND messages).

The final parameter is, for Windows 3.0, reserved, and NULL. For Windows 3.1, it's a pointer to a rectangle structure that the user can click inside of without dismissing the menu. In other words, this area enables you to define an area where the user can click and have the menu remain up—sticky menus!

The MenuDraw App—an Advanced Menuing Application

You certainly covered quite a few concepts just now—bitmaps, owner-draw menus, custom check boxes, and floating menus. Build a sample application that throws all these things together at once, in one massive menuing app — build MenuDraw, the advanced menuing application. Figure 8.4 shows the MenuDraw application at work.

Looking at the Source Code to MenuDraw

Listings 8.9 through 8.15 give the source code for the MenuDraw application.

Figure 8.4.
The MenuDraw
App in action,
demonstrating
an owner-draw
menu item.

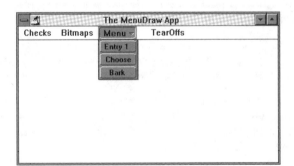

Listing 8.9. MENUDRAW.C—C source code for the MenuDraw App.

```
//File name: MENUDRAW.C
//"MENUDRAW" Generated by WindowsMAKER Professional
//Author: Alex Leavens, for ShadowCat Technologies

#include <WINDOWS.H>
#include "MENUDRAW.H"

WMPDEBUG
#include "MENUDRAW.WMC"

//----------------- Global variables -----------

// Menu handle for your owner-draw pop-up menu

HMENU           hPopUp;

// Bitmaps that contain your custom check marks

HBITMAP         checkMark1;
HBITMAP         checkMark2;
HBITMAP         unCheckMark2;

// These variables deal with your tear-off menus

#define         TEAR_OFF_INACTIVE       0
#define         NORMAL_TEAR             1
#define         CUSTOM_TEAR             2

WORD            tearOffActive;  // Are you in tear-off mode?
HMENU           hTearOff;       // Handle to normal tear-off pop-up menu

//-------------------------------------------------

//***********************************************************
//                  WinMain FUNCTION
//***********************************************************

    int PASCAL
WinMain(HINSTANCE hInstance,
        HINSTANCE hPrevInstance,
        LPSTR     lpCmdLine,
        int       nCmdShow)
```

continues

575

Listing 8.9. continued

```c
{
    MSG msg;                     // message

    hInst = hInstance;           // Saves the current instance

    if (!BLDInitApplication(hInstance,hPrevInstance,&nCmdShow,lpCmdLine))
        return FALSE;

    if (!hPrevInstance)          // Is there another instance of the task
        {
        if (!BLDRegisterClass(hInstance))
            return FALSE;        // Exits if unable to initialize
        }

    MainhWnd = BLDCreateWindow(hInstance);
    if (!MainhWnd)               // Check if the window is created
        return FALSE;

    ShowWindow(MainhWnd, nCmdShow);  // Show the window
    UpdateWindow(MainhWnd);          // Send WM_PAINT message to window

    BLDInitMainMenu(MainhWnd);   // Initialize main menu if necessary

    while (GetMessage(&msg,      // message structure
                    0,           // handle of window receiving the message
                    0,           // lowest message to examine
                    0))          // highest message to examine
    {
        if (BLDKeyTranslation(&msg)) // WindowsMAKER code for key translation
            continue;
        TranslateMessage(&msg);  // Translates character keys
        DispatchMessage(&msg);   // Dispatches message to window
    }

    BLDExitApplication();        // Clean up if necessary
    return(msg.wParam);          // Returns the value from PostQuitMessage
}


//*************************************************************
//              WINDOW PROCEDURE FOR MAIN WINDOW
//*************************************************************
```

```
    LONG FAR PASCAL
BLDMainWndProc(   HWND hWnd,
                  UINT message,
                  UINT wParam,
                  LONG lParam )
{

    switch (message)
    {

    case WM_CREATE:                 // window creation

        //-------------------------
        //
        // This block deals with initializing your
        // tear-off menu entries

        tearOffActive = TEAR_OFF_INACTIVE;        // Tear-off not active

        // Create a pop-up menu for your tear-off menu...

        hTearOff = CreatePopupMenu();   // Create a pop-up menu for a tear-off

        // Now append some menu entries to your tear-off menu

        AppendMenu ( hTearOff,
                     MF_STRING,
                     ID_TearOff1,
                     "Floater" );

        AppendMenu ( hTearOff,
                     MF_STRING,
                     ID_TearOff2,
                     "Sinker" );

        AppendMenu ( hTearOff,
                     MF_STRING,
                     ID_TearOff3,
                     "Swimmer" );

        //---------------------------
        //
        // This block deals with initializing your
        // custom check marks for menu entries
```

continues

577

Listing 8.9. continued

```
{

    // Get the menu handle of your window

    HMENU        hMenu = GetMenu ( hWnd );

    //--------------

    // Load your custom check-mark bitmaps here

    checkMark1 = LoadBitmap ( hInst,
                               "check1" );

    checkMark2 = LoadBitmap ( hInst,
                               "check2" );

    unCheckMark2 = LoadBitmap ( hInst,
                                 "uncheck2" );

    // Now set the check marks for some of the menu
    // entries...

    SetMenuItemBitmaps ( hMenu,
                         IDM_CustomCheck1,
                         MF_BYCOMMAND,
                         NULL,
                         checkMark1 );

    SetMenuItemBitmaps ( hMenu,
                         IDM_CustomCheck2,
                         MF_BYCOMMAND,
                         unCheckMark2,
                         checkMark2 );

}

{
    // You're going to be extensively modifying the menus
    // here to do some special things. First, you need
    // to get the menu handle of the main menu
```

```
HMENU        hMenu = GetMenu ( hWnd );

// Next, you create a new pop-up menu, for the fourth
// menu entry; this serves to hold the new
// owner-draw menu entries that you use

hPopUp = CreatePopupMenu();

// Now modify the menu so that you replace the
// menu entry at position 2 (zero-based offset)
// with an owner-draw pop-up menu

ModifyMenu ( hMenu,
             2,
             MF_BYPOSITION ¦ MF_OWNERDRAW ¦ MF_POPUP,
             hPopUp,
             MAKEINTRESOURCE ( ID_TopMenu4 ) );
// Now add some entries to the new owner-draw
// pop-up. Each of the entries is itself an owner-draw
// menu, with the ID given in the third parameter

AppendMenu ( hPopUp,
             MF_OWNERDRAW,
             ID_OwnDraw1,
             NULL );

AppendMenu ( hPopUp,
             MF_OWNERDRAW,
             ID_OwnDraw2,
             NULL );

AppendMenu ( hPopUp,
             MF_OWNERDRAW,
             ID_OwnDraw3,
             NULL );

// Now you're going to modify the menu entries in the
// third menu; this menu contains not owner-draw objects,
// but bitmap objects. Note the difference in how the
// two types get drawn when the application is run...
```

continues

CHAPTER 8

Listing 8.9. continued

```
        }
        // Send to BLDDefWindowProc in (.WMC) for controls in main window
        return BLDDefWindowProc(hWnd, message, wParam, lParam);
        break;

    case WM_MEASUREITEM:
    {

        LPMEASUREITEMSTRUCT       lpMi;
        WORD                      checkWidth;
        WORD                      checkHeight;

        //------------------

        // Get pointer to the info struct that you need to fill in

        lpMi = (LPMEASUREITEMSTRUCT) lParam;

        // Get width of the check mark, and subtract that size out
        // of the size of your bitmap. This is done to prevent Windows
        // from adding whitespace (enough to hold a check mark) on the
        // left edge of the window.

        checkWidth = LOWORD ( GetMenuCheckMarkDimensions() );
//      checkHeight = HIWORD ( GetMenuCheckMarkDimensions() );

        // Now check for what item this is; note that for standard owner-
        // draw menu items, you can switch off of the ID value
        // (because they have one). However, for pop-up menus (menu bar
        // entries and drag rights) this won't work, because these don't
        // have an ID. However, they do have the data field that you set
        // when you created them, and this is what you switch off of.

        switch ( lpMi->itemID )
        {
            case ID_OwnDraw3:
            case ID_OwnDraw2:
            case ID_OwnDraw1:

                lpMi->itemWidth = 64 - checkWidth ;
                lpMi->itemHeight = 21;
                break;
```

```
        // If you didn't recognize the menu item, then
        // check here to see if it's a pop-up menu

        default:
            switch ( lpMi->itemData )
            {
                case ID_TopMenu4:

                    lpMi->itemWidth = 64;
                    lpMi->itemHeight = 21;
                    break;

                default:
                    lpMi->itemWidth = 64 - checkWidth;
                    lpMi->itemHeight = 21;
                    break;
            }
        }
    }
    break;

    case WM_DRAWITEM:
    {
        LPDRAWITEMSTRUCT        lpDis;

        //------------------

        lpDis = (LPDRAWITEMSTRUCT) lParam;

        switch ( lpDis->itemID )
        {
            case ID_OwnDraw3:

                if (lpDis->itemState & ODS_SELECTED)
                {
                    BLDDrawBitmap ( lpDis,
                                    (char *)"ENTRY3D",
                                    FALSE );
                }
                else
```

continues

Listing 8.9. continued

```c
            {
                BLDDrawBitmap ( lpDis,
                                (char *)"ENTRY3U",
                                FALSE );
            }
            break;

        case ID_OwnDraw2:

            if (lpDis->itemState & ODS_SELECTED)
            {
                BLDDrawBitmap ( lpDis,
                                (char *)"ENTRY2D",
                                FALSE );
            }
            else
            {
                BLDDrawBitmap ( lpDis,
                                (char *)"ENTRY2U",
                                FALSE );
            }
            break;

        case ID_OwnDraw1:

            if (lpDis->itemState & ODS_SELECTED)
            {
                BLDDrawBitmap ( lpDis,
                                (char *)"ENTRY1D",
                                FALSE );
            }
            else
            {
                BLDDrawBitmap ( lpDis,
                                (char *)"ENTRY1U",
                                FALSE );
            }
            break;

        default:
```

```
            // OK, you didn't recognize the ID (this is true
            // for pop-up menus, which don't have them). Now check
            // the itemData field, which you set to the ID for pop-ups...

            switch ( lpDis->itemData )
            {
                case ID_TopMenu4:

                    if (lpDis->itemState & ODS_SELECTED)
                    {
                        BLDDrawBitmap ( lpDis,
                                        (char *)"MENUDOWN",
                                        FALSE );
                    }
                    else
                    {
                        BLDDrawBitmap ( lpDis,
                                        (char *)"MENUUP",
                                        FALSE );
                    }
                    break;

                default:
                    break;
            }

            break;

    }
}
    return FALSE;
    break;

case WM_SETCURSOR:              // Handle cursor set
{
    int     hitTest;

    //--------------------

    if ( wParam != MainhWnd )
        return DefWindowProc ( hWnd, message, wParam, lParam );

    hitTest = LOWORD ( lParam );

    if ( hitTest != HTCLIENT )
```

continues

Listing 8.9. continued

```
                return DefWindowProc ( hWnd, message, wParam, lParam );

        return TRUE;
    }
        break;

    case WM_SETFOCUS:           // window is notified of focus change
        // Send to BLDDefWindowProc in (.WMC) for controls in main window
        return BLDDefWindowProc(hWnd, message, wParam, lParam);
        break;

    case WM_DESTROY:            // window being destroyed

        // Clean up all your check-mark bitmap resources here

        if (checkMark1)
        {
            DeleteObject(checkMark1);
            checkMark1 = NULL;
        }
        if (checkMark2)
        {
            DeleteObject(checkMark2);
            checkMark2 = NULL;
        }
        if (unCheckMark2)
        {
            DeleteObject(unCheckMark2);
            unCheckMark2 = NULL;
        }

        // Done cleaning up check-mark bitmap resources

        PostQuitMessage(0);
        return BLDDefWindowProc(hWnd, message, wParam, lParam);
        break;

    case WM_LBUTTONDOWN:        // Left mouse button down

    {
        // Here you check to see if you do a tear-off menu...

        POINT   clToSc;         // area to convert client to screen coords
```

```
        //----------------------------

        // In order to display the pop-up in the proper place,
        // you need to convert the mouse coordinates (which are
        // given in client coords) to screen coords. You use the
        // ClientToScreen() function call to do this.

        clToSc.x = LOWORD ( lParam );
        clToSc.y = HIWORD ( lParam );

        // Now convert the client point to a screen point

        ClientToScreen ( hWnd,
                         (LPPOINT)&clToSc );

        switch ( tearOffActive )
        {
            case NORMAL_TEAR:
                TrackPopupMenu ( hTearOff,
                                 0,
                                 clToSc.x,
                                 clToSc.y,
                                 0,
                                 hWnd,
                                 NULL );
                break;

            case CUSTOM_TEAR:
                TrackPopupMenu ( hPopUp,
                                 0,
                                 clToSc.x,
                                 clToSc.y,
                                 0,
                                 hWnd,
                                 NULL );
                break;

            default:
                break;
        }
    }
        break;

    case WM_COMMAND:                // command from the main window
```

continues

Listing 8.9. continued

```
{
    WORD    menuState;      // Current menu state of a menu item
    HMENU   hMenu = GetMenu ( hWnd );        // Menu handle

    HCURSOR loadCur;        // Used for tear-off menus

    //--------------------

    // First, get the menu state of the selected menu
    // entry. Note that this works even for other
    // things that are processed by WM_COMMAND (such as
    // buttons), because this call returns a -1 for
    // non-existent menu items.

    menuState = GetMenuState ( hMenu,
                               LOWORD ( wParam ),
                               MF_BYCOMMAND );
    // Now check to see if the menu entry is -1; if it isn't, then
    // reset the tearOffActive flag to be FALSE. This allows you to
    // globally turn this flag OFF, and then turn it on for the two
    // cases where you need to.

    if ( menuState != -1 )
    {
        if ( LOWORD (wParam) != IDM_Standardtearoff &&
             LOWORD (wParam) != IDM_CustomTearoff )
        {
            SetCursor ( LoadCursor ( NULL, IDC_ARROW ) );
        }

        tearOffActive = TEAR_OFF_INACTIVE;
    }

    // Now determine the menu entry...

    switch ( LOWORD ( wParam ) )
    {
        //---------------------
        //
        // Handle your tear-off menus here

        case IDM_Standardtearoff:
            loadCur = LoadCursor ( hInst,
                                   "MENUCURS" );
```

```
        if ( loadCur )
        {
            SetCursor ( loadCur );
        }
        tearOffActive = NORMAL_TEAR;
        break;

    case IDM_CustomTearoff:
        loadCur = LoadCursor ( hInst,
                                "MENUCURS" );
        if ( loadCur )
        {
            SetCursor ( loadCur );
        }
        tearOffActive = CUSTOM_TEAR;
        break;

//-------------------------
//
// Here you handle your custom bitmap menu entries

    case IDM_Bitmaps1:
        MessageBox ( hWnd,
                    "Put the boot in, eh?!",
                    "BootBox",
                    MB_OK );
        break;

    case IDM_Bitmaps2:
        MessageBox ( hWnd,
                    "Happy face menu entry triggered...",
                    "HappyBox",
                    MB_OK );
        break;

    case IDM_Bitmaps3:
        MessageBox ( hWnd,
                    "Ttttthhhththppppppp!",
                    "RaspberryBox",
                    MB_OK );
        break;

//-------------------------
//
// This handles your custom check-mark menu entries,
```

continues

Listing 8.9. continued

```
// as well as your standard check-mark entries. Because
// the mechanics of testing and setting the check marks
// are the same, you can use the same code; the custom
// check marks, having had custom check-mark bitmaps set into
// them, displays the custom check-mark bitmaps automatically.

case IDM_CustomCheck1:
case IDM_CustomCheck2:
case IDM_CheckMe:
case IDM_Checkmetoo:

    // If item is already checked, uncheck it...

    if ( menuState & MF_CHECKED )
    {
        CheckMenuItem ( hMenu,
                        LOWORD ( wParam ),
                        MF_BYCOMMAND ¦ MF_UNCHECKED );
    }
    else    // Check menu item
    {
        CheckMenuItem ( hMenu,
                        LOWORD ( wParam ),
                        MF_BYCOMMAND ¦ MF_CHECKED );
    }
    break;

//---------------------------
//
// This code handles your radio check toggle buttons;
// when one radio button is checked, the other is
// unchecked, and vice versa.

case IDM_Radiocheckone:
case IDM_Radiochecktwo:
{
    WORD    rbOne;
    WORD    rbTwo;

    // Determine which button is being clicked here;
    // that way you can set the two button IDs so that
    // your check code works for either case

    if ( LOWORD ( wParam ) == IDM_Radiocheckone )
```

```
        {
            rbOne = IDM_Radiocheckone;
            rbTwo = IDM_Radiochecktwo;
        }
        else
        {
            rbOne = IDM_Radiochecktwo;
            rbTwo = IDM_Radiocheckone;
        }


        // Now determine what the current state of the
        // menu entry being selected is; if it's checked,
        // then uncheck this one and check the other one (it
        // doesn't matter which one it is, since you set the
        // proper IDs above). If it's unchecked, check
        // it, and uncheck the other one.

        menuState = GetMenuState ( hMenu,
                                   rbOne,
                                   MF_BYCOMMAND );

        if ( menuState & MF_CHECKED )
        {
            CheckMenuItem ( hMenu,
                            rbOne,
                            MF_BYCOMMAND | MF_UNCHECKED );
            CheckMenuItem ( hMenu,
                            rbTwo,
                            MF_BYCOMMAND | MF_CHECKED );
        }
        else
        {
            CheckMenuItem ( hMenu,
                            rbOne,
                            MF_BYCOMMAND | MF_CHECKED );
            CheckMenuItem ( hMenu,
                            rbTwo,
                            MF_BYCOMMAND | MF_UNCHECKED );
        }
    }
    break;

case ID_OwnDraw1:
    MessageBox ( hWnd,
                 "Owner draw menu entry #1",
```

continues

Listing 8.9. continued

```
                          "",
                          MB_OK );
            break;


    case ID_OwnDraw2:
        MessageBox ( hWnd,
                          "You chose owner draw menu entry #2",
                          "Owner draw menu",
                          MB_OK );
            break;


    case ID_OwnDraw3:
        MessageBox ( hWnd,
                          "Woof!  Woof!  Woof!",
                          "The Bark Button",
                          MB_OK );
            break;


    //-------------------------
    //
    // This section deals with handling the tear-off entries
    // from your standard tear-off menu.

    case ID_TearOff1:
        MessageBox ( hWnd,
                          "Tear-off: Floater",
                          "",
                          MB_OK );
            break;


    case ID_TearOff2:
        MessageBox ( hWnd,
                          "Tear-off: Sinker",
                          "",
                          MB_OK );
            break;


    case ID_TearOff3:
        MessageBox ( hWnd,
                          "Tear-off: Swimmer",
                          "",
                          MB_OK );
            break;
```

```
        default:
            break;
    }
}

    if (BLDMenuCommand(hWnd, message, wParam, lParam))
        break;                  // Processed by BLDMenuCommand.
    // else default processing by BLDDefWindowProc.

default:
    // Pass on message for default processing
    return BLDDefWindowProc(hWnd, message, wParam, lParam);

}

return FALSE;                   // Returns FALSE if processed
}
```

Listing 8.10. MENUDRAW.H—header file for MenuDraw.

```
//File name: MENUDRAW.H
//"MENUDRAW" Generated by WindowsMAKER Professional
//Author: Alex Leavens, for ShadowCat Technologies

// These definitions are provided to support
// compilers with older versions of WINDOWS.H.
typedef unsigned int        UINT;
#ifndef WINAPI
typedef HANDLE              HINSTANCE;
#endif

#ifndef WM_SYSTEMERROR
#define WM_SYSTEMERROR          0x0017
#endif
#ifndef WM_QUEUESYNC
#define WM_QUEUESYNC            0x0023
#endif
#ifndef WM_COMMNOTIFY
#define WM_COMMNOTIFY           0x0044
#endif
#ifndef WM_WINDOWPOSCHANGING
#define WM_WINDOWPOSCHANGING    0x0046
#endif
```

continues

Listing 8.10. continued

```c
#ifndef WM_WINDOWPOSCHANGED
#define WM_WINDOWPOSCHANGED     0x0047
#endif
#ifndef WM_POWER
#define WM_POWER                0x0048
#endif
#ifndef WM_DROPFILES
#define WM_DROPFILES            0x0233
#endif
#ifndef WM_PALETTEISCHANGING
#define WM_PALETTEISCHANGING    0x0310
#endif


// Give access to handles in all code modules
extern HINSTANCE hInst;
extern HWND      MainhWnd;

// Constants for error message strings
#define BLD_CannotRun           4000
#define BLD_CannotCreate        4001
#define BLD_CannotLoadMenu      4002
#define BLD_CannotLoadIcon      4003
#define BLD_CannotLoadBitmap    4004

#if !defined(THISISBLDRC)

int  PASCAL WinMain( HINSTANCE hInstance,
                     HINSTANCE hPrevInstance, LPSTR lpCmdLine, int nCmdShow );
LONG FAR PASCAL BLDMainWndProc( HWND hWnd, UINT message,
                                UINT wParam, LONG lParam );
LONG FAR PASCAL BLDDefWindowProc( HWND hWnd, UINT message,
                                  UINT wParam, LONG lParam );
BOOL BLDKeyTranslation( MSG *pMsg );
BOOL BLDInitApplication( HANDLE hInst, HANDLE hPrev,
                         int *pCmdShow, LPSTR lpCmd );
BOOL BLDExitApplication( void );
HWND BLDCreateClientControls( char *pTemplateName, FARPROC lpNew );
BOOL BLDInitMainMenu( HWND hWnd );
BOOL BLDMenuCommand( HWND hWnd, UINT message, UINT wParam, LONG lParam );
BOOL BLDRegisterClass( HANDLE hInstance );
HWND BLDCreateWindow( HANDLE hInstance );
int  BLDDisplayMessage(HWND hWnd, unsigned uMsg, char *pContext, int iType );
```

```c
BOOL BLDSwitchMenu( HWND hWnd, char *pTemplateName );
BOOL BLDDrawBitmap( LPDRAWITEMSTRUCT lpDrawItem,
                    char *pBitmapName, BOOL bStretch );
BOOL BLDDrawIcon( LPDRAWITEMSTRUCT lpDrawItem, char *pIconName );
void BLDMoveWindow( HWND hWnd, int x, int y, int nWidth,
                    int nHeight, BOOL bRepaint );

BOOL BLDInitMenuBitmaps(HWND);  // Function proto for putting bitmaps in menus
BOOL BLDDeleteMenuBitmaps(void);// Function proto for deleting bitmap objects

//**************************************************************
// Variables, types, and constants for controls in main window.
//**************************************************************

extern HWND     hClient;        // Handle to window in client area.
extern FARPROC  lpClient;       // Function for window in client area.

#define CLIENTSTRIP WS_MINIMIZE¦WS_MAXIMIZE¦WS_CAPTION¦WS_BORDER¦
WS_DLGFRAME¦WS_SYSMENU¦WS_POPUP¦WS_THICKFRAME¦DS_MODALFRAME

typedef struct
    {
    unsigned long dtStyle;
    BYTE dtItemCount;
    int dtX;
    int dtY;
    int dtCX;
    int dtCY;
    } BLD_DLGTEMPLATE;

typedef BLD_DLGTEMPLATE far      *LPBLD_DLGTEMPLATE;

#endif

#define WMPDEBUG void static WMPDebugDummy(){}

// User Defined ID Values

#define ID_TopMenu4                     8000
#define ID_OwnDraw1                     8001
#define ID_OwnDraw2                     8002
#define ID_OwnDraw3                     8003
#define ID_TearOff1                     8004
#define ID_TearOff2                     8005
```

continues

Listing 8.10. continued

```
#define ID_TearOff3                        8006

// WindowsMAKER Pro generated ID Values


#define IDM_CheckMe                        15000
#define IDM_Checkmetoo                     15001
#define IDM_Radiocheckone                  15002
#define IDM_Radiochecktwo                  15003
#define IDM_CustomCheck1                   15004
#define IDM_CustomCheck2                   15005
#define IDM_Bitmaps1                       15006
#define IDM_Bitmaps2                       15007
#define IDM_Bitmaps3                       15008
#define IDM_OwnerDraw                      15009
#define IDM_Standardtearoff                15010
#define IDM_CustomTearoff                  15011
```

Listing 8.11. MENUDRAW.WMC—special include file for MenuDraw.

```
//File name: MENUDRAW.WMC
//"MENUDRAW" Generated by WindowsMAKER Professional
//Author: Alex Leavens, for ShadowCat Technologies


//***************************************************************
//              DEFINITIONS FOR BITMAPS IN MENUS
//***************************************************************


#define MAXBITMAPS     3


HBITMAP hBitmap[MAXBITMAPS];


//***************************************************************
//                    GLOBAL VARIABLES
//***************************************************************


HBRUSH      hMBrush = 0;        // Handle to brush for main window.
HINSTANCE   hInst   = 0;        // Handle to instance.
HWND        MainhWnd= 0;        // Handle to main window.
HWND        hClient = 0;        // Handle to window in client area.
FARPROC     lpClient= 0L;       // Function for window in client area.
```

```
//****************************************************************
//               PROCESSES KEYBOARD ACCELERATORS
//               AND MODELESS DIALOG BOX KEY INPUT
//****************************************************************

BOOL BLDKeyTranslation(MSG *pMsg)
    {
    return FALSE;                    // No special key input
    }


//****************************************************************
//         CUSTOM MESSAGE PROCESSING FOR MAIN WINDOW
//****************************************************************

LONG FAR PASCAL BLDDefWindowProc(HWND hWnd, UINT message,
                                UINT wParam, LONG lParam )
    {

    switch (message)
        {

        default:
        // Pass on message for default processing by Windows
        return DefWindowProc(hWnd, message, wParam, lParam);
        }
    return FALSE;                    // Returns FALSE if not processed by Windows
    }


//****************************************************************
//              PROCESSES ALL MENU ITEM SELECTIONS
//****************************************************************

BOOL BLDMenuCommand(HWND hWnd, UINT message, UINT wParam, LONG lParam )
{

    switch( LOWORD(wParam) )
        {

        // Processing of linked menu items in menu: MENUDRAW

        default:
            return FALSE;            // Not processed by this function.
        }
    return TRUE;                     // Processed by this function.
    }
```

continues

Listing 8.11. continued

```
//****************************************************************
//     FUNCTIONS FOR INITIALIZATION AND EXIT OF APPLICATION
//****************************************************************

BOOL BLDInitApplication(HANDLE hInst, HANDLE hPrev,
                        int *pCmdShow, LPSTR lpCmd)
    {
    // No initialization necessary
    return TRUE;
    }


// Registers the class for the main window
BOOL BLDRegisterClass( HANDLE hInstance )
    {
    WNDCLASS WndClass;

    hMBrush=CreateSolidBrush(GetSysColor(COLOR_WINDOW));

    WndClass.style         = 0;
    WndClass.lpfnWndProc   = BLDMainWndProc;
    WndClass.cbClsExtra    = 0;
    WndClass.cbWndExtra    = 0;
    WndClass.hInstance     = hInstance;
    WndClass.hIcon         = LoadIcon(NULL,IDI_APPLICATION);
    WndClass.hCursor       = LoadCursor(NULL,IDC_ARROW);
    WndClass.hbrBackground = hMBrush;
    WndClass.lpszMenuName  = "MENUDRAW";
    WndClass.lpszClassName = "MENUDRAW";

    return RegisterClass(&WndClass);
    }


HWND BLDCreateWindow( HANDLE hInstance )  // Creates the main window
{
    HWND hWnd;                  // window handle
    int coordinate[4];          // Coordinates of main window

    coordinate[0]=CW_USEDEFAULT;
    coordinate[1]=0;
    coordinate[2]=CW_USEDEFAULT;
    coordinate[3]=0;
```

```
        hWnd = CreateWindow("MENUDRAW",  // window class registered earlier
            "The MenuDraw App",             // window caption
        WS_OVERLAPPED¦WS_THICKFRAME¦WS_SYSMENU¦WS_MINIMIZEBOX¦WS_MAXIMIZEBOX,
                                // window style
            coordinate[0],       // x position
            coordinate[1],       // y position
            coordinate[2],       // width
            coordinate[3],       // height
            0,                   // parent handle
            0,                   // menu or child ID
            hInstance,           // instance
            (LPSTR)NULL);        // additional info

        return hWnd;
        }


// Called just before entering message loop
BOOL BLDInitMainMenu(HWND hWnd)
    {
    BLDInitMenuBitmaps(hWnd);   // Adds bitmaps to menu

    return TRUE;
    }


BOOL BLDExitApplication()        // Called just before exit of application
    {
    if (hMBrush)
        DeleteObject(hMBrush);
    BLDDeleteMenuBitmaps();      // Destroys all bitmaps to free up memory
    return TRUE;
    }

//********************************************************
// ERROR MESSAGE HANDLING (Definitions can be overruled.)
//********************************************************

#ifndef ERRORCAPTION
#define ERRORCAPTION "The MenuDraw App"
#endif

#ifndef LOADERROR
#define LOADERROR "Cannot load string."
```

continues

Listing 8.11. continued

```c
#endif


int BLDDisplayMessage(HWND hWnd, unsigned uMsg, char *pContext, int iType)
    {
    int i, j;
    char Message[200+1];

    if (uMsg)
        {
        if (!LoadString(hInst,uMsg,Message,200))
            {
            MessageBox(hWnd,LOADERROR,ERRORCAPTION,
                      MB_OK¦MB_SYSTEMMODAL¦MB_ICONHAND);
            return FALSE;
            }
        }
    else
        Message[0]=0;

    if (pContext)
        {
        i = lstrlen(Message);
        j = lstrlen(pContext);
        if (i + j + 1 <= 200)
            {
            lstrcat(Message, " ");
            lstrcat(Message, pContext);
            }
        }

    return MessageBox(hWnd,Message,ERRORCAPTION,iType);
    }


//***************************************************************
//          FUNCTIONS FOR DRAWING GRAPHICS BUTTONS
//***************************************************************

BOOL BLDDrawIcon(LPDRAWITEMSTRUCT lpDrawItem, char *pIconName)
    {
    HICON hIcon;

    hIcon = LoadIcon(hInst,pIconName);
    if (!hIcon)
```

```
            {
        BLDDisplayMessage(GetActiveWindow(),BLD_CannotLoadIcon,
                         pIconName, MB_OK | MB_ICONASTERISK);
        return FALSE;
        }

    SetMapMode(lpDrawItem->hDC,MM_TEXT);
    return DrawIcon(lpDrawItem->hDC,0,0,hIcon);
    }


BOOL BLDDrawBitmap(LPDRAWITEMSTRUCT lpDrawItem,
                  char *pBitmapName, BOOL bStretch)
    {
    HBITMAP hBitmap;
    HDC hMemDC;
    BITMAP Bitmap;
    int iRaster;

    iRaster = GetDeviceCaps(lpDrawItem->hDC,RASTERCAPS);
    if ((iRaster&RC_BITBLT)!=RC_BITBLT)
        return FALSE;               // Device cannot display bitmap

    hBitmap = LoadBitmap(hInst,pBitmapName);
    if (!hBitmap)
        {
        BLDDisplayMessage(GetActiveWindow(),BLD_CannotLoadBitmap,pBitmapName,
                         MB_OK | MB_ICONASTERISK);
        return FALSE;
        }

    if (!GetObject(hBitmap,sizeof(BITMAP),(LPSTR)&Bitmap))
        {
        DeleteObject(hBitmap);
        return FALSE;
        }
    hMemDC = CreateCompatibleDC(lpDrawItem->hDC);
    if (!hMemDC)
        {
        DeleteObject(hBitmap);
        return FALSE;
        }
    if (!SelectObject(hMemDC,hBitmap))
        {
        DoletcDC(hMemDC);
```

continues

Listing 8.11. continued

```
            DeleteObject(hBitmap);
            return FALSE;
            }

    if (bStretch)
        {
        StretchBlt(lpDrawItem->hDC,
                lpDrawItem->rcItem.left,
                lpDrawItem->rcItem.top,
                lpDrawItem->rcItem.right-lpDrawItem->rcItem.left,
                lpDrawItem->rcItem.bottom-lpDrawItem->rcItem.top,
                hMemDC,
                0,
                0,
                Bitmap.bmWidth,
                Bitmap.bmHeight,
                SRCCOPY);
        }
    else
        {
        BitBlt(lpDrawItem->hDC,
                lpDrawItem->rcItem.left,
                lpDrawItem->rcItem.top,
                lpDrawItem->rcItem.right-lpDrawItem->rcItem.left,
                lpDrawItem->rcItem.bottom-lpDrawItem->rcItem.top,
                hMemDC,
                0,
                0,
                SRCCOPY);
        }
    DeleteDC(hMemDC);
    DeleteObject(hBitmap);
    return TRUE;
    }

//*************************************************************
//        FUNCTION FOR CREATING CONTROLS IN MAIN WINDOW
//*************************************************************

// Startup procedure for window in client area
HWND BLDCreateClientControls(char *pTemplateName, FARPROC lpNew)
{
    RECT rClient,rMain,rDialog;
    int dxDialog,dyDialog,dyExtra,dtXold,dtYold;
```

```
HANDLE hRes,hMem;
LPBLD_DLGTEMPLATE lpDlg;
unsigned long styleold,style;
HWND hNew;

if (!IsWindow(MainhWnd))
    return 0;
if (IsZoomed(MainhWnd))
    ShowWindow(MainhWnd,SW_RESTORE);

if (IsWindow(hClient))
    DestroyWindow(hClient); // Destroy Previous window in client area

// Get access to data structure of dialog box containing layout of ctrls
hRes=FindResource(hInst,(LPSTR)pTemplateName,RT_DIALOG);
if (!hRes)
    return 0;
hMem=LoadResource(hInst,hRes);
if (!hMem)
    return 0;
lpDlg=(LPBLD_DLGTEMPLATE)LockResource(hMem);
if (!lpDlg)
    return 0;

// Change dialog box data structure so
// it can be used as a window in client area
styleold      = lpDlg->dtStyle;
style         = lpDlg->dtStyle&(CLIENTSTRIP);
lpDlg->dtStyle = lpDlg->dtStyle^style;
lpDlg->dtStyle = lpDlg->dtStyle | WS_CHILD | WS_CLIPSIBLINGS;
dtXold        = lpDlg->dtX;
dtYold        = lpDlg->dtY;
lpDlg->dtX    = 0;
lpDlg->dtY    = 0;

hNew = CreateDialogIndirect(hInst,(LPSTR)lpDlg, MainhWnd,lpNew);
if (!hNew)
    return 0;

// Restore dialog box data structure.
lpDlg->dtStyle = styleold;
lpDlg->dtX    = dtXold;
lpDlg->dtY    = dtYold;

UnlockResource(hMem);
```

continues

601

Listing 8.11. continued

```
    FreeResource(hMem);

    // Move and size window in client area and main window
    GetClientRect(MainhWnd,&rClient);
    GetWindowRect(MainhWnd,&rMain);
    GetWindowRect(hNew,&rDialog);
    dxDialog=(rDialog.right-rDialog.left)-(rClient.right-rClient.left);
    dyDialog=(rDialog.bottom-rDialog.top)-(rClient.bottom-rClient.top);
    BLDMoveWindow(MainhWnd,rMain.left,rMain.top,
            (rMain.right-rMain.left)+dxDialog,
            (rMain.bottom-rMain.top)+dyDialog,
            TRUE);
    MoveWindow(hNew,0,0,
            (rDialog.right-rDialog.left),
            (rDialog.bottom-rDialog.top),
            TRUE);
    GetClientRect(MainhWnd,&rClient);

    // Compensate size if menu bar is more than one line.
    if ((rDialog.bottom-rDialog.top)>(rClient.bottom-rClient.top))
        {
        dyExtra=(rDialog.bottom-rDialog.top)-(rClient.bottom-rClient.top);
        BLDMoveWindow(MainhWnd,rMain.left,rMain.top,
                (rMain.right-rMain.left)+dxDialog,
                (rMain.bottom-rMain.top)+dyDialog+dyExtra,
                TRUE);
        }

    ShowWindow(hNew,SW_SHOW);
    hClient=hNew;
    lpClient=lpNew;
    return hClient;
    }


// Ensure that window is within screen.
void BLDMoveWindow(HWND hWnd, int x, int y,
        int nWidth, int nHeight, BOOL bRepaint)
    {
    int xMax,yMax,xNew,yNew;

    xMax = GetSystemMetrics(SM_CXSCREEN);
    yMax = GetSystemMetrics(SM_CYSCREEN);
```

```
    if ((nWidth<=xMax)&&(x+nWidth>xMax))
        xNew=xMax-nWidth;
    else
        xNew=x;


    if ((nHeight<=yMax)&&(y+nHeight>yMax))
        yNew=yMax-nHeight;
    else
        yNew=y;


    MoveWindow(hWnd,xNew,yNew,nWidth,nHeight,bRepaint);
    return;
    }


//*************************************************************
//          FUNCTIONS FOR PLACING BITMAPS IN MENUS
//*************************************************************

BOOL BLDInitMenuBitmaps(HWND hWnd)
    {
    HMENU hMenu;

    hMenu=GetMenu(hWnd);            // Get handle to window menu
    if (!hMenu)                     // Get handle to window menu
        return FALSE;

    hBitmap[0]=LoadBitmap(hInst,(LPSTR)"BOOT");
    hBitmap[1]=LoadBitmap(hInst,(LPSTR)"HAPPY1");
    hBitmap[2]=LoadBitmap(hInst,(LPSTR)"HAPPY2");

    if (hBitmap[0])
        ModifyMenu(hMenu,IDM_Bitmaps1,
                   MF_BYCOMMAND|MF_BITMAP,IDM_Bitmaps1,
                   (LPSTR)MAKELONG(hBitmap[0],0));
    if (hBitmap[1])
        ModifyMenu(hMenu,IDM_Bitmaps2,
                   MF_BYCOMMAND|MF_BITMAP,IDM_Bitmaps2,
                   (LPSTR)MAKELONG(hBitmap[1],0));
    if (hBitmap[2])
        ModifyMenu(hMenu,IDM_Bitmaps3,
                   MF_BYCOMMAND|MF_BITMAP,IDM_Bitmaps3,
                   (LPSTR)MAKELONG(hBitmap[2],0));
    DrawMenuBar(hWnd);
    return TRUE;
    }
```

continues

Listing 8.11. continued

```
BOOL BLDDeleteMenuBitmaps()        // Code to delete bitmap objects
    {
    int i;
    BITMAP bitmap;

    for (i=0;i<MAXBITMAPS;++i)
        if (hBitmap[i]&&GetObject(hBitmap[i],sizeof(BITMAP),(LPSTR)&bitmap))
            DeleteObject(hBitmap[i]);

    return TRUE;
    }


//****************************************************************
//               FUNCTION FOR SWITCHING MENU SET
//****************************************************************

BOOL BLDSwitchMenu(HWND hWnd, char *pTemplateName)
    {
    HMENU hMenu1,hMenu;
    DWORD style;

    style = GetWindowLong(hWnd,GWL_STYLE);
    if((style & WS_CHILD) == WS_CHILD)  // Called from control in main window?
        {
        hWnd=GetParent(hWnd);
        if (!hWnd)
            return FALSE;
        style = GetWindowLong(hWnd,GWL_STYLE);
        if((style & WS_CHILD) == WS_CHILD) // No menu in a WS_CHILD window.
            return FALSE;
        }
    if((style & WS_CAPTION) != WS_CAPTION) // No menu if no caption.
        return FALSE;

    hMenu1 = GetMenu(hWnd);
    hMenu = LoadMenu(hInst,pTemplateName);
    if (!hMenu)
        {
        BLDDisplayMessage(hWnd,BLD_CannotLoadMenu,pTemplateName,
                        MB_OK ¦ MB_ICONASTERISK);
        return FALSE;
        }
```

```
    if (!SetMenu(hWnd,hMenu))
        return FALSE;
    if (hMenu1)
        DestroyMenu(hMenu1);

    if (lstrcmpi(pTemplateName,"MENUDRAW")==0)
        {
        if (hBitmap[0])
            ModifyMenu(hMenu,IDM_Bitmaps1,
                        MF_BYCOMMAND¦MF_BITMAP,IDM_Bitmaps1,
                        (LPSTR)MAKELONG(hBitmap[0],0));
        if (hBitmap[1])
            ModifyMenu(hMenu,IDM_Bitmaps2,
                        MF_BYCOMMAND¦MF_BITMAP,IDM_Bitmaps2,
                        (LPSTR)MAKELONG(hBitmap[1],0));
        if (hBitmap[2])
            ModifyMenu(hMenu,IDM_Bitmaps3,
                        MF_BYCOMMAND¦MF_BITMAP,IDM_Bitmaps3,
                        (LPSTR)MAKELONG(hBitmap[2],0));
        }

    DrawMenuBar(hWnd);
    return TRUE;
    }
```

Listing 8.12. MENUDRAW.RC—resource file for MenuDraw.

```
//File name: MENUDRAW.RC
//"MENUDRAW" Generated by WindowsMAKER Professional
//Author: Alex Leavens, for ShadowCat Technologies

#define THISISBLDRC

#include <WINDOWS.H>
#include "MENUDRAW.H"

MENUDOWN BITMAP MENUDOWN.BMP
MENUUP BITMAP MENUUP.BMP
ENTRY1D BITMAP ENTRY1D.BMP
ENTRY1U BITMAP ENTRY1U.BMP
ENTRY2D BITMAP ENTRY2D.BMP
```

continues

Listing 8.12. continued

```
ENTRY2U BITMAP ENTRY2U.BMP
ENTRY3D BITMAP ENTRY3D.BMP
ENTRY3U BITMAP ENTRY3U.BMP
BOOT BITMAP BOOT.BMP
HAPPY1 BITMAP HAPPY1.BMP
HAPPY2 BITMAP HAPPY2.BMP
MENUCURS CURSOR MENUCURS.CUR
CHECK1 BITMAP CHECK1.BMP
CHECK2 BITMAP CHECK2.BMP
UNCHECK2 BITMAP UNCHECK2.BMP


//*********************************************************
//                Resource code for menus
//*********************************************************


MENUDRAW MENU
    BEGIN
    POPUP "Checks"
        BEGIN
            MENUITEM  "Check Me", IDM_CheckMe
            MENUITEM  "Check me, too", IDM_Checkmetoo
            MENUITEM SEPARATOR
            MENUITEM  "Radio check one", IDM_Radiocheckone
            MENUITEM  "Radio check two", IDM_Radiochecktwo
            MENUITEM SEPARATOR
            MENUITEM  "Custom Check 1", IDM_CustomCheck1
            MENUITEM  "Custom Check 2", IDM_CustomCheck2
        END
    POPUP "Bitmaps"
        BEGIN
            MENUITEM  "Bitmaps-1", IDM_Bitmaps1
            MENUITEM  "Bitmaps-2", IDM_Bitmaps2
            MENUITEM  "Bitmaps-3", IDM_Bitmaps3
        END
        MENUITEM  "OwnerDraw", IDM_OwnerDraw
    POPUP "TearOffs"
        BEGIN
            MENUITEM "Standard tear-off...", IDM_Standardtearoff
            MENUITEM "Custom Tear-off...", IDM_CustomTearoff
        END
    END


//*********************************************************
//      Resource code for error message strings
//*********************************************************
```

```
STRINGTABLE
    BEGIN
        BLD_CannotRun          "Cannot run "
        BLD_CannotCreate       "Cannot create dialog box "
        BLD_CannotLoadMenu     "Cannot load menu "
        BLD_CannotLoadIcon     "Cannot load icon "
        BLD_CannotLoadBitmap   "Cannot load bitmap "
    END
```

Listing 8.13. MENUDRAW.DEF—module definition file for MenuDraw.

```
;File name: MENUDRAW.DEF
;"MENUDRAW" Generated by WindowsMAKER Professional
;Author: Alex Leavens, for ShadowCat Technologies


NAME          MENUDRAW
DESCRIPTION   'MENUDRAW generated by WindowsMAKER Professional'
EXETYPE       WINDOWS
STUB          'WINSTUB.EXE'
DATA          MOVEABLE MULTIPLE
CODE          MOVEABLE DISCARDABLE PRELOAD
HEAPSIZE      1024
STACKSIZE     5120
EXPORTS

              BLDMainWndProc
```

Listing 8.14. MENUDRAW.LNK—link file for MenuDraw.

```
/align:16 /NOD /co MENUDRAW ,MENUDRAW.EXE ,, LIBW SLIBCEW, MENUDRAW.DEF
```

Listing 8.15. MENUDRAW—makefile for MenuDraw.

```
#File name: MENUDRAW
#"MENUDRAW" Generated by WindowsMAKER Professional
#Author: Alex Leavens, for ShadowCat Technologies

comp=/c /AS /W3 /GA /Gy /GEf /Zip /BATCH /f /Od /D_DEBUG /DWINVER=300
co-ol
```

continues

Listing 8.15. continued

```
ALL : MENUDRAW.EXE

MENUDRAW.RES : MENUDRAW.RC MENUDRAW.H MENUDOWN.BMP MENUUP.BMP \
          ENTRY1D.BMP ENTRY1U.BMP ENTRY2D.BMP ENTRY2U.BMP \
          ENTRY3D.BMP ENTRY3U.BMP \
          BOOT.BMP HAPPY1.BMP HAPPY2.BMP MENUCURS.CUR CHECK1.BMP CHECK2.BMP \
          UNCHECK2.BMP
    rc.exe -r MENUDRAW.RC

MENUDRAW.OBJ : MENUDRAW.C MENUDRAW.WMC MENUDRAW.H
    $(cc) $(comp) MENUDRAW.C

MENUDRAW.EXE : MENUDRAW.OBJ MENUDRAW.DEF MENUDRAW.RES
    link.exe @MENUDRAW.LNK
    rc.exe /30 $*
```

Understanding the MenuDraw Source Code

Custom Check Boxes

This one's pretty easy. The only thing you do special here is in the `WM_CREATE` message handler. There, you load the bitmaps you want to use for your custom check marks, and then use the `SetMenuItemBitmaps()` call to set them for two of your menu entries ("Custom Check 1" and "Custom Check 2"). Using the check marks is identical to using standard check marks—in the `WM_COMMAND` code you make no distinction between custom check marks and regular check marks; they all get handled by the `CheckMenuItem()` call.

Bitmaps

Bitmaps are even easier than custom check marks—actually, for the demo app, I cheated. I used WindowsMaker Pro to load the bitmaps in, because one of the options in WindowsMaker Pro when creating a menu item is to have that menu item be a bitmap. If you specify bitmap, you can then specify what bitmap you want, and WindowsMaker Pro generates all the code you need to support the bitmap.

This code is in the MenuDraw.wmc file. If you look, you can see it's doing the same thing you would: loading a bitmap, doing a `ModifyMenu()` call on the specified menu entry to set that entry to a bitmap, and passing in the handle of the just-loaded image.

Owner Draw

In the `WM_CREATE` message, you create a new pop-up with the `MF_OWNERDRAW` attribute. You then stick the new pop-up handle into the second slot in your menu. (If you look in the .rc file, notice there's a menu-entry placeholder that has the text string "OwnerDraw" in it.) Then you add some owner-draw menu entries to this new pop-up with the `AppendMenu()` call.

The next bit is the `WM_MEASUREITEM` message, which lets you specify how big your bitmaps are. Note that I'm using the trick I mentioned earlier, of subtracting the check-mark size out of the size so that Windows won't create the whitespace for the check mark. Actually, it *does* create the whitespace; it's just that you fill it up, because your bitmap is bigger than Windows thinks it is.

Also note that if you don't recognize the menu entry from the `itemID` parameter, you should check the `itemData` parameter. This is because you're stuffing a unique ID into that area, when you first do the `ModifyMenu()` call. As I mentioned earlier, this enables you to easily add an ID to all your pop-up menus (or at least all the owner-draw ones).

The final bit is the `WM_DRAWITEM` message, which looks very similar to the `WM_DRAWITEM` handler for bitmap buttons. Thus, you get the ID of the object being drawn, and then simply display a bitmap, based on that ID. Note that here, too, I'm using the `itemData` field to check for the pop-up IDs.

Note that the TearOffs menu has two entries, standard and custom. The standard tear-off is a text pop-up menu. It gets created in the `WM_CREATE` message handler, where you create a pop-up handle and put it into the local variable `hTearOff`. Then when the user selects the standard tear-off, you simply stick that menu handle into the `TrackPopupMenu()` call.

For custom tear-offs, you stick the `hPopUp` menu handle into the `TrackPopupMenu()` call. This is the pop-up handle of your owner-draw menu, which means all the stuff for the owner-draw menu happens automatically for your tear-off. When you run the app and select Custom from the TearOffs menu, it looks as though it's the same menu being displayed as under the Menu (your owner-draw pop-up) entry. In fact, it *is* the same menu being displayed. Furthermore, because it's the same menu, it generates the same messages, which are responded to the same way. This means tear-offs are essentially free when you've got the code to support the normal form of the menu. (Try it and see. Select Bark from either the tear-off or the standard Menu entry—in either case, a message box comes up that says "Woof! Woof! Woof!" in it!)

Tracking the pop-up is a bit interesting; you do this in response to the WM_LBUTTONDOWN message, which is a left mouse down. When the user clicks, you pop the appropriate pop-up menu at the mouse point. Remember, though, the WM_LBUTTONDOWN returns the current mouse position with respect to your *client* window, whereas the `TrackPopupMenu()` call expects the position it gets to be in *screen* coordinates. This is why you use the function `ClientToScreen()` to convert one to the other.

Summary

Menus provide a broad array of tools for interacting with the user. It's no wonder they do, because menus are one of the primary ways users interact with applications. It's important, then, to be able to use menus in a useful fashion, by providing the user with feedback on what has happened and what that means.

To this end, several things can be done with menus. You can place (or remove) a check mark next to a menu, as well as alter the text in the menu entry itself. You can also gray-out a menu selection, which gives that menu a different visual attribute, as well as making it no longer selectable by the user.

For more sophisticated menu handling, you can create on-the-fly menus, as well as change the visual attributes of a menu. You can change the bitmap used as a check mark, as well as substitute the standard text menu for a graphics one by making the menu a bitmap.

You can go even further and make the menu an owner-draw object, at which point you can do just about anything you can think up in visual terms. Of course, you also have to support the owner-draw menus yourself, because Windows no longer paints them for you. Finally, you can add to your application the capability to track free-floating, or tear-off, menus by using the `TrackPopupMenu()` call.

Function Reference

The following list of functions does not cover all menuing functions, but lists those you are most likely to use day-to-day in menuing. In particular, it lists functions that are harder to put into use, as well as those whose parameters might have changed from 3.0 to 3.1.

AppendMenu()

```
BOOL AppendMenu(    HMENU       hMenu,
                    WORD        mFlags,
                    WORD        idNewItem,
                    LPSTR       lpNewItem)
```

WHAT IT DOES:

Appends a menu item to the end of the menu specified by hMenu. The type and state of the new item is specified by the mFlags parameter.

PARAMETERS:

hMenu   Handle of the menu to append the item to.

mFlags   Specifies the state of the new menu entry. See the lpNewItem entry for details.

idNewItem   Specifies the ID of the new menu item. If mFlags is set to MF_POPUP, this field specifies the menu handle of the pop-up menu.

lpNewItem   Specifies the contents of the new menu item. The interpretation of this value is dependent on the setting in the mFlags parameter.

mFlags	lpNewItem is
MF_STRING	A long pointer to the text string of the menu entry.
MF_BITMAP	A handle to the bitmap for the menu entry. (The handle is in the low-order word. NULL should be in the high-order word.)

MF_OWNERDRAW   A pointer to an application-supplied 32-bit value. This value is used to maintain additional information about the menu item, and is typically a long pointer to an application-created data structure. When the application receives the WM_MEASUREITEM or WM_DRAWITEM messages, this value is passed back in the itemData member of the structure pointed to by lParam. This enables your application to create a private data structure, hook it to a menu item, and then forget about it—you can retrieve the data when you receive one of these two messages.

WHAT IT RETURNS:

TRUE if the function is successful, and FALSE otherwise.

THINGS TO WATCH FOR:

☐ When you change a menu using this function, you should call the **DrawMenuBar()** function. This is true even if the particular window that the menu entry is in is not visible. Failure to do this can cause the menu to be improperly updated or not updated at all.

☐ Several sets of flags are available for the mFlags parameter. Each set of flags is mutually exclusive (meaning you can't use more than one of them). Listed next are the various settings; in addition, they are grouped by mutual exclusivity.

MF_BITMAP—Uses a bitmap for the menu entry. The low-order word of lpNewItem contains the handle of the bitmap. Mutually exclusive with MF_STRING and MF_OWNERDRAW.

MF_OWNERDRAW—Specifies that the menu entry is an owner-draw item (meaning you get to draw it). Very similar in effect to an owner-draw button, in that your application receives a WM_DRAWITEM message each time the entry needs to be drawn. In addition, when the menu is displayed for the first time, your application receives a WM_MEASUREITEM message immediately before the menu is displayed for the *first* time, so you can inform Windows of the width and height of the entry. Mutually exclusive with MF_STRING and MF_BITMAP.

MF_STRING—Specifies that the menu entry is a text string. This is the standard kind of menu entry. In this case, lpNewItem is a pointer to the string that's inserted into the menu entry. Mutually exclusive with MF_BITMAP and MF_OWNERDRAW.

MF_DISABLED—Specifies that the menu entry is unavailable for use (and does not generate a message back to your application), but it is not grayed. Mutually exclusive with MF_ENABLED and MF_GRAYED.

MF_ENABLED—Specifies that the menu entry is available. Mutually exclusive with MF_DISABLED and MF_GRAYED.

MF_GRAYED—Specifies that the menu entry is unavailable for use (and does not generate a message back to your application). In addition, the text string for the menu entry (if the menu entry is, in fact, a text string) is displayed in a lightened gray state. If the menu entry is an owner-draw item, the itemState of the DRAWITEMSTRUCT is set to ODS_GRAYED. Mutually exclusive with MF_ENABLED and MF_DISABLED.

MF_MENUBARBREAK—For static menu-bar items, places the item on a new line. For pop-up menus, places the item in a new column and divides the columns with a vertical line. Mutually exclusive with MF_MENUBREAK.

MF_MENUBREAK—For static menu-bar items, places the item on a new line. For pop-up menus, places the item in a new column with no dividing line between the columns. Mutually exclusive with MF_MENUBARBREAK.

MF_CHECKED—Places a check mark next to the item. If the application has supplied check-mark bitmaps (see **SetMenuItemBitmaps()**), the supplied bitmap check mark is displayed next to the menu entry. Mutually exclusive with MF_UNCHECKED.

MF_UNCHECKED—Displays no check mark next to the menu entry. (This is the default.) If the application has supplied check-mark bitmaps (see **SetMenuItemBitmaps()**), the supplied bitmap indicating "no check" is displayed next to the menu entry. Mutually exclusive with MF_CHECKED.

Additionally, the mFlags parameter can have the following two values set:

MF_POPUP—Specifies that the menu item has a pop-up menu associated with it. The idNewItem parameter specifies the handle of the pop-up menu to be associated with the item (meaning, of course, you have to have created the pop-up menu in advance of trying to append it here). This flag is used for adding either a top-level menu pop-up (that is, a menu entry in the main menu bar) or a drag-right menu pop-up.

MF_SEPARATOR—Draws a horizontal dividing line above the menu item. This flag can be used only in a pop-up menu. The line cannot be grayed, disabled, or highlighted. If this flag is set, the `idNewItem` and `lpNewItem` parameters are ignored.

SEE ALSO:

```
CreateMenu()
DeleteMenu()
DrawMenuBar()
InsertMenu()
RemoveMenu()
SetMenuItemBitmaps()
```

CheckMenuItem()

```
BOOL CheckMenuItem(    HMENU      hMenu,
                       WORD       idCheckItem,
                       WORD       checkStyle)
```

WHAT IT DOES:

Places or removes a check mark from a menu entry in a pop-up menu.

PARAMETERS:

hMenu	Handle to the menu containing the entry.
idCheckItem	ID of the menu entry to be checked or unchecked.
checkStyle	Specifies how the menu entry is being specified, and what action should be taken. See the "Things to watch for" section for more information.

WHAT IT RETURNS:

The previous state of the menu item, either MF_CHECKED or MF_UNCHECKED. It returns a − 1 if the menu entry doesn't exist. (This makes the prototype return value of BOOL somewhat misleading, eh?)

THINGS TO WATCH FOR:

▪ The checkStyle parameter can have the following flag settings, which are OR'd together. Note that only one of each of the two sets of settings can be used at a time.

MF_BYCOMMAND—idCheckItem contains the menu-item identifier of the menu entry (that is, the ID passed in with the **AppendMenu()** function or created with a dialog editor). This is the default setting. Mutually exclusive with MF_BYPOSITION.

MF_BYPOSITION—idCheckItem contains the *offset* of the particular menu item in the menu. The first item in a menu is zero. For example, if this flag is set and idCheckItem contains a 4, this command affects the fourth menu entry in the specified menu. Mutually exclusive with MF_BYCOMMAND.

MF_CHECKED—Places a check mark next to the item. If the application has supplied check-mark bitmaps (see **SetMenuItemBitmaps()**), the supplied bitmap check mark is displayed next to the menu entry. Mutually exclusive with MF_UNCHECKED.

MF_UNCHECKED—Clears the check mark from the menu entry. If the application has supplied check-mark bitmaps (see **SetMenuItemBitmaps()**), the supplied bitmap indicating "no check" is displayed next to the menu entry. Mutually exclusive with MF_CHECKED.

You can check not only individual menu entries, but pop-up menus as well (that is, drag-right menus). When you want to put a check mark next to a drag-right menu, you have to specify the menu entry by position, because pop-up menus do not have identifiers associated with them.

Top-level menu entries (that is, menu-bar entries) cannot have check marks.

SEE ALSO:

GetMenuState()
SetMenuItemBitmaps()

CreateMenu()

HMENU **CreateMenu**(void)

WHAT IT DOES:

Creates an empty menu and returns a handle to it.

PARAMETERS:

None

WHAT IT RETURNS:

A handle to the new menu, or NULL if a menu cannot be created.

THINGS TO WATCH FOR:

☐ If the menu is not hooked to a window when your application shuts down, you must free the system resources used by the menu with the `DestroyMenu()` function. This is unnecessary if the menu is hooked to a window, because Windows automatically deletes any menu associated with a window when the window is deleted.

☐ To insert menu entries into a created menu, use the `AppendMenu()` or `InsertMenu()` functions.

SEE ALSO:

`AppendMenu()`
`DestroyMenu()`
`InsertMenu()`
`SetMenu()`

CreatePopupMenu()

HMENU **CreatePopupMenu**(void)

WHAT IT DOES:

Creates and returns a handle to an empty pop-up menu.

PARAMETERS:

None

WHAT IT RETURNS:

A handle to the new pop-up menu, or NULL if the menu cannot be created.

THINGS TO WATCH FOR:

☐ To insert menu entries into a created menu, use the `AppendMenu()` or `InsertMenu()` functions.

☐ There are two ways to use a pop-up menu. One way is to use `AppendMenu()` or `InsertMenu()` to put the pop-up menu into a standard menu in a window. The other is to use `TrackPopupMenu()` to track the entries of the pop-up yourself.

☐ As with a standard menu, if the pop-up menu is not hooked to a window when your application shuts down, you must free the system resources it uses by the `DestroyMenu()` function. This is unnecessary if the menu is hooked to a window, because Windows automatically deletes any menu (and child pop-ups) associated with a window when the window is deleted.

SEE ALSO:

```
AppendMenu()
CreateMenu()
InsertMenu()
SetMenu()
TrackPopupMenu()
```

DeleteMenu()

```
BOOL DeleteMenu(    HMENU       hMenu,
                    WORD        idItem,
                    WORD        mFlags)
```

WHAT IT DOES:

Somewhat of a misnomer, this function actually deletes an *item* from a menu. If the menu item being deleted has a pop-up associated with it (that is, the menu item is a menu-bar entry or a drag-right entry), this function also deletes the pop-up menu and frees the memory associated with it.

PARAMETERS:

hMenu   Handle to the menu that contains the item to be deleted

idItem   Menu item to be deleted

mFlags   Flags that govern the behavior of this function (see "Things to watch for" for details)

WHAT IT RETURNS:

TRUE if the function is successful, and FALSE otherwise.

THINGS TO WATCH FOR:

The mFlags parameter can be set to one of the following values:

MF_BYCOMMAND—idItem contains the menu-item identifier of the menu entry (that is, the ID passed in by the **AppendMenu()** function or created with a dialog editor). This is the default setting. Mutually exclusive with MF_BYPOSITION.

MF_BYPOSITION—idItem contains the *offset* of the particular menu item in the menu. The first item in a menu is zero. For example, if this flag is set, and idItem contains a 3, this command affects the third menu entry in the specified menu. Mutually exclusive with MF_BYCOMMAND.

When you change a menu using this function, you should call the DrawMenuBar() function. This is true even if the particular window the menu entry is in is not visible. Failure to do this can cause the menu to be improperly updated or not updated at all.

SEE ALSO:

AppendMenu()
CreateMenu()
DrawMenuBar()
InsertMenu()
RemoveMenu()

DestroyMenu()

BOOL **DestroyMenu**(hMenu)

WHAT IT DOES:

Destroys the menu specified by the hMenu parameter and frees any memory used by the menu.

PARAMETER:

hMenu   Handle of the menu to be destroyed

WHAT IT RETURNS:

TRUE if the menu is destroyed, and FALSE if it isn't.

THINGS TO WATCH FOR:

At application shut-down time, you do not need to call this function if the menu in question is hooked to a window, because Windows automatically destroys any menu associated with a window.

SEE ALSO:

CreateMenu()

DrawMenuBar()

void **DrawMenuBar**(HWND   hWnd)

WHAT IT DOES:

Causes the menu bar of the window in question to be redrawn. You must call this function after you have changed menu entries, or modified the menu in some other fashion, for the changes to appear.

PARAMETER:

hWnd   Window handle whose menu should be redrawn

WHAT IT RETURNS:

Nothing.

THINGS TO WATCH FOR:

It isn't necessary to call this function after each change you make to a menu. Typically, your application does quite a bit of menu manipulation in response to the WM_INITMENU message, and calling this function after each change would significantly slow things down. It is enough to ensure that this function is called once before you display the new menu states.

SEE ALSO:

CheckMenuItem()
EnableMenuItem()
SetMenuItemBitmaps()

EnableMenuItem()

BOOL **EnableMenuItem**(HMENU   hMenu,
                      WORD   idEnableItem,
                      WORD   mEnable)

WHAT IT DOES:

Enables, disables, or grays a menu entry in the specified menu.

PARAMETERS:

hMenu   Specifies the menu containing the menu entry.

idEnableItem	Specifies the item to be enabled or disabled.
mEnable	Specifies the manner in which the item is enabled or disabled, as well as how the menu item is being specified.

WHAT IT RETURNS:

0 if the menu item was previously disabled, 1 if the item was previously enabled, or – 1 if the menu item doesn't exist.

THINGS TO WATCH FOR:

☐ The mEnable parameter specifies both what should be done to the menu entry (enable it, disable it, or gray it) and how the menu entry is being specified in the idEnableItem parameter (either by command or by position). You can OR together one flag of each type from the following sets of flags. Within each set, the flags are mutually exclusive.

MF_DISABLED—The menu entry is made unavailable for use (and does not generate a message back to your application when the user moves the mouse over it), but it is not grayed. Mutually exclusive with MF_ENABLED and MF_GRAYED.

MF_ENABLED—The menu entry is made available. Mutually exclusive with MF_DISABLED and MF_GRAYED.

MF_GRAYED—The menu entry is made unavailable for use (and does not generate a message back to your application). In addition, the text string for the menu entry (if the menu entry is, in fact, a text string) is displayed in a lightened gray state. If the menu entry is an owner-draw item, the itemState of the DRAWITEMSTRUCT is set to ODS_GRAYED. Mutually exclusive with MF_ENABLED and MF_DISABLED.

MF_BYCOMMAND—idEnableItem contains the menu-item identifier of the menu entry (that is, the ID passed in by the **AppendMenu()** function or created with a dialog editor). This is the default setting. Mutually exclusive with MF_BYPOSITION.

MF_BYPOSITION—idEnableItem contains the *offset* of the particular menu item in the menu. The first item in a menu is zero. For example, if this flag is set and idEnableItem contains a 6, this command affects the sixth menu entry in the specified menu. Mutually exclusive with MF_BYCOMMAND.

To set the state of a top-level menu entry (that is, an entry in the menu bar), you need to specify the menu bar handle of the window's menu bar, which can be gotten in the following fashion:

```
hMenuBarMenu = GetMenu ( hWnd );
```

Here `hWnd` is the window handle of your application's main window (or the window that has the menu bar you're interested in). Additionally, you need to specify the menu item by *position,* because pop-up menus don't have menu IDs. For example, the following code fragment would gray the fourth menu bar entry in a menu bar:

```
hMenuBarMenu = GetMenu ( hWnd );         // Get handle to the menu
                                         // bar...

EnableMenuItem (        hMenuBarMenu,  // Disable the fourth menu
                        4,
                        MF_BYPOSITION | MF_GRAYED );

DrawMenuBar ( hWnd );                    // Update menu bar to reflect
                                         // changes...
```

The `CreateMenu()`, `InsertMenu()`, `LoadMenuIndirect()`, and `ModifyMenu()` functions also can set the state of a menu item.

To set the state of a pop-up menu entry (that is, a drag-right menu), you must use the `MF_BYPOSITION` setting and correctly specify the menu handle of the parent pop-up. For example, to gray a drag-right menu that is the third menu entry in a first-level drop-down menu (the pop-up menu of a menu bar menu), you must specify the menu handle of the pop-up menu, the value 3, and the settings `MF_BYPOSITION` and `MF_GRAYED`, like this:

```
EnableMenuItem (    parentPopMenu,
                    3,
                    MF_BYPOSITION | MF_GRAYED );
```

When using the `MF_BYCOMMAND` flag, Windows walks all child pop-up menus of the menu handle specified. This means if all of your menu entries have unique menu IDs, you can (for all standard menu entries) simply specify the menu handle of the main menu bar and the function works. If you have duplicate menu IDs (which isn't a good idea anyway), you must specify the menu handle of the particular pop-up menu you're interested in.

SEE ALSO:

```
CheckMenuItem()
HiliteMenuItem()
```

621

GetMenu()

HMENU **GetMenu**(HWND hWnd)

WHAT IT DOES:

Gets the main menu handle of the window specified by hWnd.

PARAMETER:

hWnd   Handle of the window whose menu is to be retrieved

WHAT IT RETURNS:

The menu handle of the menu associated with the window, or NULL if the window doesn't have a menu. This value is undefined if the window is a child window. (Can you say "Spurious UAEs?" Sure you can! <grin>)

THINGS TO WATCH FOR:

This function is used only for top-level menus (that is, the main menu bar) of a window. To get the pop-up menu of a menu item, use the **GetSubMenu()** call.

SEE ALSO:

GetSubMenu()
SetMenu()

GetMenuCheckMarkDimensions()

DWORD **GetMenuCheckMarkDimensions**(void)

WHAT IT DOES:

Returns the size of the default check-mark bitmap. This is the bitmap that Windows displays next to menu entries set to MF_CHECKED.

PARAMETERS:

None

WHAT IT RETURNS:

A DWORD, specifying the size of the bitmap used for the check mark. The high-order word contains the height, and the low-order word contains the width. Both values are in pixels.

```
cmHeight = HIWORD ( GetMenuCheckMarkDimensions() );
cmWidth = LOWORD ( GetMenuCheckMarkDimensions() );
```

THINGS TO WATCH FOR:

Before calling the **SetMenuItemBitmaps()** to replace the check-mark bitmaps, your application should call this function to find out what size the check mark should be. You should then scale your bitmaps accordingly.

SEE ALSO:

SetMenuItemBitmaps()

GetMenuItemCount()

```
int GetMenuItemCount(    HMENU    hMenu)
```

WHAT IT DOES:

Determines the number of menu entries in a pop-up or top-level menu.

PARAMETER:

hMenu   Handle to the menu you want an item count for

WHAT IT RETURNS:

The number of items in the menu if the function is successful, and – 1 if the function fails.

THINGS TO WATCH FOR:

None.

SEE ALSO:

GetMenu()
GetMenuItemID()
GetSubMenu()

GetMenuItemID()

```
WORD GetMenuItemID(    HMENU    hMenu,
                       int      menuPos)
```

WHAT IT DOES:

Retrieves the menu item ID of the menu item at the specified position in the menu.

PARAMETERS:

hMenu   Menu handle of the menu to retrieve the ID of the particular entry from

menuPos   Position within the menu of the desired item (zero-based)

WHAT IT RETURNS:

The ID of the specified menu item if the function is successful. If hMenu is NULL, or if the specified item is a pop-up menu itself (that is, the item is a drag-right menu), the return value is −1. If the item specified by menuPos is a SEPARATOR menu item, the return value is 0.

THINGS TO WATCH FOR:

This function can be used to determine whether the menu item in question is a drag-right menu by checking the return value for −1.

SEE ALSO:

```
GetMenu()
GetMenuItemCount()
GetSubMenu()
```

GetMenuState()

```
WORD GetMenuState(    HMENU    hMenu,
                      WORD     idItem,
                      WORD     mFlags)
```

WHAT IT DOES:

Gets the current status of the specified menu entry. If the menu entry is a pop-up menu, this function also returns the number of items in the pop-up.

PARAMETERS:

hMenu   Handle to the menu that contains the item you're interested in

idItem   Menu ID of the menu entry you're interested in

mFlags   The format of idItem (see the "Things to watch for" section)

WHAT IT RETURNS:

If the specified menu entry doesn't exist, the return value is −1. If idItem specifies a pop-up menu, the high-order byte specifies the number of items in the pop-up menu. The low-order byte always contains a set of flags that indicate the status of the menu item. The flag settings are OR'd together. The individual flag bits are

MF_BITMAP	Item is a bitmap.
MF_CHECKED	Item has a check mark (not applicable to top-level menus).
MF_DISABLED	Item is disabled (but not grayed).
MF_ENABLED	Item is enabled (this constant is defined as zero, which means you can't test for this value (or even use it as a mask), because it won't work.
MF_GRAYED	Item is disabled and grayed.
MF_MENUBARBREAK	Item starts a new column; column is separated by a vertical line.
MF_MENUBREAK	Item starts a new column; column has no line separating it.
MF_SEPARATOR	Horizontal dividing line is drawn. Separators cannot be enabled, checked, grayed, or highlighted.
MF_UNCHECKED	Item does not have a check mark next to it. (This constant is also defined as zero, which means again that you cannot test directly for it.)

THINGS TO WATCH FOR:

The mFlags parameter can be set to one of the following values:

MF_BYCOMMAND—idItem contains the menu-item identifier of the menu entry (that is, the ID passed in by the **AppendMenu()** function or created with a dialog editor). This is the default setting. Mutually exclusive with MF_BYPOSITION.

MF_BYPOSITION—idItem contains the *offset* of the particular menu item in the menu. The first item in a menu is zero. For example, if this flag is set and idItem contains a 3, this command affects the third menu entry in the specified menu. Mutually exclusive with MF_BYCOMMAND.

SEE ALSO:

```
GetMenu()
GetMenuItemCount()
GetSubMenu()
```

GetMenuString()

```
int GetMenuString(  HMENU    hMenu,
                    WORD     idItem,
                    LPSTR    nameBuff,
                    int      buffMax,
                    WORD     mFlags)
```

WHAT IT DOES:

Copies the text string of a menu entry into a buffer.

PARAMETERS:

hMenu   Handle to the menu that contains the menu entry you want

idItem   ID of the menu entry you want

nameBuff   Pointer to the buffer the name is placed into

buffMax   Maximum length of the string that can be placed in the buffer

mFlags   How the idItem field should be interpreted

WHAT IT RETURNS:

The length, in bytes, of the string that was put into the buffer pointed to by nameBuff. The length does not include the NULL terminator.

THINGS TO WATCH FOR:

▢ mFlags governs how the idItem field is interpreted. mFlags can be one of the following:

MF_BYCOMMAND—idItem contains the menu-item identifier of the menu entry (that is, the ID passed in by the **AppendMenu()** function, or created with a dialog editor). This is the default setting. Mutually exclusive with MF_BYPOSITION.

MF_BYPOSITION—idItem contains the *offset* of the particular menu item in the menu. The first item in a menu is zero. For example, if this flag is set, and idItem contains a 6, this command affects the sixth menu entry in the specified menu. Mutually exclusive with MF_BYCOMMAND.

buffMax should be set to one larger than the largest desired text string to allow for the NULL terminator (which, remember, is not counted in the return value).

SEE ALSO:

GetMenu()
GetMenuItemID()

GetSubMenu()

```
HMENU GetSubMenu(    HMENU    hMenu,
                     int      nPos)
```

WHAT IT DOES:

Gets the menu handle of a pop-up menu inside of the menu specified by hMenu.

PARAMETERS:

hMenu   Handle to the menu that contains the pop-up menu

nPos   Position of the menu entry that contains the pop-up menu. Menu entries are zero-based.

WHAT IT RETURNS:

A handle to the pop-up menu, or NULL if the specified position isn't a pop-up menu entry.

THINGS TO WATCH FOR:

This function represents the only way your application can retrieve the handle to a menu that isn't the top-level menu of your application.

SEE ALSO:

CreatePopupMenu()
GetMenu()

GetSystemMenu()

```
HMENU GetSystemMenu(    HWND      hWnd,
                        BOOL      mnReset )
```

WHAT IT DOES:

GetSystemMenu() enables you to access the System menu for copying and modification.

PARAMETERS:

hWnd   Window handle that owns a copy of the System menu

mnReset   Specifies the action to be taken:

FALSE—Function returns a handle to a copy of the System menu currently being used. The copy is initially identical to the System menu, but your application can modify it.

TRUE—Function resets the System menu to its default state. The previous System menu (if any) is destroyed, and all resources associated with it are freed.

WHAT IT RETURNS:

If mnReset is FALSE, the return is a handle to a copy of the System menu. If mnReset is TRUE, the return value is undefined.

THINGS TO WATCH FOR:

■ If your application does not use the **GetSystemMenu()** function, it receives the standard System menu.

■ You can use the handle returned by this function in the **AppendMenu()**, **InsertMenu()**, and **ModifyMenu()** functions to change the menu entries of the System menu. The initial System menu entries have menu-entry IDs based on the possible values of the message to WM_SYSCOMMAND (that is, SC_CLOSE, SC_MOVE, SC_SIZE, and so on). Menu entries on the System menu send WM_SYSCOMMAND messages when touched, rather than WM_COMMAND messages. Any menu entries you add also send WM_SYSCOMMAND messages, and not WM_COMMAND messages. In addition, all predefined System menu entries have IDs of greater than 0xF000. This means your menu-entry IDs for the system menu should be less than 0xF000. Furthermore, the low four bits of the wParam message in a WM_SYSCOMMAND message are used internally by Windows, and should be masked off by your application when responding to this message—this means that your menu-entry IDs for System menus must not be different only in the low four bits. That is, menu-entry IDs of 0x1F00 and 0x2F00 are able to be distinguished by the WM_SYSCOMMAND message; menu-entry IDs of 0x1F00 and 0x1F01 are not.

You can set up menu entries in the System menu just as you do regular menu entries, by the WM_INITMENU message. There is no separate message for initializing System menu entries.

SEE ALSO:

```
AppendMenu()
InsertMenu()
ModifyMenu()
```

HiliteMenuItem()

```
BOOL HiliteMenuItem(    HWND     hWnd,
                        HMENU    hMenu,
                        WORD     idItem,
                        WORD     mFlags )
```

WHAT IT DOES:

Adds or removes a highlight from a top-level (that is, menu bar) menu item.

PARAMETERS:

hWnd	Window handle of the window that contains the menu bar
hMenu	Menu handle that contains the menu entry to highlight
idItem	Menu entry that you want to highlight
mFlags	What you want to do to the menu entry (see the "Things to watch for" section)

WHAT IT RETURNS:

TRUE if the function is successful, and FALSE otherwise.

THINGS TO WATCH FOR:

mFlags can have one each of the two following sets of flags. One set of flags specifies how the item is to be highlighted or unhighlighted, and the other specifies how you are specifying the menu entry.

MF_BYCOMMAND—idItem contains the menu-item identifier of the menu entry (that is, the ID passed in by the **AppendMenu()** function, or created with a dialog editor). This is the default setting. Mutually exclusive with MF_BYPOSITION.

MF_BYPOSITION—idItem contains the *offset* of the particular menu item in the menu. The first item in a menu is zero. For example, if this flag is set, and idItem contains a 6, this command affects the sixth menu entry in the specified menu. Mutually exclusive with MF_BYCOMMAND.

MF_HILITE—The menu item is highlighted. If this value is not specified, the highlight is removed from the menu item. Mutually exclusive with MF_UNHILITE.

MF_UNHILITE—Removes the highlight from the menu item. Mutually exclusive with MF_HILITE.

The MF_HILITE and MF_UNHILITE flags can only be used with this function call. They cannot be used with the **ModifyMenu()** function.

SEE ALSO:

```
CheckMenuItem()
EnableMenuItem()
ModifyMenu()
```

InsertMenu()

```
BOOL InsertMenu(    HMENU       hMenu,
                    WORD        idItem,
                    WORD        mFlags,
                    WORD        idNewItem,
                    WORD        lpNewItem)
```

WHAT IT DOES:

Inserts a new menu entry into a menu, moving other menu entries below the insertion point down. It also sets the initial state of the new menu entry.

PARAMETERS:

hMenu	Handle of the menu.
idItem	ID of current menu entry you want to place the new entry *before*.
mFlags	Specifies how idItem is interpreted, and what the state of the new menu entry should be.

idNewItem   ID of the new menu entry.

lpNewItem   32-bit quantity which can be used to associate additional data with the menu entry. The interpretation of lpNewItem is governed by the setting of mFlags.

mFlags	lpNewItem is
MF_STRING	A long pointer to the text string of the menu entry.
MF_BITMAP	A handle to the bitmap for the menu entry (the handle is in the low-order word, NULL should be in the high-order word).
MF_OWNERDRAW	A pointer to an application-supplied 32-bit value. This value is used to maintain additional information about the menu item, and is typically a long pointer to an application-created data structure. When the application receives the WM_MEASUREITEM or WM_DRAWITEM messages, this value is passed back in the itemData member of the structure pointed to by lParam. This enables your application to create a private data structure, hook it to a menu item, and then forget about it—you can retrieve the data when you receive the WM_MEASUREITEM or WM_DRAWITEM messages.

WHAT IT RETURNS:

TRUE if the function is successful, and FALSE otherwise.

THINGS TO WATCH FOR:

▢ mFlags governs the interpretation of the idItem field, as well as specifying the initial state of the new menu entry. It can have one flag from each of one or more of the following sets:

MF_BYCOMMAND—idItem contains the menu-item identifier of the menu entry (that is, the ID passed in by the **AppendMenu()** function, or created with a dialog editor). This is the default setting. Mutually exclusive with MF_BYPOSITION.

MF_BYPOSITION—idItem contains the *offset* of the particular menu item in the menu. The first item in a menu is zero. For example, if this flag is set,

and `idItem` contains a 6, this command affects the sixth menu entry in the specified menu. Mutually exclusive with `MF_BYCOMMAND`.

These flag settings govern how the new menu entry is going to appear. They are identical to the settings listed under the **AppendMenu()** call.

`MF_BITMAP`—Uses a bitmap for the menu entry. The low order word of `lpNewItem` contains the handle of the bitmap. Mutually exclusive with `MF_STRING` and `MF_OWNERDRAW`.

`MF_OWNERDRAW`—Specifies that the menu entry is an owner-draw item (meaning that you get to do it). Very similar in effect to an owner-draw button, in that your application receives a `WM_DRAWITEM` message each time the entry needs to be drawn. In addition, when the menu is displayed for the first time, your application receives a `WM_MEASUREITEM` message immediately before the menu is displayed for the *first* time, so you can inform Windows of the width and height of the entry. Mutually exclusive with `MF_STRING` and `MF_BITMAP`.

`MF_STRING`—Specifies that the menu entry is a text string. This is the standard kind of menu entry. In this case, `lpNewItem` is a pointer to the string that's going to be inserted into the menu entry. This setting is mutually exclusive with `MF_BITMAP` and `MF_OWNERDRAW`.

`MF_DISABLED`—The menu entry is unavailable for use (and does not generate a message back to your application), but it is *not* grayed. Mutually exclusive with `MF_ENABLED` and `MF_GRAYED`.

`MF_ENABLED`—The menu entry is available. Mutually exclusive with `MF_DISABLED` and `MF_GRAYED`.

`MF_GRAYED`—The menu entry is unavailable for use (and does not generate a message back to your application). In addition, the text string for the menu entry (if the menu entry is, in fact, a text string) is displayed in a lightened gray state. If the menu entry is an owner-draw item, the `itemState` of the `DRAWITEMSTRUCT` is set to `ODS_GRAYED`. Mutually exclusive with `MF_ENABLED` and `MF_DISABLED`.

`MF_MENUBARBREAK`—For static menu-bar items, places the item on a new line. For pop-up menus, places the item in a new column and divides the columns with a vertical line. Mutually exclusive with `MF_MENUBREAK`.

`MF_MENUBREAK`—For static menu-bar items, places the item on a new line. For pop-up menus, places the item in a new column with no dividing line between the columns. Mutually exclusive with `MF_MENUBARBREAK`.

MF_CHECKED—Places a check mark next to the item. If the application has supplied check-mark bitmaps (see **SetMenuItemBitmaps()**), the supplied bitmap check mark is displayed next to the menu entry. Mutually exclusive with MF_UNCHECKED.

MF_UNCHECKED—No check mark is displayed next to the menu entry. (This is the default.) If the application has supplied check-mark bitmaps (see **SetMenuItemBitmaps()**), the supplied bitmap indicating "no check" is displayed next to the menu entry. Mutually exclusive with MF_CHECKED.

Additionally, the mFlags parameter can have the following two values set:

MF_POPUP—The menu item has a pop-up menu associated with it. The idNewItem parameter specifies the handle of the pop-up menu to be associated with the item (meaning, of course, that you have to have created the pop-up menu in advance of trying to append it here). This flag is used for adding either a top-level menu pop-up (that is, a menu entry in the main menu bar), or a drag-right menu pop-up.

MF_SEPARATOR—Draws a horizontal dividing line above the menu item. This flag can only be used in a pop-up menu. The line cannot be grayed, disabled, or highlighted. If this flag is set, the idNewItem and lpNewItem parameters are ignored.

If this function is inserting a pop-up menu entry into an MDI application window using MF_BYPOSITION, and the child window of the MDI application is maximized, the menu is inserted one position farther left than expected. This occurs because the System menu of the active MDI child window is inserted into the first position of the MDI frame window's menu bar. To avoid this behavior, the application must add 1 to the position value that would otherwise be used. An application can use the WM_MDIGETACTIVE message to determine whether the currently-active child window is maximized.

Whenever you change a menu using this function, you should call the **DrawMenuBar()** function. This is true even if the particular window the menu entry is in is not visible. Failure to do this can cause the menu to be improperly updated (or not updated at all).

SEE ALSO:

AppendMenu()
CreateMenu()
DrawMenuBar()
RemoveMenu()
GetMenuItemBitmaps()

LoadMenu()

```
HMENU LoadMenu(    HINSTANCE    hInst,
                   LPSTR        lpMenuName)
```

WHAT IT DOES:

Loads a menu resource from the instance of the executable file specified by hInst.

PARAMETERS:

hInst   Handle to the instance of the application that contains the menu resource.

lpMenuName   Name of the menu to load. This can also be the numeric identifier of the menu, if the menu was created with a numeric ID. In this case, use the MAKEINTRESOURCE macro with the ID here.

WHAT IT RETURNS:

A handle to the menu, or NULL if the function fails.

THINGS TO WATCH FOR:

As with other resource load functions, this function works equally well with other application instances if you know the name of the menu ID. You can also use the handle returned by the **LoadLibrary()** function in the hInst parameter of this function.

SEE ALSO:

```
DestroyMenu()
SetMenu()
```

ModifyMenu()

```
BOOL ModifyMenu(    HMENU     hMenu,
                    WORD      idItem,
                    WORD      mFlags,
                    WORD      idNewItem,
                    LPVOID    lpNewItem)
```

WHAT IT DOES:

Changes an existing menu item.

PARAMETERS:

hMenu   Handle to the menu containing the menu entry to change.

idItem   Menu-entry ID of menu entry to change.

mFlags   How to change the entry.

idNewItem   ID of the new entry (if new menu is a pop-up, handle to the pop-up).

lpNewItem   32-bit quantity which can be used to associate additional data with the menu entry. The interpretation of lpNewItem is governed by the setting of mFlags.

mFlags	lpNewItem is
MF_STRING	A long pointer to the text string of the menu entry.
MF_BITMAP	A handle to the bitmap for the menu entry (the handle is in the low-order word, NULL should be in the high-order word).
MF_OWNERDRAW	A pointer to an application-supplied 32-bit value. This value is used to maintain additional information about the menu item, and is typically a long pointer to an application-created data structure. When the application receives the WM_MEASUREITEM or WM_DRAWITEM messages, this value is passed back in the itemData member of the structure pointed to by lParam. This enables your application to create a private data structure, hook it to a menu item, and then forget about it—you can retrieve the data when you receive the WM_MEASUREITEM or WM_DRAWITEM messages.

WHAT IT RETURNS:

TRUE if successful, and FALSE if it fails.

THINGS TO WATCH FOR:

Like some of the other menu functions, the mFlags parameter of **ModifyMenu()** can have different bit flags set. The possible values are

MF_BYCOMMAND—idItem contains the menu-item identifier of the menu entry (that is, the ID passed in by the **AppendMenu()** function, or created with a dialog editor). This is the default setting. Mutually exclusive with MF_BYPOSITION.

MF_BYPOSITION—idItem contains the *offset* of the particular menu item in the menu. The first item in a menu is zero. For example, if this flag were set, and idItem contained a 6, this command would affect the sixth menu entry in the specified menu. Mutually exclusive with MF_BYCOMMAND.

These flag settings govern how the new menu entry is going to appear. They are identical to the settings listed under the **AppendMenu()** call.

MF_BITMAP—Uses a bitmap for the menu entry. The low-order word of lpNewItem contains the handle of the bitmap. Mutually exclusive with MF_STRING and MF_OWNERDRAW.

MF_OWNERDRAW—Specifies that the menu entry is an owner-draw item (meaning that you get to do it). Very similar in effect to an owner-draw button, in that your application receives a WM_DRAWITEM message each time the entry needs to be drawn. In addition, when the menu is displayed for the first time, your application receives a WM_MEASUREITEM message immediately before the menu is displayed for the *first* time, so that you can inform Windows of the width and height of the entry. Mutually exclusive with MF_STRING and MF_BITMAP.

MF_STRING—Specifies that the menu entry is a text string. This is the standard kind of menu entry. In this case, lpNewItem is a pointer to the string that's going to be inserted into the menu entry. This setting is mutually exclusive with MF_BITMAP and MF_OWNERDRAW.

MF_DISABLED—The menu entry is unavailable for use (and does not generate a message back to your application), but it is *not* grayed. Mutually exclusive with MF_ENABLED and MF_GRAYED.

MF_ENABLED—The menu entry is available. Mutually exclusive with MF_DISABLED and MF_GRAYED.

MF_GRAYED—The menu entry is unavailable for use (and does not generate a message back to your application). In addition, the text string for the menu entry (if the menu entry is, in fact, a text string) is displayed in a lightened "gray" state. If the menu entry is an owner-draw item, the itemState of the DRAWITEMSTRUCT is set to ODS_GRAYED. Mutually exclusive with MF_ENABLED and MF_DISABLED.

MF_MENUBARBREAK—For static menu-bar items, places the item on a new line. For pop-up menus, places the item in a new column and divides the columns with a vertical line. Mutually exclusive with MF_MENUBREAK.

MF_MENUBREAK—For static menu-bar items, places the item on a new line. For pop-up menus, places the item in a new column with no dividing line between the columns. Mutually exclusive with MF_MENUBARBREAK.

MF_CHECKED—Places a check mark next to the item. If the application has supplied check-mark bitmaps (see **SetMenuItemBitmaps()**), the supplied bitmap check mark is displayed next to the menu entry. Mutually exclusive with MF_UNCHECKED.

MF_UNCHECKED—No check mark is displayed next to the menu entry. (This is the default.) If the application has supplied check-mark bitmaps (see **SetMenuItemBitmaps()**), the supplied bitmap indicating "no check" is displayed next to the menu entry. Mutually exclusive with MF_CHECKED.

Additionally, the mFlags parameter can have the following two values set:

MF_POPUP—The menu item has a pop-up menu associated with it. The idNewItem parameter specifies the handle of the pop-up menu to be associated with the item (meaning, of course, that you have to have created the pop-up menu in advance of trying to append it here). This flag is used for adding either a top-level menu pop-up (that is, a menu entry in the main menu bar), or a drag-right menu pop-up.

MF_SEPARATOR—Draws a horizontal dividing line above the menu item. This flag can only be used in a pop-up menu. The line cannot be grayed, disabled, or highlighted. If this flag is set, the idNewItem and lpNewItem parameters are ignored.

SEE ALSO:

```
CheckMenuItem()
DrawMenuBar()
EnableMenuItem()
SetMenuItemBitmaps()
```

RemoveMenu()

```
BOOL RemoveMenu(    HMENU    hMenu,
                    WORD     idItem,
                    WORD     mFlags )
```

```
HMENU hmenu;              /* handle of the menu       */
UINT idItem;              /* menu item to delete      */
UINT fuFlags;             /* menu flags               */
```

WHAT IT DOES:

Deletes a menu entry from a pop-up menu, but doesn't delete the pop-up menu handle. This enables your application to re-use the pop-up menu handle again (by refilling it with new items). This function is somewhat misnamed, and should really be called something like RemoveMenuItem.

PARAMETERS:

hMenu   Handle to the pop-up menu that contains the entry to remove

idItem   ID of the item to be deleted

mFlags   Flags governing the interpretation of the idItem field (see the "Things to watch for" section)

WHAT IT RETURNS:

TRUE if the function is successful, and FALSE if it fails.

THINGS TO WATCH FOR:

Before calling this function, your application should call the **GetSubMenu()** routine to retrieve the handle to the pop-up menu that you're interested in.

mFlags controls how the idItem field is interpreted in determining which menu entry to delete. It can have one of the two following values:

MF_BYCOMMAND—idItem contains the menu-item identifier of the menu entry (that is, the ID passed in by the **AppendMenu()** function, or created with a dialog editor). This is the default setting. Mutually exclusive with MF_BYPOSITION.

MF_BYPOSITION—idItem contains the *offset* of the particular menu item in the menu. The first item in a menu is zero. For example, if this flag were set, and idItem contained a 6, this command would affect the sixth menu entry in the specified menu. Mutually exclusive with MF_BYCOMMAND.

SEE ALSO:

```
AppendMenu()
CreateMenu()
DeleteMenu()
```

```
DrawMenuBar()
GetSubMenu()
InsertMenu()
```

SetMenu()

```
BOOL SetMenu(    HWND      hWnd,
                 HWND      hMenu)
```

WHAT IT DOES:

Sets the window specified by the hWnd parameter to the menu specified by the hMenu parameter.

PARAMETERS:

hWnd   Handle to the window whose menu you're setting

hMenu   Handle to the new menu for the window

WHAT IT RETURNS:

TRUE if the menu was changed, and FALSE if it wasn't.

THINGS TO WATCH FOR:

▢ SetMenu() automatically causes the window's menu bar to be redrawn to reflect the change in the menus.

▢ This function does *not* destroy any previously associated menu; your application must call the DestroyMenu() function to destroy an old menu. Note: Your application should not call DestroyMenu() until *after* you have replaced the old menu with the new menu.

SEE ALSO:

```
DestroyMenu()
LoadMenu()
```

SetMenuItemBitmaps()

```
BOOL SetMenuItemBitmaps(    HMENU     hMenu,
                            WORD      idItem,
                            WORD      mFlags,
                            HBITMAP   bmNoCheck,
                            HBITMAP   bmCheck )
```

WHAT IT DOES:

Associates the specified bitmaps with the specified menu item for checking and unchecking. Subsequent calls to `CheckMenuItem()` for this menu entry causes one of the two bitmaps to be displayed.

PARAMETERS:

hMenu   Menu handle of the menu containing the menu entry to change

idItem   ID of the menu entry that has the bitmaps hooked to it

mFlags   Governs how the `idItem` field is interpreted (see the "Things to watch for" section)

bmNoCheck   Handle to the bitmap representing the "unchecked" state

bmCheck   Handle to the bitmap representing the "checked" state

WHAT IT RETURNS:

TRUE if the function is successful, and FALSE otherwise.

THINGS TO WATCH FOR:

- `mFlags` controls how the `idItem` field is interpreted in determining which menu entry has the bitmaps associated with it. It can have one of the two following values:

  `MF_BYCOMMAND`—`idItem` contains the menu-item identifier of the menu entry (that is, the ID passed in by the `AppendMenu()` function, or created with a dialog editor). This is the default setting. Mutually exclusive with `MF_BYPOSITION`.

  `MF_BYPOSITION`—`idItem` contains the *offset* of the particular menu item in the menu. The first item in a menu is zero. For example, if this flag is set, and `idItem` contains a 6, this command affects the sixth menu entry in the specified menu. Mutually exclusive with `MF_BYCOMMAND`.

- If either `bmNoCheck` or `bmCheck` is NULL, Windows displays nothing next to the menu item during the appropriate state. (That is, if `bmNoCheck` is NULL, then when the menu entry is set to `MF_UNCHECKED`, Windows won't display any bitmap there.) If *both* fields are set to NULL, Windows uses the standard check-mark behavior (that is, it displays the default check mark next to the menu entry when it's checked, and displays nothing when it's unchecked).

■ When a menu is destroyed, any associated check-mark bitmaps are *not* destroyed. It's your application's responsibility to destroy them (usually in response to the WM_DESTROY message).

■ Before substituting your own check-mark bitmaps, you should call the GetMenuCheckMarkDimensions() function to determine the default width and height of a check mark. You should size your bitmaps accordingly.

SEE ALSO:

CheckMenuItem()
GetMenuCheckMarkDimensions()

TrackPopupMenu()

```
BOOL TrackPopupMenu(    HMENU     hMenu,
                        WORD      mFlags,
                        int       x,
                        int       y,
                        int       nReserved,
                        HWND      hWnd,
                        LPRECT    lpRect )
```

WHAT IT DOES:

Displays a floating pop-up menu at the specified location, and tracks the selection of items from the pop-up menu. Also known as a tear-off menu.

PARAMETERS:

hMenu	Handle of the pop-up menu to be used.
mFlags	Screen position and mouse button flags (see the "Things to watch for" section).
x	Horizontal position of the pop-up menu (governed by mFlags)
y	Specifies the upper edge of the position of the pop-up menu
nReserved	Reserved, must be set to 0.
hWnd	Window handle of window that owns the pop-up menu. This is important, because it's this window's message loop that receives messages regarding the menu.
lpRect	Pointer to a rectangle structure containing the upper-left and lower-right coordinates of the box within which the user

can click without dismissing the pop-up menu; if NULL, the menu is dismissed as soon as the user clicks outside the pop-up. (Windows 3.1 *only*.)

WHAT IT RETURNS:

TRUE if the function is successful, and FALSE otherwise.

THINGS TO WATCH FOR:

This function can either use a newly created pop-up menu (that is, `CreatePopupMenu()`) or it can use an already existing pop-up menu, retrieved by the `GetSubMenu()` call.

For Windows 3.0, the `mFlags` and `lpRect` fields are unused, and must be set to 0. The position of the pop-up menu under Windows 3.0 is that x and y define the upper-left corner of the point at which the menu appears.

For Windows 3.1, `mFlags` specifies a screen position setting and a mouse button setting. It can have one of each kind of flag, from the following sets of mutually exclusive values:

Alignment flags:

TPM_CENTERALIGN—Centers the pop-up menu horizontally relative to the coordinate specified by the x parameter.

TPM_LEFTALIGN—Positions the pop-up menu so that its left side is aligned with the coordinate specified by the x parameter.

TPM_RIGHTALIGN—Positions the pop-up menu so that its right side is aligned with the coordinate specified by the x parameter.

Mouse button flags:

TPM_LEFTBUTTON—Pop-up menu tracks the left mouse button.

TPM_RIGHTBUTTON—Pop-up menu tracks the right mouse button.

SEE ALSO:

```
CreatePopupMenu()
GetSubMenu()
```

ICE/Works:
A Brief
Introduction

ICE/Works is an icon editor designed for programmers, software engineers, graphics artists, and any others who find themselves needing a tool with which to create graphics images for MS Windows 3.0 programs. It provides a powerful editing engine for the creation of icons, cursors, and bitmaps, and it enables you to save them in the proper format for inclusion in your programs.

ICE/Works also incorporates an Icon Library Manager, which enables you to group icons together and save them in a library. The Icon Library Manager has the capability of importing these images from a variety of file formats. It supports the Windows Clipboard and gives you what I think is the most powerful set of image manipulation tools available anywhere.

To begin using ICE/Works, double-click the ICE/Works Icon (the silver diamond), or select **R**un Program from the **F**ile menu of Program Manager. (Users of alternative desktops should follow the manual's instructions for executing a program.) The first time you run ICE/Works, it comes up in Novice User mode. In this mode, you are warned about many types of actions that can alter or erase your work. As you become more familiar with the operation of ICE/Works, you can eliminate many of these warning messages by choosing the Expert User mode.

After ICE/Works begins execution, it displays the main editing window. This window, where you do most of your work, is broken into several areas. (See Figure A.1.)

ICE/Works has been designed so that objects that are logically related are physically grouped as well. For example, all the *Image Creation Tools* are grouped together in the lower-right section of the main window. This is because they all perform similar functions—they enable you to actually create pieces of the image that you're working on. The Image Creation Tools include the pencil, paint brush, paint can, spray can, linetool, circle tool, and rectangle tool. (The area select and mover tools are actually Image Editing Tools. They are grouped with the Image Creation Tools because they share the qualities of direct manipulation.) You can get started right away by single-clicking the left mouse button on the button representing the tool you want to use. In addition, double-clicking the paint brush, paint can, and spray can tools brings up the options for these tools. Use these options to determine how you want each of the tools to behave.

Figure A.1.
The ICE/Works
Pro main
window.

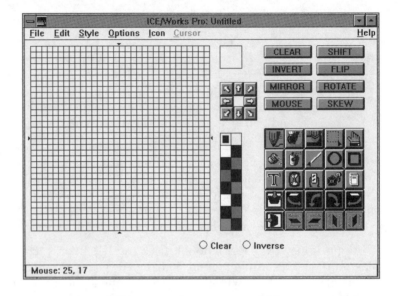

The *Image Editing Tools* are grouped as a stack of buttons above the Image Creation Tools. The Editing Tools do not create an image, but instead modify an already-existing image. Click the tool you want; most of the tools bring up a dialog box, enabling you to further define and control the action you want taken. Two of the Editing Tools (CLEAR and INVERT) do not bring up dialog boxes, but instead perform the requested action immediately.

The *Color Palette* enables you to select the color used by the Image Creation Tools, so it's located near them. Click the color you want used for subsequent graphics operations; the color you clicked shrinks into the center of its square, indicating that it has been chosen. (Note: When editing Icons, you also have two additional colors—Clear and Inverse—that you can use. These colors are available on the two radio buttons directly below the Color Palette.)

The *Fast Shift* buttons are located near the *Editing Grid* so that you can easily move an image around for accurate positioning. (More sophisticated positioning operations are available through the SHIFT Editing Tool.)

The *Menu Bar* has seven entries, each related to a different aspect of using ICE/Works Pro:

File	Commands for loading, saving, and managing icons
Edit	Commands for undoing, cutting, pasting, and snatching icon images
Style	Specifications for how ICE/Works Pro treats various editing tools

Options	Specifications for how ICE/Works Pro behaves under various circumstances
Icon	Editing options specific to icons
Cursor	Editing options specific to cursors
Help	Help with ICE/Works Pro

The final area is the *Editing Grid*. This is where you actually construct your images. Each of the large boxes corresponds to a single pixel in the final image, which is represented by the *Image Display,* which is the small box to the top-right of the edit window. Every time you manipulate one or more of the large pixels in the edit window, the corresponding change is reflected in the display window, enabling you to see how the resulting image is actually displayed.

You create images in ICE/Works by selecting an image creation tool and then using it to draw or paint in the editing grid. To get a feel for this, select the pencil tool by clicking it; the button appears to go down, indicating that it is selected. (If the pencil tool is already selected, clicking it will have no effect.) Move the cursor over to the color palette and choose a color. Now move the cursor into the editing grid; the cursor changes to the pencil cursor. To draw a single-pixel line in the selected color, simply press and hold down the left mouse button, and move the mouse. As you do so, each pixel the cursor crosses over is filled with the selected color. It's that easy! It's also easy to erase the selected color (that is, turn it back to white) by pressing the left mouse button while the cursor is over a pixel of the current color.

If you change from the pencil tool to the paint brush tool, you can see that the cursor changes shape also, from a pencil to a paint brush. Each of the Image Creation Tools has its own cursor. This lets you know at a glance which drawing mode you're in.

This is a brief introduction to ICE/Works; more information is available in the on-line help that comes with the package.

Index

D

K-L

M

N-O

P-Q

Installing the Disk

The accompanying disk contains the source code for the examples in the book, as well as a special version of ICE/Works, a sophisticated utility for creating icons, cursors, and bitmaps.

To install ICE/Works, copy the files in the \iceworks directory to your hard disk.

To install the source code, copy the file SOURCE.EXE to your hard disk. Run the self-extracting archive file by typing

```
source /x
```

> **Note:** It is very important to use the /x option to maintain the directory structure of the source code examples.

License Agreement

By opening this package, you are agreeing to be bound by the following agreement.

This software product is copyrighted, and all rights are reserved by the publisher and author. You are licensed to use this software on a single computer. You may copy and/or modify the software as needed to facilitate your use of it on a single computer. Making copies of the software for any other purpose is a violation of the United States copyright laws.

This software is sold *as is* without warranty of any kind, either expressed or implied, including but not limited to the implied warranties of merchantability and fitness for a particular purpose. Neither the publisher nor its dealers or distributors assumes any liability for any alleged or actual damages arising from the use of this program. (Some states do not allow for the exclusion of implied warranties, so the exclusion may not apply to you.)